SOCIOLOGY OF CRIME

SOCIOLOGY OF CRIME

edited by

JOSEPH S. ROUCEK

GREENWOOD PRESS, PUBLISHERS
NEW YORK

CONTENTS

EXPERIMENTAL EFFORTS AT TREATMENT AND "SOLUTIONS"

THE SOCIOLOGY OF THE POLICE

SELECTED GLOBAL ASPECTS

THE USSR AND THE EUROPEAN SATELLITES

PREFACE

The wrongdoing among children has become so outrageous and such a frequent factor in day-to-day news, not only in the United States but also in nearly all parts of the globe, that some people have reached a state of alarm that makes them think the word "juvenile" is inseparably joined to the word "delinquent." But this universal apprehension over antisocial acts committed by persons under a certain age (usually between sixteen and eighteen) can be approached only as one aspect of the whole problem of crime—a social phenomenon which has intrigued men for centuries as shown in numerous stories, songs and poems in the literature of many cultures. Today this interest in the deviant behavior is even more featured in all media of communications—in contemporary literature, periodicals, radio and television plays and motion pictures.

Yet, interestingly enough, the scientific aspects of criminal behavior began to be studied only seven or eight decades ago, when the speculations about crime started to be replaced by the more scientific approaches of Cesare Lombroso, and his followers, Enrico Ferri and B. Raffaele Garofalo. It was only with the advance of knowledge based upon systematic investigations of social phenomena that criminal behavior began to be investigated scientifically.

Every social problem can be approached from numerous, and often conflicting viewpoints: religious, educational, philosophical, psychological, ethical, moral, patriotic, and the like. The sociologist has a definite contribution to make by his persistent search for the uniformities involved in social behavior related to criminal acts. He tends to set aside considerations of venge-

1

ance, justice, and moral condemnation in general, and addresses himself to the study of crime as a social and socio-psychological phenomenon with the goals of reducing criminal behavior to a relatively small number of principles, or laws, testing these principles through prediction, and ultimately affording techniques of control.

The aim of the present symposium is to synthesize the vastness of available sociological knowledge by having the most important fields of the subject covered by the authorities, by bringing into sharp focus the facts available in different areas and in their bearing upon related sectors. That the chapters have been prepared by specialists is an outstanding feature of this work. Insulation from the findings of specialists was a normal matter only a few decades ago; but today the student can hardly be led through the complex and ever growing mountains of knowledge by a "generalist."

Two other outstanding features, it is hoped, characterize the present publication. With the exception of specialized monographs, the usual run of textbooks in the field of criminology and penology do not even bother to handle the sociological aspects of the police work. The section covering this field is a distinctly valuable feature of the present volume. In addition, we have also added a section treating another one of the most neglected aspects of the problem of crime—the comparative international ramifications. Crime and delinquency, particularly certain aspects of it, are being recognized more and more as an international, rather than a local problem. Nearly all general studies dispose of this field by making passing remarks here and there about the "crime abroad," although knowledge regarding crime in its multifarious forms, expressions and definitions can be best attained through cooperative comparative studies and surveys of the situations in various parts of the globe. Unfortunately, the problem of crime and the ideas about criminology and penology cannot be covered in this volume on a global scale. The lack of available space has forced the inclusion here of only the chapters on Great Britain, Western Europe, and the countries behind the Iron Curtain. At the same time, the present publication claims the distinction of being the latest, and one of the very few works dealing "head-on" with the problem from the sociological standpoint.

JOSEPH S. ROUCEK

University of Bridgeport

THE FRAMEWORK

SOCIOLOGY AND CRIME

Gilbert Geis
Los Angeles State College

The marriage in the United States between the academic discipline of sociology and the scientific study of criminal behavior has now passed its 40th anniversary. It was in 1918, with the publication of Maurice Parmelee's textbook, *Criminology,* that the union was officially consummated. Since then, a considerable number of brilliant offspring have issued from the liaison, as well as a number of mésalliance products. It will be the purpose of the present paper to examine this relationship between sociology and analyses of criminal behavior, both from an historical perspective and against a contemporary background. We shall also consider the interaction between criminology and criminal law, theoretical formulations in criminology (in particular, the theory of differential association), and current research emphases. An attempt will also be made to chart what appear to be the more promising elements in the future of criminology.

It might be noted at the outset that such an endeavor involves at times careful evaluative steps through the debris of intramural dispute that often marks current affairs in criminology. Examples abound of clashes of views which sometimes give way to sharp and almost intemperate outbursts of annoyance and impatience with what the other person is doing or, equally likely what he isn't doing. One short chain of documentation will suffice to illustrate this situation. Take, for instance, the review of a current English textbook in criminology. The reviewer, Donald Cressey, himself the leading current exponent of the differential association theory, notes that the English author, after stating his general approval of the theory, does not use

7

"differential association or something like it . . . as a principle for organizing and systematizing our knowledge of crime and criminals." [1] Not long after, Howard Gill publishes a long critical article on differential association claiming, among other things, that the theory provides a skewed and misleading interpretation of commonsense items.[2] Gill's article, in turn, is labelled "incomprehensible" by Hartung,[3] while Hartung, in his turn, is castigated by Caldwell for putting forth a "morass of misconceptions, distortions, and half-truths . . . [which] . . . rarely rise above a hysterical denunciation of everyone who does not agree with a certain cult of criminology." [4] It can only be added, with perhaps facetious whimsy, that if internal conflict represents an index of the health of a discipline, criminology might well lay claim to being one of the most vigorous areas of current academic research.

It is semantically significant that both "sociology" and "crime" present curious etymological histories. The term sociology, coined by Auguste Comte, represents a deliberate combination of Greek and Roman roots, undertaken to vivify linguistically the omniscient role of the new science of society. The life history of the word "crime" offers but little help in resolving its meaning so that it might be of greater value in the catalogue of scientific terminology. The Romans, who passed the word along, were wayward and erratic about defining it. *Crimen* first referred to a judicial decision or verdict, then came to be used more loosely to include a charge, accusation, or reproach, especially, interestingly enough, if the accusation was unfounded. Still later, dating particularly from the reign of the Emperor Augustus (27 B.C.-14 A.D.), the word *crimen* was expanded further to include the item complained of by the accuser, whether or not the complaint was accurate.[5] The classical poet Ovid, exiled from Rome by Augustus for reasons that still remain unknown, illustrates this verbal flexibility by using interchangeably the words *crimen* and *error* (mistake) to describe his offense.[6]

In popular usage today, both "sociology" and "crime" are employed with a looseness of definition that has represented a stumbling block in attempts to delineate clearly the province of the sociology of crime. Sociology itself is often equated with social welfare, a vocational field with an explicit value orientation, and even occasionally with the economic doctrines of socialism. It is in fact this latter misconception, it is sometimes alleged, which has brought forth the term "behavioral science," a designation innocuous enough to carry no negative connotations to the fund-granting foundations. Among professional sociological initiates, who agree on the more general characteristics of their field, there remains considerable dispute as to its proper sphere and function.

As loosely as "sociology" is sometimes employed, the word "crime" is treated even more cavalierly in popular speech. In common usage it covers, literally, a multitude of sins, and includes acts which deviate from the imperatives of various ethical systems, and numerous other acts which, at one time or another, appear to some persons, by some standards, to represent improper behavior. At the same time—and this fact has never been adequately investigated and formulated—the category of crime includes an impressive hard core of acts which, *in a general form,* have been regarded by most, if not all, societies as detrimental to their well-being. Reference might be made, in this sense, to acts such as the killing of a socially-blameless person without his consent.

The inexactness of the definition of the word crime and the ineptness of its ability to characterize homogeneous units of behavior has proven to be a formidable barrier against sophisticated interpretations of criminal behavior. It is one of the major tenets of the present paper that investigations of causes or correlates of crime per se, using crime to describe a gross behavioral entity, are inevitably doomed to a degree of vastness and vagueness that will vitiate whatever probative value they may seem to contain.

EARLY HISTORY OF CRIMINOLOGY

The early history of studies of criminal behavior as well as the story of the emergence of sociology as a formal academic discipline, when considered together, shed considerable light on the present status of the sociology of crime. The life story of sociology is well-documented but, unfortunately, there exist no parallel tracings of the history of criminology. DeQuiros prepared a rather thorough report on the state of criminology about the time of the First World War,[7] and Sellin has published in a Swedish symposium a brief but useful survey of criminological thought.[8] More recently, a series of short biographical sketches of pioneers in criminology have been appearing in the *Journal of Criminal Law, Criminology, and Police Science,* with the plan to bring these together in book form, while in 1958 George Vold published a general critique on various aspects of theoretical criminology.[9] The tradition in Europe has been to restrict criminology to an offshoot of legal science, documented by such monumental works as Leon Radzinowicz' three-volume history of English criminal law,[10] and in the United States to publish either empirical studies relating to contemporary aspects of crime or general-purpose textbooks with their recapitulation and reformulation of research and theory. The pattern of developments in criminology as these blended with sociological progress must be woven together from diverse historical sources.

It is a curious sidelight on the relationship between sociology and studies of crime that the scholar now generally acknowledged to be the forerunner of scientific efforts in criminology was Adolphe Quetelet (1796-1874), the Belgian statistician who preempted the term "social physics" to describe his work, and thus forced Comte, who had intended to use this term for his emergent science, to coin the word "sociology." [11] Quetelet charted the ecological distribution of crime and then related his findings to social conditions in diverse urban areas and national regions.[12] In retrospect, it is self-evident that the scientific study of crime made a bad detour when it by-passed Quetelet and André-Michel Guerry (1802-1866), the French scientist who conducted similar research, to concentrate its attention upon the contributions of the Italian school of positivistic criminology.

The doctrines of Cesare Lombroso (1836-1909), Raffaele Garofalo (1852-1934), and Enrico Ferri (1856-1920), leaders of the Italian school, have often been chronicled. It is significant that the works of these men constituted three of the nine books chosen in the early 1900's by a committee of the American Institute of Criminal Law and Criminology to epitomize current thinking in criminology. These works were to serve as an introduction for Americans to an "entire scientific movement" about which they had "remained ignorant . . . or indifferent." The works of the Italian group were heralded as among "the most useful treatises now extant in the Continental languages"—a judgment, incidentally, not shared on the Continent[13]—and their content was alleged to be some forty years in advance of American thought.[14] The six-man committee choosing the works in this Modern Criminal Science series included law professors John Wigmore of Northwestern University, Ernest Freund of the University of Chicago, and Roscoe Pound of Harvard University, three of the most intellectually influential men of the American bar at the time. Their wholehearted endorsement of the Italian school may be pointed to as a first landmark along the path that led to disenchantment among the rank-and-file of American lawyers with social science efforts in criminology.

The hard-shelled biological views of Lombroso have generally been regarded with more intellectual compassion than they seem to merit. Because Lombroso scorned the armchair and employed the laboratory for his work is no cause for endorsement, unless it can be maintained that poor science is by definition always superior to first-rate philosophy. Lombroso's caricatured case histories (". . . a demi-type . . . her ears stand out, she has big jaws, and cheek bones, and very black hair, besides other anomalies, such as gigantic canine teeth and dwarf incisors . . ."), and his elaborate torturings of logic, such as the serio-comic attempt to relate the fatness of prostitutes, which "strikes those who look at them en masse" to the obesity of Hottentots, and then to relate both of these to a theory of atavism, represent dolorous twistings of a scientific approach.[15]

Lombroso's work was labelled "criminal anthropology" and this rather awkward designation was the precursor of the more felicitous term, "criminology," which was suggested at the Second International Congress of Criminal Anthropology in 1889 by

11

Paul Topinard (1830-1911), a professor at the École d'Anthropologie in Paris.[16] The suggestion was adopted with enthusiasm by the popular press to describe "the branch of anthropological science which has the best promise of affording results of immediate practical value."[17] It was the same Topinard, incidentally, who, when shown a collection of Lombroso's pictures of asymmetric and stigmatic criminals, remarked wryly that the pictures looked no different than those of his own friends.[18] It took several decades before the main body of American criminological thought accepted the validity of this singularly accurate criticism of Lombroso's work.

SOCIOLOGICAL CRIMINOLOGY

Criminology was nudged from the confines of anthropology into those of sociology primarily by Ferri, who attempted to reconcile social elements in the genesis of criminal behavior with the physical and anthropological views of Lombroso. It was the publication of Ferri's *Sociologia criminale* (1884) that probably more than anything else ordained the eventual resting place of studies of crime within the discipline of sociology in the United States. Ferri, in retrospect, appears to represent a keen mind fatally encumbered by the heritage of an intellectual fetter from which he could not disengage himself. He brings to mind Thorstein Veblen's classic statement, made in an attempt to explain the intellectual preeminence of Jews, that social marginality does not carry with it vested interests and social taboos which block a panoramic view of reality.[19] Ferri, shackled by the Lombrosian tradition, could only go as far as an amalgamation of anthropological and telluric conditions with social phenomena in his explanation of crime.[20]

The academic affiliations of European pioneers in criminology partially explain its current status on the Continent. Lombroso was a doctor who later taught legal medicine at the University of Turin; Garofalo, a jurist who became professor of criminal law at the University of Naples; and Ferri, a member of parliament who taught criminal law at the University of Rome. Their investigations were incorporated as part of the work of the traditional disciplines. Criminology took root as a new and distinct field only in the United States. In Great Britain, a typical European example, early stress was placed on physical correlates of criminals in studies undertaken by medical doctors, and formal research in criminology soon became attached to legal faculties where, after a long history of agitation for reform, they concentrated on providing pragmatic research findings upon which enlightened legislation might be founded.[21]

Its academic nesting place has greatly influenced emphases in criminological research throughout the world. It is with considerable truth that Norval Morris, an Australian, has remarked that the close relationship of criminology to law on the European continent has provided scholars there with an understanding of relevant questions to be investigated though, unfortunately, they lack the research sophistication to perform this task adequately. In the United States, on the other hand, Morris believes, methodology in sociological research has reached a highly sophisticated level, but criminology suffers from the absence of a concomitant awareness of or interest in significant problems towards which to direct its research skills.[22]

The comparatively amorphous state of American academic affairs in the early 1900's appears more responsible than anything else for the incorporation of criminology into the fold of sociology in the United States. It has been noted that sociology itself, coming upon the academic scene about 1885, almost the same year that Ferri published his *Sociologia criminale,* gained its initial acceptance and strength only in those institutions, particularly in the midwest, which were not yet committed to traditional European patterns. Because of its housing in sociology departments, criminology inevitably became highly responsive to shifts in emphasis in its parent field, whether or not these were altogether suited to its particular needs. It also became responsive, of course, to such items as the status implications for sociologists of different forms and methods of research, as well as to the type of graduate training to which recruits to criminological research were exposed.

In its early period, criminology fit snugly into the strong emphasis in sociology on what Howard P. Becker has labelled the three S's—sin, sex, and sewage.[23] Early writings clearly reflect both a moral concern over the waywardness of criminals, as well as a crusading drive to ameliorate the more brutal treatment procedures used to punish offenders. The shift in sociology proper away from overtly value-laden areas readily carried criminology with it, particularly since Parmelee, author of the earliest criminology textbook, spearheaded the campaign against contamination of "the scientific character and objectivity of sociology" by social welfare considerations.[24]

It should be noted, however, while considering value commitments, that criminology continues to contain an element of reformist zeal, though this zeal is better camouflaged than previously. There is at least a strong subvert belief that one of the more compelling reasons for studying crime is to be able eventually to reduce it. A rather clear indication of this feeling seems to be reflected in part in the quick proliferation of college courses in juvenile delinquency, courses which arose not from interest in a unique form of human behavior, but from public concern with a defined social problem. Bergman, a psychiatrist, has attempted to illustrate this value commitment by pointing out that no one seems to have thought of investigating the hypothesis that the criminal by maintaining an original hostile defiance against the frustration of man's environment might be able to achieve a higher degree of integration than the average honest citizen, and that nobody has bothered to determine what personality assets are buried when "youngsters who might find harmonious fulfillment of their unique individuality in a criminal career are at all costs and with all imaginary pressures led towards an honest way of life."[25]

EARLY STUDIES IN CRIMINOLOGY

Before Edwin H. Sutherland came along to give sociological criminology a distinctive theoretical viewpoint, the field concentrated heavily on a variety of rather eclectic approaches to its subject matter. Among other things, intensive efforts were directed toward embellishing Lombroso's carcinomatous ideas about the physical condition of criminals. These and similarly-rooted efforts were widespread enough to provide material for a 50-page bibliography in Fink's monograph on biological studies on crime causation in America between 1800 and 1915.[26] In addition, particularly during the period when the field of human ecology flourished at the University of Chicago, studies concentrated on the spatial distribution of crime and criminals.

Research also concerned itself with a wide variety of relationships between criminal behavior and such identification variables as age, sex, place of origin, family conditons, and urban-rural residence. Such investigations rarely made any serious attempt to move beyond readily discernible correlations into the wider realm of theoretical formulations and generalized statements of causal linkage. Nonetheless, these studies provided a large measure of worthwhile insight into the dynamics of criminal activity. They represented scientifically wholesome attempts to grapple with crime in its natural habitat, and they gathered together a vast array of information that has since supplied a core lode for more advanced efforts, and for critical essays, themselves significant contributions pointing the way to refined techniques. A comparison between this early American work and criminological investigations throughout the remainder of the world serves to highlight the significance of the American contributions as pathfinding ventures. Foreign criminologists today are often just beginning to undertake field research of the type that is now considered naive in the United States.

Despite its positive elements, however, this initial work possessed at least two serious shortcomings, shortcomings which still seem to represent major unresolved questions in contemporary work on sociology and crime:

1. The first shortcoming was an inability to bring together the diffuse findings into a theoretical framework which would both explain the findings in a more meaningful manner and point the way to significant subsequent research. This shortcom-

15

ing was, it is only fair to point out, one shared with the general body of both sociological and psychological thought. Criminology's present difficulties in this area appear to be related as much to the nature of its subject matter and to a certain academic insularity as to anything else. Unable to theorize on a grand scale in the manner envisaged originally by Comte, sociology began to examine items, such as small groups, which were suggested by its accumulated work, by academic priorities and protocol, and by its general ethos. Sociology possessed a basic flexibility denied to criminology. Only if sociology could command all the keys to human behavior could criminology, subsumed strictly under sociology, come to possess a monopoly in the explanation of criminal behavior. Sociology made no pretense to such heights, and its findings blended with those of other disciplines to form something of a variegated explanation of criminal behavior. Sociological criminology, with a parochial approach to its subject, tended to produce a skewed view of the behavior it dealt with.[27]

Criminology, in addition, had to wait upon sociological theory for general schemes of interpretation of human behavior. Sociology and its middle-range theories, however, particularly when they moved away from their original social welfare concern, paid scant attention to criminology which rapidly became a peripheral member of the sociological group. This development is clearly reflected in the tendency among criminologists to "advance" in their interests beyond substantive and theoretical criminology into areas carrying more professional prestige, areas such as methodology, general theory, the investigation of administrative and organizational groups, and statistics.

2. The second shortcoming, containing a number of facets, was related to the delineation of the subject matter of criminology. Early studies accepted uncritically commonplace characterizations as to who constituted criminals. In them, a criminal became no more or less than a person whom everyone regarded as a criminal. It is from such a perspective that Burgess insists that white-collar offenders cannot be real criminals because they

do not think of themselves as criminals.[28] In addition, each study based its findings on available criminal populations, which almost invariably consisted of persons apprehended and in custody. Contemporary studies in criminology have made but little progress toward obtaining more legitimate representation of the offenders they study, though they are better aware of this disadvantage and attempt to compensate for it. The problems in this general category fall into three areas: 1) the defined limits of criminal activity; 2) meaningful behavior typologies within these limits; and 3) adequate representation of the types for study.

It cannot be overemphasized that *for real progress in criminology, all the dilemmas outlined above must be resolved together, not unilaterally.* Theoretical breakthroughs without concomitant advance toward definitional integrity may confound more than they contribute. Sutherland's differential association theory, attempting to embrace indiscriminately the broad sweep of all criminal behavior, soared beyond the point of utility. On the other hand, definitional resolutions without theoretical awareness often represent little more than futile exercises in semantics. The present state of the sociology of crime, bearing the above items in mind, seems to be clearly represented by Wolfgang's recent monograph, *Patterns in Criminal Homicide.*[29] Wolfgang's investigation is based upon the definitions of homicide in Pennsylvania law, as he amends these slightly to fit logical prerequisites and the nature of his material. He gathers together in painstaking fashion a wealth of numerical information on homicide as it occurred in Philadelphia from 1948-1952. Bloch's pertinent observation that Wolfgang's study lacks theoretical integration[30] is not essentially a criticism of Wolfgang, but a comment on the present state of criminology and the fact that it previously by-passed the task of gathering basic data on forms of criminal behavior in favor of studies and theories of crime in general, and must now retreat to the necessary level of fact-finding about relevant problems before re-integration at a more meaningful theoretical level.

THE DIFFERENTIAL ASSOCIATION THEORY

The sociology of crime, as noted, has been permeated by the theory of differential association, a theory expounded in 1939 by Edwin H. Sutherland (1883-1950). Differential association actually offers an explanation for all human behavior, though it has been singularly ignored in areas of sociological concern other than criminology.

In a statement on the "biography" of differential association, Sutherland pointed out the intellectual paths, sometimes direct, sometimes meandering, which he had followed to arrive at this theoretical position.[31] The theory itself,[32] well-known to professional criminologists, centers particularly about the twin propositions that "crime is a symptom of social disorganization" and that "criminal behavior is learned behavior." The body of the theory attempts to explain the learning of criminal behavior through a process in which behavioral items are reproduced by the individual to the degree that he has absorbed them. From a vast panorama of possible behavior, a panorama analytically clouded by its very diversity, the individual comes to engage in that behavior which has been most effectively impressed upon him through "differential association" which may "vary in frequency, duration, priority, and intensity." The major attempt in the theory to distinguish criminal behavior from all other human behavior is the statement that criminal motives and drives are "learned from definitions of legal codes as favorable or unfavorable."

Differential association has been subjected to a considerable amount of professional abuse, and defended with equal vehemence by those partial to its theoretical approach. In general, criticisms of Sutherland's theory may be summarized under four headings:

1. The theory is not predictive. Differential association, as an explanation of all human behavior and not just criminal behavior, represents nothing more than a somewhat simplicistic collection of truisms.

2. Differential association does not deal with measurable quan-

tities, therefore it can neither be verified nor rejected by means of empirical demonstration.

3. The theory is skewed in its emphasis. By concentrating on the effect of experience in learning it tends to ignore the significant fact that the same experiences have different meaning for different individuals.

4. The theory has actually been shown to be inaccurate in field studies which demonstrated that the precise behavior involved in the criminal action was not, in fact, learned by differential association but in many cases was merely the utilization of prior knowledge of potentially illegal methods.

It has sometimes been maintained that no one was more keenly aware of the shortcomings of the differential association theory than Sutherland. William Healy thought that Sutherland put forth the theory "a little tentatively and without evidence of complete faith" [33] In 1944, Sutherland wrote one of the most penetrating critiques of his own theory in a paper facetiously called "The Swan Song of Differential Association" which he circulated among his colleagues, but never published. Following his death, the paper was included in a collection of Sutherland's writings, with the rather unconvincing editorial hyperbole that Sutherland was not "in the main" taken with his own criticisms because he restated the theory "with the same vigor" in the subsequent edition of his book.[34]

In this paper, Sutherland notes that differential association can perhaps be regarded only as one of the important processes in the genesis of criminal behavior rather than a universal explanation of such behavior. He mentions that under ideal conditions differential association may be a totally adequate explanation, but under others only a partial explanation. He cites an analogy from the field of medicine, pointing out that in tuberculosis not only the tubercle bacilli are necessary factors in the onset of the disease, but other factors are also relevant, factors which may be grouped under the vague heading of "susceptibility." So, too, in criminal behavior Sutherland implies, it may be that in some instances similar differential associations may produce divergent behavior because of the general susceptibility of the individuals involved. This same point has been made by Olaf Kinberg, dean of Scandinavian criminologists, who stressed that Sutherland's theory reduced men to "a passive, homogeneous, amorphous, plastic mass, acted upon in a similar manner by the milieu" and that "the environment is not an objective reality . . . but a function of the individual." [35]

Severest criticism of the differential association theory has been leveled by Sheldon Glueck, a Harvard law professor whose own work on juvenile delinquency, which is eclectic and actuarial, has in turn been the object of extremely harsh treatment by many sociologists. [36]

The following represents a general summary of Glueck's strictures against differential association: The theory, he says, "fails to organize and integrate the findings of respectable research and is, at best, so general and puerile as to add little or nothing to the explanation, treatment and prevention of delinquency." Persons can invent criminal behavior or commit crime without training, an "obvious" fact. Differential association ignores such primitive impulses as aggression, sexual desire, and acquisitiveness, which lead children to various forms of anti-social conduct before they have learned it from others. It is therefore not delinquent behavior which is learned; that comes naturally. It is rather non-delinquent behavior which must be learned. Besides this, it is impossible to count the number of definitions favorable to violations of law and demonstrate that these exceed the definitions unfavorable to violation of law. Finally, few, if any, worthwhile policy recommendations can be derived from the differential association theory. Glueck maintains that "a wise eclecticism, guiding research in which investigations, examinations and tests are thorough, and sociocultural data are carefully verified and collated, is still the only promising and sensible credo for the modern criminologist." [37]

Empirical studies using differential association as their theoretical base have tended to point to some chinks in the theory's conceptualization, though these have generally been regarded as minor flaws rather than irreparable gaps. Thus, Cressey, in

20

his study of embezzlers, rejected as an initial hypothesis the statement that embezzling techniques were learned in association with identifiable criminal patterns.[38] Clinard has reported that the differential association theory proved to have "limitations" in its application to black market offenses since it did not "adequately explain why some individuals who are familiar with the techniques of violation, as well as frequently associate with persons similarly familiar do not engage in such practices."[39] Weinberg has indicated also, after studying incest offenders, that differential association is not of valid applicability to a considerable portion of his sample.[40] Finally, Robert Lindner, writing from a Freudian position, rejects differential association as a "fancy and elaborate" explanation stated in terms of "resonant and palate-pleasing superficialities." Lindner maintains that the evidence he gathered in day-to-day study of inmates of penitentiaries does not line up with Sutherland's theory,[41] though, it might be added, few criminologists would be able to discern any theoretical advance through acceptance of the highly jargonized and speculative assumptions of psychoanalytical approaches to crime such as those championed by Lindner.

CRIMINOLOGY AND CRIMINAL LAW

Sutherland's theory is built on a deterministic philosophy of human behavior in contrast to the allegiance in the system of criminal law to a doctrine of free will. This philosophical distinction is one of the major explanations for the continuous rupture between criminology and criminal law. The rupture is particularly evident in flailing attempts in criminological literature to come to grips with the definition of crime, and equally evident in the failure of the disciplines of law and sociology to cooperate to produce material of particular value to the main body of thought in either discipline, or to resolve important matters of joint concern to both disciplines.

There is at the moment a tendency in studies in the sociology of crime to move away from legal characterizations of criminal activity into the more malleable area of "deviant behavior." Deviant behavior is considered to be represented by variations from the complex of normative standards in the society or in its sub-groups. These normative standards are to be found not only in the elements of criminal law, but also in such social items as the mores of the society. The study of deviant behavior is, of course, an area of legitimate concern to sociologists and it might be, as it seems to be, a more productive sociological field than that of criminology, with its restricted subject-matter.

It also seems apparent, however, that criminology is obligated to function from the base of statutory and judicial definitions of criminal acts. In this respect, therefore, it is important that attention be paid not only to the causes of criminal behavior but also to the elements within the society which lead particular acts to be legally proscribed, and the procedures through which this is accomplished. The relationship between changes in the criminal law and changes in the behavior circumscribed by the law is a matter of considerable importance, for it is, as Tappan maintains, "axiomatic" that "the norms of criminal law do exert some measure of effective control over human behavior." [42]

The gap between criminology and criminal law requires a moment's attention. It is a peculiar rupture particularly when viewed in the light of the strong moves toward inter-disciplinary rapprochement by distinguished figures in the history of the American bar, men such as Roscoe Pound, Jerome Hall, and Louis Brandeis, to mention but a few. It was Brandeis, for instance, originator of the famous "Brandeis briefs"—elaborate documentations of the social science relationship between such things as health and hours of work—who quoted with approval the observation that "a lawyer who has not studied economics and sociology is very apt to become a public enemy." [43] More recently, William J. Brennan, an associate justice of the United States Supreme Court, urged lawyers to "turn their minds to the knowledge and experience in particular of those disciplines that investigate and report on the functioning and nature of our society." [44] Nor can it be overlooked that several outstanding persons in American criminology have combined sociological training with the acquisition of law degrees, men such as Nathaniel Cantor, Robert Caldwell, and Paul Tappan.

That the disenchantment between criminal law and criminology is real and not imagined seems self-evident. David Riesman, who knows both disciplines well, has noted that lawyers are "very apt to be scornful of the findings of social science." [45] Robert Kramer, commenting recently on law and inter-disciplinary research, advises fellow lawyers to avoid such entanglements lest they find themselves caught up in a never-never land of confusion.[46] Julius Cohen, an eminent legal philosopher, has attempted to explain this disciplinary breach in terms of three items: 1) Social science resources are not shaped to answer many specific and practical problems with which law is concerned; 2) Social science findings are much too unripe and tentative for reliable use in predicting human behavior; 3) Social science resources, being so "enormous" produce a certain reluctance and inertia in legal minds.[47]

Cohen's items lead to consideration of some other barriers blocking better relationships between criminology and law. Criminologists, as sociologists, are pulled toward the main line of sociological thought which, in turn, contains among other things a large element of jargon—such as hyphenated linguistics inventions which Schlesinger, Jr., maintains are considered "chic" in sociological circles.[48] It also places a strong emphasis on methodological sophistication in contrast to substantive investigation and humanistic disputation. There is, as Cohen notes, a denegation of research dealing with segmentalized problems which might prove to be of some pragmatic relevance to law.[49] Sociologists also tend to stand in a certain awe of colleagues who, as Riesman notes, "with no philosophical training, consume their time affixing exact degrees of significance to insignificant correlations and never get around to discovering anything new about society." [50]

In regard to what sometimes approaches a fetish with methodology in sociology, inevitably filtering down to criminology, a number of comments seem worth reproduction: First, Poincaire's rather harsh judgment that physical scientists devote their time to solving their problems, while social scientists devote theirs to discussing their methods" [51] and second, the observation of Percy W. Bridgman, a Nobel Prize winner, that ". . . there is no scientific method as such . . . The most vital feature of the scientist's procedure has been merely to do his utmost with his mind, no holds barred . . . This means that . . . one makes continued checks to assure onself that one is not making mistakes, and that any line of inquiry will be followed that appears at all promising." [52] In relation to criminology, Schur has made the challenging point that a "general disdain of political, economic, and historical considerations, exaggerated stress on methodological precision, and ascetic efforts at ethical neutrality, may all tend to support an outlook stressing individual, rather than social, pathology." [53]

These internal elements of the sociological ethos serve as part of an inter-disciplinary Maginot Line between criminal law and criminology, particularly in view of the fact that practicing lawyers have a strong need for predictable certainty and surety, regardless of the price in logic or empirical reality at which this certainty is sometimes purchased. Lawyers trade on their ability to predict the outcome of the legal system *before* the system itself arrives at its results. Any interference with this process, real or imagined, represents a formidable threat.

It is also true, of course, that the lawyer is at least as ethnocentric as the rest of us and uses his profesional training and position as a system of barbed wire to keep outsiders, such as social scientists, on the nether side. Equally important too is the fact that the lawyer is traditionally a man of affairs; the social scientist, though he is becoming more so,[54] still suffers from the déclassé fact of his almost total immersion in academia. These real differences in status seemingly manifest themselves in the reluctance of lawyers to pay more serious attention to the findings of social science. They might also explain the open-arm welcome that sociologists receive from business concerns, and particularly the advertising affiliates of such concerns, where the professional status of the academic consultant lends

24

an aura of prestige to a pursuit not notable for its own public image, and where sociological contributions are considered to be capable of producing financial gain.

Not all of the signs, however, are disheartening, and mention might be made of several current attempts at rapprochement between the disciplines of law and sociology and, in particular, criminal law and criminology. Highly significant has been the combined work of legal scholars and social scientists in investigating the work of juries as part of the program in Law and the Behavioral Sciences at the University of Chicago. Fragmentary reports so far issued indicate that the work will provide an extremely valuable body of information on a much-debated but little understood legal institution.[55] It is both amusing and significant that when the jury project ran into early difficulties because of its wiring of a jury room during a federal trial, the New York *Times* editorially commented that such irresponsibility might likely "appeal to sociologists" but the newspaper could not understand the equivalent lack of public conscience on the part of lawyers.[56]

Additional cooperative efforts between law and the social sciences have been taking place in several law schools, including Yale and Chicago. Ford Foundation fellowships for sociologists at the latter school may likely produce a new group of criminologists with a more abiding interest in criminal law and its concerns, a necessary item for the future growth of criminology. There is also a program of inter-disciplinary research attached to the School of Law at the University of Pennsylvania. Despite these portents of goodwill, however, the foregoing comments on the difficulties inherent in the academic position of criminology inevitably lead to a stress upon the recommendation of a UNESCO report based on a world-wide survey of criminology. The study of criminology, the report maintained, "is essentially a multi-disciplinary affair" and "should not be attached to a single discipline"[57] The implementation of this recommendation, unlikely as it presently appears, would seem to hold the prospect for one of the soundest developments in the future of criminology.

THE PRESENT STATUS OF CRIMINOLOGY

There are many signs of present vitality and health and progress in the sociology of crime, despite the preceding strictures. The growing awareness that criminology can only advance by breaking down its subject matter into more manageable units of behaviorally homogeneous illegal activity is widespread in the field today, though there remains the difficult task of gathering together material on particular units of criminal behavior.

In the field of criminological theory, there seems to be particular promise in Bloch's approach to criminal behavior through use of what he labels *psychogenetic patterns*. Admittedly a "crude" beginning, Bloch nonetheless feels that his approach is significant "in putting into some coherent form the conditioned effects of his developmental history upon the culturally oriented and organically vulnerable individual as they fall into a pattern and tend to impart consistency to his behavior." [58] The theory needs greater application to field material in order to test and refine its scope and statement, but it may provide a beginning toward bridging the wide gap in criminology between sociological and psychological approaches, which at times seem to operate as if they were dealing with two totally different kinds of behavior rather than two aspects of the same behavior.

Bloch's theory, using self-consistency as part of its framework, runs parallel to one of the more intriguing findings that has grown out of recent criminological field research. Investigating shoplifters in Chicago's Marshall Field's department store, Mary Beth Cameron grouped offenders, as previous workers had done, as either amateurs or professionals. She observed that store detectives, after apprehending amateur shoplifters, made strenuous efforts to break through their self-conceptualizations in attempts to force them to re-define their behavior in terms which led inescapably to the conclusion that they were criminals. "Yes, I took the purse," one woman sobbed, "but that doesn't mean I'm a thief." Store detectives had to point out again and again to the amateur that she is in fact a thief, and had to reiterate that she was under arrest and would in the due course of events be taken in a police wagon to the police station, booked and finger-printed, and then brought before a judge and sentenced. Cameron found this technique was so effective, though the procedures threatened were not often carried out, that the amateur shop-lifters rarely repeated their offense either at Marshall Field's or elsewhere in Chicago.[59]

"From the general viewpoint of criminology," Cameron later wrote, after reflecting on her original study, "this is a very sig-nificant fact and an understanding of the why's and how's of it might be important to our total treatment program for first offenders."[60]

There have been other noteworthy recent contributions to the literature of criminology which are aimed at filling factual and theoretic gaps in knowledge. Only a few of the book-length studies will be mentioned here; other major contributions will be noted in subsequent articles in this symposium.

In the area of organized crime, the intensive hearings by the Senate Subcommittee to Investigate Organized Crime in Inter-State Commerce (1950-1951) and the Senate Select Committee on Improper Activities in the Labor or Management Field (1958-1959) both provide considerable documentation on a form of behavior rather neglected by criminologists. In the area of homicide, *Suicide and Homicide* (1954) by Henry and Short, and Wolfgang's *Patterns in Criminal Homicide* (1958), both add measurably to data in these areas, as does a brief monograph, *Homicide* (1955) by Albert Morris, long a pioneering advocate both of studies in white-collar crime and of analyses of particular forms of criminal behavior.

Kinsey's well-known investigations of sexual behavior in vari-ous strata of American society provided both popular discussion and empirical data on offenses against sexual laws. The promised study by Kinsey's Institute for Sex Research in Indiana on sexual offenders should approximate a definitive study on this subject. In the area of professional crime, works such as Sutherland's *The Professional Thief* (1937) have been complemented by Martin's *My Life in Crime* (1953) and *Men of the Underworld* (1952), edited by Charles Hamilton, and by two classics by David

Maurer, *The Big Con* (1940), and *The Whiz Mob* (1955), the last a study of pickpockets published unobtrusively by the American Dialect Society.

In the field of white-collar crime, still the rather exclusive bailiwick of sociologists, Sutherland's original work, *White Collar Crime* (1949), has been followed by a growing awareness that white-collar crime might be more reasonably handled under a number of analytically discrete headings rather than, as Sutherland did, treated as a vast and rather vaguely defined entity. Full-length studies in this area include Cressey's investigation of embezzlers, *Other People's Money* (1953), using analytic induction as its approach, and Clinard's *The Black Market* (1952). Recent joint announcements by the Federal Trade Commission and the Department of Justice that advertising offenders will increasingly be prosecuted under criminal statutes rather than dealt with administratively seem to undercut partially criticisms of white-collar crime voiced at times by persons who believe it to be more of a moral than a criminal category.[62] This emergent sign of alignment between sociological theory and criminological fact represents, in summary, but one of the many hopeful signs pointing to a growing factual and theoretical maturity in sociological criminology.

SELECTED BIBLIOGRAPHY

Barnes, Harry Elmer and Negley K. Teeters. *New Horizons in Criminology*, third edition, Prentice Hall, Englewood Cliffs, N. J., 1959. A provocative, readable book that comes to direct grips with many current problems in crime and criminology. Extremely authoritative in regard to correctional history and procedures.

Branham, Veron C. and Samuel B. Kutash. *Encyclopedia of Criminology*, Philosophical Library, New York, 1949. More than 500 pages of material, contributed by 61 authorities, on various aspects of crime and correction.

Caldwell, Robert G. *Criminology*, Ronald Press, New York,

1956. The only current textbook in criminology written by a scholar with scrupulous concern for the system of criminal law. Many teachers regard it as more "realistic" than the other texts.

Cavan, Ruth, *Criminology*, second edition, Crowell, New York, 1955. This text, widely used, is somewhat more elementary than the remainder, but well-written and coordinated. Much new material on military corrections.

Elliot, Mabel A. *Crime in Modern Society*, Harpers, New York, 1952. A long and somewhat discursive general textbook. Notable particularly for its concentration upon female crime and the treatment of female offenders.

Hall, Jerome. *Theft, Law, and Society*, second edition, Bobbs Merrill, Indianapolis, 1953. A classic study attempting to relate changes in criminal law and criminal procedure to changes in social structure and social values.

Korn, Richard R. and Lloyd W. McCorkle. *Criminology and Penology*, Henry Holt, New York, 1959. The most recent textbook in criminology, representing a collaboration between two scholars with extensive field experience in correctional institutions and agencies.

Michael, J. and Mortimer J. Adler. *Crime, Law, and Social Science*, Harcourt Brace, New York, 1933. A thorough review of the scientific aspirations of criminology and a polemic for a legal approach to its subject matter.

Reckless, Walter C. *The Etiology of Delinquent and Criminal Behavior*, Social Science Research Council, New York, 1943. A brief for an actuarial, multiple factor approach to the investigation of criminal behavior. Stresses the need to study many diverse items which blend together to produce criminals.

Reckless, Walter C. *The Crime Problem*, second edition, Appleton Century Crofts, New York, 1955. A textbook built around the multiple factor approach. Particularly noteworthy for its use of case histories of criminal careers.

Sellin, Thorsten. *Culture Conflict and Crime*, Social Science Research Council, New York, 1938. An important statement concerning the cultural influences which lead to criminal activity, with particular stress on conflicting and ambiguous elements within American culture.

Sutherland, Edwin H. *The Sutherland Papers* (edited by Albert Cohen, Alfred Lindesmith, and Karl Schuessler), Indiana

University Press, Bloomington, 1956. A collection of Sutherland's published and unpublished essays, representing keen critical analyses of various aspects of criminology, and presenting basic material on the theory of differential association.

Sutherland, Edwin H. *Principles of Criminology*, fifth edition, revised by Donald R. Cressey, Lippincott, Philadelphia, 1955. The most widely-used criminology textbook. A terse critical presentation of research in the field. Built around the differential association theory.

Sykes, Gresham M. *Crime and Society*, Random House, New York, 1956. An interpretation of the current status of criminology. "The study of crime is a focus for that central issue of sociology: the relationship between the individual and the group."

Taft, Donald R. *Criminology: A Cultural Interpretation*, third edition, Macmillan, New York, 1956. A well-written, stimulating general textbook in criminology, concentrating particularly on cultural factors as etiological items in the genesis of criminal behavior.

Vedder, Clyde B., Samuel Koenig, and Robert E. Clark. *Criminology: A Book of Readings*, Dryden, New York, 1953. A carefully-selected collection of the more important writings in historical and contemporary criminology. A gold mine of excellent material.

Vold, George B. *Theoretical Criminology*, Oxford, New York, 1958. A general presentation of the more promising avenues in theoretical attempts to understand crime and criminals and a critique of the shortcomings of other such attempts.

Gilbert Geis has been an associate professor of sociology at Los Angeles State College since 1957. He was on the faculty of the University of Oklahoma from 1952-1957 and also served during this period at various times as consultant and research director with the Oklahoma Crime Study Commission. Geis received his Ph.D from the University of Wisconsin in sociology in 1953. He lived in Scandinavia two years—in 1947 as a student at the University of Stockholm, and in 1952 as a Social Science Research Council and Fulbright fellow in Oslo. His publications include articles in the *Journal of Criminal Law, Criminology, and Police Science*, the *NPPA Journal, Social Problems*, the *Rocky Mountain Law Review*, the *Oklahoma Law Review*, the *Minnesota*

Law Review, the *American Bar Association Journal, Journal of Legal Education, Marriage and Family Living,* the New York *Times* Magazine, *Phylon, Revue de Criminologie,* and a number of other periodicals.

NOTES

1. Cressey, Donald R., Book Review, *American Sociological Review*, XXII, 5, October, 1957, 614.

2. Gill, Howard, "An Operational View of Criminology," *Archives of Criminal Psychodynamics*, I, 1, 1957, 3-55.

3. Hartung, Frank E., "A Critique of the Sociological Approach to Crime and Correction," *Law and Contemporary Problems*, XXIII, 4, Autumn 1958, 703-734.

4. Caldwell, Robert G., Book Review, *Journal of Criminal Law, Criminology, and Police Science*, L, 3, September-October 1959, 281-283.

5. Andrews, E. A., *A New Latin Dictionary*, American Book Company, New York, 1878, 482.

6. Ovidius Naso, Publius, *Tristia* (translated by Henry Riley), Bell, London, 1912, 9, 64.

7. de Quiros, C. Bernaldo, *Modern Theories of Criminality* (translated by Alfonso De Salvio), Little, Brown, Boston, 1911.

8. Sellin, Thorsten, "Et Historisk Aterblick," in *Kriminologi* (edited by Ivar Agge, et. al.), Wahlstrom & Widstrand, Stockholm, 1955, 1-22.

9. Vold, George B., *Theoretical Criminology*, Oxford, New York, 1958.

10. Radzinowicz, Leon, *A History of English Criminal Law*, Macmillan, New York, 1948-1953.

11. Timasheff, Nicholas S., *Sociological Theory: Its Nature and Growth*, Doubleday, New York, 1955, 3.

12. Lindesmith, Alfred and Yale Levin, "The Lombrosian Myth in Criminology," *American Journal of Sociology*, XLII, 5, March 1937, 653-671.

13. Hall, Jerome, "Criminology," *Twentieth Century Sociology* (edited by Georges Gurvitch and Wilbert E. Moore), Philosophical Library, New York, 1945, 645.

14. Wigmore, John, et. al., "General Introduction to the Modern Criminal Science Series," in all volumes, Little, Brown, Boston, 1911-1917, v-viii.

15. Lombroso, Caesar and William Ferrero, *The Female Offender*, T. F. Unwin, London, 1895.

16. Ellis, Havelock, *The Criminal*, Scribner's, New York, 1892, 30.

17. "Science," *The Athenaeum*, No. 3280, September 6, 1890, 325.

18. Tarde, Gabriel, *Penal Philosophy* (translated by Rapelje Howell), Little, Brown, Boston, 1912, 220.

19. Veblen, Thorstein, "The Intellectual Pre-Eminence of Jews in Modern Europe," *Political Science Quarterly*, XXXIV, March 1919, 33-42.

20. Ferri, Enrico, *Criminal Sociology* (translated by Joseph I. Keely and John Lisle) , Little, Brown, Boston, 1917.

21. Rose, Gordon, "Trends in the Development of Criminology in Britain," *British Journal of Sociology*, IX, 1, March 1958, 53-65.

22. Morris, Norval, "The Lawyer and Criminological Research," *Virginia Law Review*, XLIV, 2, February 1958, 163-183.

23. Becker, Howard, "Anthropology and Sociology," in *For a Science of Man: Convergences in Anthropology, Psychology, and Sociology* (edited by John Gillin), Macmillan, New York, 1954, 102-159.

24. House, Floyd Nelson, "Social Pathology and Criminology," in *The Development of Sociology*, McGraw-Hill, New York, 1936, 331-337.

25. Bergman, Paul, "The Objectivity of Criminological Science," in *Searchlights on Delinquency* (edited by K. R. Eissler) , International Universities, New York, 1949, 275-283.

26. Fink, Arthur E., *Causes of Crime*, University of Pennsylvania Press, Philadelphia, 1938, 252-302.

27. Geis, Gilbert, "Sociology, Criminology, and Criminal Law," *Social Problems*, VII, 1, Summer 1959, 40-47.

28. Burgess, Ernest W., Comment, *American Journal of Sociology*, LVI 1, July 1950, 32-34.

29. Wolfgang, Marvin E., *Patterns in Criminal Homicide*, University of Pennsylvania Press, Philadelphia, 1958.

30. Bloch, Herbert A., Book Review, *American Sociological Review*, XXIII, 6, December 1958, 756-757.

31. Sutherland, Edwin H., "The Development of the Concept of Differential Association," in *The Sutherland Papers* (edited by Albert Cohen, Alfred Lindesmith, and Karl Schuessler) , Indiana University Press, Bloomington, 1956, 13-29.

32. Sutherland, Edwin H., *Principles of Criminology* (revised by Donald R. Cressey) , 5th edition, Lippincott, Philadelphia, 1955, 74-81.

33. Healy, William, Book Review, *American Journal of Orthopsychiatry*, XX, 4, October 1950, 846-847.

34. Sutherland, Edwin H., "Critique of the Theory," in *The Sutherland Papers, op. cit. supra* note 32, 30-41.

35. Kinberg, Olaf, "Kritiska Reflexioner Over Den Differentiella Associationshypotesen," in *Kriminologi, op. cit. supra* note 8, 415-429.

36. See, for instance, Reiss, Albert J., Jr., "Unraveling Juvenile Delinquency: An Appraisal of the Research Methods," *American Journal of Sociology*, LVII, 2, July 1950, 115-120.

37. Glueck, Sheldon, "Theory and Fact in Criminology," *British Journal of Delinquency*, VII, 2, October 1956, 92-109.

38. Cressey, Donald R., *Other People's Money*, Free Press, 1953.

39. Clinard, Marshall B., "Criminological Theories of Violations of Wartime Regulations," *American Sociological Review*, XI, 3, June 1946, 258-270.

40. Weinberg, S. Kirson, *Incest Behavior*, Citadel, New York, 1955.

41. Lindner, Robert M., *Stone Walls and Men*, Odyssey Press, New York, 1946, 84-85.

42. Tappan, Paul W., "Who Is the Criminal," *American Sociological Review*, XII, 1, February 1947, 96-103.

43. Brandeis, Louis D., "The Living Law," in *The Curse of Bigness*, Viking, New York, 1935, 318-325.

44. The New York *Times*, November 26, 1958.

45. Riesman, David, "Law and Sociology: Notes on Recruitment, Training, and Colleagueship," *Stanford Law Review*, IX, 4, July 1957, 643-673.

46. Kramer, Robert, "Some Observations on Law and Interdisciplinary Research," *Duke Law Journal*, XII, 4, February 1959, 563-570.

47. Cohen, Julius, "Factors of Resistance to the Resources of the Behavioral Sciences," *Journal of Legal Education*, XIII, 1, 1959, 67-70.

48. The New York *Times*, Book Review, December 20, 1959.

49. For an example of such research see Kunkel, Marilyn and Gilbert Geis, "Order of Final Argument In Minnesota Criminal Trials," *Minnesota Law Review*, XLII, 4, March 1958, 549-558.

50. Riesman, David, *Thorstein Veblen: A Critical Interpretation*, Scribner's, New York, 1953, 48.

51. Cairns, Huntington, *Law and the Social Sciences*, Harcourt Brace, New York, 1935, 6.

52. Bridgman, Percy W., *Reflections of a Physicist*, Philosophical Library, 1950, 370.

53. Schur, Edwin M., "Theory, Planning and Pathology," *Social Problems*, VI, 3, Winter 1958-1959, 221-229.

54. Riesman, David, "The Academic Career: Notes on Recruitment and Colleagueship," *Daedulus: Proceedings of the American Academy of Arts and Sciences*, LXXXVIII, 1, Winter 1959, 147-169.

55. Kalven, Jr., Harvey, "Report on the Jury Project of the University of Chicago Law School." Address at the Conference on Legal Research, Ann Arbor, November 5, 1955.

56. The New York *Times*, October 13, 1955.

57. Carroll, Dennis and Jean Pinatel, "Report on the Teaching of Criminology," in *The University Teaching of Social Science: Criminology*, UNESCO, Paris, 1957, 16-48.

58. Bloch, Herbert A. and Frank Flynn, *Delinquency: The Juvenile Offender in America Today*, Random House, New York, 1956, 90-94.

59. Cameron, Mary Beth, *Department Store Shoplifting* (Ph.D. Dissertation), University of Indiana, Bloomington, 1953.

60. Cameron, Mary Beth, in Loren E. Edwards, *Shoplifting and Shrinkage Protection for Stores*, Thomas, Springfield, Ill., 1958, x.

61. Washington, Herald Tribune News Service, December 12, 1959.

62. For instance, Jones, Howard, *Crime and the Penal System*, University Tutorial Press, London, 1956, 6-8.

JUVENILE DELINQUENCY

W. G. Daniel
Virginia Union University

Juvenile Delinquency has been the subject of extensive discussion for the past three decades. Especially since 1950 have we witnessed a growing concern on the part of the public and the publication of more research literature. In spite of new information, efforts to explain the nature and the causes have sometimes been more confusing than clarifying and real meaning is often obscured. Whether juvenile delinquency has increased greatly remains debatable. The problem is centuries old and a study of statistics and publications shows that it seems to rise and fall in cycles, like many other social phenomena. The need to understand it remains, nevertheless, and the subject should be explored with all diligence.

THE MULTIPLE DIMENSIONS OF JUVENILE DELINQUENCY

Authorities in the field differ appreciably in their definitions and in the types of offenses and behavior which they include in treating the subject. Among them, however, there is an enhanced awareness that juvenile delinquency constitutes a problem of many dimensions that must be studied by a variety of approaches.

Differences of opinion as to the way that juvenile delinquents are regarded have been expressed by a newspaper reporter somewhat as follows. To most parents, juvenile delinquents are other people's children who behave objectionably. To lawyers, they are minors who are accused of offenses from which they are immune to the punishment that is usually administered to adults. To psychologists, they are youngsters whose social behavior patterns show deviations from acceptable norms. To court judges, they are simply neglected children who have been brought into the world by parents who have turned their backs on their offspring and left them to shift for themselves. The court is trying "to break the vicious cycle in which delinquent children become delinquent parents of more delinquent children." [1]

For our purposes, we accept the definition formulated by the NEA Juvenile Delinquency Project Staff. Juvenile delinquency is characterized as "behavior by non-adults which violates specific legal norms or the norms of a particular societal institution with sufficient frequency and/or seriousness so as to provide a firm basis for legal action against the behaving individual or group." [2]

Delinquency, thus, is a form of adopted or learned social behavior that is manifested in individuals or groups in their personal relations with other individuals or groups. This definition takes into account the fact that the term applies to conduct that may be peculiar to youth since adult society has accepted some standards for youth situations not faced by adults (such as school truancy or pranks of vandalism). Moreover, emphasis is placed on recurrence, persistency and seriousness of the offense.

We take the position that deviant behavior must be studied in the framework of our understanding of all forms of behavior— normal and exceptional. Then we may unravel the tendencies toward anti-social behavior and determine why some individuals become deviants or delinquents. In other words, it is necessary to study normal behavior and then see how social maladjustment develops to the extent of becoming juvenile delinquency.

Students of the subject have been approaching some agreement in their explanations. For example, it has become clearer that the study of the nature and causes of juvenile delinquency cannot be limited to one discipline or subject area. Rather, there must be an interdisciplinary undertaking that utilizes insights from a variety of disciplines, such as psychology, psychoanalysis, sociology, anthropology and ethics. Some authorities have tried to polarize two major viewpoints as psychodynamic and sociological. Such an attempt, however, seems unfruitful because of the interrelatedness of the factors which are involved. A single cause cannot be isolated and disagreement is sharp regarding the influence or significance of primary, secondary or contributory causes.

Our approach may be named socio-psychological, for it seeks for causes in the interaction of the individual with his immediate environment. Some of the influences responsible for delinquency cannot be neatly labeled as psychological and others sociological. Further, inasmuch as the definition already accepted has stressed the interaction of behavior with societal norms, the many factors tend to converge and intertwine rather than to become separated and isolated.

The study of the causes of delinquent behavior must be, then, in the area of personality development or socialization. In the pursuit of information, the most pertinent sources are investigations based on data using the genetic method, supported and checked by experimental, empirical and combinations of methods based upon sound hypotheses.

PERTINENT LITERATURE

Fortunately, there are many publications which supply data, findings and conclusions that may be utilized in formulating concepts, in developing working hypotheses, and in guiding programs of prevention and rehabilitation. Two series of studies, conducted in Massachusetts, are particularly significant. The Cambridge-Somerville Youth Study was initially reported and interpreted by Edwin Powers and Helen Witmer and later reevaluated by William and Joan McCord. The other investigations, directed by Sheldon and Eleanor Glueck, have been continuing for more than three decades. Considered together these independent teams of researchers utilize the two approaches useful in determining the critical factors in delinquency.

The Cambridge-Somerville Youth Study, published in 1951, illustrates the genetic method.[3] Its explicit hypothesis was that delinquency could be prevented by providing boys with an adult counselor who would supply friendship, understanding and a good example. These were the three elements deemed essential for developing a pattern of adequate social living. Approximately 650 boys were carefully paired into control and treatment groups and studied for about ten years. Many tests were given and the results reported statistically. Roughly, forty per cent of the boys in each of the categories obtained criminal records. Stable character traits had not been instilled and the incidence of delinquency was about the same for both groups. Such findings failed to prove the hypothesis and served to discourage many social workers and theorists.

The re-evaluation study, which appeared eight years later, reported a follow-up of the individuals by the use of case studies and the re-examination of the great mass of accumulated data.[4] This later investigation sought (1) to determine the part that the original study played in actually deflecting a boy from a life of crime, and (2) to discover what forces turned some of the boys into criminals. Further evidence of the value of case studies was ascertained and the cases were sufficient in number to permit reliable and valid statistical treatment. The authors proved the falsity of many popular notions on the subject, demonstrated the importance of the individual conscience in determining delinquency, and gave encouragement to those who believed in the value of the study.

Among the numerous volumes authored by the Gluecks, two are outstanding. They are *Unraveling Juvenile Delinquency*[5] and *The Problems of Delinquency*.[6] The former title reports the major research on which most of the publications have been based. Five hundred matched pairs of delinquents and non-delinquents (or a total of 1000 boys) were studied. Rigid procedures were administered in the selection of the cases and in the application of statistical measures. Some patterns of behavior differentiating the two groups were established and some reliable prediction tables were developed.

The other title is the most recent one to date. It is a compilation of selected writings representing the most accepted or recognized viewpoints on the subject, with introductions to each section by the editor, Sheldon Glueck. He quotes generously from his own work, and answers criticisms of his previous investigations. The implicit assumptions underlying the research through the years are made explicit. The compiler felt that the evidence from his prediction tables and the follow-up had provided an answer to the question, can the delinquent behavior be successfully predicted from the presence of the supposed criminogenic pattern and, relatedly, does it disappear when that pattern, or its major constituents, are blotted out?

A study stemming from a concern about the role of the schools in dealing with delinquency problems was directed by William B. Kvaraceus for the National Education Association.[7] The final two-volume report is the product of a team composed of recognized authorities in the fields of cultural anthropology, criminology, sociology, psychology, psychiatry, and pediatrics.

Four valuable symposia appeared in the two-year span of 1957-58. *Juvenile Delinquency*, edited by Joseph Roucek,[8] presented the views of fourteen competent authors whose combined contributions covered the important aspects of the subject. Both psychodynamic and sociological factors were discussed.

Preventing and reducing juvenile delinquency was the subject of the Law Enforcement Institute on Youth and Crime held at New York University. The proceedings were not published until two years later (1957). Edited by Frank J. Cohen, the published volume was titled *Youth and Crime*[9] and stressed the role of law enforcing agencies as well as giving consideration to psychological and sociological factors. Emphasis was on prevention.

Another symposium stressing prevention was published as a volume of *The Annals of the American Academy of Political and Social Science* under the title "Prevention of Juvenile Delinquency."[10] The book consists of reports of small programs directed toward prevention, gives some appraisals of their effectiveness and interrelates the knowledge from social science and psychology in offering valid explanations of socially deviant behavior. Most of these programs have not been subjected to scientific evaluation.

Appearing the same year was the Summer Yearbook number of *The Journal of Negro Education* entitled "Juvenile Delinquency Among Negroes." [11] This issue presented the views of many competent writers regarding the status of a marginal group in the context of a national problem. The role of society in contributing to the problem and some penetrating analyses of the issues involved are included.

The researches of Gough and Peterson indicate an approach that may help to identify some factors which explain tendencies toward delinquency.[12] They have developed a measuring device of predictive items to test the hypothesis that the delinquent is an individual who is unable to evaluate his own conduct in terms of its effects or consequences upon other persons and their welfare.

DEVIANT BEHAVIOR AND THE SOCIALIZATION OF CHILDREN AND YOUTH

The process of socialization takes place by the development within the individual of the adaptive mechanisms "which become part of the personality through the introjection (or internalizing) of standards and behaviors of individuals who have played a vital part in the characteristic forms of interaction" to which he has been exposed. Especially significant is the fact that there are two parallel lines of development; that is, "types representative of different social groups emerge within cultural settings, while at the same time individual variations occur within each one of these acculturated forms." [13]

The groundwork for the beginning of socialization lies in the early affiliative needs of the individual. These needs have been defined by one social psychologist as dependence, succorance and attachment. "They demand a basic rapport with the world before growth proper can start. Aggression and hatred, by contrast, are reactive protests, aroused only when affiliative tendencies are thwarted." [14] Feeling precedes intellectual understanding in the process of interacting with people. Built into the personality structure are habits and skills, frames of reference and cultural values that make for warmth, unity and a sense of personal worth. When these personality elements are absent or undeveloped, the individual becomes socially maladjusted. Much delinquency has been traced to affectional deprivation and disturbance in early childhood.[15]

The first reference group for the infant is his family. From its members he gets his first help in fulfilling needs or in obtaining recognition, reward or rebuff. In this frame of reference he learns to love and hate. A wide variety of family types is producing individuals with fundamental differences in culture. These differences "induce a series of behavior expectancies on the part of the child that are wholly indigenous to the peculiar social environment in which they are found." [16] Research points to the quality of the home and family life as the critical factor in social adjustment. Children who live in an emotionally frustrating home seek gratification for their affiliative needs elsewhere. William and Joan McCord concluded that a general family ethos provides an important reason that prevents children in some of the disorganized communities from turning to crime.[17]

The most fundamental influence, according to the McCords, is the mother's attitude, her behavior and family discipline. The effect of discipline is complicated and dependent upon many other factors. Whether of a punitive or love-oriented nature, consistent discipline is the best preventive for criminal behavior. Lax discipline in the home produces a large number of property, violent and sex delinquents. Youth reared in such a manner, however, are more likely to reform than offenders whose punishment has been erratically administered. Erratic punishment is most likely to induce delinquent behavior. Generally speaking, the effect of lax or punitive discipline is most strongly felt when other desirable socializing influences are absent in the home life of the offender.

As the child becomes older, his family group becomes larger and more inclusive of persons toward whom he has warm or

40

hostile feelings. His reference groups widen to include playmates, pals, friends, etc. in both informal and formal groups. As he achieves adolescence, he becomes conscious of the need to define his role in adult society. The process of role-determination is an individual one which evolves out of his own experiences in interacting with the social environment. As a young adolescent, his primary concern relates to status with his peers as he strives to be as much like the others as possible. Development as an older adolescent requires that he find an identity for himself, rather than limit himself to his role as a member of a particular sociological group, such as a family or gang.

The individual, however, continues to relate himself to some group with whose members he feels compatible. He accepts their values and social standards and they accept him as a person. The youth who become the members of gangs are those for whom home has failed to provide satisfaction. The solidification of the gang serves to increase their loyalty and dependence. "It is a source of adventure, social approval, training in the skills and lore of the streets, and of collective support. It becomes an agency for transmitting to new recruits the delinquent values of the older venerated members." [18] Thus, it develops a subculture of its own that conflicts with the adult community. For the individual, delinquency becomes a way of life that determines his outlook, mode of livelihood, use of leisure time and personality fulfillment. The juvenile delinquent becomes the adult criminal offender and a social liability.

The chances that individuals will become delinquents are increased if they are members of the subcultural groups which live on the margin of the community. These are the people who "(1) cannot readily make ordinary socio-economic adjustments; (2) are employed largely in marginal and unskilled occupations; (3) are handicapped in their search for normal avenues of assimilation by powerful cultural barriers erected against them; and (4) find it difficult because of language, culture, and other reasons to identify with the predominant public culture." [19] They are the scapegoats of the community who are blamed for its difficulties, ranked in the lowest strata of the social scale and permitted no voice in the democratic processes of community organization.

Many youth drop out of school when they reach the age at which school is no longer compulsory. The drop-out sees no value in his school experience, has trouble in getting a job and is likely to join an anti-social group whose members carry hostile feelings toward the world in which they live. Such youth are likely to be members of a marginal group whose adults have psychological and social problems. In fleeing from a school which they dislike, they go to job discrimination and social deprivation. Ofttimes the agencies which are supposed to help them compound their problems. Some of those who get jobs enter a social structure which permits members of prestige groups to violate the generally professed norms of behavior and go unpunished. Many soon find themselves under indictment by the law for some minor offense; but our governmental agencies for personal and social adjustment continue the emotional and social deprivations which they have already experienced.

As the result of their experiences during these important formative years of childhood and adolescence, definite personality patterns emerge. Researchers have observed differences between the composites of traits of the delinquents and those of non-delinquents. The studies of the Gluecks, the McCords, Gough and Peterson supply evidence for our conclusions.

Especially germane to our position are the findings originally reported in *Unraveling Juvenile Delinquency* and later re-interpreted in *Problems of Delinquency* regarding intelligence, mental pathology and the dynamics of temperament. On the Wechsler-Bellevue Scale, the delinquents made lower average scores on verbal intelligence items than the non-delinquents, but on the performance intelligence items, the resemblance was close. In the qualitative and dynamic aspects of intelligence that are measured by the Rorschach Test, the resemblance is close in originality, creativity, banality, intuition, phantasy and over-verbalizing intelligence.

The investigators comment that "Reflection upon these findings suggests that the differences between the delinquents and non-delinquents are concerned with intellectual tendencies that are interwoven with emotional dynamics, and that they are likely to be involved, not only in the ability to cope with school tasks, but also in the general process of socialization or maladjustment." [20]

By the use of the Rorschach Test, validly significant differences were found in the mental pathology patterns of the normal and socially deviating boys. The latter were more socially assertive, defiant and ambivalent to authority, more resentful of others, far more hostile, suspicious and destructive.

The two groups of boys were also interviewed by psychiatrists, who reported differences in many aspects and manifestations of personality. Delinquents are more inclined to impulsive and non-reflective expression of their energy drives for they are more dynamic, much more agressive, adventurous, stubborn and positively suggestible but emotionally unstable and less adequate in the capacity to operate on a fairly efficient level. They are, moreover, less sensitive to aesthetic values, less conventional and practical in considering the consequences of behavior and far less critical of their own conduct. On the other hand, this group was desirous of acquiring material things, more self-centered and more extroverted in resolving conflicts.

These findings give support to the importance of the inner-springs or dynamics of human adjustment. Fritz Redl has said that delinquent behavior results from a disturbance in any one or several of the following personality areas: (1) the organism's defense against something that was done to it; (2) the result of growth confusion; (3) the result stemming from the impact of excitement and group intoxication; (4) the consequence of neurotic afflictions, all the way from mild hangovers from childhood difficulties to well-defined neuroses; (5) the need to implement severe impulses or compulsions; (6) the inability to stabilize the individual's control system; and (7) the reflection of the exposure to the mores of a delinquent community or neighborhood.[21]

The conclusions of Redl indicate the internal nature of cause. The researches of the Gluecks and the McCords give him further support. The latter team concluded "that criminality is generally the result of a basic deficiency in conscience, a failure to internalize basic inhibitions." [22] And Allport says that conscience is the crucial agent in socialization for it produces the controls which govern "transitory impulse and opportunistic adjustment in the interests of long-range aim and consistency with self-image." [23]

Previously in the chapter, the most significant variables in determining delinquency were mentioned. According to our present knowledge, the development of conscience depends upon three of them. Its base is established when the needs for affiliation are satisfied. The content of conscience comes from exemplary models and relationships supplied by parents or parental substitutes, while consistency of discipline insures the internalization of this content. The absence of these conditions leads to delinquency. Their presence provides the ingredients for the maturing and functioning of conscience.

THE DELINQUENT AND THE COMMUNITY

Implicit in this discussion has been the view that the nature of a delinquent offense is largely a matter of cultural definition and is influenced by varying community norms, pressures and practices. Sociologists have established the fact that cities and towns are aggregates of several neighborhoods, communities or subcultures. In fact, for many years, slums were regarded as the cause and breeders of juvenile delinquency. Although there is a correlation between the rate of delinquency and neighborhood deterioration, the preponderance of recent research does not support a cause-and-effect relationship. Of itself, an environmental factor is not a cause. It contributes to the cause when it becomes a part of the motivating factor. In this manner, the environment helps or hinders the maturing of conscience.

A major fallacy in the environmental approach to the explanation of delinquency has been the use of "trappings" or outward manifestations rather than the inner dynamic qualities which cause significant differences. Sometimes the observer is unable to distinguish between cause and effect. A good example of this difficulty is the role of the gang as a subcultural group. The juvenile may turn to the gang because it is the group that approves his behavior. There is evidence that delinquent tendencies are well on their way before many boys become gang members.

The neighborhood or local community, nevertheless, provides the conditions which nurture the development of criminal tendencies and the environment which fosters the operations of the influential antisocial subcultural groups. The juvenile whose personality pattern predisposes him to choose socially inadequate ways of living finds certain cultural and social conditions more conducive to delinquency than others.

In discussing the community, it is helpful to distinguish between the cultural and social structures. Merton suggested rough working definitions at a conference held under the auspices of the United States Children's Bureau. Cultural structure is "that organized set of normative values which is common to members of a designated group" while social structure is "that organized set of social relationships in which members of the group are variously implicated or involved." [24]

The conflicting values prevalent in our culture are readily recognized. Our culture signals in so many directions that the bewilderment of many children and youth should not be surprising. Mass media of communication, overtly and subtly, transmit to most Americans a common set of values which are conflicting and confusing to adults and juveniles alike. Each person accepts the values of the subculture with which he identifies most easily and comfortably. Most people give lip-service to certain high and lofty ideals expressed in the official documents of church, state and school; but their deeds are not consistent with their words.

Observing the cultural and social structures which control our lives, many sociologists write about the delinquent community rather than the delinquent juvenile. Some characterize our society as sick, socially underdeveloped or morally immature.

Some also consider the number and variety of social deviants as indices of community fragmentation.

According to Barron, our values are conducive to delinquency.[25] In describing the typology of American values, he selects six for special emphasis and treatment. These are (1) success, (2) status and power ascendance, (3) pecuniary and material wealth, (4) resistance to authority, (5) toughness and (6) dupery. Others which he mentions are (1) American culture is dynamic; (2) American culture offers alternate norms; (3) social relationships in American society have become increasingly impersonal; and (4) a multi-group society fosters a duality of loyalty and ethics.

Contained in this value orientation is the model of the successful, aggressive, self-made man. His major qualities which youth are taught to admire are self-reliance, acquisitiveness, inventiveness, and the ability to manipulate people and things. He is typified in our financial wizard, industrial giant or labor boss, whose attitudes toward others are quite likely to be based upon their usefulness in accomplishing the ends of the enterpriser. "Traditional values are used to support the ends of power, authority and wealth, and emphasis is on the need of unlimited freedom to make a triumphant struggle through the human jungle. Business is business; expediency and self-interest are primary."[26]

Exerting tremendous influence in the community are the prestige subgroups. Research has shown that what they do sets norms of behavior as much as what they say. Or what they exact of others sets the model of behavior. Among the more prominent prestige subgroups mentioned by Taft are lawyers, politicians, government agents, business men, labor leaders, physicians, clergymen and leaders in sports.[27] They influence and are affected by law-making and law enforcement. They help determine the nature and effectiveness of agencies of social control other than the law. Our newspapers report daily the prosecution and conviction of men in the aforementioned groups. Testimony, expressed opinions, attitudes show a curious mixture of respect and disrespect for the law itself, the law-makers and the agents

46

of law enforcement. Recent exposures of rackets involving legislators, police and businessmen do not provide youth with values or models which are essential to character-building.

Taft lists three ways in which our culture and social structure make for crime.[28] First, on the seeming theory that some persons must fail or be underprivileged, differentiated experiences and restricted opportunities are provided for a large part of the population. Second, our society involves the relative tolerance, acceptance and even the approval of exploitive behavior, either of the white-collar crime type or that of the non-criminal exploiter. Third, although they are not necessarily positively valued, such characteristics as the complexity of our society and the decline of personal relations among its members help to explain the way in which delinquency and crime become possible.

There are other environmental influences that affect human behavior and consequent delinquency. Among them are social disorganization, urbanization, internal migration and rapid technological change. The social institutions determine the manner in which the community is organized. When their services are suddenly disrupted, there is an immediate sociopsychological response, such as a lowering of morale, vandalism, anti-social conduct, and the like. Every community has a system for protecting its citizens, administering justice to all and dealing with offenders. The effectiveness of the work of the police system and the courts has a tremendous influence upon inducing, preventing or abetting illegal behavior.

In a symposium concerned with delinquency among the largest racial minority in the United States, the contributors highlighted the significance of social factors and community institutions. Lohman suggested two crucial agencies in the career of the socially deviating or disturbed child which afford an opportunity for meeting his needs on a group basis. These are (1) the school and (2) the police and court system.[29] Today every juvenile who is classified as a delinquent has had experiences with representatives of these institutions and the community has given them certain responsibilities for handling the problems involved. Their work will not be discussed in this chapter, since other contributors to this volume are treating them in some detail. At this point, however, it should be said that their failure to perform their functions adequately contributes to norm-violating behavior on the part of children and youth. Youth gangs are formed in schools, juvenile detention homes and correctional institutions. Juveniles turn to anti-social gang life when home, school and other agencies are unattractive. On the other hand, many teachers, school administrators, judges, police officers and group workers have contributed the leadership necessary to help potential delinquents and juvenile offenders in following socially satisfying ways of life.

The NEA Juvenile Delinquency Project report stresses the significance of social class in influencing behavior[30] and is corroborated by many recent publications. It suggests that lower-class behavior is diffusing itself into our community life at all levels but most successfully through adolescents. Americans have generally thought that the middle class sets most of our norms. Many examinations of the sources of our values and tastes indicate that our practices are on a low level and that even our ideals or standards are not those which we thought prevailed. When the adults appeal to physical prowess, masculine or feminine vanity, personal comfort, selfish interests or getting ahead in a competitive society, the youth response may very likely be the pattern of a lower social class rather than the middle class norm which is accepted by the church, school and other character-building agencies.

Some writers maintain that the attempt of the middle class to impose its norms upon others causes a revolt by youth. The pressure for conformity is thought to result in non-conformity. It would be well to remember, however, that our understanding might not be complete because the investigations have been conducted mainly with lower class groups.

Another finding of the NEA Project relates to attitude. It is the attitude of the adults rather than a phenomenal increase in the rate of delinquency that has caused more concern for juvenile deviant behavior. For some law-abiding adults the psychological functions of vicarious thrill, guilt or escape are fulfilled by their overt expressions of alarm about the norm-violating behavior of youngsters.

FRAMEWORK FOR UNDERSTANDING JUVENILE DELINQUENCY

The research and publications of the last ten years provide materials for the development of a theory regarding juvenile delinquency. It would be helpful if a new publication would refer less to existing differences and begin the construction of a set of principles or workable hypotheses. On some viewpoints, there seem to be some growing agreements.

In this chapter, we have started from the premise that juvenile delinquency is learned antisocial behavior. Such behavior is learned by non-adults in violation of the specific norms codified in law or required by a particular societal institution "with sufficient frequency and/or seriousness so as to provide a firm basis for legal action against the behaving individual or group."

Our approach is the socio-psychological one. The principal technique for investigation is the genetic method which must be supported by all other relevant methods. An interdisciplinary approach must be used to bring to bear pertinent information which cannot be found in one discipline or approach. The growth and development of the socialization process from infancy to adulthood must be studied scientifically. Special stress needs to be given to the way in which the affiliative needs of youngsters are being met, the presence of cohesiveness in the home and family relationships and the interaction between juveniles and the local community. To the extent to which they influence their interacting, such social factors as cultural values, transitional neighborhoods, social disorganization, social stratification, adult attitudes and social or community institutions need to be considered.

Many popular notions and unproved theories must be discarded. Prominent among them are views that juvenile delinquency is caused by poverty, slum neighborhoods, low in-

49

telligence or sick minds. There are helpful publications already available.

Careful study of the sources which we have mentioned, their findings and conclusions, will give some answers to the questions (1) Who are the juvenile offenders? (2) How do they get to be offenders? (3) How did the environment assist in the process of developing norm-violating behavior? and (4) What are the factors which come closest to providing an explanation for the differences between those who choose to follow socially accepted norms and those who deviate?

SELECTED BIBLIOGRAPHY

Allport, Gordon. *Becoming: Basic Considerations for a Psychology of Personality*, Yale University Press, New Haven, 1955. An important treatment of the process of personality development.

Barron, Milton I. *The Juvenile in Delinquent Society*, Alfred A. Knopf, New York, 1954. Analyzes the way in which the American society is more responsible for delinquents than the juveniles.

Bloch, Herbert A., and Flynn, Frank T. *Delinquency: The Juvenile Offender in America Today*, Random House, New York, 1956. A comprehensive treatment of the problem from the viewpoint of modern sociology.

Cohen, Albert K. *Delinquent Boys: The Culture of the Gang*, Free Press, Glencoe, Illinois, 1955. Presents the thesis regarding the way in which the gang operates as a subculture in producing delinquency.

Dahlke, Otto H. *Values in Culture and Classroom*, Harper and Brothers, New York, 1958. How the value system in the culture of the school and community socializes the students.

Glueck, Sheldon and Eleanor. *Unraveling Juvenile Delinquency*, Commonwealth Fund, New York, 1950. A ten-year study of 500 pairs of delinquent boys that provides material for determining some causes of delinquency. Useful prediction tables are given.

Glueck, Sheldon, (ed.), *The Problem of Delinquency*, Houghton, Mifflin, Boston, 1959. A valuable and comprehensive survey of the delinquency problem edited by an authority and containing representative selections of competent researchers and writers.

Kvaraceus, William C., *et al. Delinquent Behavior*, National Education Association, Washington, 1959. Reports in two volumes the results of the NEA Juvenile Delinquency Study. An excellent statement of the social environment viewpoint.

Martin, William E. and Stendler, Celia B. *Child Behavior and Development*, (revised edition), Harcourt, Brace, New York, 1959. Explains the way in which children learn their social behavior in the light of an inter-disciplinary approach to the psychology of behavior.

McCord, William and Joan. *Origins of Crime*, Columbia University Press, New York, 1959. Re-appraisal of the Cambridge-Somerville Youth Study with an encouraging view of how the data may be used. The most useful publication for developing workable hypotheses.

Powers, Edwin and Witmer, Helen. *An Experiment in the Prevention of Delinquency*, Columbia University Press, New York, 1951. An extensive research investigation of 325 pairs of boys based upon the hypothesis of preventing delinquency by providing guidance. Very suggestive as to types of data needed.

Roucek, Joseph S. (ed.). *Juvenile Delinquency*, Philosophical Library, New York, 1958. A symposium in which 14 authors treat the most significant phases of deviant behavior among non-adults.

Ruch, Floyd L. *Psychology and Life*, Scott, Foresman and Co., fifth edition, Chicago, 1958. Contains a brief summary of important studies on illegal behavior with suggestions of programs for improvement.

Stein, Herman D. and Cloward, Richard A. *Social Perspectives on Behavior*, Free Press, Glencoe, Illinois, 1958. Presents the viewpoints of a variety of recognized scholars regarding the social influences on human behavior.

Sutherland, Edward H. and Cressey, D. T. *Principles of Criminology*, fifth edition, J. B. Lippincott, Philadelphia, 1955. A revision of a well-known work of a famous sociologist who developed a theory of crime and evaluated pertinent research.

Taft, Donald. *Criminology*, third edition, Macmillan, New York, 1956. An explanation of the background and nature of crime and of the treatment of criminals. Special emphasis is given to the dominant role of culture and particularly prestige groups.

Teeters, Negley K., and Reinemann, John O. *The Challenge of Delinquency*, Prentice-Hall, New Jersey, 1950. In spite of the fact that this book is ten years old, the presentation is extensive and well supported. Includes an interesting statement of basic theory.

Thompson, Charles H. (ed.). "Juvenile Delinquency Among Negroes in the United States," *Journal of Negro Education*, 1959. Although this symposium was concerned with Negroes, the contributors treated the subject in national perspective.

Wattenberg, William W. *The Adolescent Years*, Harcourt, Brace and Company, New York, 1955. Excellent chapters on the stages of progress before and during adolescence and the interaction of personality with the environment.

Witmer, Helen, and Kotinsky, Ruth. *New Perspectives for Research on Juvenile Delinquency*, Government Printing Office, Washington, 1956. Reports the deliberations and conclusions of a conference held under the auspices of the U.S. Children's Bureau for the purpose of gaining new insights and leads for further study and investigation.

Walter G. Daniel, Director of the Division of Education and Psychology at Virginia Union University, was born on June 21, 1905. He received his A.B. from Virginia Union University; his Ed.B. and A.M. from the University of Cincinnati; and his Ph.D. from Columbia University. He pursued two years of formal post-doctoral study at Teachers College, Columbia University in human relations and psychological foundations and services. As a senior college student, he did volunteer YMCA work in the Virginia State Penitentiary at Richmond and for three years was on the residential staff of William Sloane House YMCA, New York City. He has held teaching positions in the field of education and psychology at the State Teachers College Winston-Salem, North Carolina State Teachers College at Bowie, Maryland, and Howard University; and for two years was specialist in higher education in the Office of Education of the United States Department of Health, Education and Welfare. His publications include more than 50 articles in *The Journal of Negro Education, School Life, Journal of Educational Sociology, College and Research Libraries,* etc. The most recent publication relevant to this volume was "The Role of Character-Building Organizations in the Prevention of Juvenile Delinquency," in *The Journal of Negro Education*, Summer 1959. Fellow of the American Association for the Advancement of Science and member of Phi Delta Kappa, Kappa Delta Pi, The National Education Association, The American Teachers Association and The Virginia Teachers Association.

NOTES

1. Adapted from a report by William B. Rosten, Jr. in the *Richmond News Leader*, November 18, 1959.
2. Kvaraceus, William, *et al.*, *Delinquent Behavior: Culture and the Individual*, National Education Association, Washington, D. C., 1959, 54.
3. Powers, Edwin and Helen Witmer, *An Experiment in the Prevention of Delinquency*, Columbia University Press, New York, 1951.
4. McCord, William and Joan, *Origins of Crime*, Columbia University Press, New York, 1959.
5. Glueck, Sheldon and Eleanor, *Unraveling Juvenile Delinquency*, Harvard University Press, Cambridge, 1950.
6. Glueck, Sheldon, *The Problem of Delinquency*, Houghton, Mifflin, Boston, 1959.
7. Kvaraceus, William B., *et al.*, *Delinquent Behavior*, National Education Association, Washington, 1959.
8. Roucek, Joseph, *Juvenile Delinquency*, Philosophical Library, New York, 1958.
9. Cohen, Frank J., *Youth and Crime*, International Universities Press, New York, 1957.
10. Witmer, Helen L. (ed.), "Prevention of Juvenile Delinquency," *The Annals of the American Academy of Political and Social Science*, The Academy, Philadelphia, Vol. 322, March 1959.
11. Thompson, Chas. H. (ed.), "Juvenile Delinquency Among Negroes," *Journal of Negro Education*, Washington, D. C., Summer 1959.
12. Ruch, Floyd L., *Psychology and Life*, Scott, Foresman, Co., 5th edition, Chicago, 1958, 410.
13. Bloch, Herbert A. and Frank T. Flynn, *Delinquency: The Juvenile Offender in America Today*, Random House, New York, 1956, 87.
14. Allport, Gordon, *Becoming: Basic Considerations for a Psychology of Personality*, Yale University Press, New Haven, 1955, 32.
15. Allport, Gordon, *op. cit.*, 31-55.
16. Bloch, Herbert A. and Frank T. Flynn, *op. cit.*, 55.
17. McCord, William and Joan, *op. cit.*
18. Lohman, Joseph, "Juvenile Delinquency: A Social Dimension," *Journal of Negro Education*, Summer 1959, 291.
19. Bloch, Herbert A. and Frank T. Flynn, *op. cit.*, 44.
20. Glueck, Sheldon and Eleanor, *Unraveling Juvenile Delinquency*, 214.
21. Witmer, Helen and Ruth Kotinsky, *New Perspectives for Research on*

Juvenile Delinquency, Government Printing Office, Washington, D. C., 1956, 58-61.

22. McCord, William and Joan, *op. cit.,* 196.

23. Allport, Gordon, *op. cit.,* 68.

24. Witmer, Helen and Ruth Kotinsky, *op. cit.,* 28.

25. Barron, Milton L., *The Juvenile in Delinquent Society,* Knopf, New York, 1954.

26. Dahlke, Otto, H., *Values in Culture and Classroom,* Harper, New York. 1958, 54-55.

27. Taft, Donald, *Criminology,* Macmillan, New York, 1956.

28. *Ibid.,* 388-9.

29. Lohman, Joseph, *op. cit.,* 286-299.

30. Kvaraceus, William, *op. cit.,* 56-86.

LEGAL NORMS AND CRIMINOLOGICAL DEFINITIONS

Donald J. Newman
St. Lawrence University

It would seem axiomatic that criminal law serves the vital function of defining, and very precisely, the subject matter of criminology. While there can be all sorts of social science originating and progressing totally independent from legal norms, criminology by its very existence as a recognized and distinct field would logically rest its definitions solidly on legal foundations. In brief, criminology is generally conceded to be that field of social science most devoted to the measurement, analysis, classification, prediction and (more esoterically) the "understanding" and possibly "control" of criminal behavior. And criminal behavior is *ipso facto* that body of culturally reprehensible behavior defined in the substantive criminal codes. The law provides the "what" and social science the "why" in a happy, mutually satisfying partnership.

Unfortunately perhaps, this relationship is not as clear cut, in either theory or practice, as would superficially appear nor has the partnership been particularly satisfying or happy. On the one hand those persons and institutions whose chief concern is the criminal law have been generally either hostile or indifferent to the problems of the social scientists working with the same behavior. There are notable exceptions, of course, but lawyers (using the title in a very generalized sense), who have no trouble understanding extremely subtle variations in legal concepts, have never clearly distinguished sociology from social welfare and criminology from prison administration.

This confusion, and in some instances antagonism, is not without grounds. Criminologists on their part have rather consistently, and even cheerfully, chosen to dismiss the whole or at least significant parts of the criminal law system as irrelevant in forming their theoretical models. As Gilbert Geis puts it "sociologists are not interested, because of disciplinary values, in dealing with the diffuse and complicated criminal law system, a system which they neither created nor can control, and therefore prefer to ignore."[1] He attributes part of the lawyers' hostility to the failure of such "sociological" experiments as the juvenile court and the problems raised by such "sociological" judicial decisions as the Supreme Court holding on school desegregation.[2] And the social scientist in addition to his impatience with legal obtuseness, points accusingly to the unreality of legalistic conceptions of behavior in the light of up to date motivational and action theory research.

Regardless of the roots of the lawyer—social scientist conflict, it is apparent that it exists and its existence adds confusion to both fields. It is our purpose here to examine some of the problems raised by this conflict, to point up some of the implications of departing from legal foundations in defining crime and to suggest, although tentatively, a rapprochement.

THE LAW AND CRIMINAL BEHAVIOR

It is neither necessary here to trace the development of codified criminal law nor to discuss in great detail the aims and ends of the law or its effectiveness as a means of social control. Suffice it to say that the great mass of criminal codes now in existence along with the multiple procedures for implementing them represents centuries of man's most noteworthy attempts to specify that behavior which is culturally reprehensible and to provide means for both correcting and preventing it. The construction of such laws poses problems of the greatest magnitude for they must at the same time be general and specific, consistent, predictable yet dynamic, uniform but tolerant of variations, scientific yet humanistic, directed more to the protection of innocent than conviction of guilty and yet efficient in the determination of guilt, and of course they must punish and reform simultaneously.

Legal norms could be easily codified if the consequences of behavior, or if the behavior itself, were the only issues. Thus "Thou Shalt Not Kill" with few modifications and some simple rules of evidence could become a reasonably sufficient homicide statute. The law as it developed, however, became as much concerned with the mental state of the actor as with his overt behavior or the consequences of his actions. It became insufficient to prove that "killing" did occur and that "thou" effected it without distinguishing the intentions of the killer. Thus inadvertent killing became clearly distinguishable from killing with "malice aforethought" and this in turn from killing because of negligence or in "the heat of passion" and so on. In short the law added to actions and consequences this very difficult conception of variable intent while, it might be added, excluding from criminal liability certain categories of persons such as children and mental incompetents. Thus the simple rule "Thou Shalt Not Kill" became recast into the multiple and complex homicide statutes of today's criminal codes. Who kills and under what mental conditions became more important in determining liability than the killing itself.

The addition of "mental state of the actor" as a considered factor in criminal liability made the law very much a behavioral science but a behavioral science of a peculiar sort. Perhaps "science" should not be the term for although the law seeks to describe all possible permutations of a number of deviant behaviors, it is not necessarily dedicated to the scientific method in developing codes or concepts nor in testing the validity of many of its premises. Unlike the ethos of social science in general, the law is predicated on a set of values devoted to enumerating behavior which *ought* to be (or perhaps more accurately which ought *not to* be) rather than describing behavioral variations which exist without making explicit moral judgments. In so doing, the law in theory rests on a set of values which are rarely questioned and which are derived from the major ideological foundations of the society. In our own society some of these would include the Constitution, conceptions of private property, and capitalistic enterprise, the supremacy of the state (with adequate controls) and the other principles of modern democracy. In elaborating its codes, lawmakers test deviation against a set of legal "fictions" such as the "reasonable and prudent" man, the hedonistically "calculating" offender, and seek to discover truth through cross-examination before a "reasonable" jury and even with modern sentencing discretion, statutes attempt to make the "punishment fit the crime." In its efforts to be uniform and consistent the law presumes an equality of motivation so that, as Anatole France put it, "The law, in its majestic equality, forbids the rich as well as the poor to sleep under bridges, to beg in the streets and to steal bread." [3] For while the law is endlessly explicit on its various meanings and uses of "intent" it is almost totally unconcerned with motivation for lawbreaking (except, of course, where motivation might help prove intent). Here, I believe, is one of the greatest distinctions between criminology, other social sciences and the criminal law. The detailed descriptions of behavior contained in law, the elaborate methods of testing facts against these behavioral standards must be admired by social scientists for their scope if not their premises. The obvious necessity of daily applying law to thousands of cases presents problems far beyond the ken of the social scientist who with his primarily microscopic studies and his measurement techniques must only evaluate, not practice. There is no assurance, either, that measurement in criminology, psychiatry, clinical psychology or any other field is one whit more accurate in determining "truth" or dispensing "justice" than the complex system of evidence, methods of cross-examination and judgment of peers found in the law. Is an attitude scale more valid than a jury decision in determing the practical results of freedom or imprisonment? This, of course, could be hotly debated with lie detectors and truth serum frequently mentioned. Let it be sufficient here to state that legal procedure, while cumbersome and slow-changing, has indeed incorporated some social science techniques, such as the frequent use of psychiatric examinations for the purpose of defense, pre-sentence investigations and even sentencing boards. Lawmakers, too, have been influenced, sometimes belatedly, by developments in such diverse fields as race relations, child development and labor economics. But the law and the social scientist still differ in emphasis on the issue of why laws are broken. The lawyer seeks to *control* lawbreaking while the social scientist is more interested in etiological analysis for its own sake. That these ends are not theoretically exclusive is apparent but the divergent developments in law and sociology have somehow made them so. To the social scientist and to the psychiatrist the legal fictions underlying criminal codes are anathema. Hedonism, the "reason-able" man and the devotion to "free will" all are viewed by more deterministic sciences as naive and archaic. But the lawyer, faced with a multitude of conflicting personality and attitude theories can best ignore them, except perhaps in sentencing. The inclu-sion of motivation into the law would appear to add merely confusion, not enlightenment. Look, for example at the problems raised by allowing insanity as a defense! No two experts can agree on its definitions, symptoms or causes; how then can psychotics be distinguished from legally liable violators except to use primarily legal rules of evidence regarding intent?[4] And won't the effect of still other motivational distinctions make the law less certain, less uniform and less just than at present?

In addition to this matter of the behavioral premises under-lying statutory descriptions, social scientists are apt to raise questions about the types of behavior defined as criminal and about the relative seriousness of offenses implicit in the gradu-ated punishment provisions of the criminal codes. Here ques-tions are directed to lawmakers rather than enforcers and the issue centers on that behavior which *ought* to be criminal rather than the reality of descriptions of behavior already so defined. The ideology of social scientists has led them to eye law*making* as a sociocultural process almost as fascinating as law*breaking* and to ask questions and raise issues basic to both this process and its results.[5] What factors lead to legislative decisions defining some offenses as misdemeanors and others as felonies? Why is embezzlement less seriously punished than some other forms of theft? Do not the interrelated variables of prestige and power converge to *build into* the law class-based inequalities regardless of the claim or the facts of uniform enforcement? Not all lawmaking analysis is critical, of course, but is directed toward a broad, analytic understanding of historical processes, popular opinions and other sociocultural vectors in legislative and judicial decisions.[6]

At any rate, the criminal law as stated has not proved behaviorally accurate enough for criminologists to accept as completely delimiting or defining for their purposes. Nevertheless, criminologists oriented to etiological discoveries in lawbreaking must reckon with the criminal law to give themselves identity no matter how much they later depart from an analysis of its norms.

THE FIELD OF CRIMINOLOGY

Criminology as a recognized academic field is as old as most of the areas of social science and as distinct and respectable. Starting, empirically at least, as an offshoot of physical anthropology it has gradually shifted to almost total inclusion within the discipline of sociology, taking theory, method and scientific ethos from this broader orientation. The action oriented companions of criminology, notably social work and psychiatry, have gone their own ways and are viewed by practicing criminologists as sort of lesser heresies fit only as subjects of periodic attack in textbook and classroom.[7] Part of the lawyer's indignation at criminology comes from a fairly persistent tendency to confuse the values of social work with sociological method and to stereotype social science with psychiatry with which the lawyer has had anything but good relations. As a matter of fact both psychiatry and social work have concentrated their efforts on the criminal as distinct from the abstraction "crime" and both maintain an action orientation seeking to cure or rehabilitate offenders while causative theories of crime receive only incidental attention, although all sorts of hypotheses are implicit in curative programs. Some theories, eclectic in social work, neo-Freudian in psychiatry, of course are continually invented or exhumed but the day-by-day duties of practitioners in both fields leaves little room for expansive theorizing and less room for worrying about such esoteric problems as whether the substantive criminal law really includes all criminal behavior, whether clinical or inmate samples are representative of all criminals and so on. Questions about such things as white collar crime and violations of ethical codes befuddle theory and practice alike.

Criminology while perhaps no less befuddled by such questions does not directly concern itself with curing criminals, although evaluation of others' rehabilitative or preventive programs is fair game. Criminology sets itself the admittedly not modest task of seeking to understand, first, the existence of crime in any given culture and, second, the processes by which some individuals in the culture become criminals while others do not. On the first level, criminologists can deal with crime in its most abstract form, measuring rates and trends of violations, values and value-conflicts concerning what behavior is called criminal, the impact of urbanization on crime and delinquency, and other facets of the crime problem without ever once referring themselves to an individual criminal or even seeing one let alone curing him. On the second level, criminologists seek to develop theories to account for differential violation within a society and here they more often come in contact with hypotheses concerning heredity, personality development, family influence, learning processes, and so forth, many emanating primarily from other fields.

Of course criminology like all modern fields of social science is empirical as well as theoretical. Measurement techniques, methods of approach to the testing of theoretical models and all the paraphernalia of empiricism form a major part of criminological activity.[8] Now perhaps methodology and conceptualization should be reciprocally dependent but for any number of reasons this is not always the case particularly in this field. In the first place, problems posed by criminologists are cast in behavioral terms while research must rest on definitions which are primarily legalistic. In some instances any differences between these two approaches may be minor but in others major problems are raised. For example, a criminologist may wish to study the broad problem of stealing. He will want to know why stealing exits, (or perhaps even why private property exists), its extent in our culture, who steals and who does not steal, types and techniques of stealing, class variations in stealing and so on. He is interested in the motivational patterns in stealing, in the "why" and the "who" of the problem but he discovers methodologically that his first problem becomes "what" is stealing. Turning to the law, as he must to discover legal norms relating to stealing, he discovers not a single conception of theft but a series of norms each with separate and sometimes quite distinct requirements for stealing. He is confronted with larceny, grand and small, stealing through "breaking and entering," stealing through force, through fraud and trickery, by embezzlement and extortion, and stealing by omission (tax frauds) as well as stealing by commission, both direct and indirect. His original problem of "stealing" now involves such diverse behavior as taking an automobile for a joy-ride, bank robbery, confidence games, racketeering and the formation of business monopolies. At this point, he must either narrow his conceptions of stealing to fit one of the legal subtypes or face almost insurmountable data-gathering problems should he maintain his "stealing" conception. If he narrows his problem, as has been customary in sociology,[9] he also narrows his results. If he should choose to study only embezzlers, as Cressey did,[10] or some other distinct legal type, he is being clearly "criminological" in the sense of studying behavior defined criminal by legal norms but he loses, of course, the generalization necessary to answer his original questions of the motivation for stealing, the extent of it and questions of differential participation in stealing. If he maintains his generalized conception he may find it hard to behaviorally reconcile divergent legal definitions or may look beyond the law to behavior similar motivationally to stealing (college students cheating, quiz-show fixes, the "payola" of disc jockeys and so forth) but not legally prohibited. At this point he is not as precisely "criminological" but can likely claim to come closer to the mark of understanding the generalized motivational patterns of stealing than he could by the narrower study.

In its early decades criminology had little interest in legal norms as such. Pioneer criminologists studied prison inmates and cheerfully generalized their results to the total universe of "criminals." Obviously convicts were criminals, duly defined, processed and incarcerated. No conflict with norms here. Furthermore early research was primarily anthropological, involving physical measurements of "criminals" (compared later with more statistical sophistication with "non-criminal" controls) or focussed on mental-testing or the searching for other personal pathologies existing in men in prison.[11] The shift in criminological emphasis from anthropology and psychometry to sociological methods took the criminologist out of the prison and away from preoccupation with individual traits. He became interested in "crime" as a cultural abstraction from "criminal" and at the same time became dedicated to the discovery of processes generalizable to the total phenomenon of law-breaking and not merely to prison samples. He became aware that, although they were neat and to a certain extent satisfying, his studies of inmates told him little of causative value except perhaps to describe the process of how an offender gets into prison and, by inference, something of the courts' biases in sentencing and something of the law's dedication to repressing lower class law violation.

On the other hand, stepping outside the walls challenged his research ingenuity. Studying undetected criminals, the criminal "in the open" became a much more difficult task.[12] Furthermore, the apparent necessity to develop definitive limitations to his field made him look squarely at the dual concepts "crime" and "criminal" and to propose both working and theoretical models based upon revised estimates of their scope.

The field of criminology thereafter progressed along two major lines. On the one hand, new methods of analysis were developed (or borrowed) while new hypotheses were constantly proposed, tested, discarded or reworked and causative theories propounded. On the other hand, no less concern was shown with the definitive problems of crime. It was apparent that no measurement of criminals or theory about crime was more accurate or useful than the definitions on which it rested. Probably as much journal space has been devoted to debates about the meaning of "crime" and the limits of the universe "criminal" as to results of empirical studies of lawbreaking. Criminology fought on one front for identity as a discrete science, obviously dependent for definitions based upon formal legal norms, but on the other for meaningful inclusion within a broader conception of behavioral science, limited and unique only in that it included as a primary source legal norms but was not bound by them. This battle is far from finished but its impact upon the field of criminology cannot be denied. The scope of the field has been extended to include the analysis of processes formerly ignored and the methodological problems have been multiplied many fold.

CONVICTION VERSUS ASSUMPTION OF GUILT

The narrowest legal conceptions of criminals (and, by their records, of "crime") view them as persons who have not only violated the provisions of penal law but who have thereafter been *convicted* of such violations by due process.[13] After all, the presumption of innocence so central to legal procedure, cannot be easily dismissed by researchers or theoreticians who talk of "undetected" violators and the "criminal in the open." Thus "convict" and "criminal" are synonymous, and as has been pointed out, positive criminology took this viewpoint in its early years. Vold, commenting on this reasoning says:[14]

> . . . such definitions are purely formal and a matter of logic and verbal consistency. They are of little assistance in helping to understand the problems of crime causation. All that

is really said is that law is the immediate cause of crime, since without the formal legal definition there would be no crime, regardless of the behavior involved. This is reflexive circularity that leads nowhere.

Criminologists point out, and quite correctly, that there are many more crimes committed than there are convicted criminals and while convicts cannot be ignored as a part of the total crime picture, they are only a part, not the total. Furthermore, they are neither representative of all criminals of their class nor do the crimes for which they are convicted represent accurately the broader universe of lawbreaking. Inmates, probationers and others duly adjudicated represent merely a risk category of apprehension, conviction and sentencing.[15] It would be both naive and, from a theoretical viewpoint, fruitless to base hypotheses of lawbreaking upon data from such samples.

Not only are convict samples non-representative in general but the crimes for which these persons are convicted may not accurately indicate either their degree of criminality or the actual criminal behavior they performed. Studies of the conviction process point to the frequency of "bargaining" in both conviction and sentencing[16] and other surveys indicate the frequency with which some individuals, through bribery and other forms of corruption can escape conviction.[17]

Furthermore, it would be a most innocent criminologist who remained unaware of the concept "known criminals" widely used by both the police and investigating committees. Analyses of organized crime, the gangsters and racketeers so prominent in our culture as to be folk heroes (or villains), would be impossible if conviction was the basis for criminological definitions. Likewise the professional thief, with his uncanny ablity to "fix" his arrests,[18] would remain primarily outside the criminological scope. And the great bulk of white-collar crime, political corruption, business and labor union bribery and the like would remain beyond theoretical models.

Therefore, in spite of the obvious difficulties posed to the empiricist, criminology has expanded its definitions beyond the conviction basis. In so doing, it can quite accurately be accused of violating the "presumption of innocence" tenet but necessarily so. Criminology seeks not to accuse persons falsely but to examine the scope of the crime problem in entirety and waiting for court convictions would, reiterating Vold, lead nowhere.

THE WHITE COLLAR CRIME PROBLEM

The major conflict between adherence to strict definitions derived from the criminal code and expansion to include other behavior, centered, and for that matter, still is focussed, on the problem of white collar crime. While criminology was peripherally interested for many years in what Morris calls "upper-world crime",[19] impetus in this area was provided by the 1949 publication of Sutherland's *White Collar Crime*[20] in which he analyzed the "criminal records" of seventy large corporations and has been kept alive by the research and writing of Clinard,[21] Hartung,[22] Lane,[23] Cressey,[24] and Newman[25] among others.

Apart from the research methods involved, the conclusions reached, and the theoretical import of this concept, all of which are in themselves of criminological interest, the inclusion of white-collar crime into the subject matter of criminology has generated a good deal of heat among those advocates of adherence to stricter legal definitions of crime and criminal behavior. The major legalistic issue centers around the fact that white-collar crimes are chiefly violations of regulatory (administrative) law rather than that of the conventional criminal codes. It is argued that such laws are at best only partially penal, having primary provision for civil and administrative sanctions and only as a last resort criminal conviction and conventional criminal punishments. Furthermore, even in criminal provisions the laws customarily define violation as misdemeanors which are, by implication, significantly lesser than the more serious felonies of conventional codes. Likewise many of the laws make no provision (except as a compounding factor) for "willful intent" as a requirement for conviction, all very much in contradistinction to the careful intent provisions in felony matters.

Then, too, it is argued that such "lawbreaking" (some writers attempt to distinguish "lawbreaking" from crime) falls outside the criminological sphere because (1) administrative laws define *mala prohibita* whereas the conventional codes reiterate *mala in se*. Thus such offenses are not a part and parcel of our mores; they are arbitrary even whimsical, and therefore, regardless of whether they are "legal" crimes, they are not "sociologically" reprehensible behavior. Professor Hart points to the different behavior assumptions underlying the two kinds of law:[26]

> To engage knowingly or recklessly in conduct which is wrongful in itself and which has, in fact, been condemned as a crime is either to fail to comprehend the community's accepted moral values or else squarely to challenge them. The maxim, *Ignorantia legis neminem excusat*, expresses the wholly defensible and, indeed, essential principle that the action, in either event, is blameworthy. If, however, the criminal law adheres to this maxim when it moves from the condemnation of those things which are *mala in se* to . . . those things which are *mala prohibita*, it necessarily shifts its ground from a demand that every responsible member of a community understand and respect the community's moral values to a demand that everyone know and understand what is written in the statute books.—Indeed, all such instances of conduct in ignorance of laws enjoining *mala prohibita* might well be thought of as constituting a single type of crime, if they constitute any crime at all—the crime of ignorance of the statutes or their interpretation.

(2) Violators of regulatory laws, whether persons or corporations, do not conceive of themselves as criminals nor are they held to be criminals by the community.[27] "Lawbreakers," "sharp" or even "dishonest" but not criminal. Thus, behaviorally criminology, if it is to remain a distinct field, should limit itself to those actions condemned as criminal by the populace. Again Professor Hart says: "Crime is not simply anything which a

legislature chooses to call a 'crime'.—It is not simply any conduct to which a legislature chooses to attach a 'criminal' penalty. It is conduct which, if duly shown to have taken place, will incur a formal and solemn pronouncement of the moral condemnation of the community." [28] Thus, presumably, unenforced laws or violation of laws passed in contradiction to the values of the community, such as prohibition legislation and certain "blue" laws would not be crimes. (3) The admission of regulatory offenses to the universe of crimes would necessarily lead to inclusion of traffic violations, infringement of health ordinances and so forth making "criminal" as general a term and as widely applicable as "neurosis." This would merely confuse the entire field of criminology and allow most arbitrary definitions of all sorts of common misconduct, intentional or otherwise, as criminal.

Advocates of the inclusion of white collar crime, among them myself, while admitting many differences, stand behind Professor Sutherland's statement: [29]

> White collar crime is real crime. It is not ordinarily called crime, and calling it by this name does not make it worse, just as refraining from calling it crime does not make it better than it otherwise would be. It is called crime here in order to bring it within the scope of criminology, which is justified because it is in violation of the criminal law. The crucial question in this analysis is the criterion of violation of the criminal law. Conviction in the criminal court, which is sometimes suggested as the criterion, is not adequate because a large proportion of those who commit crimes are not convicted in criminal courts.

They argue that behavior which is *triable* in a criminal court should be the basis of the decision; the fact that some comparable actions are handled by warnings, seizures, treble-damage suits and the like does not *behaviorally* make them distinct from white collar offenses tried in courts of record. Furthermore, the felony-misdemeanor dichotomy is arbitrary and does not indicate the relative "seriousness" of offenses but merely reflects the influence of white collar classes upon legislatures.[30] Likewise while technically white collar violations are *mala prohibita* the behavior involved is merely a modern manifestation, a sort of corporate guilt, of older forms of theft, fraud and even homicide. New laws must meet new conditions and merely because a manufacturing concern rather than an individual is the object of laws regulatory to theft does not distinguish this "prohibited evil" from the "intrinsically wrongful" individual theft.[31]

The fact that white collar violators choose to define themselves as "lawbreakers" rather than criminals is neither as important a distinction as it is made out to be nor necessarily valid. It is doubtful if most persons, no matter how many laws they have broken, think of themselves with any consistency as "criminals." If this were the determining variable, not even all prison inmates would be included in criminological studies. Variations in self-conception, reference groups, ideological identifications and the like are of course of paramount interest to criminologists but are not in themselves determiners of the type of behavior to be studied.

The lack of public condemnation of white collar violators is too easily assumed. Does the community condemn the burglar but not the corporate violator? Certainly they may not be classified together but it is abundantly obvious that both evoke condemnation. The very existence of laws making prestige class behavior criminal argues for this. True, white collar crimes rarely are melodramatic. Both the perpetrator (many times a corporate body) and the victim (the public) are diffuse and the effects of law violation indirect, complex, and not as easily apparent as in robbery or murder. And while many Americans, cynically to be sure, seem to accept the existence of corruption and financial manipulation as expected of those in prestigeful roles, condemnation of such activities is seen time and again in investigation of "scandals" at all levels of our economic system.[32]

While possibly some violators of regulatory law are themselves victims of legal obtuseness or are otherwise unintentional criminals, studies of white collar violations lead to an obvious conclusion that willful intent, though not a requirement, is rarely absent, particularly in those offenses tried in courts of record. Sutherland showed an average of fourteen violations per corporation, hardly accidental, in his study[33] (four convictions in ordinary felony cases are usually enough to label, and imprison, a man as a "habitual criminal") and Clinard demonstrated the knowledgeable and intentional nature of black market crimes.[34]

It is apparent, in spite of the resistance mentioned, that violations of regulatory laws are now an integral part of criminology and the significance of this inclusion is manifest. In the first place, particularistic theories of lawbreaking based as they chiefly have been on description of essentially lower class characteristics—poverty, unemployment, substandard living conditions in general—of inmate populations are herewith shattered much as Goring shattered the Lombrosian myth. Broken homes, low intelligence, emotional disturbance, Freudian hypotheses of infantile sexual trauma and similar explanations appear grossly inadequate when cast in the light of upper-strata violations. The criminologist must become more "sociological" and less "pathological" in both method and theory when examining this phenomenon. As I have commented elsewhere:[35]

> Whether he likes it or not, the criminologist finds himself involved in an analysis of prestige, power, and differential privilege when he studies upperworld crime. He must be as conversant with data and theories from social stratification as he has been with studies of delinquency and crime within the setting of the urban slum. He must be able to cast his analysis not only in the framework of those who *break* laws, but in the context of those who *make* laws as well. This, of course, necessitates the development of enlarged, if not wholly new, theoretical models. There remains for the criminologist the task of relating white-collar crime to class differences in interaction, in styles of life, aspirations, child-rearing, mobility patterns, prestige symbols, and the host of other sociological variables important to the understanding of motives and differential behavior patterns in a multiclass society.

Above all since white-collar crime represents deviation either of or within occupational roles,[36] criminology must focus upon role analysis and develop both method and theory within this framework. Careful analysis of norms, conflicts, status differentials all within a framework of *processes* of attitude formation, recruitment, differential identification,[37] cultural value-conflicts and the like must necessarily replace older methods of comparing "criminals" with "non-criminals" on a host of demographic characteristics and concluding "cause" from any differences found.

Perhaps criminologists have spent too much effort trying to prove white-collar offenses are "real crimes" and not enough analyzing the reasons for differences between regulatory and conventional code provisions. In this respect Aubert comments:[38]

> For purposes of theoretical analysis it is of prime importance to develop and apply concepts which preserve and emphasize the ambiguous nature of white-collar crimes and not to "solve" the problem by classifying them as either "crimes" or "not crimes." Their controversial nature is exactly what makes them so interesting from a sociological point of view and what gives us a clue to important norm conflicts, clashing group interests, and maybe incipient social change.

IDEOLOGICAL CRIMES: TREASON, SEDITION, COMMUNISM AND RELIGIOUSLY MOTIVATED LAWBREAKING

White collar crime represents only one type of lawbreaking at variance with the conventional definitions of crime. Another type is made up of what might be called political and religious crimes; crimes which are usually defined as felonies (unlike most white collar violations) but which are atypical in the sense that the behavior occurs within a value framework totally different from robbery or murder. These are crimes that are ideologically motivated, that present the criminologist with the dilemma of reconciling the conventional image of the criminal with the Jehovah's Witness draft evader and the communist conspirator, with the imprisoned member of a snake-handling cult and with "peace-time traitors" in the deathhouse. Ideological crimes include all forms of subversion including treason, espionage, sabotage, sedition, conspiracy to overthrow the government by force or violence and also violation of military, tax, public health or safety laws by members of religious sects which condone or tolerate such activities. These are "value-laden" crimes in the sense that they are core issues of civil rights and central in debates, legal and otherwise, about the meaning of political and religious freedom in our society.

Because these crimes are value-laden, because they are not traditional subjects of criminological study, and perhaps because they present motivational patterns different from either burglary or white collar crime, they have been ignored by American criminologists. Theories of lawbreaking or studies of criminals rarely, if ever, include such conceptions, and yet they are crimes. Conviction as a Communist under the Smith Act is as surely "legal" crime as conviction as a kidnapper under the Lindbergh Law. Subversives and pacifists have been sentenced to prisons, thereby becoming "practical" problems for wardens if not "theoretical" problems for academic criminologists.

In order to give consistency to theoretical generalizations and to avoid criticisms based upon narrowness of concepts and limited samples, ideological crime must be included within criminological definitions. Obviously, the ideological violator must not be confused or equated with the petty thief or the armed robber.

Ideological crime must be treated as a separate behavior system (or perhaps as two with a distinction made between political subversives and religious outlaws) much as the criminologist now treats the organized criminal as a systematic type distinct from the professional thief or the white collar violator. The legal, demographic, and behavioral uniqueness of this type can thus be preserved but any generalized statements of crime causation must nevertheless account for this form of behavior as well as the more traditional types of lawbreaking.

The inclusion of ideological crime within criminological definitions raises many of the same methodological and theoretical problems as the inclusion of white collar crime. At the same time, it has much the same significance and offers the criminologist another opportunity to test hypotheses and validate etiological generalizations about lawbreaking within this new expanded perspective. Once again, many of the deprivation hypotheses, like mental retardation, broken homes, or poverty become inadequate to explain the state-department communist or the pacifist who refuses to pay taxes which are used to support military developments. On the other hand, theories broader, more sociological, than the "factor" hypotheses may be applicable to these types. The differential association hypothesis, reference group theory, group conflict theories and their modifications may not be invalidated, but strengthened, by analysis of the recruitment and training processes of the Communist party, the evaluation of reference standards of religious fanatics, and the processes necessary to explain disproportionate members of racial, religious, economic and intellectual minorities in subversive activities.

Furthermore, parallels of organization may be drawn between ideological and other systematic types. The organization of the Communist party or the Ku Klux Klan, for example, has much in common with gangster organization in terms of hierarchal power distribution, its underground (underworld) nature, the use or threat of violence, the development of cellular structure to isolate and conceal member identities (much as the organized criminal uses in narcotic distribution) and the international nature of its network. Of course, the crimes themselves differ as do the ideational patterns of the criminals. Here subversion and the subversive approximate more closely the white collar type (although subversive rationalizations may be similar to the "distribution of wealth" philosophies of the confidence man). As in white collar crime, the offenders, at least in subversion, often come from social class levels a cut above the ordinary offender and from intellectual circles closer to the businessman violator than to the racketeer. Of course there is a spread, and there may prove to be marked differences in background and ideational patterns between fascistic and communistic subversives. Likewise, religious lawbreaking draws dichotomously from intellectual-radical circles on the one hand and anti-intellectual fundamentalist groups on the other. The offenses themselves are complex (conspiracy, inciting riots, etc.), their effects indirect, distant and diffuse. Communism or Fascism, by the very abstractness of their consequences, parallel the criminal formation of monopolies more than murder or robbery where the victim is concrete and the act and consequences directly linked.

While ideological crime might parallel other systems, it is abundantly distinct and forces the criminologist to new levels of analysis. Political and religious antagonisms world-wide in scope become relevant to his understanding. The very foundation of legal and economic "rights" come under scrutiny. The burglar, for example, may rationalize his crimes in numerous ways, but rarely does he *justify* burglary by arguing that it should be tolerated or is otherwise historically "good." The ideological deviant, on the other hand, challenges the very right of the state to define certain behaviors as criminal and seeks historical or religious justifications for his actions. While the common thief in a sense challenges private property, the ideological conspirator challenges the entire system on which private property is based. All this raises some new issues for the criminologist and forces him, to some extent, to examine the premises on which law and legal philosophies are based.

Ideological crime has further significance for the administration of justice, a field of interest to both lawyer and social scientist. Among other things, the investigation of political and religious deviants in recent years has raised controversies about (1) the limitations of federal police investigatory powers, (2) the use of wire-tapping by congressional investigators, (3) protections against self-incrimination, particularly the use of the Fifth Amendment, (4) the procedural limits of congressional hearings, (5) the effect of television coverage of hearings, (6)

74

senatorial immunity from slander, (7) the tests of conspiracy, (8) loyalty oaths, and (9) the limits of religious, political and even academic freedom.

Certainly ideological deviation is not, or should not be, exclusively the theoretical or research property of criminologists. But the fact that such behavior is defined as criminal and that the violators in question are subject to penal sanctions, makes this an area that cannot be ignored in criminological works.

CRIME AS DEVIANT BEHAVIOR

That aspect of sociology devoted primarily to studying "problem" behavior has undergone a series of changes in emphasis in the past few years. The most important development has been the emergence of "social deviation" as a conceptual replacement for "disorganization" which in turn had earlier supplanted "social pathology" and the more eclectic "social problems" approaches. Social deviation treats all sorts of conventional problem behaviors, crime included, as culturally relative, functionally interrelated and the product of variations on exactly the same processes and forces creating non-deviant, normatively conforming behavior.[39] Thus criminals and physicians, psychotics and housepainters all are products of enculturation processes no more mysterious, no more pathological, in one case than another.

Central to the deviation concept is the idea of the relative, continuum-like nature of problem behavior varying, not absolutely, but by degrees from various cultural norms. The dichotomy "criminal" versus "non-criminal" is non-existent; in reality there are only "degrees" of deviation from legal and moral norms. The person called a criminal is done so arbitrarily; he violates the law selectively and for the most part the far greater percentage of his behavior is conforming, lawabiding. Likewise, since everyone in modern society by virtual necessity breaks some laws at some time, the non-criminal is, like the reasonable man, a fictional standard. Furthermore, the law provides only one set of norms and one description of deviation from these standards.

The criminologist should be as aware of a continuum of norms as of a continuum of deviation from any single one.

The methodological problem of deviation is to determine various norms, in some cases culture-wide, in others narrowed to neighborhoods or to occupational roles, and to measure deviation from them. "Working" definitions of deviant behavior can, and must, be made but absolutism in either definitions or conclusions is to be avoided.

The application of the deviation conception to criminology opens the possibility of expansion of the field beyond the limits set by legal definitions. Criminal law in this view provides only one normative base which can be used as merely a point of behavioral departure. There is a good deal of immoral, unethical and general non-conforming activity among our citizenry that is clearly not criminal if one looks into the codes but is certainly deviant from other normative bases. And this behavior involves, presumably, much the same etiological patterns as conventional criminal misconduct. Can the criminologist limit his analysis to burglary and ignore "fixed" television quizzes? Some think he must do just this and decry the expansion of definitions beyond criminal codes. Tappan says:[40]

> Vague, omnibus concepts defining crime are a blight upon either a legal system or a system of sociology that strives to be objective. They allow judge, administrator, or—conceivably—sociologist, in an undirected, freely operating discretion, to attribute the status "criminal" to any individual or class which he conceives nefarious. This can accomplish no desirable objective, either politically or sociologically. . . . (The) law has defined with greater clarity and precision the conduct which is criminal than our anti-legalistic criminologists promise to do; it has moreover promoted a stability, a security and dependability of justice through its exactness, its so-called technicalities, and its moderation in inspecting proposals for change.

Part of the problem has been a confusion of the ends of the law with the goals of social science and an assumption that the criminologist is committing a grave error and taking upon himself legislative functions if he uses a concept of crime different from that of lawyers who are so carefully bound by the principle *nullem crimen, nulla poena, sine lege* (no crime, no punishment, without a law). Over twenty years ago, Sellin made the point:[41]

> The unqualified acceptance of the legal definitions of the basic units or elements of criminological inquiry violates a fundamental criterion of science. The scientist must have freedom to define his own terms, based on the intrinsic character of his material and designating properties in that material which are assumed to be universal . . It should be emphasized . . . that this does not imply that the criminal law or the data about crimes and criminals assembled in the process of its enforcement are not useful in scientific research. They are indeed a rich source for the scientist, but the application of scientific criteria to the selection and classification of these data independently of their *legal* form is essential to render them valuable to science . . . what *is* claimed is that if a science of human conduct is to develop, the investigator in this field of research must rid himself of shackles which have been forged by the criminal law. If psychiatry had confined itself to the study of persons declared legally incompetent by criminal courts— the psychiatrist would have learned little indeed.

This viewpoint and Tappan's comment seem diametrically opposed. However, a good deal of confusion results from the assumption that criminologists are attempting or should attempt to replace legislatures. This confusion can be reduced if it is kept in mind that criminologists are not, and should not be, seeking to define crime differently from behavior legislatively so described. When the criminologist studies deviation from nonlegal norms he is not saying "This activity *is* crime" nor even that the activity *should be* criminal. What is claimed is that the deviation is *similar behaviorally* to violation of legal norms and must be considered along with conventional legal deviation in testing etiological hypotheses. Does this then destroy the intrinsic identity of criminology as a discrete discipline and categorize it with the broader area of social deviation? The answer can only be "yes" if by discrete is meant strict adherence to legal definitions. But the point has been made, I think, that criminology is first and foremost social science and with the general trend away from absolute categorization of behavior, no aspect of social science can claim discreteness. Criminology is distinct from such other areas as social psychology and social theory only in the relative emphasis it places upon the study of criminal behavior. There is no aspect of behavior, nor of scientific theory or method, that criminology can ignore as intrinsically irrelevant. Criminology will remain that aspect of sociology (and of other social science disciplines) most devoted to the study of lawbreaking but by no means bound by it. In this respect there are a number of forms of deviation that are essentially non-legal but which are increasingly attracting criminological attention. Most of these remain currently deficient in adequate research but hold promise for the future.

THE VIOLATION OF ETHICAL CODES OF CONDUCT

One of the major trends of modern industrialization has been the "professionalization" of a widely divergent number of occupational roles. For a variety of reasons, including the emergence of the scientist as a preferred cultural image and the disillusionment with the businessman prototype, professional status today carries the highest social prestige. Formerly limited to medical practitioners, lawyers, college professors, ministers and a select few other categories, "professional" has become the goal of, and at least partially achieved by, many new, technical occupations and some formerly non-professional old ones. Thus architects, engineers, social workers, laboratory technicians and the like today claim professional admittance. Undertakers have become "morticians", druggists "pharmacists", publicity is now "public relations", paperhangers are "interior decorators", gardeners "landscape architects" and house salesmen "realtors". All this is accompanied by increased training standards, licensing, formal organization into union-like structures and, above all, a set of internal and external "ethical" standards of behavior agreed upon by the occupational membership and enforced by them. These ethical codes, patterned on those of the older professions, seek to define role obligations, professional responsibilities and, increasingly, even personal conduct outside the strictly professional role. These then are in reality extra-legal "laws" controlling the occupational membership and carrying sanctions of "fines," suspension or complete expulsion from the role. They are enforced by "grievance committees" who both investigate and try alleged violations.

Not only have "ethics" come to professions but there is also a trend toward setting conduct standards for entire non- or quasi-professional industries and for government personnel. Mink coat scandals, followed by McCarthyism, led to the creation of a senate committee to investigate the possibility of establishing "ethics in government" and the Teamsters Union case has revitalized this same interest in the case of labor unions. The recent expose of deceitful television quiz shows and the influence of "payola" on popular music have caused broadcasting and television companies to re-examine their ethical principles and to develop hurriedly, before legislation to point appears, methods of enforcing these principles.

All of this is, or should be, meat for the criminologist. These occupationally based conduct norms provide relatively microscopic legal systems in which hypotheses freed from the deprivation emphasis of conventional criminology can be tested. And while deviation from these norms does not constitute (in many cases, at least) "real" crimes, no causal theory of law-breaking today can be considered worth its salt unless the same variables of the thesis can account for both conventional theft, let us say, and the behavior of television's "fixed" intellectuals. These are not absolutely the same, admittedly, but the processes involved, the pressures, the value-conflicts and all the rest of the cultural variables can be studied in both, contrasted, and (hopefully) generalizations, the aim of all science, made.

THE VIOLATION OF OTHER CONDUCT NORMS

All social behavior exists of course in a framework of normative proscriptions. In addition to the norms of occupational roles, individuals are bound by a multitude of conduct expectations in virtually all aspects of their existence. Perhaps these conduct norms other, and ordinarily much less precise, than ethical codes of professions can be made the basis of criminological inquiry. This is precisely what Sellin proposed when he rejected the law as the sole basis of criminological activity. He argued that criminologists should also be "ethologists" and, if possible, expand their research to include violations of "conduct norms" which he defined as "rule(s) which prohibit and conversely enjoin a specific type of person, as defined by his status in (or with reference to) the normative group, from acting in a certain specified way in certain circumstances." [42] He admitted the difficulties inherent in isolating norms and gaining research consensus on their limits but felt this was a necessary step in criminological development.

The methodological problems of Sellin's proposal have not been generally solved but it is possible to see the applicability of such an approach in some areas in addition to violation of codified ethical standards. Floyd Allport and his followers, for example, have attempted a quantitative formulation of conformity and deviation from a variety of norms in terms of what they call the "J-curve Hypothesis." [43]

All institutional structures have rules of organization and procedures which govern the conduct of participants. Thus factory workers are normatively expected to behave in a certain manner while on the job, (apart from the ethical codes of unions to which they may belong and the technical requirements of their jobs) and soldiers must obey military protocol, monks behave in a monkish manner, and college students refrain from cribbing on examinations. The list could be endless and in some instances, for example the military, the protocol may be written out. But in most cases the conduct codes of a variety of statuses are transmitted by recruitment and indoctrination procedures,

80

by all the socialization subtleties of learning any role components. Written or not, all statuses have lists of expected actions and certain deviations from these expectations are punished by others in the same or in reciprocal roles in ways ranging from slight loss of esteem to expulsion from the status with attendant loss of prestige.

It would seem possible, and hopefully valuable, for criminologists to attempt not only to study deviations from selected roles but to perhaps experiment with the production of role deviation. Quite obviously a criminologist cannot induce crime without himself becoming legally liable. But he may with greater impunity experiment with small groups to discover variables conducive to norm deviation.

Can this have implications for actual lawbreaking? Obviously, no absolute answer can be given. But let us suppose a criminologist sets himself the task of analyzing college students cheating on examinations or papers. Is the middle-class student who cheats in college doing so on the basis of significantly different behavioral traits than the lower class youth who steals? True, the law looks differently at the behavior but cannot the same processes, the same or similar motivational models, be used to analyze both behaviors? It is not necessary to call them both crime, or even delinquency, to draw parallels, to test similar hypotheses and even to develop interchangeable methods of study. The advantage to the criminologist of a microscopic cheating study is further enhanced by the possibilities of manipulating the incidence of cheating or of testing various methods of control. It is quite possible, perhaps, that criminological theories and a variety of research proposals could be developed experimentally with non-criminal conduct norm violations and the results or the methods tested later with more criminologically orthodox samples. Furthermore, since ordinary crime in some instances represents socially integrated, rather than dissociated or disorganized, behavior (as in certain types of professional and white-collar offenses particularly) it may be possible for the criminologist to use conduct norm analysis to test some of the theoretical implications of Merton's claim that "certain phases of social structure generate the circumstances in which infringement of social codes constitutes a normal response." [44] Behavior defined as deviant by law or in the mores may, in many instances, be defined as expected and proper within certain sub-cultural conduct codes. Conformity to general moral standards, when exposed to the opposite in reality is itself of criminological interest. Thus as criminologists become interested in studying the "good boy in the slums" and methods of "insulating" the exposed person from law violation,[45] studies of comparable behavior in non-criminal, experimental samples may add substantively to the results.

CRIMINOLOGY AND THE LAW: RAPPROCHEMENT

The numerous points of conflict between criminological definitions and the criminal law are perhaps inevitable in view of the different approaches which the two fields take to roughly the same problem behavior but these differences are not necessarily bad. Criminologists need not be lawyers, nor lawyers criminologists. Criminologists have been primarily dedicated to studying causes, not consequences, of behavior and have tried to cast the entire phenomena of crime into a broad sociological framework of analysis that includes but is not limited by the criminal law.

Lawyers are very much interested in the consequences of law violation and daily face multitudes of cases of lawbreaking that must be viewed, analyzed, adjudicated and treated within legislatively prescribed methods. Little wonder their impatience with causes when immediate disposition of diverse cases is their primary duty and continuing criminal consequences their bane.

Both lawyer and criminologist have been guilty of this impatience, if nothing more, with each other's problems. If some rapprochement can be achieved it will involve not surrender of one position to another but greater understanding and closer cooperation, exchange of methods and interanalysis of mutual problems all based upon a more complete exchange of information about each respective field. It is sometimes surprising to discover how little lawyers know of criminology and to uncover almost total ignorance of the criminal law, of procedure and of legal methods and processes, among criminologists. Yet if any two fields are naturally destined for interdisciplinary research it is criminal law and criminology.

On their part, lawyers and lawmakers have only reluctantly, and fairly recently at that, taken sociological evaluation of law-breaking and its treatment into account and Michael and Alder's warning that "criminological research . . . represents an attempt to do the impossible" [46] still has legal adherents.

Undoubtedly there are many methodological skills developed by social scientists that can be utilized by lawyers, at least by that band of research-minded legal scholars now in ascendancy. Some of the problems posed by criminologists, particularly those directed to the aims of law, the efficacy of traditional punishments, and the evaluation of such legal procedures as arrest, charging and sentencing, are of particular significance to lawyers.

Within recent years the legal profession has turned to examining itself and its subject matter with an intensity and a sophistication promising great things. Attack on the problems of recoding and attempts to develop a model penal code must be given great credit.[47] Furthermore the American Bar Association has "surveyed" itself with particular emphasis on studies of the criminal lawyer,[48] and the American Bar Foundation is currently engaging in an intensive study of the administration of criminal justice in the United States.

Criminologists on their part can do much more with legal matters than has been customary. If the criminal law is viewed, as it should be, as a *process* rather than a set of static proscriptions, then this process itself becomes of criminological interest. Instead of avoiding things legal, or accepting legal terminology out of its procedural context, criminologists can study intensively not only legal norms but the processes by which these norms are implemented, the interaction of roles involved and any discrepancies between legal models and legal practices.

Even that aspect of criminology most devoted to studying

behavior legally enjoined has been guilty of selectivity of subject matter and a sociological bias in research choices. Geis accuses criminologists of being both overconcerned with "methodological sophistication" to the detriment of content and being tyrannized by the IBM machine so the "the problem to be investigated becomes tailored to the talents of the machine rather than . . . more desirable considerations." He concludes: "The criminologist often selects for investigation those aspects of criminology tailored to sociology and by-passes other (and often more important) matters which do not fall within the sociological compound." [49] Thus even when it is claimed that criminology studies law violation, the meaning of "criminal" is neither as broad as the law nor does it include analysis of behaviors important to jurisprudence even if disdained by social scientists. Criminologists saying "crime" have typically studied the more dramatic, and overt, forms of lawbreaking. They have rarely concentrated their efforts on *conditions* defined as illegal, such as vagrancy or *omissions* such as non-support. They have not typically included in their samples clearly illegal but "value-laden" behaviors such as "conspiracy to overthrow the government by force or violence," treason, sedition or religiously motivated crimes (as outlawed cults) or failing to register for military draft because of "conscientious objections" or tax evasion by pacifists. Then too, they have fallen into the lay error of failing to distinguish juvenile delinquency from adult crime, except by chronological age. Results of studies based on delinquency samples are generalized to crime without, apparently, an awareness that the two phenomena are fundamentally distinct in behavioral content and in the legal processes of definition.[50]

All this may be futile. Perhaps rapprochement is more complex than shared knowledge and is a matter of overcoming status differentials between practitioners in both fields and removing various vested interests in certain phases of the crime problem. Be that as it may, a closer relationship between both fields is desirable for both methodology and results. Both can only gain by greater interdisciplinary understanding and, hopefully, greater cooperation.

SELECTED BIBLIOGRAPHY

Carr, Robert K., *The House Committee on Un-American Activities, 1945-1950*, Cornell University Press, Ithaca, 1952. The record of the post-war Dies Committee and the many controversies surrounding such investigations.

Clinard, Marshall B., "Sociologists and American Criminology," *Journal of Criminal Law and Criminology*, Vol. 41, No. 5, January-February, 1951. Summarizes briefly the history and new developments in American criminology with particular attention to research methods.

Clinard, Marshall B., *Sociology of Deviant Behavior*, Rinehart, New York, 1957. The most up to date and systematic treatment of deviation as a conceptual replacement for disorganization and pathology.

Geis, Gilbert, "Sociology, Criminology and Criminal Law," *Social Problems*, Vol. VII, No. 1, Summer, 1959. Discusses the conflicts between legal and sociological approaches to crime.

Glaser, Daniel, "Criminality Theories and Behavioral Images," *American Journal of Sociology*, Vol. 56, 1956. A brief but fruitful critique of existing criminological theories.

Hall, Jerome, *Theft, Law and Society* (second edition), Bobbs-Merrill, Indianapolis, 1952. Shows the relationship of cultural changes and modifications in the law.

Hart, Henry M., Jr., "The Aims of the Criminal Law," *Law and Contemporary Problems*, Vol. XXIII, No. 3, Summer, 1958. A lawyer's discussion of the criminal law as a process and its philosophies and methods.

Hartung, Frank E., "A Critique of the Sociological Approach to Crime and Correction," *Law and Contemporary Problems*, Vol. XXIII, No. 4, Autumn, 1958. Not a critique of all criminology but only the worst in it. Stresses the sociological rather than the biological or pathological method of understanding crime.

Hoover, J. Edgar, *Masters of Deceit*, Henry Holt, New York, 1958. A policeman's view of the Communist Party in the United States and what the FBI has done about it.

Michael, Jerome and Mortimer J. Adler, *Crime, Law and Social Science*, Harcourt-Brace, New York, 1933. Puts forth the narrowest conception of criminal behavior and challenges criminology as a scientific endeavor.

Newman, Donald J., "White Collar Crime," *Law and Contem-*

porary Problems, Vol. XXIII, No. 4, Autumn, 1958. A discussion of the conflicts surrounding the inclusion of white collar crime into the subject matter of criminology and the research and theoretical implications of this concept.

Ohlin, Lloyd E. and Frank J. Remington, "Sentencing Structure: Its Effect Upon Systems for the Administration of Criminal Justice," *Law and Contemporary Problems,* Vol. XXIII, No. 3, Summer, 1958. A sociologist and lawyer collaborate on an analysis of an important sociological process.

Sellin, Thorsten, *Culture, Conflict and Crime,* Social Science Research Council Bulletin 41, New York, 1938. The pioneer statement of the desirability of extending criminology beyond legal norms.

Stroup, Herbert E., *The Jehovah's Witnesses,* Columbia University Press, New York, 1945. An analysis of a sect whose members have been imprisoned because of ideological lawbreaking.

Sutherland, Edwin H., *White Collar Crime,* Dryden, New York, 1949. This is the definitive work on white collar criminality, defining the topic and answering major criticisms of its inclusion in the subject mater of criminology.

Sutherland, Edwin H. and Donald R. Cressey, *Principles of Criminology* (fifth edition), Lippincott, New York, 1955. Probably the most prominent text in the field of criminology.

Tappan, Paul, "Who is the Criminal?," *American Sociological Review,* Vol. 22, No. 1, February, 1947. A strong statement of the pitfalls of using sociological rather than legal definitions of crimes.

Vold, George B., *Theoretical Criminology,* Oxford, New York, 1958. Summarizes the development of criminology and the implication of criminological theories in research.

Donald J. Newman, Ph.D., Associate Professor of Sociology at St. Lawrence University, Canton, New York. He was born in 1924 in Janesville, Wisconsin; and attended the University of Wisconsin where he received bachelor (1949) masters (1952) and doctorate degrees (1954). He has been a Fellow of the American Bar Association, participating in their nation-wide "Survey of Criminal Law and Litigation," and is the author of various articles and research papers in the field of criminology and juvenile delinquency. For the past five years he has participated in and is now a member of the planning committee of The Frederick A.

Moran Memorial Institute on Delinquency and Crime and has recently been appointed a consultant-analyst to the American Bar Foundation's study of "The Administration of Criminal Justice in the United States."

NOTES

1. Geis, Gilbert, "Sociology, Criminology, and Criminal Law," *Social Problems*, VII, No. 1, Summer, 1959, 45.

2. *Ibid.*, 42-43.

3. France, Anatole, *Crainquebille*, Dodd-Mead, New York, 1922.

4. As a matter of fact, The "Durham Rule" (*Durham v. United States*, 214 F. 2d. 862-76) seeks to determine legal insanity by psychiatric evidence rather than by the older legal test of "right or wrong" under the M'Naughten Rule. Whether this is an improvement is debatable. See "Insanity and the Criminal Law—a Critique of Durham v. United States," *University of Chicago Law Review*, Winter, 1955, 317-404.

5. See particularly Sutherland, Edwin H., *White Collar Crime*, Dryden, New York, 1949, Chaps. I, III, XIII and Georg Rusche and Otto Kirchheimer, *Punishment and the Social Structure*, Columbia, New York, 1939.

6. See Hall, Jerome, *Theft, Law and Society*, second edition, Bobbs-Merrill, Indianapolis, 1952 and N. S. Timasheff, *An Introduction to the Sociology of Law*, Harvard, Cambridge, 1939 as well as Roscoe Pound, "Sociology of Law" in Georges Gurvitch and Wilbert Moore, *Twentieth-Century Sociology*, Philosophical Library, New York, 1945, 297-341.

7. See especially Hakeem, Michael, "A Critique of the Psychiatric Approach to Crime and Correction," *Law and Contemporary Problems*, XXIII, No. 4, Autumn, 1958, 650-682. And for a criticism of the individualistic, eclectic approach characteristic of social work see Frank Hartung "A Critique of the Sociological Approach to Crime and Correction" in the same issue as the Hakeem article, pp. 704-717 especially.

8. Clinard, Marshall B., "Sociologists and American Criminology," *Journal of Criminal Law and Criminology*, XLI, No. 5 January-February, 1951, 566-577.

9. *Ibid.*, 560-566.

10. Cressey, Donald R., *Other People's Money*, Free Press, Glencoe, Illinois, 1953.

11. For a discussion of these developments see Vold, George B., *Theoretical Criminology*, Oxford, New York, 1958.

12. See especially Thrasher, Frederic, *The Gang*, University of Chicago Press, Chicago, 1927, and James S. Wallerstein and Clement J. Wyle, "Our Law-Abiding Law-Breakers," *Federal Probation*, XXV, April, 1947, 107-112; Austin Porterfield, *Youth in Trouble,* Leo Potishman Foundation, Fort Worth, Texas, 1946.

13. Michael, Jerome and Mortimer J. Adler, *Crime, Law and Social Science*, Harcourt-Brace, New York, 1933, Chapter 1.

14. Vold, *op. cit.*, 268.

15. Reckless, Walter C., *The Crime Problem*, second edition, Appleton-Century-Crofts, New York, 1955, Chapter 3.

16. Newman, Donald J., "Pleading Guilty for Considerations: A Study of Bargain Justice," *Journal of Criminal Law, Criminology and Police Science,* XXXXVI, No. 6, March-April, 1956.

17. See for example Hopkins, Ernest J., *Our Lawless Police*, Viking, New York, 1931; National Commission on Law Observance and Enforcement (Wickersham), "Report on Lawlessness in Law Enforcement," No. 11 Government Printing Office, Washington, 1931, and Estes Kefauver, *Crime in America*, Doubleday, New York, 1951.

18. Sutherland, Edwin H., *The Professional Thief*, University of Chicago Press, 1937.

19. Morris, Albert, *Criminology*, Longmans-Green, New York, 1934.

20. Sutherland, *op. cit.*

21. Clinard, Marshall B., *The Black Market*, Rinehart, New York, 1952.

22. Hartung, Frank E., "White Collar Offenses in the Wholesale Meat Industry in Detroit," *American Journal of Sociology*, LVI, July, 1950, 25-34.

23. Lane, Robert, "Why Businessmen Violate the Law," *Journal of Criminal Law and Criminology*, XXXXIV, No. 2, July-August, 1953, 151-165.

24. Cressey, *op. cit.*

25. Newman, Donald J., "Public Attitudes Toward a Form of White Collar Crime," *Social Problems*, IV, No. 3, January 1957, 228-232.

26. Hart, Henry M. Jr., "The Aims of the Criminal Law," *Law and Contemporary Problems*, XXIII, No. 3, Summer, 1958, 419.

27. Burgess, Ernest W., "Comment" on Hartung's "White Collar Offenses in the Wholesale Meat Industry in Detroit," *American Journal of Sociology*, LVI, No. 1, July, 1950, 32-33.

28. Hart, *op. cit.*, 405.

29. Sutherland, Edwin H., "White Collar Criminality," *American Sociological Review*, V, February, 1940, 5.

30. Sutherland, *White Collar Crime*, op. cit., 46-47.

31. For a more detailed discussion of this whole problem, see Newman, Donald J., "White Collar Crime," *Law and Contemporary Problems*, XXIII, No. 4, Autumn, 1958, 735-753.

32. See the discussion in Clinard, *op. cit.* on attitudes toward violation of wartime regulations.

33. Sutherland, *White Collar Crime, op. cit.*, 20.

34. Clinard, *op. cit.*, 235-236.

35. Newman, "White Collar Crime," *op. cit.*, 746-747.

36. *Ibid.*, 737.

37. See Glaser, Daniel, "Criminality Theories and Behavioral Images," *American Journal of Sociology*, LXI, 1956.

38. Aubert, Vilhelm, "White Collar Crime and Social Structure," *American Journal of Sociology*, LVIII, November, 1952, 264.

39. See Clinard, Marshall B., *Sociology of Deviant Behavior*, Rinehart, New York, 1957, especially chapters 1 and 2.

40. Tappan, Paul, "Who is the Criminal," *American Sociological Review*, XXII, No. 1, February, 1947, 99-100.

41. Sellin, Thorsten, *Culture Conflict and Crime*, Social Science Research Council Bulletin 41, New York, 1938, 23-24.

42. *Ibid.*, 32, 33.

43. Allport, Floyd H., "The J-Curve Hypothesis of Conforming Behavior," *Journal of Social Psychology*, V, 1934, 141-183.

44. Merton, Robert K., "Social Structure and Anomie," *American Sociological Review*, III, October, 1938, 672.

45. Reckless, Walter, Simon Dinitz and Ellen Murray, "Self Concept as an Insulator Against Delinquency," *American Sociological Review*, XXI, December, 1956, 744-746. See also by the same authors, "The 'Good' Boy in a High Delinquency Area," *Journal of Criminal Law, Criminology and Police Science*, XXXXVIII, 1957, and Gresham Sykes and David Matza, "Techniques of Neutralization: A Theory of Delinquency," *American Sociological Review*, XXII, No. 6, December, 1957, 664 670.

46. *Op. cit.*, 85.

47. American Law Institute, *Model Penal Code* (tent. draft No. 2, 1954) (tent. draft No. 3, 1955).

48. Blaustein, Albert P. and Charles O. Potter, *The American Lawyer; A Summary of the Survey of the Legal Profession*, University of Chicago, 1954. See also Arthur Wood, "Informal Relations in the Practice of Criminal Law," *American Journal of Sociology*, LXII, 1956. Professor Wood directed that aspect of the American Bar Association's study devoted to a "Survey of Criminal Law and Litigation."

49. Geis, *op. cit.*, 45.

50. See Newman, Donald J., "Legal Aspects of Juvenile Delinquency," Chapter 2, in Joseph Roucek (editor), *Juvenile Delinquency*, Philosophical Library, New York, 1958.

SOCIO-PSYCHOLOGICAL ASPECTS

PSYCHOPATHOLOGY OF THE SOCIAL DEVIATE

Nathan Masor, M.D.
Staten Island, New York

THE PSYCHOPATHIC PERSONALITY AND CRIME

The psychopathic personality, known also as the constitutional psychopath, is an individual who is unable to adjust satisfactorily to the accepted code of ethical, social and moral climate. The term is generally applied to the large army of misfits who cannot be succinctly classified as definitely neurotic or psychotic, but who, because of inherent character and behavioral tendencies, often find themselves in conflict with the law. Sexual perverts, prostitutes, drug addicts, chronic alcoholics, cranks, hoboes, criminals and ne'er-do-wells lend themselves well to this label. No apparent physical cause within the brain or glandular make-up can be identified as a basis for the behavioral tendencies of the psychopath. This does not rule out the possibility of bio-chemical causation which may parallel the very recent findings of the schizophrenic personality.

Theories of Causation. The theory of Dr. Cesare Lombroso that the criminal is identified by certain stigmata of body build, as well as his receptivity to pain (either too much or too little) once had many adherents. Dr. Lombroso tried to correlate these characteristics with psychological attitudes, and considered the criminal a throwback to primitive man. His classification of criminals into various types and subtypes was responsible for the origin of the Italian or Positive School of criminology, (a scientific attempt at understanding crime.) His theories are now only of historical importance, chiefly due to the work of Dr. Charles Goring of England, who disproved his findings.

Attempts at identification of crime with differences in body build have now been completely discounted. Similarly, Dr. Ashley-Montagu and many others questioned any assigned role of heredity in the causation of crime, a position challenged by Dr. Walter C. Alvarez.

Not all psychopaths come into conflict with the law, because queer as their behavior may be, they are not all anti-social. One school believed that psychopaths were influenced by inborn constitutional inferiority, but the motivations are too complex to be limited to a genetic origin *alone*.

The environmental school contends that the outlet for the psychopathic personality (unlike the psychotic) is purely social. Frustration of his needs may render him hostile to society. Rejected and alienated by a lack of the more tender emotions like love, consideration, warmth and kindness, his impressionable and sensitive makeup produces feelings of resentment and distrust, as evidenced by irrational retribution. This explanation may be quite applicable with reference to only a certain percentage of psychopathic individuals, but not to all. Some psychopaths emanate from families and social atmospheres of distinction. Unwholesome associations at times transcend the restraining influences of a good family background. A sense of inferiority through physical defect has been known to accelerate individual resentment with consequent leaning towards a psychopathic state.

The psychopathic personality is beset with a gamut of anti-social feelings with a firm seed often planted in early childhood. By analogy to the neurotic who may respond to his anxiety by personality disorders, it is possible that the psychopath manifests his expressions through anti-social behavior instead. Thus, this theory supposes that the acts of the criminal may be social expressions of symptoms that are compulsive, illogical and repetitive in spite of an innate conscious desire for reform.

At best, these are only hypotheses as is the psycho-analytical explanation of the psychopathic personality, viz: result of forces residing in the unconscious which are never fully gratified, and which produce compulsively repetitive action. The explanations may elucidate an isolated case, but with the increased incidence of crime their true origins defy clarification. The ultimate truth more likely embraces a combination of the above theories, with the most important causative factor still at large.

Symptoms of the Psychopath. Very often the childhood of the psychopath portends the omen of his later adult behavior. A wide variety of anti-social conduct may be evident in early years, typifying compulsive, irrational and emotional characteristics. Stubbornness, cruelty to children and animals, sensitivity, temper tantrums, deceit, stealing, introspection, arrogance and prevarication are common findings of these problem children. Antagonism to one or both parents, siblings, or neighbors, is frequent, as he resists their attempts at social correction. As he gets older, he becomes more defiant and irresponsible, and seems to lose a sense of ethical and moral values because good conscience is lacking. He may repeatedly run away from home. Personality defects then accompany his emotional immaturity, though they are not in the forefront as in truly psychotic states. He is thus recognized as queer, and more integrated people avoid undue association with him, so that he stands alone in his egocentric, distorted appreciation of his everyday environment. Thus the vicious cycle of his social inadequacies and personality defects is further accentuated in rejection, and his compensation consists of exercising unjust demands. Being self centered, his motivation is always self satisfaction even at the expense of others. Hence any judgment he may exercise is warped in favor of the attainment of immediate pleasure or material benefit, regardless of future consequence. It is not surprising, therefore, that the psychopath generally makes no attempt at correction since the sense of guilt or fear of punishment is far removed from his thinking processes. He is in constant search for the unknown and engages in restless pursuit of a phantom that is unreachable. He is like an instinctive animal **functioning on a spinal cord level rather than an individual** who can accept the realities of everyday existence. He is a round peg in a square hole who must either dominate a given situation or change the circumstances for his selfish benefit. The psychopath is easily influenced in shady transactions since society's condemnation is of little import. If caught in misbehavior, he is quite adept at rationalizations and often effectively pretends that he was outraged. There are of course varying degrees of deviant behavior from the barely unrecognized to the homicidal criminal.

Although the term psychopath usually refers to the unproductive irresponsible elements of society, there is a large group within this classification whose motivation is nevertheless social and productive. Reformers, prima donnas of the theatrical profession, extreme dissidents within scientific and literary fields, and moralists have all at one time or another been stigmatized with this term. Perhaps a more deserving title should be nonconformist. When we keep in mind the lessons of history, namely that public approval to a given ethical, moral or scientific problem is often a circumstance of the era in which we live, we realize that the concept of psychopathy is also subject to change from time to time. If the non-conformist succeeds in moulding public opinion to his side, he is no longer regarded as a psychopath. If he fails, the appellation stays. The genius too is only a shade away from the psychopath, spared by the fact that his productive usefulness to society outweighs his eccentricities.

Treatment of the Psychopath. It is almost futile to speak of effective rehabilitation of the psychopath during this period when crimes of delinquency and violence are rising out of proportion to the increase in population. Certainly the repeated attempts at applying psychoanalytic methods to social deviates has been no more effective than in the field of mental ailments. All too often, the psychopath, just as the psychotic, is unreachable, and not only does not understand why he misbehaves, but resents any attempts to be helped.

Undoubtedly, the best treatment is prophylactic, such as clearing of slum areas, avoidance of overcrowding of dwellings, providing ample space for playgrounds, organizing of clubs and scouting activities, emphasis upon vocational guidance, recreational camps during vacation periods, and participation in manual skills, art, music and theater, as wholesome preventive measures. A sympathetic understanding on part of trained and inspired personnel, such as social workers, supervisors, sociologists, physicians, clergymen and other interested individuals should play a major part, and special attention should be given to the individual conduct of the problem child. The goal is no different with adults, whether in penal institutions or the outside, for as Wm. Cowper has so well expressed it, "Absence of occupation is not rest; a mind quite vacant is a mind distressed."

Contribution of Religion in Crime Prevention. An essential aim in any religion is identical, namely, the development of character. If this goal could be reached, there would be no behavioral problems and hence no crime, for sin occurs only when character decays. Should the great incidence of crime thereby be looked upon as a failure of religious influence in deterring evil? Not at all, for there can be no adequate religious inspiration without the individual being conditioned and being made to understand the many ways that the church may help him. Thus many psychopaths who merely expose themselves to pastoral contact, are rendering passive lip service, rather than an active desire to cleanse their souls. It is they who fail their God, rather than the reverse, regardless of the frequency of exposure to Bible classes or services. On the other hand, there are those delinquents who might have been subjected to reform, and could have been salvaged had they been exposed to religious influences. One must therefore not blame the seeming impotency of the church in failing to develop character, for it is a paradox. The fault lies not with too much religion, but rather with too little rapport with it. The goal should therefore be to inculcate an active desire for religious teachings, instead of moralizing to deaf ears.

The Occult Psychotic, a Newly Formulated Concept. The term occult, as applied to a sudden violent anti-social manifestation, with little or no predatory warning in a person erroneously believed to be well integrated, was recently described for the first time in my book, "The New Psychiatry." The word *occult* is used synonymously with latent or hidden rather than in the context of mysterious. It is best described in the vernacular as the individual "going berserk," and who commits what appears to be a sudden act of violence aimed at himself or others. The factor of seeming normality until just prior to commission of the crime, does not imply that the occult psychotic was actually well integrated. In fact, the contrary is often the case. However, up to the instant of his asocial behavior, he possessed the faculty to suppress and contain his abnormal feelings to the point of non-recognition by his daily contacts. To be sure, his immediate family and close friends may have been able to detect recent flaws in his personality. By and large, however, the occult psychotic had been successful in presenting quite another face outside his home. The inner tensions, angers, resentments and desires that he was superbly able to mask, finally would burst through the emotional container, so to speak, to the point of commission of an overt act of tragedy.

The newspapers daily illustrate this criminopathic type. Not too long ago, for example, there was a description of the railroad tycoon in seemingly good health and spirits, and with no known pressing problems, who destroyed himself. Another headline featured the case of a well liked patrolman who suddenly went on a shooting rampage in midtown New York, killing a number of people before he was himself mortally wounded by pursuing police. Many a community has at one time or another learned of its own local bank executive, or "do-gooder," who for the first time departed from the role of exemplary citizen, and then committed an act of embezzlement, rape, murder or some other felony.

The occult psychotic may well have fitted into the diagnosis of a paranoid with a real or imaginary background, or else may have been compulsively neurotic. All too often, however, his background offered no premonition of events to come. When we consider the staggering incidence of crimes of the "one time performer" we must look for signs of recognition. He is adept at perpetrating a social ruse, and every effort should be made for his detection if tragedy is to be avoided.

By the nature of this description, it is evident that the burden of recognition falls mainly upon the family and intimates of the occult psychotic, rather than upon the occasional observer, trained as he may be in medical or allied professions. The most radical sign to be noted in the occult psychotic is a *sudden* change in personality, especially depression, not heretofore evident. Sullenness, introspection, general apathy, loss of appetite, fatigability, somatic complaints without physical basis, loss of powers of concentration, and irritability in a previously well integrated person, are the most important satellite symptoms arising out of depression.

Sometimes, a situational conflict due to an overwhelming stress experience may dominate the waking thoughts of the individual. Present environmental stress, regardless of cause, must be ventilated and resolved. Excess stress loads (through hormonal interplay especially mitigated through the body's natural supply of adrenalin and its breakdown products) only accentuate brooding, with its possible anti-social consequences.

The occult psychotic may be particularly adept in concealing his inner conflicts even at home, but may reveal an impending personality breakdown through newly acquired strange habits. Thus he may decide to walk in the rain for long periods, lock himself in his room, or expose himself to any intemperate situation without wanting to be observed. Such activity is a means of self-preoccupation, and avoidance of detection by escapism. However, one must not be overly suspicious to read into every unusual social expression as evidence of an impending derangement. The difference lies in duration and degree of the asocial conduct exhibited. An occult psychotic may have successfully masked a compulsive neurosis or paranoia for years. In any case, sympathetic counsel to situational problems and psychiatric aid become mandatory when early premonitory signs of personality breakdown are noted. The prevention of crime, therefore, ofttimes begins in the recognition of the occult psychotic.

In a study of 10,000 convicted criminals in the psychiatric clinic of the Court of General Sessions, N.Y.C., and reported widely throughout newspapers of the country in November 1959, the conclusion was reached that personality disorders play a minor role in causing crime. The overall percentages showed that:

89.2% of criminals were mentally sound
6.9% " " were neurotic
2.4% " " were mentally defective
1.5% " " were psychotic

Nevertheless, the statistics reveal that personality derangement (because of loss of the faculties of judgment and reason) is still responsible for a substantial incidence of crime. The writer has therefore postulated the existence of a third grouping in the causation of crime, namely the occult psychotic, because at least the latter group offers a possible method for his detection and rehabilitation.

Marginal Crime (or Personal Deviations). The question of honesty is identified as a relative term that could be qualified by various considerations. It is almost universally accepted that there is a bit of larceny in all of us, and that a modern Diogenes would need a strong lamp indeed to find an honest person in this day and age. Of course the great masses of people are "impeccably" honest only to the extent that either:

(a) they would steal under the circumstances that would offer less than one chance in a million of being caught, or

(b) they will attempt but one act of stealing in a lifetime, and enjoy the material gain thereby without hazarding a second risk, or

(c) they will steal only the most trifling objects, and rationalize their misconduct because of the smallness of the theft, or

(d) they will steal only that which offers them an exorbitant return, which would radically alter their mode of living, or

(e) they will start suit against individuals or corporations for non-existent or trifling damages to their person or property, or

(f) they will misrepresent that which they are and/or that

which they can accomplish, for selfish monetary or other reasons, or

(g) they use influence in obtaining employment, selling products, and in the problems of inter-personal relations, eliminate the less favorably connected, or

(h) they are a willing tool in the hands of influencing parties in glamorous adventures, such as occurred on T.V. Quiz show scandals.

Obviously most every adult has at one time or another been guilty, therefore, of theft, if not in primary motivation, then certainly in its more subtle secondary considerations. The following incidents are examples of personal deviations:

At the close of World War II, a well known chain restaurant in New York City closed several of its establishments because the extent of the petty theft of its clientele reached such proportions that it made it unprofitable to continue in business.

A contestant on a T.V. Quiz show was given the correct answers to advance questions, while his opponent regretted that he was not given the same opportunity for dishonesty. In the interim, interviewers, program directors, and other so called people of integrity who always lived exemplary lives, were not immune to compounding the public ruse.

The linen closets of many homes do more than furnish silent testimony to the fine hotels patronized.

Many people falsify applications for health insurance policies by "forgetting" their past ailments, when it would have been more practical to compose instead their last will and testament. Other examples are legion.

In the above classification of marginal dishonesty, apprehension regardless of the extent of theft would lead to shame, possibly a sense of guilt and remorse. If such tendency is universal, then one must be impressed by the irrational nature of stealing. Subtlety, ease of operation and failure to visualize a *"bleeding" victim* are characteristics of personal dishonesty. The essential motivation in this type of marginal dishonesty appears to be as much egocentric in nature as it is mercenary.

The most detestable margin culprits are those who spin their evil webs under the deceptive veil of pretending to do good. There is virtually no defense against them in the absence of legal limitations of their activities. Certain types of faith healers, under the relative immunity of their religious robes, who pretend to heal the physical and mental states of their followers by virtue of unproven anachronisms, are dishonest. This is evidenced in some instances by the so called "healing clinics" they conduct, and their bulletins on ("scientific") prayers and treatments, cloaked in metaphysical tones, with liberal sprinklings of blessings from the Scriptures. (God has made a great deal of money for such charlatans). Somehow from this planned misalliance, the soul, the mind and the body are simultaneously healed. Actually such "healers" are spiritual voyeurs, for they delight in the nakedness of the soul.

There exist also psychotherapists who consider deliberate use of phantasy as an important source of new empirical knowledge, and who recognize intuition or insight as the dominant factors in treatment. This delusion that awareness can exist not only beyond the five senses, but can actually be of aid in therapy is fraught with danger. Since supernatural overtones pervade these therapeutic sessions, (a more apt term is séance) troubled minds cannot even count upon their dreams as their sole undisputed property. Such probers into depth are psychological voyeurs, for they vicariously delight in laying bare the nakedness of the imagination.

If marginal or personal dishonesty is a crime, then virtually no one is immune, and the identification is a quantitative rather than a qualitative point of view.

The Sexual Deviate (As a Group). Gratification of the sensual impulse is manifest in many diverse ways, making the absolute concept of normality indecisive. Changing standards of morality make it exceedingly difficult to strictly delineate normal from pathologic modes of sexual contact. What is considered proper in one community may constitute a violation of the criminal code if committed across its border. The emancipation of the female from consideration as a chattel in most civilized areas has not affected one iota the variations of modes of sexual conduct still extant, nor in the interpretations placed by individuals, society and the law upon the meaning of normality. There is, therefore, an inexorable intertwining of right and wrong as applied to sexual congress. Opinion has often been expressed that were spouses to be criminally punished for sexual offenses in their marital lives as defined in the statute books, there would be very few adults fortunate enough to have escaped incarceration.

Sexual expression is probably the greatest single factor in the life of the individual that influences his course of social conduct and ethical values. Sex in all its subtle forms is the appetite supreme, and the springboard for all human ambition, inventiveness and creativity.

Medically, the sexual psychopath does not differ from the normal person in any way. From an anatomic, physiologic or glandular point of view there is no demonstrable disparity. The deviations at present can only be postulated on the basis of social and environmental factors upon individuals of limited moral fiber. Decisive criminality in the sexual sphere, being essentially a psycho-emotional induced state, is not primarily a function, therefore, of the intellect. It is as likely to be prevalent in people of great skill, intelligence or means, as it is in those of moronic caliber. The sex deviate is a product of unbridled, aberrant sexual appetite, which has transcended the intellectual processes. In such an instance, there is complete loss of capacity for individual restraint.

The actual origin of the sexual instinct resides in the cerebral cortex. The presence of external stimulation by the opposite sex through the senses of sight, touch, hearing or smell, evokes in the brain certain chains of erotic ideas and images which produces effects upon the reproductive organs, namely, tumescence and increased internal secretions. Actual external stimulation of the senses is not at all necessary for the same effect. Phantasies, impulses and dreams accomplish similar libidinous tendencies.

The reflex stimulation of the reproductive organs is dependent upon basic hormonal requirements within the male and female gonads. Specifically, there are certain types of cells in testicles, known as interstitial cells of Leydig, which secrete the essential hormone responsible for sexual appetite in the male. In the female there are two hormones residing within the ovaries responsible for her desire, but unlike the male, the sexual urge is not completely lost in case of her castration. In such an event, there is partial restitution of the sexual drive through a complex interaction of other glandular secretions, mitigated through the pituitary, adrenal and thyroid axis. The actual stimulation of sexual organs is transmitted through the erigente or pelvic nerves which by distending the venous spaces of the sex organs with blood, is responsible for an erection.

There are numerous influences of neurological diseases and spinal cord injuries upon the reflex excitation apparatus of the sexual organs. However, these mechanisms are unrelated to specific contribution to sexual psychopathy. There are instances when local irritation of the penis may be responsible for excessive sexual impulses as in the condition of phimosis, wherein the foreskin cannot be retracted, resulting in local irritation and excessive erotic stimulation of the penis. By and large, however, there is no statistical evidence to prove that local pathology of the sex organs, while increasing the sex urge, is a specific cause for sex crime. Isolated cases may in specific instances indict brain damage in an etiological role, but these are the exceptions rather than the rule.

Those committing sex offenses generally are not involved in criminal prosecution. Most sex crimes are those of rape, the majority of cases being statutory, where the female is below the age of consent. Often such cases find their origin in "framing" the male, jilting, or remorse at voluntary submission. Edwin H. Sutherland reports that 60% of rape murders were perpetrated by relatives or intimate associates of the slain woman.[1]

Those who commit sex offenses are probably in greater need of psychiatric treatment than incarceration, for there is virtually no treatment in prison. Dr. Walter Bromberg considers the sex offender to be more likely a person without any distinct psychopathic constitution. He believes that youthful offenders most often resort to violence, and the middle aged to homosexualism and pedophilia.[2] Although the stigmata of alcoholism, mental deficiency, or personality defects are not essentially characteristic of the sex offender, nevertheless, their problems demand study and treatment.

Both Denmark and Holland have castration laws against sex offenders. The Danish system of rehabilitation is especially noteworthy. Sex offenders are cared for in a hospital prison attended by a professional staff of high competence. The general aim is rehabilitation through personality and behavior evaluation, consistent with the intelligence of the sex deviate. Castration is performed for offenders past age 26 whose prognosis for rehabilitation is poor, generally confined to repeaters whose victims were children.

All too often sexual psychopathy resides alone in an otherwise integrated personality. The individual may be the embodiment of virtue in every respect save in departure from accepted sexual code. He may otherwise demonstrate, (and most frequently does) ample psychical balance in his thoughts and actions, but his departure from accepted sex mores of the community in which he lives, labels him a sexual psychopath.

Dr. Albert Ellis in his "Psychology of Sex Offenders", rightly contends that there is no absolute criterion of sexual normality; that sex behavior is anything and everything that society chooses to make it at any particular time. He further departs from most current opinion in his contention that those people who are exclusively oriented to one form of sexual activity to exclusion of all others are guilty of irrationality of behavior out of fear, which in itself constitutes a form of sexual deviation or neurosis. His theory indicts homosexualism, (for example), not as an immoral or degradative way of life, but because it is a fixated exclusive means of sexual gratification. He blames the restrictive sexual covenants of society in inculcating prejudices upon the individual, overburdening him with guilt, which in turn is responsible for his illogicalities and sexual devationism. Thus, to Dr. Ellis, homosexualism is the individual's rebellious fix-ation against society for banning this act and not others. It can be looked upon too as a case of the forbidden fruit being exceptionally tempting. Dr. Ellis further applies the restrictive sexual taboos of society to the interpretation of other forms of sexual psychopathy. However, it is my opinion that there is an additional factor of the sex deviate's behavior to be considered, viz: at the time of the commission of his sexual offense, he is *ignorantly defiant* of society's taboos in favor of giving expression to his own *innate* cravings. His compulsive desire is so great that he loses sight of any guilt feelings imposed by society.

In any description of sexual aberration, the reader must determine for himself whether he considers the various types as normal or as deviant expressions of sexuality. Certain types of sexual activity in early life are distinctly normal, which if continued into adulthood, might assume another aspect. Thus it is normal for a small child to exhibit his sexual organs which in adulthood would label him an exhibitionist.

Excessive male sex drive is known as satyriasis and in females is described as nymphomania. These basic impulses form the settings for departures from the socially accepted norms of heterosexual contact. The more common forms of sexual deviation are as follows:

Pederasty is unnatural intercourse between men by the anus.

Pedophilia is a pathological sexual interest in children through anal assault.

Sodomy is often applied to either term.

Fetichism is an attachment on the part of the male for certain portions of the female body or her attire, as an obedience to sex impulses. Krafft-Ebing draws the analogy to religious cultism wherein the individual worships holy objects and relics. In such an instance there exists the delusion of the idol which transcends mere symbolism, and possesses divine attributes and miraculous powers. He further describes an erotic fetichism wherein individual qualities of charm, voice, mental qualities, etc. are sufficient to induce ecstasy. A more modern version is the "swoon" of the adolescent female at the altar of the crooner.

Exhibitionism is indecent exposure to the opposite sex, without aggressive intent.

Sadism is the attainment of sexual satisfaction through infliction of cruelty in varying degrees, which may include rape and murder.

Masochism is violence wherein the acts of cruelty are directed towards oneself rather than another party. It may take subtle forms, such as personal castigation and humiliation as well as the desire to be whipped (flagellation).

Masturbation is the mechanical manipulation of the genitals for purposes of orgasm.

Homosexualism is the perverse feeling for sexual contact between individuals of the same sex.

Bisexualism is the indiscriminate sexual desire for either sex.

Frottage is a sense of pleasure by rubbing against someone.

Mixoscopia is the achievement of sex pleasure by observing intercourse.

Coprolalia is sexual excitation from the use of obscenity.

Effemination is the condition wherein a male possesses the feelings and tastes of a female. He assumes the part of a woman in homosexual intercourse and will often masquerade in female attire (transvestism).

A voyeur is a person who attains sexual gratification by looking at sensuous objects.

Bestiality implies contact by either sex with an animal.

A cunnilinguist is one whose sexual outlet is licking the vulva.

Fellatorismis is the act of introduction of the penis into the mouth.

Necrophilia is sexual indulgence with a corpse.

Incest implies sexual intercourse with a member of the immediate family.

The characteristic of all of the above forms of sexual behavior is the tendency for compulsive illogical repetition in a search for relief from inner tension. Numerous theoretical considerations have been evolved for the origins of sexual inconsistencies. The best known, of course, deals with the universal application of infantile sexuality residing in the dynamics of the unconscious, as evolved by Freud in his underlying theory of psychoanalysis, a concept challenged by numerous writers including the author.

It is difficult to conceive how the personality and sexual disturbances of an adult may be resolved either by identification with the perplexities of his childhood toilet habits, or his alleged incestual tendencies at an age when his main preoccupation was toys. The actual background for the development of deviational desires may well have arisen from prolonged denial of sex, miseducation, basic feelings of inferiority, misdirected religious fervor, imitation, desire for conformity within a given social or anti-social set, weak moral fiber and as a protest against society's mores as theorized by Dr. Albert Ellis. Just as nature abhors a vacuum, so does man. He seeks to know why, but the answers are not immediately forthcoming. If he can ever unequivocally differentiate right from wrong in sex practices, only then will it be possible to work towards an ultimate cure of what is proven to be abnormal. Sometimes the differential is one of degree and not of kind.

Sadism in its fullest connotation is an act of cruelty and undoubtedly symbolic of psychopathy. Reduce its physical or emotional manifestations in intensity and virtually all people become sadists. For example, it is difficult to separate sexual orgasm from its combined pleasurable and painful state. Kissing may be accompanied by lip biting, and the marriage bed ofttimes produces its share of bruises not motivated by malice. The teases of the lover are expressions of a sadistic yearning. There is yet a delight in suffering, but it reaches a point of satiety beyond which sadism erupts in psychopathic fury.

THE PROBLEM OF HOMOSEXUALITY

Whatever variant opinions psychologists, physicians or laymen may entertain regarding the propriety of homosexual practices, one certain aspect is evident, namely, that civilized society considers it to be reprehensible and usually translates its moral indignation into law. Of course, the great majority of homosexual expressions are clandestine, and habitués, as long as they confine solicitation to dens and known places where they assemble, are rarely taken into custody.

Dr. William J. Robinson, in his book, "Our Mysterious Life Glands", expresses his opinion that homosexuality is innate and cannot be changed. Any claims of cure, he states, was never homosexuality in the first place, but rather pseudo-homosexuality. He bases his contention on the very definition of the term as a feeling, and not as action towards the same sex, an opinion also held by Krafft-Ebing. Thus, will power may be sufficiently great to overcome the overpowering urge so that the individual may never have indulged in overt homosexual practice. Yet by virtue of this emotional perversion, he must be identified as homosexual. On the other hand, the man participating in pederasty, or mutual masturbation is not necessarily a true homosexual, unless his motivation is actually a feeling for the act. Thus, many weak-willed individuals may indulge in homosexual practice because of monetary considerations or because of limitation of outlet of their sexual emotions, such as occurs in boarding schools, jails or any other places where prolonged confinement is necessary. When the temptation of money is removed or heterosexual stimulation is substituted, homosexual practice is curtailed in many instances. Such people, perverted though their action may be, are not true homosexuals and so are readily amenable to cure. It is ironic, therefore, that such perverted practices can often be an asocial expression without actual homosexual feeling, and conversely, the true homosexual with intense desire may escape detection by avoiding contact out of strong social conscience and will power.

In a certain proportion of homosexual men, there is a demonstrable difference in body build. Thus, the shoulders may be narrower, the hips wider, the voice higher pitched, and the distribution of body fat and pubic hair similar to the female. Similarly, the genital region may indicate sexual physical immaturity. Conversely, the lesbian may possess the secondary characteristics more of the male than of the female. Such individuals may actually parade in the full attire of the opposite sex, in which case they are known as transvestites. However, the great majority of homosexuals present no physical stigmata for positive identification.

Theories of Homosexuality. The actual cause of this perversity remains an enigma. It is not failure in anatomical or endocrinal maturation, but a defect in psychosexual development that is manifest, often in early childhood. Thus, when they were children, homosexuals often were predisposed to games involving sex play with the same sex, or witnessing nude bodies. Their fantasies too, showed the tendencies of perversities that were to be later identified as homosexual. To be sure, the history of the prepubertal homosexual stage of development may stand out in homosexuals, but so has it been evident in adults whose sexual outlets are perfectly normal. To adopt the psychoanalytic viewpoint that failure of the child to form a wholesome identification with the parent of the same sex out of hate or fear, or to say it differently, that if the child forms an identification with the parent of the opposite sex, homosexual tendencies may later appear, is stretching credulity beyond the boundaries of naivité. Even most analysts now disown the Freudian theory that the persistence of the oedipus complex causes homosexuality.

The question is often raised whether homosexuality is a neurosis due to fear of the opposite sex. Yet if fear *against* the opposite sex exists, it does not explain the perverse feeling *for* the same sex. If homosexuality is a neurosis it is unique in that all too often other evidences of personality defects are lacking as well as not being amenable to treatment with drug therapy. It is more valid to theorize that fear of sexual contact with the opposite sex is responsible for avoidance of heterosexual relations, commonly termed celibacy. A negative attitude for the opposite sex is an illogical explanation for a positive one towards the same sex.

Although the actual cause or causes of true homosexuality remains an enigma, actual homosexual practices (as distinguished from innate desire) are nurtured in variable degree in people of weak moral fiber via the depravity of society's dark alleys.

There have been various claims made that homosexuality in males or females can be cured. Yet this type of sexual deviate presents one of the most complex psychological problems in all sexual aberrations. This is attributed to the kaleidoscopic nature of homosexualism, and its great incidence even in people who have never actually participated in such practice. Homosexuality may thus remain latent in some individuals although they may not even be aware of it, until they are seduced by other homosexuals.

The first problem in the effective treatment of homosexuality is the understanding of what type is being dealt with. The innate or true organic type offers virtually a hopeless prognosis. His or her sexual attitude is built in, and the therapist can no more effectively change the unnatural desire through inculcating understanding, than a physician can curtail a patient's inclination to smoke with the rational argument that smoking is injurious to the heart and lungs. There are many who will dispute this claim and will devote long hours of deep psychiatric and psychoanalytic probing and guidance in attempts at cure. There are equal numbers who share the opposite viewpoint, in particular, Havelock Ellis, who said, "I do not know of any cases in which a complete and permanent transformation of homosexuality into heterosexuality was achieved."

On the other hand, pseudo-homosexuals can often be cured, because the motivating factor in their misbehavior is other than actual desire. The task is made easier if moral values are taught to them at a time when they become receptive to re-education and guidance through psychiatric and religious efforts.

According to Dr. Edmund Bergler, in "1000 Homosexuals", the homosexual who has the will to change and is receptive to giving up the desire for self-punishment (which Dr. Bergler claims is responsible for his predicament) can be cured. I challenge this assertion. A will to change is admirable, but there is another essential ingredient to be considered if the homosexual is to be cured, and that is the feeling of sexual attraction for the

111

same sex. Just as many criminals have the will to go straight but are powerless to do so by an inner compulsion, similarly, is the true homosexual a slave to his passions, will notwithstanding. As long as *feeling* for the same sex remains, treatment is futile.

PROSTITUTION

Prostitution is here to stay as long as sex remains. No legislation or police force can effectively cope with a problem that attempts to bridle as solid an emotional core as man's sexual appetite. Neither the pulpit nor the school, appeal to morals or reason, can effectively contain the biologic urge which prostitution attempts to satisfy.

The appetite supreme, in seeking expression, respects neither caste, education nor status. Thus, a constant theme of "A House is Not a Home," the experiences of one of the most active "madames" this country has ever known, emphasized the fact that one can find some of the most respected people from all walks of life, in common with the psychopath, patronizing houses of ill repute.

The business of prostitution knows no slack seasons, and recognizes no cycles of depression. It caters in a highly marketable commodity, namely sex. Although now illegal in virtually every town, hamlet and city of the United States, prostitution still manages to flourish through diverse subterfuges. Certain officials not only close their eyes to the existence of brothels in their communities, but actually facilitate their existence. In fact the economy of local legitimate business establishments in such localities designated as "sin cities," is directly dependent upon the influx of traffic for the purpose of sex.

Prostitution grows wherever males assemble and is especially popular at convention places and holiday resorts. In the past its organization was often but not always a function of underworld syndicates, operating with methodical efficiency, sometimes with judicial and police connivance. Now, however, the brothel itself, in most cities is rapidly disappearing, its place often being taken by streetwalkers, bar flies, and such fronts as massage parlors, dance halls, taxi and bellhop contacts.

There have always been two main schools of thought in handling the problem. The moralists, believing prostitution an instrument of pure evil, adopt a frontal head-on attack, with jail sentences for miscreants, as their means of coping with the problem. A more liberal school concords with the philosophy of Lincoln Steffens in recognizing that people cannot be legislated into morality. This school advocates segregation of districts, licensing and inspection of prostitutes as more practical measures. Dr. Harry Benjamin, in his treatise, "Prostitution Re-Assessed," expounds his views that in a social setup such as ours, prostitution has a function. He states that an increase in sex crimes and other undesirable effects would result in an attempt to suppress it.

There are those people who claim that wiping out all prostitution through the medium of apprehension and punishment will reduce automatically the incidence of venereal disease. There are equal numbers who claim that this action only results in the increase of venereal disease, by virtue of numerous clandestine outlets. One must not be so naive to believe that the medical supervision of prostitutes under governmental regulation is an effective means of control of venereal disease. There are certain medical facts to be kept in mind in this connection, viz:

1. Any venereal exposure can lead to venereal disease.
2. It is extremely difficult, impractical, often impossible to diagnose every kind of venereal disease without resorting to extensive tests in each case.
3. A prostitute may prove negative to all tests, but become infected subsequent to medical examination.

However, the fact remains that the effectiveness of the antibiotics used both in prophylaxis as well as in treatment of vene-

113

real disease, has now relegated to a secondary role the medical aspects of this problem.

Prostitutes are recruited from all walks of life, from the servile to high society, from the moronic to the university trained. The motivation is generally a combination of economic and psychological factors, with no sharp line of demarcation. Some housewives, unknown to their husbands and families, accept part-time occupation as prostitutes, as do those who desire to augment their income for various reasons.

There are numerous reasons why men visit prostitutes, most common being the excitement of sexual outlets, freedom from responsibility for pregnancy and other personal considerations.

The arrest and apprehension of prostitutes is only a minor solution to the problem. It is a means of pacifying the outraged conscience of society, seeking redress for an offense of moral degradation. Believing that water seeks its own level, and that nature abhors a vacuum, it is my firm opinion that destroying prostitution at the organization level results in a home-grown variety of independent prostitutes. Such programs as sex education, including venereal diseases, hygiene of pregnancy, counseling services, child guidance courses for young girls, etc., all constitute an ambitious and laudatory program, but are ineffectual instruments of morality.

The effects of prostitution are social. The causes are only partially so, being mainly interwoven with biologic and psychological considerations. Therefore, one must not expect a solution to this age old problem by a purely sociological approach.

As long as men are men, and women are women, prostitution will exist. Although brothels may continue to be raided and preventive legislation like the Mann Act may be passed, nevertheless passion will still reign supreme. When mankind has at last learned to alter his biological and psychological yearnings, and to influence his genetic characteristics, only then will prostitution be completely eradicated. Until such time, may it not be advisable to harness this social problem through a suitable governmental program, which would at least minimize the accessory criminopathic influences?

NEUROSES, PSYCHOSES AND CRIME

Regardless of the true etiologic nature of neurosis, the fact remains that the neurotic individual has failed to make a satisfactory adjustment to his environment. As a result of this failure, there are numerous sympton complexes which affect the individual's happiness through a reaction of anxiety and/or behavioral characteristics.

The problem is of interest chiefly because of its causal relation to crime. There are certain types of crimes which are peculiar to mentally disturbed people as a direct result of their personality disorder. Arson is probably the best example of pyromania, a compulsive desire to start fires. The arsonist delights in the excitement incident to fires, especially at the sight of racing fire engines and police cars. The act itself is purposeless and wanton, born of a persistence in ideation (obsession) with an impulse to act (compulsion). Another example of a compulsion neurosis leading to larceny is kleptomania. Although there is no economic motive for stealing, the excitement of the exploit is nevertheless a compulsive type of neurosis. Some authorities believe that voyeurism of the "Peeping Tom" is still another compulsive type of psychoneurosis, in which the afflicted thrills at the sight of females in state of undress. Similarly, they consider all sexual perversity as compulsive types of neuroses.

The most noticeable feature of all neurosis is the great variety and complexity it may assume in different individuals. The symptoms may be either purely subjective, or combined with physical signs of distress, even though laboratory and X-ray confirmation of a pathological breakdown of tissue are lacking. The minor group of neuroses are characterized chiefly by restlessness and fatigue. Accompanying these states are variable symptoms, such as headaches, dizziness, depression, irritability, difficulty in concentration, insomnia, sleeplessness and waning sex appetite. The face may express evidence of distress in form of apprehensiveness, tics, bizarre mannerisms, and the person may bite his nails.

Ofttimes the signs and symptoms can be classified into distinct specific syndromes, such as psychogenic rheumatism, migraine, spastic colitis, neurocirculatory asthenia (undue preoccupation with cardiac consciousness), menopausal states, etc. Obviously, a good many of the symptoms are hypochondriacal, have no basis in fact and arise out of a deep seated anxiety. A complete discussion of the theories of origin, descriptions of types and treatment of the minor or major neuroses or of psychoses, is beyond the aims and scope of this chapter. In view of the fact that some crimes, especially those due to compulsion neuroses, arise from personality disorders, an overall survey is of help in understanding the causation of some types of crime.

It is understandable that a restless body, disturbed in spirit, with little conscious knowledge of the motivating mechanisms, and with various somatic equivalents to a state of anxiety, can sometimes give actual expression to its incapacity by anti-social behavior. In other words, if the neurosis is severe enough, the disturbed mind may seek physical retribution on an innocent offspring, relative or bystander, when unhappiness gives vent to anger.

The behavioral characteristics of the hysterical person stand out especially in this major type of neuroses. The symptom complex that develops in this condition can simulate every organic manifestation, and occurs at any age. The personality is infantile, with very labile emotional overtones, including moodiness, impulsiveness, hypersensitivity, ambivalency in feelings towards the same person—at one moment affectionate and at another resentful. The hysteric is impressionable, as well as a fanciful liar. Hysteria may assume many forms, from sensory paralysis to pain, or sensory loss of any of the five senses in whole or in part. The hysteric in his many emotional expressions of an anxiety over which he has no conscious control, is in the unfortunate position to utilize his suggestible makeup to cross into the boundary of crime.

Obsessive Reactions. A phobia is a defensive reaction whereby the individual experiences an intense fear, and although recognizing that no actual danger exists, he is powerless to control his emotion. Among the phobias are fear of germs, dirt, animals,

116

travel, or fear of confined spaces, etc. Exposure to the object of fear inevitably leads to panic, faintness, nausea, sweating, tremors and other somatic equivalents. Often the phobia is associated with some activity that he may or may not be aware of which previously accounted for psychic trauma. Such phobias are also of an obsessional nature. At times they assume a milder form, such as avoidance of walking on cracks of sidewalk, or skipping every other step when walking up a flight of stairs. Obviously, phobic activities are all too often translated to asocial behavior, though usually not to an extreme.

Sometimes the individual is unable to control his compulsive obsessions, in spite of recognition of the unreasonablensss of his thoughts and actions. The obsession may be ideational in content or combined with repetitive activity, ofttimes criminal. Sometimes the obsessed individual is preoccupied with content repugnant to his ethical and moral values, including themes of sexual aberrancies, larceny, incest or murder. At times the ideational components are of metaphysical, religious or philosophical content. The obsessive thoughts often lead to anxiety with exclusion of other important interests. Suicidal impulses are often said to arise from obsessional thoughts, and when the ideas dwell on unimportant objects the phenomenon is known as rumination.

The repetition of obsessive thinking leads to considerable indecision and doubting, and in its simplest form to activity aimed at removing the illogical thoughts, examples being, re-checking if lights were turned out, if a door was closed, or excessive bathing. Thus the individual reacts to his anxiety and achieves some measure of satisfaction through a semi ritualistic behavior. An extreme form of such compulsive behavior may result in homicidal activity, of which the most alarming recent example is the case of the "mad bomber," who, in spite of his awareness of wrong doing, habitually erupted into his maniacal fury. Larceny of all sorts, rape, tribal rituals of primitive peoples utilizing human victims, frequently belong to the category of obsessive compulsive reactions. Hypochondriasis may be classified as an obsessive awareness of the individual's concern with

117

his bodily sensations which normal people would ordinarily disregard. The developing anxieties can lead to compulsions which may be translated into anti-social activity.

Dissociation. Dissociation is the process by which the individual possesses the means of eliminating that part of the personality which troubles him. A new emergent personality with no recollection of the original, and functioning on its own, is capable of acting independently at times. Thus, a common form is somnambulism, in which a certain aspect of the individual's personality participates in some complicated activity while he is asleep. At times, the patient may wander considerable distances, a condition known as fugue, which is variable in emotional content, duration, and degree of amnesia. A number of secondary personalities may emerge, each acting independently, to which the name, multiple personalities, is given. Although crimes are rarely committed in such state, they have occurred in the past. The reader will recall the recent controversy concerning a woman who committed murder during an alleged state of somnambulism. The unsettled question, of course, is the extent to which the primary personality was accountable by virtue of her awareness or lack of awareness of her secondary personality. In some cases of dissociative reactions, the fugue state may be accompanied by loss of personal identity, with the assumption of the name and characteristics of another. It is simple to visualize criminal complications in such a state of dissociation. The termination of the fugue often leads to complete amnesia of these new experiences, and the latter has often been offered as excuses by criminals for their acts.

The tales some prisoners tell of blacked out memories, are often false, and the prime tool of the malingerer, for it offers a readily available excuse for the criminal who knows how to act. Sometimes the malingerer will also feign temporary insanity when he is caught for misbehavior. There are other motives for pretending insanity, such as escape from unpleasant situations or associates, and the desire to demonstrate superior intelligence by "putting it over" on the authorities. There are varying degrees of malingering from the crude to that with finesse. Various forms of physical illness may also be mimicked by the apprehended criminal, in order to obtain the obvious advantages of hospital care in preference to the drab life in a prison cell. The differential characteristic of malingering in contrast to the neurotic or the dissociative individual is that the motivation of the former is entirely conscious, while the others have no pernicious intent.

Psychoses and Crime. As stated, the great majority of crimes are committed by the psychopathic personality rather than by the truly psychotic (insane). There is a difference between the legal and the medical interpretation of insanity, so that not all psychoses can be interpreted as being free from legal responsibility. In the U.S. the rule that is followed is patterned after M'Naghten's case (10 CL. and Fin. 200), namely, "To establish a defense on the ground of insanity it must be clearly proved that, at the time of the committing of the act, the party accused was laboring under such a defect of reason from disease of the mind as not to know the nature and quality of the act he was doing, . . ." This legal interpretation has often been under attack by psychiatrists, because the medical concept of insanity is based on other considerations than being able to distinguish right from wrong.

The main characteristic of the psychotic is the dissociation of himself and his environment, and the factor of emotions gaining control of his intellectual processes. Unlike the neurotic, the insane person is unaware that he is sick. He displays anti-social characteristics and his personality is often beset with delusions of sex, persecution, grandiosity, etc., or hallucinations in any of the five senses.

There are two main groupings of psychoses, those due to organic causes, and the affective without definitive causology.

I. *Organic Psychoses.*

There are numerous causes for the organic deterioration of personality with its attendant behavioral picture. The classification of psychoses of the American Psychiatric Association, lists numerous categories of organic psychoses resulting from infection (such as syphilis, tuberculosis), intoxication (alcohol, toxins, metals, gases, drugs), head injuries, disturbances in circulation (embolism, arteriosclerosis, heart disease), convulsive disorders (epilepsy), disturbances of nutritional, metabolic or endocrine function (pellagra, uncontrolled diabetes, etc.), brain tumor and hereditary causes (Huntington's chorea, Parkinson's disease.)

The personality and anti-social changes are extremely variable from mild to severe. From a sociological point of view we need be concerned most with the atherosclerotic type of psychoses because of its great incidence and occasional criminopathic tendencies on the part of those so afflicted. The following summation taken from *The New Psychiatry*, gives ample evidence of the variable effects of cerebral atherosclerosis:

> "Probably the best known organic psychosis is due to arteriosclerotic and/or senile changes within the brain, resulting in slow circulation of blood nutrients within the walls of cerebral vessels, and a consequent lowering of available oxygen concentration in arteries below a critical value of approximately 90%. Similarly, the peculiarities of personality changes are brought about by an inability of the blood of narrowed, sclerosed cerebral vessels to properly circulate, accumulated by-products of cerebral metabolism. The manifestation of cerebral atherosclerosis may be mild in onset, with a gradual blunting of fine traits of personality previously exhibited, loss of social and ethical values, lapses of memory, inattention, disorientation, loss of powers of concentration, constant reminiscing, strange utterances, or behavioral departure from previous normal actions; or it may be fulminating due to sudden withdrawal of oxygen from vital portion of brain as occurs in strokes, with a parade of psychic disturbances simulating all nervous syndromes." [3]

The Affective or Functional Group of Psychoses, offers no definitive cause or causes, although there is virtual agreement now among medical authorities that the greatest factor in its etiology is metabolic in nature. Thus, environmental stress of past and present are merely ancillary components that modify the individual psychology of the mental disorders.

120

A description of the characteristics of the Affective group of psychotics is mandatory, in order to obtain a clearer perspective of the anti-social behavioral tendencies. The following summary is taken from the same source.

II. *The Affective Group of Psychoses.*

(a) Schizophrenia. In this connection there is a dissociation of the patient's emotional system from reality, with the element of affect having complete dominance over the patient's intellectual processes. Ofttimes the manifestations are precipitated by undue stress. Four distinct types are recognized, viz:

1. Simple. There is a gradual transformation of personality, with changes in interest and modes of behavior. There generally are no delusions, hallucinations, though they can occur; no frank depression, though irritability and suspicion are inherent trends. Unusual absorption in some sort of activity, such as religion, or seclusiveness, apathy (loss of interest), preoccupation with own subjective symptoms are often present. There develops a tendency to misconstrue the attitude of associates, and the environment is translated to personal fears, suspicions and desires. There is generally no memory disintegration, though the thinking apparatus is compromised.

2. Hebephrenia. The irritability of mood, adolescent mentality, tendency toward fantasy, delusion, hallucinations serve to identify this advanced state. The patient is rather inaccessible due to lack of coherency, and responses to questions are often silly and disjointed. Particular mannerisms, lack of sphincteric control of urine and feces serve to emphasize the depersonalization that has taken place.

3. Catatonia. There are phases of alternating stupor and of excitement, although one phase may predominate. Patients in the former stage exhibit inattention to bodily needs, as well as to external pressures and often exhibit mutism, negativism, and immobility. The duration of the phase is unpredictable and is often followed by an excitement stage, or even temporary periods of relative normality.

121

4. Paranoia. Illogical delusions, chiefly of persecution, negativism, hallucinations. There is often a feeling of conspiracy at play in even the simplest behavior of associates, with tenacious retention of fixed ideas on the subject of the delusion. Although the classic paranoiacs rarely recover, they may not require hospitalization because their conduct often does not become antisocial, though they may be looked upon as "cranks."

(b) Manic-Depressive Psychoses. This disorder is characterized by alternating periods of mania and depression, or of only one of either phase, with tendency to periodic recurrence. The depressive phase may vary from mild to stuporous. There is a marked psychomotor retardation and suicidal tendencies are common. The manic phase too runs the gauntlet from mild to delirious, and the patient is distracted from anything around him. The increased psychomotor activity results in a veritable parade of completely asocial behavior, with destructive tendencies, not born of malice, obscenities and purposeless activity.

(c) Involutional Psychoses. Starting at a time of waning physical and sexual vigor, after 40 in females and after 50 in males, the disorder is one of tremendous anxiety to patient and is accompanied by agitation, hypochondriasis, with delusions, hallucinations as prominent byplay. There is no psychomotor retardation, nor history of earlier attacks of mania, or depression, although pre-morbid traits of intolerance, sensitivity, stubbornness, apprehension and meticulousness had been evident previously."

It is obvious, from the description of the mentally afflicted, especially the compulsively neurotic and the psychotic types, that there exists a behavioral component as well as a defect of personality, and it is often reflected through conflict with society. The paranoid in particular, because of a well organized delusional system is in frequent conflict with the law. He may be of superior intelligence and thus be able to build up most effective arguments to prove a point that may ultimately erupt into violence due to a wrong basic premise.

It is not the psychosis itself that is responsible for crime, but rather some unknown factor in the behavioral component of

122

the disturbed personality. The fact remains that the great majority of psychotics, whether of organic or affective origin, offer no criminopathic tendencies and are usually quite docile in manner.

The Neuropathic Individual and Crime. There are individuals who show personality and behavioral changes as a result of injury or intoxication to the central nervous system, without actual signs of insanity. Although they may also be classified under the organic psychoses, they merit separate classification because the symptoms are more benign and resemble those of the psychopath more than the psychotic. The various types of epilepsy, such as Jacksonian (due to irritation of motor area of brain following injury, infection, etc.) and idiopathic (of unknown cause) are cases in point, also as are addiction to drugs and to alcohol. The Italian criminologist, Cesare Lombroso, erroneously identified criminality and epilepsy as similar terms, crime being, he thought, the analogue of epilepsy. However, there is a type of epilepsy accompanied by an act of violence with complete amnesia, for the anti-social activity. Similarly, temper tantrums may actually resemble an epileptic seizure, although there is usually no loss or only partial loss of recollection of what transpired. As with psychotics, most epileptics are not criminally inclined.

Psyche, Soma and Behavior. We have seen in the description of the organic psychoses wherein a disturbed somatic state, such as arteriosclerosis, intoxication, infection, etc. can lead to psychic sequelae. The resultant changes in personality in turn are reflected unfavorably in deterioration of interpersonal relations resulting in crime. All too often, even with treatment that includes the primary somatic conditions, brain damage is considerable, especially in instances where deprived of oxygen (anoxia) for any length of time. In such cases prognosis is unfavorable, for therapy leaves much to be desired. It is far more practical to exert efforts at preserving normal body equilibrium, if secondary more permanent effects upon the brain are to be avoided. The task of prevention, therefore, by means of the teaching of body hygiene, nutrition, sex education, spiritual training, and through recreation, is a more rewarding method of approach.

We have also noted the many physical manifestations of disturbed emotions upon bodily functions in a discussion of the affective psychoses and neuroses. The impacts of a disturbed psyche are exerted upon all organs (including the heart, lungs, stomach, etc.), and upon behavioral tendencies as well. There is therefore, a mutual dependency of the soma and psyche, that may well overflow into the individual's social attitudes.

ALCOHOLISM

Alcoholism is a state of drunkenness. There are two types, acute and chronic, which are sometimes indistinguishable.

The effects of alcohol on the human body depend upon whether ingestion is acute or chronic, and upon individual sensitivity. These manifestations are exerted primarily upon the central nervous system. Alcoholism occurs much more readily if no food is present in the stomach, and in individuals not accustomed to drinking. Absorption through the stomach and small intestines takes place much more readily in such cases. The behavioral characteristics of an inebriate will approximate the alcohol concentration in the blood. A feeling of exhilaration generally occurs with a blood concentration of 1 to 3 milligrams, and correspondingly higher levels will remove inhibitions, impair judgment, speech, powers of observation and muscular coordination. After a brief period of nervous system stimulation, depression ensues with consequent disturbances in sensation, vision, hearing and numbness. Further effects of depression of the nervous system consist of nausea, vomiting, flushing of face, quickening of pulse, fall in blood pressure, sweating, incoherency and loss of consciousness. Hence intoxication often leads to incontinence of urine and feces, drop in body temperature, and even death. Alcohol sometimes precipitates a form of amnesia or automation, whereby the person will exhibit a stereotyped form of behavior, enter into a trance, or perhaps wander away in a sort of fugue state. In such instances alcoholism is secondary to the primary psychic disturbance that exists. These trends may occur periodically, with individual behaving normally between sprees without any craving for alcohol except at intervals, a condition known as dipsomania.

The physical effects of acute alcoholism, known commonly as "hangover" consist of a feeling of lassitude, light-headedness and headaches. More severe cases result in dehydration with effects upon the internal organs and vascular system, and pneumonia resulting from exposure.

The behavioral effects of acute alcoholism are probably most apparent in the multiplicity of its anti-social manifestations. Placid individuals may sometimes feel the need to belligerently demonstrate any latent prowess they think they may have. Ancient submerged animosities, long since buried, may suddenly be disinterred and their flames rekindled. Ethical and moral restraints may temporarily vanish so that all varieties and grades of offenses may be committed during a period of inebriation. Probably the greatest problem incident to alcoholism is the driving of a vehicle while drunk. It is not surprising that sexual crimes and incidence of venereal diseases always rise during holidays and festive occasions. Of course, trangressions in interpersonal relations are greater in those of weak will and nervous constitution.

The sociological implications of alcoholism are amply testified by the fantastic number of intoxicants who pass through the city court systems, hospitals and jails, each day. Of course, jail terms can hardly serve as cures but rather as opportunities for reflection and sobering up processes. Dr. Dagobert D. Runes, in his book, "Dictionary of Thought", has aptly expressed alcoholism as "Society's legitimatized drug addiction."

The chronic indulgence in alcohol is very often but not always found in persons where they or their families have a history of psychic disturbance. This oft apparent observation was recently statistically proven by Dr. Walter C. Alvarez who documented thousands of clinical cases over many years' duration of his patients and their relatives.[4] His investigation led to the conclusions that:

(a) alcoholism was genetically determined and took preference over environmental influences and/or Freudian pain-pleasure theories;
(b) alcoholism was associated with a common core of familial tendencies towards psychoses, severe neuroses and epilepsy;
(c) any type of stigma may be genetically altered to appear in its related form in later generations.

This investigator's equating of clinical data among alcoholics and their relatives against known environmental factors, which led to the above scientifically validated conclusions, is a distinct forward step in the understanding of genetic and biochemical motivation of mental disease and alcoholism.

The effects of chronic imbibing of alcohol on body organs are numerous and often devastating. However, it is primarily the personality structure and resultant character decay that is of greatest sociological import. The alcoholic, though jovial, is frequently unreliable and untrustworthy, not out of volition but rather due to lack of self control. Not only the liver, spleen and other organs are subjected to deterioration, but the continuous effects of alcohol upon the brain and central nervous system are responsible for the gradual decline in personality. Sometimes a transient psychosis known as delirium tremens occurs. This may last as long as 10 days. The alcoholic then is disoriented, suffers from visual and auditory hallucinations, and exhibits a veritable train of excitatory phenomena often with paranoid overtones. A closely allied picture of the chronic alcoholic is that of Korsakoff's Psychosis. This condition starts with delirium, but exhibits a strong element of confabulation and loss of memory. These states are evidences of alcoholic deterioration of the brain and clashes with society often become inevitable.

Treatment of the Alcoholic. Probably the best known and most effective method of treatment of the alcoholic is through

Alcoholics Anonymous. This organization operates on a national scale, and its members are actively devoted to the alcoholic's problems. Their approach, although non-medical, is often more effective than present day medical care.

There are numerous drugs used to treat the excitement, dehydrative and depressive phases of acute alcoholism. These include parenteral fluids with vitamin additives, tranquilizers and stimulative medicaments, such as caffeine and dextro-amphetamine in event of depression. The social rehabilitation of the chronic alcoholic who may be temporarily sober is a more difficult problem. It is mainly psychiatric in nature, with due attention to be paid to current stress situations requiring solution. The physical harm must similarly be thoroughly assessed and treated medically. Recently two drugs, antabuse and temposil, have been used in attempting to break the habit. The drugs interfere with the metabolism of alcohol and cause the accumulation of a toxic metabolite, acetaldehyde. Should the patient drink alcohol while on this therapy, the accumulation of acetaldehyde produces great discomfort, such as difficulty in breathing, vomiting, flushing of face, and he must desist from further drinking. However, a drawback is that the alcoholic must be sufficiently motivated to want to be cured of his habit. Very recently hypnosis has been used in alcoholics to create an aversion to drinking by having patients relive the unpleasant hangover effects of alcohol.[5] Good results are claimed.

The real solution to the great social problem of alcoholism may still be a long way in coming. Though strides have been made, especially in the management of the acute alcoholic, the problem of the chronic imbiber remains a formidable one.

DRUG ADDICTION

Any medicament that has the potential for relieving pain, may be similarly responsible for addiction. The reason is that the action of a drug in relieving pain depends also upon its ability to alter mood, in order for pain stimuli to become lessened. Numerous drugs, including opiates such as morphine, heroin; synthetics as demerol; sedatives as bromides, barbiturates, marihuana; and cortical stimulants as cocaine and amphetamine, come under the classification of addictive drugs.

Habituation to drugs may be accidental as a result of their therapeutic use, such as the presence of opiates in diarrhea and cough mixtures. The widespread use of barbiturates among those suffering from emotional disturbances and insomnia is a still more pernicious form of accidental addiction.

The intractable pain of cancer and other conditions may require large doses of narcotic drugs. Not infrequently, the patients thereby become addicted to their use. However, this presents no social problem since the hopelessness of the physical state demands relief of pain, and there is no danger of moral degradation in such individuals.

A far greater problem of addiction than that incident to relief of pain, involves the deliberate use of habituating drugs. In such cases, addiction serves as an escape from the realities of everyday existence into a make-believe world. It is a personality problem which is most likely to appear in those people of unstable psyche. Thus, Dr. Walter C. Alvarez was able to correlate in numerous case studies the close relationships of drug addiction to prior existing psychiatric disorders.

The manifestations of addiction vary with the causative drug. Habituation to any drug is characterized by a strong emotional dependency, especially with regard to opiates. This group, in addition, will produce a tolerance, or diminishing effect on repetition of the same dose. It will also cause a physical dependency so that if the opiate is not continued, withdrawal signs and symptoms will develop. Cocaine derivatives, amphetamine, marihuana, unlike the opiates, will produce neither tolerance nor physical dependency, but will exert their influence predominantly on emotional cravings. The records of the U. S. Public Health Service Hospital at Lexington, Kentucky indicate that morphine is the most commonly used narcotic with heroin second. It has been estimated that there are 46,226 addicts in the United States, 79% males, with 7 out of 10 under the age of thirty. Some estimates place the total number of addicts as higher.[6] A description of the individual characteristics of the addictive drugs is necessary in order to understand the social implications of the problem.

The opiate drugs exhibt no characteristic (pathognomonic) signs of addiction. Frequently, evidences of needle marks and scars of the veins, arms and legs are noted. Withdrawal of this group of drugs results in restlessness and depression, provided the addict is in the early stages of addiction. However, if the drug is sharply curtailed in a confirmed addict, the above symptoms become more severe with perspiration, tearing of eyes and catarrh of nose ensuing. After 24 hours, the addict exhibits a progressively greater restlessness, muscle twitching and pupillary dilatation. He may begin to suffer from insomnia, vomiting, diarrhea or loss of appetite. In about a week, these acute manifestations subside although generalized weakness and nervousness continue for some time. These abstinence symptoms are common with opium, heroin, morphine and dilaudid. Codeine and the synthetic analgesic demerol, produce milder forms of abstinence symptoms.

Barbiturate addiction is highly prevalent in the United States and to a lesser degree is addiction to chloral hydrate and paraldehyde. The manifestations of toxic dosage in the addict include mental confusion, drowsiness, loss of memory. Crimes have been committed while under barbiturate influence, with no remembrance of the crime by the addict. The abrupt withdrawal of barbiturates may produce severe emotional disturbances and epileptiform convulsions.

Habitués to the smoking of marihuana are more common among adolescents than older people. It is probably indulged in because of the thrill of loss of contact with reality regarding time and space. Reference is often found in newspaper media to sex crime occurring in the midst of marihuana parties. The actual cause lies in the personality of the users, rather than in the drug itself. There is neither a developed tolerance nor abstinence symptoms with marihuana.

Peyote, which comes from certain varieties of cactus in

western United States and Mexico, contains a hallucinatory drug, mescaline. Its effect is upon the senses, especially sight. Though widely used, especially experimentally, it is not an addictive problem.

Cocaine is capable of producing a feeling of exhilaration, although its effects are short lived. Hence, frequent injections may be repeated by the addict within a space of minutes for the psychic stimulation and temporary endurance against the fatigue it affords. It is not unknown, therefore, for an occasional criminal to use cocaine as a method of reinforcement of a lagging enthusiasm for the commission of a contemplated act of violence.

There is probably no more widely used and abused drug than amphetamine. It is ingested alone and in combination with various medications, especially when used as an appetite depressant. Most users are probably unaware that they are taking the drug. Many thrill seekers, morphine addicts, and ill-advised adolescents find it quite easy to obtain. The exhilaration it produces is somewhat similar to cocaine, though milder. Athletes have used it for the increased muscular efficiency it produces, and the armed services find it helpful in keeping the forces awake at crucial times.

There is a great deal of misinformation regarding drug addicts in the United States, occasioned by distortions of the problem through television and newspaper media. They are often visualized as criminals and rapists, although it has been proved by many authorities that addicts generally comprise a highly useful segment of society.[7] In fact, professional criminals rarely choose to associate with narcotic users because of the unreliability of users as consorts in crime. The habitué to drugs becomes dangerous only when the drug is denied to him, and not when the supply is available. Whenever the addict does not have the means to purchase drugs and must resort to stealing or begging he becomes a potential social problem. Sometimes, to support his habit he must become a dope peddler. By and large, he is a useful citizen. To quote Michael Pescor, "If an individual has an unfailing source of supply for his drug and an income adequate to support his habit in addition to maintaining a good standard of living, he can live the life of a respectable, honored citizen in his home community." [8]

There are many authorities who consider the Harrison Anti-Narcotic Act of 1914 and the Federal Narcotics Control Act of 1956 as contributing to rather than solving the narcotic problem.[9] The latter act calls for severe penalties for illegal possession of drugs. In failing to distinguish between possession of drugs for use or for sale, and failure to evaluate the medical problem of the addict, Lindesmith and others consider it to be vengeful legislation.[10]

The consensus of opinion among enlightened sociologists, physicians and criminologists is that narcotic addiction should not be treated as crime, but rather as an unfortunate ailment. Since the social implications generally become apparent only when the addict can ill afford to support his habit, the community must of necessity become an interested party by providing whatever medical and economic aid is necessary for rehabilitation.

Regrettably, the percentage of permanent cure is pitifully small, even when the addicts are fortunate enough to obtain admission to the hospitals maintained by the Federal Government at Lexington, Kentucky and at Fort Worth, Texas. Actually, there are very few beds available anywhere in the United States for psychiatric care of addicts.

The Council of Mental Health of the American Medical Association[11] concurred that narcotic addiction should be looked upon as an illness and should, therefore, be treated medically and not punitively. The report favored:

(a) institutional care in localities where the problem existed;
(b) continuation of treatment on discharge of patient;
(c) that addicts be committed to institution by civil and not criminal action;
(d) elimination of punitive aspects for addict violators which would interfere with treatment;
(e) that voluntary admission of addicts should be extended and encouraged.

131

The suggestion whether government regulated clinics for the addict be established, is an insoluble problem. Although this method might eliminate much of the anti-social elements who prey on illicit traffic in drugs, there is doubt of the efficacy of such ambulatory treatment, especially when narcotics thus become readily accessible. The clinic scheme was tried in the United States in 1920 and discontinued after being judged a failure. Drs. Larimore and Brill contend that possibly a fair trial was not given.[12] They maintain that the British Narcotic system which makes narcotics available to addicts under medical supervision, offers effective control in that country. However, the authors point out the apparent lack of a cultural susceptibility of the British to narcotic addiction in general, and that their success with the clinic plan does not guarantee similar results in this country.

PREMENSTRUAL TENSION AND CRIME

In recent years it has been recognized that the syndrome of premenstrual tension is of paramount importance in medicine. The reason is attributed to the fact that more than 15 million women suffer from this condition, with a resultant annual loss to industry of more than $15,000 per 100 women employees.[13]

Premenstrual tension is a cyclic occurrence of a multiplicity of symptoms, both physical and mental, starting approximately ten days preceding the menstrual period, and usually abating with the start of the flow. From a sociological point of view, we need concern ourselves only with its behavioral aspect, because of the changes in mood, temperament and emotional lability that may adversely affect the sufferer. Various theories involving ovarian and/or pituitary dysfunction have been postulated, without adequate proof for the cause of premenstrual tension. The theory has also been advanced that this condition is actually a neurosis, possibly related to marital and sexual problems, in tense, sensitive women.[14]

Although the cause is obscure, there is little doubt that the personality and behavior of an afflicted female assumes its most anti-social characteristics during the premenstrual phase of the cycle. Some authorities have even gone so far as to identify the condition with criminopathic tendencies. Dr. John D. Campbell noted that a Parisian prefect of police tabulated the incidence of crime in women of menstruating age, and reached the conclusion that 84% of all violent crimes were committed during the premenstrual period. Numerous lay periodicals have sought to indict this phase of a woman's cycle as the actual causative mechanism of violence, by reference to specific cases occurring during the premenstrual phase. However, the awareness of a specific time in a woman's cycle when she is most prone to committing a crime is not conclusive evidence. It merely identifies this phase of a woman's cycle in which she is most vulnerable to anti-social actions.

The predominant factor of criminality in females remains the same as with males, namely, the predisposition to psychopathy. The fact exists that the overwhelming majority of women with premenstrual tension, who exhibit extreme signs of irritability, moodiness and depression, are not homicidal. Even if the premenstrual syndrome could be completely alleviated by drug therapy, as it sometimes is, there is still no indication that the incidence of crime in females could be reduced. It would seem to me that any alleged relationship between premenstrual tension and causation of crime is highly exaggerated.

SELECTED BIBLIOGRAPHY

Alvarez, Walter C., M.D., Dr.Sc., *Practical Leads to Puzzling Diagnosis*, J. P. Lippincott Co., Philadelphia, 1958. A guide to the physician in determining the factors leading to detection of nervous ailments.

Alvarez, Walter C., M.D., Dr.Sc., *Live at Peace with Your Nerves*, Prentice-Hall, Inc., Englewood Cliffs, New Jersey, 1958. A helpful and practical guide in alleviating nervous tensions.

Anslinger, J. J., & Tompkins, William F., *The Traffic in Narcotics*, Funk & Wagnalls Co., New York, 1953. Surveys the problem and summarizes the various programs proposed to control addiction.

Barnes, Harry Elmer, & Teeters, Negley K., *New Horizons In Criminology*, Prentice-Hall, Englewood Cliffs, New Jersey, 1959, (3rd edition). A text of sociological aspects of criminology.

Cecil, R. L., & Loeb, R. F. (editors), *A Textbook of Medicine*, Saunders, (10th edition), 1959. A textbook covering the general field of medicine.

Chessman, Caryl, *Trial by Ordeal*, Prentice-Hall, Inc., Englewood Cliffs, New Jersey, 1955. The personal record of a prisoner awaiting execution, with his analysis of crime in relation to possible causes and mismanagement by society.

Clinard, Marshall B., *Sociology of Deviant Behavior*, Rinehart & Co., Inc., New York, 1957. Deals with certain deviations from social norms.

Cohen, Louis H., M.D., *Murder, Madness & The Law*, The World Publishing Co., Cleveland, New York, 1952. Examines the growing problem of criminal insanity with its legal implications.

Comfort, Alex, M.D., *Sexual Behavior in Society*, The Viking Press, New York, 1950. An evaluation of social attitudes with regard to sex.

DeWitt, William A., *Drinking and What To Do About It*, Grosset & Dunlap, Inc., New York, 1952. Deals with major aspects of the liquor problem including sociological and medical manifestations.

Ellis, Albert, Ph.D., *Sex Without Guilt*, Lyle Stuart, New York, 1958. An analysis of our sex code in helping the individual evaluate anxieties relating to sex guilt.

Fry, Monroe, *Sex, Vice & Business*, Ballantine Books, New York, 1959. Deals with the breakdown of morality in Post War America.

Lombroso, Cesare, *The Female Offender*, Philosophical Library, New York, 1958. A study in criminal biology.

McCarthy, Raymond G. (editor), *Drinking & Intoxication*, Vail-Ballou Press, Inc., Binghamton, New York, 1959. Selected readings in social attitudes and controls.

Masor, Nathan, M.D., *The New Psychiatry*, Philosophical Library, New York, 1959. Deals with criticisms of present day psychiatry, offering hope to the mentally disturbed through entirely new approaches to mental health.

Modell, Walter, M.D., *The Relief of Symptoms*, W. B. Saunders Co., Philadelphia, 1956. Alleviation of symptoms from medical point of view.

Murtagh, John M., & Harris, Sarah, *Cast the First Stone*, McGraw-Hill Book Co., New York-Toronto-London, 1957. Discusses the secret world of prostitution with a review of our laws.

Murtagh, John M., & Harris, Sarah, *Who Live in Shadow*, McGraw-Hill Book Co., New York-Toronto-London, 1959. A graphic, authoritative and compassionate view of drug addiction.

Noyes, Arthur P., & Kolb, Lawrence C., *Modern Clinical Psychiatry* (5th edition), W. B. Saunders & Co., Philadelphia, 1958. An exposition of clinical methods in psychiatry.

Oursler, Will, & Smith, Laurence Dwight, *Narcotics: America's Peril*, Doubleday & Co., Inc., Garden City, New York, 1952. A factual report on the shrouded area of narcotics and its people.

Robinson, Wm. J,. M.D., *Our Mysterious Life Glands*, Eugenics Publishing Co., Inc., New York, 1934. A discussion of the endocrine glands, their inter-relationships, and their role in relation to sexual deviation.

Scudder, John J., *Prisoners Are People*, Doubleday & Co., Garden City, New York, 1952. An unembellished account of men in prison to prepare them constructively for the day of release.

Wilson, J. G., M.D., & Prescor, M. J., M.D., *Problems in Prison Psychiatry*, Caxton Printers Ltd., Caldwell, Ohio, 1939. An evaluation of the prisoner from the point of view of insanity, psychopathic tendencies, sexual deviationism, feeble-mindedness and epilepsy, in relation to the prison environment.

Nathan Masor, M.D., practicing physician and surgeon, author and lecturer. He was born in New York City and went to school there (elementary through college). He was graduated from the New York Medical College, Flower-Fifth Avenue Hospital; and did his post-graduate work at Metropolitan, Mt. Sinai and Beth Israel Hospitals, and the University of Wisconsin General Hospital. After his interneship at Christ Hospital, Jersey City, N. J., he entered the armed services several months prior to Pearl Harbor as a 1st Lieutenant in the Medical Corps. He participated in the invasion of **Oran Beach, North Africa**, with Combat "B" of the 1st Armored Division, and served in the Tunisian Campaign. He then became the Surgeon of the Prisoner of War Camps in French Morocco and Commanding Officer of its Prisoner of War Hospital and attained the rank of Major. Degrees: B.S., Brooklyn College; M.D., New York Medical College, Flower-Fifth Avenue Hospital; Diplomate, National Board of Medical Examiners. *Affiliated Hospitals*: St. Vincent's Hospital, Staten Island, N. Y.; Staten Island Hospital, Staten Island, N. Y.; Richmond Memorial Hospital, Staten Island, N. Y., Italian Hospital, New York City. Awarded life membership in the American Legion (1948); Surgeon, Jewish War Veterans, (Richmond Borough Post); was medical member of numerous court-martial and disciplinary boards throughout army career, as well as boards for discharge of psychopathic personalities from service. Author, *The New Psychiatry*, Philosophical Library, New York, July, 1959; has written a number of scientific articles for such publications as Journal of Nervous & Mental Diseases, New York State Journal of Medicine, Journal of American Geriatrics Society, etc. Lectured at the International Congress for Psychiatry (Zurich), as well as at hospitals, etc., on the subject of various aspects of health, with predominant emphasis on nervous ailments, mainly through the biochemical approach.

NOTES

1. Sutherland, Edwin H., "The Sexual Psychopath Laws," *Journal of Criminal Law*, XXXX, No. 5, January-February, 1950, 543-554.

2. Bromberg, Dr. Walter, *Crime and the Mind*, Lippincott, Philadelphia, 1948, 85.

3. Masor, Nathan, *The New Psychiatry*, Philosophical Library, New York, 1959.

4. Alvarez, Walter C., M.D., *Practical Leads to Puzzling Diagnosis*, Lippincott & Co., Philadelphia, 1958, 5.

5. Miller, Michael M., M.D., "Treatment of Chronic Alcoholism by Hypnotic Aversion," *Journal of American Medical Assn.*, CLXXI, No. 11, November 14, 1959, 163-167.

6. Report by *New York State Journal of Medicine*, LX, #1, January 1, 1960, 124.

7. Lindesmith, A. R., "Dope Fiend Mythology," *Journal of Criminal Law*, XL, #2, July-August, 1949, 199.

8. Pescor, Michael J., M.D., *Encyclopedia of Criminology* (edited by Branham & Kutash), New York, Philosophical Library, 1949, 132.

9. Karpman, Ben, "Laws That Cause Crime," *American Mercury*, XXIII, #89, May 1931, 77.

10. Lindesmith, A. R., "Dope Fiend Mythology," *Journal Criminal Law*, XL, #2, July-August, 1949, 205.

11. (Report), *Journal American Medical Association*, CLXV, #15, December 14, 1957, 1972-73.

12. Larimore, Granville W., and Henry Brill, M.D., "The British Narcotic System," *New York State Journal of Medicine*, LX, #1, January 1, 1960.

13. *MD Newsmagazine*, XL, #1, January 1960, 75.

14. *British Medical Journal*, II, 1318, December 12, 1959.

THE IMMIGRANT AND CRIME

Samuel Koenig
Brooklyn College

Among the most popular reasons given for the wide-spread existence of crime and delinquency in the United States is the settling in this country of large numbers of immigrants. Immigrants, from the time they have begun to arrive here in considerable numbers, have been blamed for all sorts of social ills, not least of which is crime. Although in the recent past it was primarily those who have come here from eastern and southern Europe, as well as such countries as Mexico, the Philippines, and Puerto Rico, who have been so blamed, there is hardly an immigrant group which was not, at the initial period of its settling here, accused of bringing with it pauperism and crime. The Germans and Irish, two of the early immigrant groups, were looked upon, around the middle of the past century when they arrived in large numbers, as hopeless idlers and criminals who were infecting the population with immorality, alcoholism, and crime.

The Irish were referred to in the 1830's by the then mayor of New York as "strangers among us, without a feeling of patriotism, or affection in common with American citizens . . ." [1] Another outstanding citizen of New York City at the time held the Irish responsible for widespread drunkenness and crime, maintaining that this was going to continue unabated "as long as we are overwhelmed with Irish immigrants. . . . Thefts, incendiaries, murders which prevail, all arise from this source." [2] Both Irish and German immigrants were blamed for the continuous increase in juvenile delinquency in the 1850's, a report by a Congressional Committee at the time accusing these two groups of contributing about four fifths of all delinquents.[3] Aside from crime and delinquency, these groups were accused of creating slums in our large cities. Action against the dangers presented by these and other immigrants was advocated in order to prevent disaster which was sure to come, if immigration were allowed to continue unabated. "As a surety", states an official report emanating from the New York State Assembly in 1857,[4] "we must, as a people, act upon this foreign element, or it will act upon us. Like the vast Atlantic, we must decompose and cleanse the impurities which rush into our midst, or, like the inland lake, we will receive the poison into our whole national system." Today those of Irish and German extraction form the part of our nation, perhaps the largest, which is held up as an example of successful assimilation and integration into the American national, cultural, and social life.

Each successive wave of immigration was, in turn, considered as a menace to the welfare of the nation, as consisting of individuals who are hopeless as far as assimilation is concerned. Following the mass immigration from northern and western Europe, which at the beginning was considered as the source of all kinds of evil and later as the most desirable stock, there began, towards the end of the past century, the mass immigration from eastern and southern Europe. The same accusations began to be levelled against them, accusations which, while gradually easing off, are far from having disappeared. This is shown by the augmentation of the immigration act of 1924, presumably designed to restrict immigration impartially but in actuality working out against eastern and southern Europeans, by the McCarran-Walter Act of 1952, which, while allegedly intended to keep out subversives and criminals, is considered by many as prejudicial to eastern and southern Europeans seeking admission to the United States. The latest victims of what appears to be traditional American prejudice against newcomers are the Puerto Ricans against whom all the usual accusations are directed, frequently by former immigrants and their descendants.

CRIMINALITY OF FOREIGN- AND NATIVE-BORN AMERICANS

The assumption that immigrants and those of immigrant stock have a high rate of crime compared with the native, or "Old American," stock, was first based on common sense and casual observations by native Americans. However, ultimately these notions began to be investigated more or less systematically, and the findings largely supported the theory that immigrants contributed to crime and delinquency out of all proportion to their numbers. These investigations were carried on primarily at the initiative of official governmental bodies. Outstanding among the studies concluding that immigrants showed an excessive crime rate were those by the commission on Crime of the Chicago City Council, in 1915, and a study by Dr. H. H. Laughlin, of the Eugenics Record Office.[5] In his report, Dr. Laughlin presented a picture showing a great preponderance of crime and vice among immigrants, especially among the more recent arrivals, by which were meant the eastern and southern Europeans.

On the other hand, a number of more carefully conducted studies disputed these findings, arriving at opposite conclusions. The United States Immigration Commission, in 1910, came to the conclusion that there was no evidence for the assumption that immigration brought about "an increase in crime disproportionate to the increase in the adult population."[6] A similar conclusion was reached in a study by the National Commission on Law Observance and Enforcement in 1931[7] in which it was concluded that the foreign-born actually showed a lower crime rate than the native-born. In comparing the rates of conviction of native-born with those of foreign-born males 17 years old and over in Chicago, it was found that the rate of the latter was lower; this was also found to be true in the case of arrests for those 15 years of age and older in 9 American cities.

More recent studies[8] have all revealed the fact that the native-born exceed the foreign-born in criminality. Sutherland[9] found that the rates of both arrests and imprisonment are in general about twice as high for the native-born whites as for the foreign-born. Similarly, an official United States report of 1946[10] found that only 3.2 per cent of the total population in state and federal prisons was of foreign birth, which was less than the percentage of the total number of foreign-born in the country. It should be noted, however, that these figures were computed on the basis of population numbers only, without consideration of such factors as age and sex distributions, which differ considerably between the native-born and foreign-born. When these factors were taken into consideration, Van Vechten[11] found the rates for the two groups to be about the same. It was only in the youngest groups, namely, age 16 to 29, that the foreign-born showed a higher rate than the native-born. On the other hand, the native-born rates were much higher than the foreign-born rates in cases involving crimes for personal gain, such as robbery (11 to 3), burglary (22 to 5), and larceny (20 to 5).

The notion that immigrants must have a high crime rate, still held by the average American, is based on the idea that settlers from abroad are racially inferior, that they come from countries with social and political systems which are below those in the United States, and hence, find it difficult to adjust properly to life here; that they refuse to assimilate; and that their poverty makes them especially prone to commit crimes. The fact is that the foreign-born, as we have seen, have been found not to have a higher crime rate than the native-born. The above-mentioned factors, therefore, cannot be considered as causes. The assumptions that the immigrants are inherently inferior racially, culturally, or socially, too, have been invalidated by a multitude of anthropological and sociological studies, as well as by the fact that, without exception, they have, after a certain lapse of time, become an integral part of the American nation, contributing significantly to its growth and development in all spheres of activity.

While it is true that most immigrant groups have been living in their homelands under conditions greatly differing from those found here and, hence, have to go through a difficult adjustment

141

period, there is no indication that the difficulty has proven insurmountable. In the course of time they find their place in the adopted country, proving an asset rather than a liability to it. It is also true that most immigrants come here poor and are forced to settle in slums, which, apropos, they find here, rather than create. But poverty per se has not been found to be connected significantly in a cause-and-effect relationship with crime. If crime, at least of the conventional type, has been found to exist to a greater extent in blighted areas than in well-ordered neighborhoods, it is the accompanying conditions of the slums, such as disorganization and the presence of criminal gangs, which find there a congenial environment, that account for it. There is nothing in poverty as such, unless it be of the extreme type, that inevitably drives a person subjected to it to crime.[12]

On the other hand, criminologists have found that far from bringing with them criminalistic behavior, most immigrants come here with a respect for law and authority which they acquired in their home countries; they come mostly from stable, homogeneous societies which exerted strict control over the behavior of individuals.[13] They come, however, into contact with the socially disorganized American city, with an environment which is highly conducive to crime. This, coupled with the facts that they have been released from the former controls of their home communities, are confused by the new standards, which frequently conflict with those they brought with them, may result in disorganization and express itself in crime and delinquency. According to Sutherland, immigrants probably have a higher crime rate here than in their home countries.[14]

In spite of the many adverse conditions and handicaps which one would expect to result in excessive criminality among them, immigrants, as we have seen, have maintained a relatively good record. What are the reasons? There are a number of factors that, taken together, account for it.

The restraining influence of the immigrants' home environment, which, as noted above, was largely one of obedience to law and authority, undoubtedly is an important factor. The fact that they tend to live in their own colonies, or ghettoes, where

142

the group exerts control over individuals is another factor of significance. Moreover, living in their own communities, with little or no contact with the society at large, diminishes oportunities for committing crimes. In this case, too, the overlooking or covering up of crimes, particularly those of a minor nature, by the community, very likely plays a role. Still another factor is ignorance, on the part of the immigrants, of the language and customs of the larger society, which makes it difficult for them to get around. Finally, there is the fact that most types of crime are committed by young people, namely, between the ages of 17 and around 30. Since immigrants belong largely to an older age group,[15] the risk for their committing crimes is relatively low. All these factors combine to produce a rather favorable crime record among the foreign-born.

CRIME RATES AMONG VARIOUS IMMIGRANT GROUPS

Crime rates vary greatly among the different immigrant groups, as do the types of crime they tend to commit. On the whole, immigrant groups, with very few exceptions, tend to commit to a lesser extent crimes involving personal gain than native-born. As far as crimes prompted by personal violence is concerned, the rate for the two groups is about the same.[16] In the afore-mentioned study by the National Commission on Law Observance,[17] it was found that the native whites committed rape twice as often as the foreign-born, three times as many robberies and four times as many burglaries. There is some indication, not sufficiently substantiated, that the immigrants stemming from eastern and southern Europe, with some exceptions, have been involved in crime to a greater extent than those of western and northern European derivation.[18] Taft[19] thinks that this might be explained by the fact that their cultural background differs much more from American culture than that of the north and west Europeans and, hence, is bound to create more severe adjustment problems, as well as by the fact that they have settled predominantly in the criminogenic environments of the cities.

When broken down according to nationality, we find that differences in the crime rates among the various groups are very great, ranging from very high to very low. Thus the afore-mentioned Commission[20] found, for New York State, a variation in the commitment rate from a high of 779.5 per 100,000 population, for Greeks to a low of 38.1 for Czechoslovaks. Another study,[21] which took into consideration the age differences existing between the different nationalities, showed that the commitment rates, per 100,000 population, ranged from a low of 16.6 for the Welsh and 23.0 for the Czechoslovaks to a high of 125.3 for the Austrians. The rates for Canadians was 112.0 (probably due largely to violations of border regulations), and those for Greeks and Italians 90.0 and 99.0, respectively.

According to computations made by Dr. Elliott,[22] of the various important offenses committed by the foreign-born of different nationality groups, 15 years and over, per 100,000 population of the same class,[23] the highest rate in homicide is to be found among the Mexicans[24] (77.2). These are followed by the Italians (53.6), Lithuanians (21.3), and the Austrians (16.0). Among the lowest ranking in crimes involving homicide are: the Yugoslavs (0.0), Czechoslovaks (2.1), and Hungarians (2.2). In crimes involving rape, the nationalities figuring highest are again the Mexicans (132.7), Italians (34.8), and Greeks (29.0); while the group having the lowest rates are the Scandinavians (1.2), Irish (1.3), and Czechoslovaks (2.1). In aggravated assault cases, the nationalities having the highest rate are, again, the Mexicans (417.4), and Greeks (146.5), but here the Lithuanians, with 161.4 outrank the Italians, whose rate is 102.3. In crimes involving burglary it is again the Mexicans who come first with 579.1. The next highest rates, but trailing far behind the Mexicans, are found among the Lithuanians (39.6), the Italians (38.7), and the Canadians (38.4). Finally, in crimes involving the carrying of weapons, the Mexicans, with 349.9, far outrank all the others. Next to them, but far below them, are the Italians (64.7), and the Greeks (58.1).

144

CULTURAL BACKGROUND AND CRIMINALITY

We thus see that the extent to which immigrants of different nationality groups commit crimes and the types of crime they commit vary a great deal. Both the rates and types of crime committed by the various groups have been found by criminologists to be determined largely by their cultural background and conditions of life here, rather than by any hereditary traits. As shown above, several of the nationality groups have a much higher crime rate than others. To a considerable extent this is consistent with the relatively high incidence of crime in their home countries. This is especially true as far as particular types of crime are concerned. As Sutherland[25] points out, the high rate of commitment to jails and workhouses of the Irish and Finns, for instance, is connected with the drinking habits of these two groups, which is often excessive and results in intoxication. Again, the high homicide rate of the Italians can be explained in terms of the high incidence of homicide in Italy, considered the highest in Western Europe. On the other hand, Italians have a low rate of arrest for drunkenness, which is consistent with the comparative absence of drunkenness in Italy.

Similar explanations can be found for the comparative low or high rates of crime, or certain types of crime, found among the other nationality groups. It is primarily a case of groups bringing with them their customs and traditions and continuing them here. The rise and development of those customs and traditions can, in turn, be explained by the conditions of life of the different nations in Europe. Thus, owing to the political situation in Italy, especially in the pre-World War I period, a distrust of government developed which has been transferred here by the Italian immigrant. The custom of one's taking the law into one's own hands and of one's seeking to settle grievances by one-self undoubtedly also accounts for the high prevalence of crimes of violence among the first-generation of Italians here.

That criminal behavior among immigrant groups is determined largely by traditions as well as by conditions under which they live here may be illustrated especially by two groups, namely, the Japanese and the Jews, who have maintained a relatively low crime rate here. These two groups come obviously from cultural environments which are as different as two environments can be. Nevertheless, there are certain characteristics they both share. Perhaps outstanding among these is the great sensitivity both display to the opinion outsiders have of them. They are anxious to appear in as good a light as possible before the world. They are, therefore, concerned about the behavior of members of their group, as, it is felt, it reflects upon the group as a whole. Now, all minority groups display these characteristics, but they are much more pronounced in the case of these two groups. In addition to these characteristics and in consequence of them, we find that these groups endeavor, perhaps more than others, to control the behavior of the individual and show a greater readiness to assume responsibility for his conduct. In the case of the Jews, the centuries-old tradition of self-help and a highly developed philanthropic sense, which expresses itself in welfare organizations of all kinds, undoubtedly play an important part. On the other hand, the above-mentioned factors also serve to prevent crimes and delinquencies committed by members of these groups from coming to light. Thus, crimes committed by Jews, which tend to be of the white-collar type primarily (again a matter of tradition and peculiar conditions of life), are, for this reason, perhaps more numerous than shown in their record.[26] The same is probably true of delinquencies committed by Jewish children.

Criminologists agree that prejudice and discrimination account to a considerable extent for crime among minority groups suffering from them. Hence, the examples of the two groups, the Jews and the Japanese, considered above, need explaining. Both of them are subjected to prejudice and discrimination and yet their crime rates are comparatively low. It would seem, as Taft[27] points out, that certain other factors, if present in the case, have a counteracting effect. Among these, Taft mentions effective institutions of control and primary relations, a consciousness of and pride in a historical ancestral culture, and appreciation of the advantages offered by democracy, such as education and economic opportunities. These factors are present in the case of those two groups, but are largely absent in the case of the American Negroes. The high Negro crime rate—the highest of any minority group in the United States—may, at least partly, be explained by this deficiency.

CRIME AS A PRODUCT OF AMERICAN CULTURE

It is quite popular to attribute lawlessness and particularly organized crime in the United States to immigrant groups, especially the Italians. The secret organization, the Mafia, and gangsters and racketeers with Italian names are usually offered as proof. One gets the impression that crime in America is an imported product, that if it were not for foreigners, this would be a law-abiding nation, with crime occupying an unimportant place among our problems. This notion, too, is hardly proved by the facts. "Opposition to law," writes Dr. Sutherland,[28] "has been a tradition in the United States." Lawlessness and crime were not lacking in the earliest period of American history and continued to constitute a problem, especially during the frontier period. Indeed, one authority maintains that many aspects of our present-day crime problem can be traced back to and explained by the past, particularly the frontier days. Writes Dr. Elliott:[29] "We sometimes forget . . . that anti-social conduct is as much rooted in the past as it is a function of the present and that, in America, as everywhere, crime bears an important relationship to our culture. In our country the frontier mores are related in a significant sense to lawlessness. . . ." "Obviously, she continues, "it is far from this author's belief that either our culture or our frontier mores explain all or most of our crime rate. Nevertheless, the frontier culture constituted an important part of our social heritage and explains much of the American's rejection of and disrespect for formal legislative controls." [30]

It is undeniable that immigration has contributed directly or indirectly to the problem of crime in the United States by creating disorganization and conflict. In a sense, this is the price the American nation had to pay for the great benefits it ultimately derived from the settling here of millions of people who contributed their brawn and brains to its upbuilding and development. It is also true that certain forms of crime were introduced here to a considerable extent by the foreign-born. The roster of the leadership in many types of organized crime and racketeering is studded with names like Capone, Luciano, Anastasia, and Genovese. But, as Barnes and Teeters point out,[31] traditionally American names such as, Dillinger, Van Meter, Floyd, Nelson, Barker, and Kelly are far from being rare in the underworld.

Thus, while a goodly number of our notorious gangsters and racketeers are immigrants, it can hardly be said that crime in America depends upon them, and that if they were not here, or were deported, the situation would be radically changed. Ours is a criminogenic society; crime of all kinds is widespread in America, and among its perpetrators are primarily natives and frequently "Old" Americans. While foreign-born gangsters and racketeers, as shown in the Kefauver report,[32] loom large, "Old" Americans, often highly respectable and occupying positions of responsibility and trust, as also brought out in this report, play a very important role. It must be understood that many types of crime, particularly those within the white-collar category, are made possible by the active or passive participation of large numbers of our so-called law-abiding citizens, including not infrequently those in charge of law-enforcement. Foreign-born criminals have been making a significant contribution to crime in America, but there is little doubt that they are not, so to speak, indispensable; crime could and very likely would go on in their absence without much loss or radical change in its character.

CRIME AMONG THE SECOND GENERATION

On the whole, children of immigrants, or the second generation, have a higher crime rate than their parents in most, if not all, types of crime. This fact is brought out in a number of studies, perhaps the most significant of which is an official report on prisoners.[33] In this report, covering 26 states, a comparison is made of the commitment rates, per 100,000 population, of male prisoners, 15 years old and over, between white native-born of native, foreign, and mixed (one parent born here and the other abroad) parentage, as well as foreign-born. The foreign-born have the lowest rate of all groups, which is 43 and which is only one third that of the natives of native parentage. The highest rate among the native-born is that of the natives of native parentage (144). Next to it is that of the native-born of foreign parentage (120), while the lowest rate is that of the native-born of mixed parentage, which is 91.

We already have noted the reasons that account for the relatively low crime rate of the foreign-born. The comparatively high rate of those born here of foreign parentage, which is, nevertheless, on the whole, lower than that of the natives of native parentage, has been considered by students as due to a number of factors. Chief among these is their cultural marginality, i.e., their position in between two cultural worlds, the American and the Old World (ancestral) environments, with neither of which they can completely identify themselves. Such a situation, unless strong counteracting forces are at work, such as a good home, understanding intelligent parents, a good neighborhood, and an appreciation of the ancestral culture, is bound to produce conflict in the individual. Confusion as to values and standards is then almost inevitable, and one of the symptoms of such a state is anti-social behavior, which often assumes the form of delinquency and crime.

It thus appears that it is the conflict situation, the clash between the cultural standards and values present in the environment of the second generation, that is one of the chief factors involved in its relatively high criminality. According to Sutherland,[34] the delinquency rate of the second-generation is relatively low during the initial period of an immigrant group's settling in a community, but rises with the increase in contact between the immigrant colony and the dominant culture. As long as the colony remains relatively isolated from the larger community surrounding it, the rate continues to be low, being lowest in the center of the colony, but increases as one moves toward the border lines, where contacts with other groups are closest. This would seem to indicate that the immigrant colony is able to control quite effectively the behavior of its American-born children as long as it can keep its Old World standards intact and as long as its children are not exposed to situations of conflict. There are indications, however, that the deteriorated areas with their generally low behavior standards are also significantly related to the relatively high crime rate of the second generation. This is shown by the fact that immigrant groups which have left deteriorated areas and settled in stable neighborhoods maintain a low delinquency rate. It is worth noting that immigrants who come here in early childhood tend to have a higher crime rate than those who arrive as adults.[35] This might be explained by the fact that young immigrants, being more impressionable, become more easily assimilated to the culture around them and, hence, among other behavior patterns, take on also the high crime rate found in their environment.

There are definite indications, as shown above, that the native-born of mixed parentage have a considerably lower crime rate than those born here of parents both of whom come from abroad. Since, as we have seen, conflict in cultural standards is considered as one of the chief causes in bringing about a high rate of crime among the second generation, why should the natives of mixed parentage have a low crime rate? One would expect in this case the conflict to be more acute than in that in which both parents were born in Europe. Taft[36] suggests that conflict actually is lessened in this case by the very fact that the immigrant who marries an American-born individual is likely to have become assimilated to a much greater extent than the one who marries a foreign-born person. He, furthermore, opines that an immigrant who has married an American-born is probably more successful economically, and, hence, is able to maintain a more stable home.

The delinquent and criminal activities of the younger age

groups in the second generation is usually carried on by means of the gang. Just as most types of crime in America tend to be organized, so crime by juveniles and youths is carried on in organized groups. In this case, again, a widespread notion is that the gang is principally an immigrant importation and that it characterizes primarily the second generation. This notion has little foundation in fact. The gang is as typically American as the corner drug store. As Taft[37] points out, among the chief forces driving a boy to join a gang is the need for recognition, a need deeply imbedded in American culture and universally shared by Americans. This, he writes, is shown by the fact that "Americans must at all costs belong and must strive for social recognition. Law-abiding Americans have many traits in common with gangsters, and ours is a gang-producing culture." The boy who is a member of a gang, he continues, is "in his basic personality traits a typical American boy. The slum which produces the gang is a by-product of our economic and social system." The high crime rate by young people of the second generation thus appears to be consistent with the generally high American crime rate. It is chiefly the result of acculturation or assimilation to the American environment on the part of the immigrant's children.

VARIATIONS IN RATE AND TYPES OF CRIME AMONG THE SECOND GENERATION

As in the case of the first-generation immigrants, the crime rate in the second generation varies greatly from one group to another and depends upon what part of Europe the group derives. Those whose parents have come from northern and western Europe have been found to have less than half the rate of those whose parents derive from southern and eastern Europe, the figures being 30.9 and 67.6, respectively, per 100,000 population.[38] On the whole, the crime rate of second-generation groups is quite consistent with that of the first generation of the same nationality. Thus, according to computations by Taft,[39] on the basis of commitment rates per 100,000 population in 26 states, the lowest rate is found among the second-generation Welsh, which is 19.4. These are followed by the Swedes, with 22.7 and the English, with 27.1. The highest rates among the northern and western European groups are found among the French (43.3), the Irish (42.4), and the Scots (41.4). Within the southern and eastern European groups, those of Spanish parentage, with 211.2, have the highest rate. Following them are the children of foreign-born Greeks (160.0), Italians (95.2), and Lithuanians (91.1). Among those of Oriental derivation, the second-generation Japanese, like their foreign-born parents, have a very low rate. This is also true of second-generation Jews. On the other hand, the native-born of foreign-born Mexicans have a relatively high crime rate.

In recent years, the great influx of Puerto Ricans to Continental United States, especially New York City, has, as in the case of the great immigration waves of Europeans towards the end of the past and the beginning of this century, resulted in a clamour to control their movement in some manner other than restriction, since Puerto Ricans are American citizens. Again, the familiar accusations have been made against them to the effect that, at least as far as New York City is concerned, they come here to be supported by relief agencies, do not want to work, create slums, and contribute all out of proportion to their numbers to crime and juvenile delinquency. There can be no doubt that mass immigration and settlement in a crowded city creates problems and that a considerable period of time has to elapse, often two or three generations, until people of a radically different culture than our own become adjusted to the way of life here. But, these people settling here at once begin contributing to the economy by usually getting into the least desirable, poorest-paid, but, at the same time, essential types of jobs. As the United States representative from New York, Emanuel Celler, at a recent Senate Subcommittee hearing on juvenile delinquency conducted in New York City, states, the Puerto Ricans, far from being a drain on the city, are actually necessary to some branches of its economy. "We should not," he said, "discourage them from coming. We need them for the hard chores and rough work. If they do not come, most of our hotels, restaurants and laundries would close." [40]

The Puerto Ricans are among the ethnic groups having a relatively high crime rate. This high rate, as in the case of American Negroes and other high-rate groups, is explainable in terms of culture conflict, discrimination, low economic status, and other factors, which cannot be gone into here. Figures for the first eight months of 1959, issued by the New York City and State Correction Departments,[41] show that while Puerto Ricans constitute 7.17 per cent of the population of Greater New York, they contributed 20.8 per cent to the prison population of the Brooklyn House of Detention, which serves all the five boroughs but admits only youthful offenders, and 19 per cent to that of Sing Sing Prison, 95 per cent of which come from Greater New York.

As far as juvenile delinquency is concerned, again, Puerto Rican children show a high delinquency rate, but it is somewhat lower than that of the general non-Puerto Rican children. A study by the New York Board of Education,[42] covering two school districts in Manhattan for the period of September 1, 1955 and May 31, 1956, reveals that, while Puerto Rican children constituted 35 per cent of the total number of children attending school in these two districts, they contributed only 32 per cent of the referrals made to the Children's Court. Again, while non-Puerto Rican children were found to be offenders at the rate of 14 per 1,000, those of Puerto Rican parentage showed a 12 per 1,000 rate. It must, however, be remembered that the non-Puerto Rican children, in this case, included the high-rate Negro children. If this were taken into consideration, undoubtedly the rate of the Puerto Rican children would be considerably higher than that of non-Puerto Rican white children. The problem of habitual truancy and of other serious behavior problems appears to be relatively high among Puerto Rican children. According to the afore-mentioned study, of the 1914 pupils enrolled in the so-called "600 Schools," designed for serious problem cases, 20 per cent were Puerto Ricans, although

153

they constituted about 12 per cent of the total school population in 1956.

DIFFERENCES IN FIRST- AND SECOND-GENERATION CRIME

While, as we have seen, the general rate of crime of second-generation individuals is considerably higher than that of their foreign-born parents, in certain types of crime their rate is lower. Thus, in homicide the rate of the second-generation Irish has been found to be less than half of that of their foreign-born parents.[43] In the case of the Italians, the foreign born showed a rate of 192, per 100,000 population, while the native-born showed a rate of 24, which is only one eighth that of their parents.[44] On the other hand, in cases involving gambling and rape the second generation has a much higher rate.

The crimes committed by second-generation immigrants tend to be characteristically American crimes, rather than those typical of their ancestral culture. Thus, native-born individuals of foreign parentage become involved primarily in crimes of a predatory nature, such as gambling, prostitution, racketeering, swindling, fraud, and forgery, rather than in crimes of violence, predominating among many first-generation groups. Moreover, the crimes of violence committed by second-generation individuals result principally from attempts at extortion and not from feelings of insult, jealousy, retribution for hurts suffered, or the protection of the family honor, as is largely true of the first generation.

Stofflet,[45] in a study of first- and second-generation Italians, among other nationality groups admitted to the New Jersey State Prison over a period of several years, arrived at some noteworthy conclusions. These may be summarized as follows: (1) crime among the different immigrant nationality groups tends to change in character with the second generation; (2) there is noticeable among the native-born of immigrant parents a shift away from crimes of violence and toward predatory types of crime; (3) crimes of violence, among the second generation, are

154

motivated by monetary gain, rather than by defense of family honor; (4) the careers of second-generation Italian criminals tend to resemble those of native whites of native parentage; (5) the latter tendency indicates that in becoming assimilated, the second generation adopts, among other patterns, also the characteristic American criminal pattern.

CONCLUSION

From the data brought out in the preceding pages, it is possible to conclude that crime, as the noted anthropologist Franz Boas[46] has pointed out some years ago, is not a matter of race or of traits passed down from one generation to the next. The behavior of the individual, like social behavior in general, instead, is a result of the culture with which he becomes identified. The immigrant to the United States brings with him a cultural heritage which guides him in his conduct. Those with criminal inclinations tend to perpetrate crimes characteristic of their group. On the whole, the crime rate of the first-generation immigrants is lower than the general American crime rate.

If, as there seems to be some indication, the immigrants' rate of crime is higher than it was in their homelands, it is due to the lessening of the former controls, on the one hand, and to the demoralizing effect of their new environment, on the other. As far as the second-generation individuals are concerned, their higher crime rate, which approximates that of native whites of native parentage, appears to be due chiefly to the cultural conflict situation in which they find themselves and to the assimilative process, which brings them close to the American pattern of behavior, as found in the environments in which they live.

SELECTED BIBLIOGRAPHY

Bonger, W. A., *Race and Crime*, Columbia University Press, New York, 1943. Discusses the relationship of race and crime.

155

Glueck, Eleanor, "Culture Conflict and Delinquency," *Mental Hygiene*, XXI, January 1, 1937, 46-66. Propounds thesis that culture conflict is the primary cause of delinquency among the second generation.

Goldberg, Nathan, "Jews in the Police Records of Los Angeles, 1933-1937, *Yivo Annual of Jewish Social Science*, V, 1950, 266-291. A study of Jewish criminality on the basis of police records in Los Angeles.

Hentig, Hans von, "The First Generation and a Half: Notes on the Delinquency of Native Whites of Mixed Parentage," *American Sociological Review*, X, December, 1945, 792-98. Analysis of criminal statistics relative to native-born persons, one of whose parents was born here and the other abroad.

Hooton, Earnest A., *Crime and the Man*, Harvard University Press, Cambridge, 1939. A highly controversial study of criminality among American racial and ethnic groups by a physical anthropologist.

Koenig, Samuel, "Second- and Third-Generation Americans," in *One America* (edited by Francis J. Brown and Joseph S. Roucek), Prentice-Hall, New York, 1952, 505-522. Analyzes the problem of cultural marginality of the second and third generations.

Ross, Harold, "Crime and the Native-Born Sons of European Immigrants," *Journal of Criminal Law and Criminology*, XXVIII, 1937, 202-9. Presents view that socio-economic conditions explain the crime rates of minority groups.

Sellin, Thorsten, *Culture Conflict and Crime*, The Social Science Research Council, New York, 1938. An examination of the relationship of culture conflict to crime.

Stofflet, "The European Immigrant and His Children," *The Annals of the American Academy of Political and Social Science*, CCXVII, September, 1941, 84-92. A study comparing the rate and type of crime committed by first- and second-generation immigrants.

Sutherland, Edwin H., *Principles of Criminology* (revised by Donald R. Cressey), J. B. Lippincott Co., Chicago, 1955, Chapter 8. A survey of facts and theories regarding the relationship of crime to race and nativity.

Taft, Donald R., *Criminology*, The Macmillan Co., New York, 1956, Chapter 8. A summary of research and theories regarding the relationship of immigration and crime.

Van Vechten, Cortlandt C., "The Criminality of the Foreign Born," *Proceedings of the American Prison Association*, LXX, 1940, 505-516. A careful analysis of the extent of criminality among the foreign born and their children.

Wood, Arthur L., "Minority-Group Criminality and Cultural Integration," *Journal of Criminal Law and Criminology*, XXXVII, March-April, 1947, 498-510. Propounds theory that crime among minority groups may be explained by the type of cultural and social integration that takes place among them.

Samuel Koenig, who received his Ph.D. degree from Yale University, is Professor of Sociology and Anthropology at Brooklyn College of the City of New York. He did extensive research on ethnic groups in Connecticut, resulting in a number of publications; served, as Research Associate, on the Committee for the Study of Recent Immigration from Europe (1944-46); was a member of the Editorial Board of the Slavonic Encyclopedia (1947-48), of the Commission for the Study of Jewish Education in the U.S. (1952-54), of the Editorial and Publication Committee of the Society for the Study of Social Problems (1953-55), and Book Review Editor of *Social Problems* (1953-56). In 1950-51 he made a study of the emerging culture patterns in Israel on a grant from the Social Science Research Council, the findings of which have appeared in a series of articles in learned periodicals, and in 1957-58 he was Fulbright Visiting Professor at Bar-Ilan University, Israel. He is the author of *Immigrant Settlements in Connecticut* and of *Sociology; An Introduction to the Science of Society*, co-author or co-editor of *Studies in the Science of Society, Jews in a Gentile World; One America, The Refugees Are New Americans, History of the Jewish Labor Movement in the United States, Criminology: A Book of Readings, Sociology: A Book of Readings*, and *Contemporary Sociology*.

NOTES

1. Nevins, Allan (editor), *Diary of Philip Hone*, 1828-51, Dodd, Mead and Co., New York, 1936, 434.
2. Barck, Dorothy (editor), *Letters of John Pintard*, New York Historical Society, New York, 1941, III, 51.

3. *Foreign Criminals and Paupers.* Report of the Committee on Foreign Affairs, Aug. 1, 1856, U.S. 34th Congress, 1st Session, House Report No. 359, 16-17.

4. *Report of the Select Committee Appointed to Examine into Conditions of Tenant Houses in New York and Brooklyn,* New York State Assembly Document No. 205, 1857.

5. *Analysis of America's Modern Melting Pot,* House of Representatives, 67th Congress, November 22, 1922.

6. *Immigration and Crime,* Senate Document 750, 61st Congress, 36, 1.

7. *Recent Statistics on Crime and the Foreign-Born,* Report No. 10, January 24, 1931, U.S. Government Printing Office, 1931.

8. There exists no more recent study comparing immigrant with native criminality than those made in the 1940's. The main reason seems to be due to the fact that with the dwindling of the immigrant population, there is little interest in undertaking such a study, except in the case of such recently arrived groups as the Puerto Ricans. Another reason is the fact that the F.B.I., in its *Uniform Crime Reports,* has ceased to distinguish native-born from foreign-born criminals.

9. Sutherland, Edwin H., *Principles of Criminology* (revised by Donald R. Cressey), J. B. Lippincott Co., Chicago, 1955, 144.

10. *Prisoners in State and Federal Prisons and Reformatories,* 1946, Washington, D. C., U.S. Bureau of the Census, 1948, 27.

11. Van Vechten, Cortlandt C., "The Criminality of the Foreign-Born," *Journal of Criminal Law and Criminology,* XXXII, July-August, 1941, 139-147.

12. *Cf.* Taft, Donald R., *Criminology,* New York, The Macmillan Co., 1956, 174.

13. Sutherland, Edwin H., *op. cit.,* 148.

14. *Ibid.,* 148.

15. According to the U.S. Bureau of the Census, (Population Series, No. 6), the median age of the foreign-born was 51.0 years, while that of the native-born whites was 26.7 years.

16. Van Vechten, *op. cit.*

17. *Recent Statistics on Crime and the Foreign-Born, op. cit.,* 116.

18. *Ibid.,* 100-102.

19. *Criminology, op. cit.,* 163.

20. *National Commission on Law Observance and Enforcement,* Report No. 10, January 24, 1931, U.S. Government Printing Office, 1931, 109.

21. Taft, Donald R., "Nationality and Crime," *American Sociological Review,* I, 5, October, 1936, 732.

22. Elliott, Mabel A., *Crime in Modern Society,* Harper and Brothers, New York, 1952, 294.

23. The data are based on police reports in 7 cities, namely: Chicago, Detroit, Cleveland, Kansas City, Mo., Rochester, N. Y., San Francisco, and Cambridge, Mass.

24. All Mexican rates are unreliable, since the estimates of their number in the various localities covered are of questionable validity.

25. *Principles of Criminology,* op. cit., 161.

26. Taft, Donald R., *Criminology, op. cit.,* 161.

27. *Ibid.*, 160.

28. *Principles of Criminology*, op. cit., 38.

29. *Crime in Modern Society, op. cit.*, 259.

30. *Ibid.*, 282.

31. Barnes, Harry E. and Negley Teeters, *New Horizons in Criminology*, Prentice-Hall, New York, 1959, 166.

32. Kefauver, Estes, *Crime in America*, Doubleday, New York, 1951.

33. *Prisoners in State and Federal Prisons and Reformatories*, Washington, 1935.

34. *Principles of Criminology, op. cit.*, 147.

35. Van Vechten, *op. cit.*

36. Taft, Donald R., "Nationality and Crime," *op. cit.*, 726-27.

37. *Criminology, op. cit.*, 231.

38. Taft, Donald R., "Nationality and Crime," *op. cit.*, 726-27.

39. *Ibid.*

40. Reported in The New York *Times*, September 25, 1959.

41. *Ibid.*

42. *The Puerto Rican Study, 1953-57: A Report on the Education and Adjustment of Puerto Rican Pupils in the Public Schools of the City of New York*, New York, 1958, 120.

43. *Principles of Criminology, op. cit.*, 146.

44. *Ibid.*

45. Stofflet, E. H., "The European Immigrant and His Children, " *The Annals of the American Academy of Political and Social Science*, 217, September, 1941, 86-87.

46. Boas, Franz, "The Effects of American Environment on Immigrants and Their Descendants," *Science*, 84, 1936, 525.

159

THE GEOGRAPHY OF CRIME

Sidney J. Kaplan
University of Kentucky

Historical speculation about the relationship between geographical factors and human behavior reminds one of the cynical observation that in psychological research with rats, German rats act like Germans and American rats act like Americans, the former being phlegmatic and the latter being energetic.[1] What has been said about rats can with greater justice be said about historical assertions concerning geographical determinism. So ethnocentric were some of the early surmises that one is bound to acknowledge that they cast less light on the significance of geographical conditioning than they do on the cultural conditioning of the social philosophers involved. Aristotle, for example, in characterizing the inhabitants of warm and cold climates suggested that both had positive and negative qualities, but that inhabitants of temperate zones, Greeks for example, combined the best qualities of both. Similarly, Ibn Khaldun in the 14th century, and Bodin in the 16th century pictured the residents of temperate zones in more flattering terms than those of warmer or colder zones.

Even with the development of modern geography during the 19th century a great many sweeping generalizations were made about the significance of geographical factors in determining human behavior. Few if any cultural attributes were left unexplained by cosmic forces: economic and political organization, population distribution, the growth and decay of civilizations, familial patterns, military prowess, health, energy, creativity, intelligence, crime, genius, forms of art, religious ritual, all accounted for by the effect of the physical environment. No attribute of the physical environment was ignored for the explanation of human events: temperature, humidity, wind, storms, soil, sun spots, atmospheric pressure, precipitation, sunshine, cloudiness, ozone, topography, and altitude were all utilized by one writer or another to make man's cultural forms intelligible.

Adding impetus to the attempt of social philosophers, historians, and geographers to explain man and his culture by reference to geographical conditioning, was the emergence during the 19th century of a materialistic scientific philosophy in search of causal laws, and the development of the theory of evolution and its application to social as well as natural phenomena. Both of these intellectual viewpoints were exhibited in their most crystallized form, as far as geographical determinism is concerned, in the works of Buckle, Demolins, Ratzel, Semple, and Huntington.[2] It was not, however, until the latter part of the 19th century and the beginning of the twentieth century that speculative anthropogeography gave way to the careful and detailed studies characterizing the contemporary behavioral sciences, although it still should be added, that the twentieth century, too, has had its share of naive geographical determinism.

Contemporary behavioral scientists give little credence to strict geographical determinism. While acknowledgment is made that man must come to terms with his environment, his adaptation is viewed more in terms of his cultural choices than in terms of the coercive force of cosmic influences. The physical environment may be a limiting factor, but within the limits provided, man on the basis of his history, ideals, and technology, adjusts to his environment. The inevitability of a one to one relationship between culture and physical environment is denied. Even geographers who would be most inclined to attribute preeminent significance to the physical environment seldom subscribe to geographical determinism. Most of them have adopted what has been termed "possibilism" in professional geography. That is, the physical environment is viewed as being permissive, or providing alternatives, and man, endowed with his cultural heritage is viewed as being active rather than submissive in his adaptation to his environment. One might even go further, as some geographers have, and assert that man, if he chose to expend the money and effort, could with his modern technology and energy sources, grow bananas at the North Pole.

What has been said of geographical determinism in general applies in particular to the relationship between geographical elements and crime. With the accelerated development of the behavioral sciences in the twentieth century etiological interest in crime has been more and more focused on psychological and sociological factors. Concern has been shown for cultural and sub-cultural variations, the effect of differential social organization, and the motivational patterns associated with criminality. Interest in geographical matters has been almost completely subordinated to investigations of sociocultural causes, indicating some considerable belief among behavioral scientists, that at best, geographical factors are of negligible importance. No better evidence of this lack of concern for the geography of crime is exhibited than in the paucity, during the past half century, of such research by either geographers or criminologists.

While it is acknowledged that geographical forces may be of negligible importance etiologically, this does not mean they are of no consequence whatsoever. To take the view that geographical factors are indirect or are "mediated by conditions of personality, culture, and social organization" does not preclude their significance even though they are admittedly of minor etiological weight.[3] It is from more than an esoteric viewpoint, then, that this lack of concern with geographical factors may be deplored. It is noteworthy in this regard that the *Uniform Crime Reports* of the Federal Bureau of Investigation does provide data on criminality and seasonal variation. Apparently to the law enforcement officer, if not to the criminologist, concern for geographical factors is not entirely a dead issue.

INVESTIGATIONS OF GEOGRAPHICAL FACTORS AND CRIME

Although interest in the relationship between cosmic forces and crime has in recent years been subordinated to interest in

162

psychological and sociological factors, the literature on this problem is great, the bulk of it being contributed in the 19th and early 20th centuries and for the most part by Europeans. Interest on the part of American criminologists is at a minimum. Only an occasional article is to be found in criminological literature. And much the same may be said of contemporary European interest as well. The lack of interest is further attested to by the absence of any serious treatment of the problem in most modern textbooks. Indeed, in some criminology texts the problem is either ignored or dealt with in a cavalier fashion.

Among the many geographical features assessed in relation to crime are the following: humidity, latitude, time of day, precipitation, season, light, cloudiness, and quite recently the amount of "aran" in the atmosphere. Investigations of most of these features, however, have been fleeting. The major concern has been the relationship between crime and season, temperature, latitude, or zone. This continuing concern may be linked historically to the early 19th century and Quetelet's "thermic law" of criminality although, as has been indicated, this idea has been apparently bandied about since man first began to speculate about behavioral variations.[4]

Of the studies including a consideration of geographical factors Dexter's appraisals of the influence of weather upon conduct is pre-eminent.[5] His findings were based upon data recorded during the latter two decades of the nineteenth century: approximately 40,000 cases of assault and battery in New York City and 184 cases of homicide in Denver. Conclusions based on the New York data were as follows: crimes of violence were most frequent when humidity and atmospheric pressure were low, when winds were mild and on clear days; contrariwise, high humidity, cloudiness, high pressure, and rain were associated with fewer crimes of violence.

While in his explanation of the relationship between weather influences and crime, Dexter entertained the idea that weather influences were mediated to some minor extent by social factors, for example, increased social contact in the summer, he assigned predominant weight to weather influences as such. For him weather influences functioned to either depress or energize the organism. For example, a decrease in barometric pressure brought an anticipation of storms and an associated emotional state that predisposed to violence. Similarly, high humidity he regarded as being physically enervating, low humidity energizing and consequently predisposing to violence. Winds, too, he regarded as energizing. Carbon dioxide in the atmosphere, he felt, was depressing. On windy days the carbon dioxide was dissipated and replaced by revivifying oxygen thus leading to an increase in vitality. And paralleling these explanations for violence was his suggestion that clear days encouraged activity, just as cloudy and rainy days, while they may call up varied emotional states, tend to depress activity.[6]

While care was exercised by Dexter in the presentation of his data, and while it may be admitted that weather phenomena do have some effect upon mental states, the conclusions drawn by Dexter about the significance of the relationship between weather and crime are more than dubious. Replications of his research would be necessary to give one assurance in his correlations. And even were these relationships reliable the enormously complicated task of separating the influence of social factors from those of weather would have to be attended to. Assuming weather factors are energizing or enervating, how might one reveal the direct relationship between these mental and physical states and crime without reference to socio-cultural factors? A person who is aroused emotionally or physically need not express his vitality in criminality. He might well channel his vitality along socially acceptable lines. In short, Dexter's weather correlations while worth serious consideration as, possibly say, part of the total context of criminal behavior, are not explanatory of the direction of the criminal response. Consideration of this problem would lead one to suspect that a more satisfying explanation might be better sought in the area of sociological and psychological enquiry. On the other hand, more sophisticated research concerning physiological response to weather variations and the relationship of these responses to behavior, would also be desirable. After all, to say that weather phenomena are mediated by social conditions is in no sense an explanation. What, one may legitimately ask, is the character of this mediation?

Among other geographical conditions investigated has been the phenomenon of light. Goedeken has suggested that light influences mood which in turn affects variation in crimes of violence particularly sex crimes although social conditions are also involved.[7] Similarly, Verkko on the basis of a statistical analysis found that assaults and other crimes against the person tend to occur in the late evening, unpremeditated murder, for example, occurring generally between 6 and 9 P.M.[8] This late occurrence Verkko attributes to alcohol consumption, so that here too, if his explanation is to be accepted, is shown the intervening effect of social practices. In a more recent investigation Falk has indicated that assault is most numerous between 10 and 12 P.M. and least frequent between 6 and 8 A.M.[9] This too, Falk attributes to evening and morning differences in alcohol consumption. Robbery, burglary, auto theft, and larceny were also examined with the following results:

> Robbery occurs mainly between 10 and 12 P.M. reaching a low point between 10 to 12 A.M. Burglary is most frequent between 2 and 4 in the morning and least frequent between 8 and 10 A.M. Larceny reaches a maximum around 8-10 P.M. which is considerably earlier than is the case with robbery and burglary. Auto theft is high between 8 and 10 P.M. also, while the lowest auto theft rate occurs between 4 and 6 in the afternoon The highest frequency of robbery takes place between 8 and 12 in the evening and that of burglary only a little later, i.e., from 12 midnight till 2 A.M. Larceny and auto theft both reach a maximum between 8 P.M. and 10 P.M.[10]

While Falk does not comment on these hours of crime it may be safe to assume that the phenomenon of light and darkness is related to these crimes as is the associated variations in social habits. In short, explanatory significance may be attributed to light and darkness variation, that is, the possibility of detection, but probably greatest significance should be attached to the periodicity in social behavior associated with night and day, such as deserted streets, empty stores, evening drinking, householders absenting themselves for evening recreation, and so forth.

In a recent article which was preceded by what was in effect an editorial apology Curry, a medical doctor, suggested that criminality can be related to an ozone-like substance in the atmosphere, an oxidizing gas, which he labelled "aran."[11] According to Curry there are two types of individuals, W and C types, differentially affected by concentrations of "aran" in the air. The W type, he suggests, tend to be suicides and the C types murderers. He provides no data and makes such absurd claims that one has no choice but to regard his notions as being blatant nonsense. It is unfortunate that his comments appeared in a reputable journal. If for no other reason, mention of his theories in this survey is calculated to point up the continuing existence in the contemporary period of the wildest of notions about geographical phenomena and criminality. Fortunately most such gratuitous speculation is in the past.

THE THERMIC LAW OF DELINQUENCY

The greatest interest in the geography of crime has been exhibited in the continuing investigation of the relationship between climate and crime, that is, climate as couched in terms of season or temperature. Most of these investigations have dealt with seasonal or monthly variations, and to a lesser extent has region, temperature, and latitude been studied. These studies have in part sprung from historical and literary weather lore, and in part from what to some appeared to be common sense observation. Supporting this interest in the nineteenth and twentieth centuries was the increasing availability of seasonal and temperature statistics gathered by governmental agencies in Europe and America.

The number of students of crime investigating this problem are legion: Champneuf, Leffingwell, Lombroso, Aschaffenburg, Herz, Von Oettingen, Bonger, Von Mayr, Mayo-Smith, Dexter,

Brearley, Cohen, Schmid, Lottier and Falk among others. The countries studied have included: France, Germany, Hungary, Italy, Denmark, Belgium, England, Finland, Austria, Argentina, and the United States.[12]

There seems to be little question that the so-called thermic law of delinquency as enunciated by Quetelet and others is substantially sound as revealed by the bulk of these studies. Cohen, in 1941, on a basis of a survey of the literature and his own analysis of American figures taken from the Uniform Crime Reports during the period 1935 to 1940, says:

> Thus, we find that the data from many countries, gathered for well over a century, show incontrovertibly that crime is a seasonal phenomenon; that is, crimes against the person, tend, on the whole, to increase in the summer time, while crimes against property predominate in the winter. The evidence of the Uniform Crime Reports for seven major offenses confirms what was deduced from the scantier data available in the United States before 1930.[13]

Similarly Falk, on the basis of a systematic survey showed that the literature dealing with the relationship between crime and delinquency supports the thermic law of delinquency.[14] It should be added, however, that Falk's own empirical study, based upon an appraisal of 10 American cities only partially verifies the thermic relationships.

Since considerable objection has been raised about this relationship, partially on the basis of its negligible significance, partially on the basis of contrary or unsupporting empirical evidence, and partially on the invalidity of questionable statistics, some assessment of these objections should be made.

With respect to the negligible significance of the relationship between season and crime, as compared, for example, to the significance of sociological and psychological conditions, little question may be raised. Perhaps the thermic law is a "minuscule mouse", too trivial to warrant serious concern. It is nonetheless, part of the total etiological context, and as such, a legitimate area of enquiry. Moreover, to the law enforcement officer,

167

whose role has been woefully ignored by criminologists, the concern may be of substantial practical use. One can further assert that until such time as sociological "imperialists" have provided a valid body of explanatory principles, an eclectic approach admitting also of the investigation of geographical phenomena, would appear to be not only legitimate, but entirely warranted, scientifically as well as practically.

Negative empirical evidence, on the other hand, deserves more serious attention. Frequently, data have shown that infanticide rather than occuring with greatest frequency in the summer, tends to occur in the winter, and this is taken to mean that the "thermic law" is contradicted.[15] It may be suggested, however, that infanticide is a special kind of crime against the person and in some respects shares characteristics with crimes against property which occur most often in the winter. The Eskimos, for example, who practice female infanticide, did this, not in the throes of anger, but out of a recognition that when food was scarce some members of the community or family would have to be sacrificed. The parallel between contemporary infanticide and Eskimo infanticide may not be entirely to the point, of course. Infanticides in Western Society are probably closely associated with illegitimate birth and the social definition of illegitimacy. But this type of infanticide is in motivation clearly different from other crimes against the person. And secondly, it may not be entirely out of place to suggest that concealing or caring for a child may be easier in the summer than in the winter.

Reference is often made to Schmid's study of homicide in Seattle as providing contradictory evidence as well.[16] According to this investigation homicides were most frequent in the winter and this frequency Schmid attributed to the influx of migratory workers in the winter, who jobless and in general distress, vented their feelings in crimes against the person. The data, of course, do not prove that seasonality is not operative; it rather suggests that seasonality is involved, but that in this circumstance that social conditions may have primacy, not exclusiveness. What, one may ask, is the nature of the relationship between the season of the year and the social factors which do appear to have primacy? Is the answer merely a commonplace? Or is the relationship worth considering as being more than a triviality to be waved aside? Would such a relationship be trivial in a framework of prevention and control? Or is the criminologist so wrapped up in problems of etiology that he need not be concerned about prevention or control?

It might be added in connection with Schmid's data on the greater frequency of homicide in the winter, that much the same findings have turned up often but usually they have been related to the festivities of the Christmas period.[17] Here again, one sees the significance of social events confounding seasonal factors. But, again, may not one enquire into the relationship between the Christmas period and weather phenomena? Is there any physiological difference between the effect of drinking in the summer and drinking in the winter? And if so, how do these differences relate to crimes against the person, even though they are mediated by social factors?

The above comments do suggest that geographical factors are indeed subordinate in importance to the impact of social factors. But the fact that this is so does not mean that seasonal factors are not involved. Few students of the geography of crime nowadays take a purely deterministic position geographically. What they are concerned with is the frequent correlation that is found between seasonality and crime and its explication in meaningful terms whether they be sociological, psychological or perhaps, as Dexter and others have suggested, physiological and geographical.

A third objection to correlations between crime and season has to do with the reliability of the statistics upon which they are founded. One can hardly dispute the many criminologists who have depreciated criminal data, particularly data made available by governmental agencies. Even the F. B. I. in publishing the Uniform Crime Reports does not vouch for the data, suggesting that it serves mainly as a collating and distributing agency for American police departments which do collect the data. And yet the crime and season correlations, based upon more than a

169

century of appraisal in many countries, appear so often, even with notable exceptions, that one is persuaded that the relationship between season and crime is a fairly reliable one.

Since greater reliability probably attaches to more recent data, and since U. S. data are readily available for careful scrutiny by the American criminologist, an examination of recent data may be desirable. Perhaps it should be said at the outset that the findings are mixed. Some research supports the "thermic law"; other research is negative. In general, however, there appears to be a more than partial basis for the correlation between season and criminality.

Dexter, in his New York and Denver study, drew the conclusion that temperature and crime were related. According to him, based upon data carefully collected between 1880 and 1900 ". . . except for the very highest temperatures, the number of assaults increases with the heat." [18] Also, adds Dexter, "This curve (temperature and assault) . . . is most beautifully regular, showing a gradual increase from January the coldest month, to July, the hottest month, and decrease for the rest of the year." [19] Unfortunately Dexter did not deal with crimes against property, so that his figures support only that part of the "thermic law" that has to do with crimes against the person.

In his examination of Uniform Crime Reports for cities over 100,000 population between 1935 and 1940, Cohen drew a similar conclusion for crimes against the person, and since he dealt with property crimes as well, also substantiated the property crime winter relationship embodied in the thermic law. Of the robbery curve, for example, Cohen says that "the amounts of robbery receded and rose from the beginning of the year to the end with a symmetry that is rare in the statistics of social data." [20] And similarly, but to a lesser extent, was this true of burglary, auto theft, and larceny. Of his data on aggravated assault Cohen offers the following: "In each case the low point came in January; the annual average was approximately early in May; the peak was reached in midsummer; there was a gradual and continuous decline through November; December showed a minor 'holiday' rise." [21] Concerning homicide Cohen says, "In general, murders are committed more frequently during the summer than during the winter, but there is a marked variation in peak and low months from year to year and area to area.[22]

In his detailed analysis of homicide, based upon South Carolina and national figures, Brearley draws the conclusion that:

> "The series of extended investigations reported . . . does not, unfortunately, enable one to unequivocally reject or support the thermic law of crime . . . Since the data are somewhat contradictory, they have been presented here in detail in order that further investigation may carry forward the study of the problem. Meanwhile the criminologist is forced to suspend judgment. Temperature trends may affect seasonal distribution of homicide in the United States, and, again they may not. The relationship may actually exist, obscured by interfering factors but the evidence already presented does not lend much support to this conclusion." [23]

Actually a close appraisal of Brearley's detailed tables as well as his analysis of them leads one to suspect that Brearley is being entirely too equivocal as far as the gross relationship between homicide and season is concerned. Careful scrutiny of his tabulated data and the curves based upon them leads this writer to assert that the bulk of his data are far more consistent with the thermic law of delinquency than contradictory. In this connection it is noteworthy that Brearley's discussion seems to emphasize data which depart from the thermic law while minimizing data which appear to support it. For example, in commenting upon Uniform Crime Report figures for 1930, he suggests that the data (supporting the thermic law) were atypical "both for its (1930) extremely hot summer and the severity of its economic depression" [24] And yet in examining homicide data for the period 1923-1928, he does not comment on the obviously atypical December of 1928 which because of its tremendous excess of homicides raises the December results for the six year period to a point such that totals and curves based upon them are distorted

171

as far as general meaningfulness is concerned. (December of 1928 had 200 homicides in excess of any of the five previous Decembers. A strange figure indeed.)[25] It is unfortunate in this regard that some students of criminology have uncritically accepted Brearley's investigation as refuting the thermic law. Even Brearley does not go this far, preferring rather to adopt the equivocal position of suspended judgment.

In 1952, Falk, on the basis of statistics for eight American cities for a ten year period appraised the relationship between crime and season.[26] Unfortunately he did not provide tabulated monthly data or curves based upon them, so that one is unable to draw any conclusions about general trends. He did, however, offer a number of conclusions which partially support the thermic law. His conclusions are as follows:

1. Whereas crimes against the person consistently reach their maximum frequency in the summer, such crimes do not always increase or decrease with the temperature as evidenced by the fact that criminal homicide is higher in December than in June and August.
2. Crimes against the person are at a minimum in the winter months.
3. Crimes against property do not always reach a maximum in the winter and a minimum in the summer. This may be observed primarily in the case of larceny.[27]

Perhaps his conclusions do not need additional comment. As has been the case in other investigations, variations from the thermic law are exhibited. Had Falk offered tabulated data more might be said. Failing this, however, one can only say that there is only partial support for the thermic law of delinquency.

In the final analysis one may draw the conclusion that the bulk of research dealing with the relationship between crime and season does show substantial support for the thermic law. Despite the contradictory evidence, patterns do emerge which show that, in general, crimes against the person reach their maximum in the summer and their minimum in the winter; and that crimes against property are highest in the winter and lowest in the summer. The explanation can perhaps be best couched in social terms. That is, in the winter economic distress may be at its height, and in the summer increased social contact makes more frequent conflicts possible. This explanation strikes one as being satisfactory even though it may be commonplace. On the other hand, this explanation may not be entirely complete. Most people would acknowledge that they are affected by weather phenomena, however slight the degree. Perhaps it is not too far fetched to suggest that an investigation of weather phenomena, physiological response, and behavior is indicated. Moreover, to say that weather conditions are mediated by social factors is also not sufficiently explanatory. What is the specific nature of this mediation? And to what extent is it reflected in criminal behavioral systems? Of course, the argument that from the point of view of the economical use of scientific resources, that weather phenomena are not worth investigating and that major effort should be expended in psychological and sociological research, is probably a sound one. And yet from the viewpoint of comprehensiveness, particularly in regard to problems of apprehension and prevention, such research may be considered justifiable. In any case the scientific attitude would seem to suggest encouragement of any effort to understand the relationship between seasonal phenomena and crime, however commonplace, or theoretically unimportant.

THE ECOLOGY OF CRIME

One theoretical approach to criminal behavior which utilizes a geographical base is that of the so-called ecological school. This approach, concerned with the distribution of crime throughout a given area, usually cities, is by no means new. Ecological appraisal of social phenomena, as has been indicated, may be found in the speculations of the earliest social philosophers. In the recent period, however, interest in ecological distributions, modest in scope, may be associated with the University of Chicago and the empirical investigations carried on in the 1920's and

1930's at that school. Prominent among sociologists subscribing to this mode of analysis at Chicago were Park and Burgess.[28] Due in part to their influence investigations were carried on dealing with the ecology of many different kinds of social phenomena: welfare cases, suicide, church attendance, delinquency, crime, mental disorders and so forth.

Among the best known of the early ecologists concerned with criminal behavior were Shaw and McKay, who in *Delinquency Areas* and *Urban Areas and Delinquency*, analyzed the relationship between ecological patterns and criminal phenomena.[29] Careful assessment of delinquency rates, for example, revealed a variation from the center of the city to the outskirts. The highest rates were in or near the center of the city and as the periphery was approached the rate of delinquency gradually diminished. A delinquency gradient was thus revealed that varied inversely with the distance from the center of the city. Particularly significant in these findings was the fact that this pattern of delinquency corresponded generally with zones delineated previously by ecological theorists.

The typical city, as described by Burgess and others, has several major ecological zones which form a series of concentric circles around the center of the city. The Central Zone includes among other features, specialty shops, hotels, department stores, and theaters. Next to this central business district is the Zone in Transition, changing in character as the central business district encroaches upon it. Here are found boarding houses, light manufacturing, small businesses, warehouse, and substandard housing. Adjacent to this interstitial zone is the area of workingmen's homes, Zone 3, which affords ready access to city employment. Beyond is Zone 4, containing single family houses and occasionally expensive apartment houses. Finally, on the perimeter of the city and in the suburbs, is to be found the Commuters Zone. It should be added that these zones were offered as ideal representations. It was anticipated that empirical research would only approximate this ecological pattern.

Appraisals of Chicago and other American cities have led ecologists to distinguish neighborhoods of high delinquency which

174

they have termed "delinquency areas." Found mainly in the Zone of Transition "delinquency areas" are usually deteriorated physically. In these substandard areas live immigrants, migrants, Negroes and other groups either unable to obtain or pay for better living accommodations. Among the characteristics often encountered in these delinquency areas are declining population, poverty, overcrowding, anti-social standards, racial and cultural heterogeneity, a transient population, few recreational facilities, and substandard housing.[30]

While the physical character of the delinquency area is accorded some importance, the more significant point is that the physical deterioration of the areas of high delinquency is construed to be an indication of social disorganization. Not only are these areas physically deteriorated but they are deteriorated socially as well. Characterized by conflicts in values and subject to ineffective techniques of social control, residents of the delinquency areas were viewed as being "socially demoralized." Out of this "lack of moral order" there emerges criminality and other behavioral deviations.

In general, studies made since Shaw's early investigations of Chicago substantiate his findings as far as the high incidence of delinquency in certain areas is concerned.[31] Explanations of the high delinquency rates, however, are still couched in abstract terms which, as far as understanding is concerned, leave much to be desired. Such terms as anomie, social disorganization, culture conflict, deprivation, competition, and the like are quite plausible, but hardly enlightening to the criminologist who would prefer to have the etiology of criminality more explicitly revealed.

Of the criticisms which may be directed toward ecological analysis of criminality, several are worth noting. In the first place, recognition of the existence of delinquency areas is a mere commonplace. In what sense does it have more than casual descriptive value? Secondly, question may be raised about juveniles, living in delinquent areas, who do not become delinquents. Then too, there are many juveniles who do not live in delinquency areas, but nonetheless do become delinquents. How may these two categories be explained? Third, it may be assumed that the gradient of delinquency is related to favoritism which is shown juveniles in non-delinquent areas due to parental influence or the social backgrounds of officials. And finally, it may be submitted again that ecological explanations are overly general. Perhaps a satisfactory understanding of delinquency can only come from a detailed consideration of the psychological characteristics of the delinquent as they interact with specific social conditions.[32]

These criticisms, of course, are quite pertinent. But they do not render ecological explanations insignificant, gross as they may be. That a disproportionate number of offenders come from delinquency areas may be accepted. The fact that many individuals living in these areas do not become delinquent does not mean that social disorganization is not involved. It rather points to the necessity of studying the factors that select out those individuals who do become delinquent.

Thus, ecological analysis has served as a point of departure for other kinds of empirical investigations, and the development of theory as well. Case studies of delinquents, for example, may be linked to the impetus provided by ecological analysis.[33] And Cohen, in his analysis of the delinquent subculture has drawn upon the commonplace findings of the ecologists in formulating a very persuasive theory of delinquency that has provoked more that commonplace interest among criminologists.[34]

Taking his cue from the high incidence of delinquency in delinquency areas, particularly as expressed in gang behavior, Cohen asks a series of questions about the nature of delinquent behavior and the adequacy of conventionally used sociological theories to explain such behavior. According to Cohen the delinquent subculture is *non-utilitarian, malicious* and *negativistic,* characterized by *short run hedonism* and *versatility,* and calculated to emphasize the importance of *self autonomy.*[35] As Cohen sees it, "social disorganization," "culture conflict," and "illicit means" theories often used to explain delinquent behavior, are not at all satisfactory. None of these concepts explain the specific direction of delinquent behavior, nor do they explain the zest

176

or "spirit" found in delinquency. Delinquency areas are not altogether disorganized, culture-conflict does not explain why delinquency is an appropriate response, and illicit means fails to explain why stolen goods are often discarded or destroyed nor does it explain the maliciousness and negativism often encountered in delinquents.

For Cohen, the behavior of the delinquent gang, that it, its subculture, emerges from the nature of American society, particularly its class system. Since the delinquent subculture is mainly a working class phenomenon, Cohen argues that many working class juveniles unequipped to cope with American middle class expectations adjust by attacking the middle class values which define them as being unworthy. Delinquency, then, as expressed in the gang, is a reaction against working class stigma and an attempt to enhance self-esteem. The delinquent gang enhances its feelings of worth by attacking and debasing middle class values and by developing group norms which rationalize their delinquencies. A group solution to the problem of status deprivation, suggests Cohen, is an effective solution since it brings with it the sustaining weight of group approval.[36] As Redl also suggests, the delinquent subculture provides "gratifications" without the onerous burden of guilt feelings.[37] Moral approval, in short, is provided for behavior which in the larger community would be defined as immoral or illegal. Thus, as Cohen views it, the delinquent subculture is related to the stratification of American society. The same values which serve to call up virtuous behavior in the middle class youth simultaneously elicit delinquent behavior from the working class youth. American middle class values calculated to encourage respectable behavior may also serve to "encourage" delinquent behavior of the kind described by Cohen in his characterization of the delinquent subculture.

The extent to which the delinquent subculture is a protest against middle class expectations has yet to be demonstrated. Doubtless, empirical scrutiny will show that Cohen's theory like other broad sociological theories demands added qualification. As Clinard has pointed out delinquent gangs may also function to meet such diverse needs as "adventure, excitement, protection

177

against other gangs, racial, ethnic, and religious identification, and dislike for the police." [38] And as far as protest is concerned, delinquent behavior may be regarded as a protest not against middle class expectations so much as protest against the expectations of the adult world. [39] In any case, even though question may be raised about the content which Cohen imputes to the delinquent subculture, and the adequacy of his theory to explain this content, he has nonetheless provided a cogent theoretical framework which will probably generate many empirical investigations.

Ecological investigations of the delinquency area have also served to focus interest on the problem of selective response. Why, one may ask, are many individuals reared in delinquency areas able to avoid becoming delinquents? Who is "The 'Good Boy' in a High Delinquency Area"? [40] On the basis of several studies of this problem in Columbus, Ohio, the conclusion was drawn that the good boy had incorporated a self image that "insulated" him from delinquency. Regarded by his parents and teachers as being a good boy, and conceiving himself to be a law-abiding person, the good boy had been relatively free from contact with delinquency patterns and had been closely supervised in a conventional home characterized by affectional and stable family relations. Theoretically, however, the significant conclusion was that the self-conception the good boys developed during their socialization served as a buffer against delinquency. Whether or not they would become delinquent in the future lay in "their ability to maintain their present self-images in the face of mounting situational pressures." [41]

It is indeed unfortunate that the conclusions offered in regard to the "good boy" were not accompanied by a presentation of the relevant data. Appraisal of these studies suggests that the investigators—of the wide variety of data they apparently had at their disposal—simply chose to emphasize the data pertaining to the self-image. Whether or not the self-image is the "basic component that steers the youthful person away from or toward delinquency" seems to be a matter of the kind of sociological or social-psychological language one prefers to use or finds most useful in analysis.[42] In any case—and this is not merely reduction-ism—the self-image itself would seem to call for explanation. And this would be necessary whether one were concerned with etiology or prevention and rehabilitation. The usefulness of the concept of the self-image, as far as criminality is concerned, is at this juncture a matter of assertion or analytical preference. The studies of the "good boy" are as yet hardly persuasive of that usefulness.

RURAL-URBAN DIFFERENCES

The 1958 Uniform Crime Reports were the first published in accordance with the revisions suggested by a special FBI Consultant Committee.[43] Prior to 1958 urban and rural data were based upon 1940 U.S. Census definitions. In 1958 the definitions used in the 1950 Census were used. Three areas were identified: the standard metropolitan area, other cities, and rural.[44] Whereas the rural category had previously included some urbanized fringes, the 1958 Uniform Crime Reports defined rural as including,

> ... neither any place of 2500 or more inhabitants, nor any of the densely populated suburban areas adjacent to our large metropolitan centers. In that sense the somewhat restricted meaning attached to the term 'rural' may actually more closely represent what has been traditionally considered rural than the term 'rural' as used in earlier Uniform Crime Reports.[45]

Because of the exclusion of areas previously labeled rural, the 1958 data are not comparable to previous data. But more than compensating are the new area definitions which may well yield rural-urban differences of a "purer" kind.

In Table I are shown rates of crime for the three population areas based upon offenses reported to the police and estimates extrapolated from this data by the FBI.[46] For the seven offenses tabulated the overall rates per 100,000 population are as follows: 1155 for the standard metropolitan areas, 632.6 for the other cities category, and 407.9 for rural. In gross terms, then, the data

179

show that the rural rate is one-third that of the metropolitan area which contains the bulk of the urban population. For each one of the 7 crimes the metropolitan area is highest except for murder for which the rural rate is highest. In the other cities category the rates are intermediate except for murder, rape, and assault for which offenses the rates are lowest. These 1958 figures, except for murder support the conclusion that urban crimes are more numerous than rural crime. Moreover, the rural rate for murder, and the other cities rate for murder, rape, and assault suggest that rural areas are characterized by relatively higher rates for crimes against the person, as is the case in murder and also for rape and assault as compared at least to the other ciites category. For the metropolitan areas, however, the rate of assault and rape are still higher than the rural rate, although as compared to crimes against the property the discrepancy is very much less.

TABLE I
CRIME RATES—STANDARD METROPOLITAN AREAS, OTHER CITIES AND RURAL, 1958
(Per 100,000 inhabitants)*

Area	Total	Murder & Non-Negligent Manslaughter	Forcible Rape	Robbery	Aggravated Assault	Burglary	Larceny over $50.	Auto Theft
Standard Metro-politan Areas	1155	4.6	9.8	62.5	79.9	486.3	296.2	215.7
Other Cities	632.6	3.3	4.1	15.9	41.6	311.5	157.1	98.9
Rural	407.9	6.0	7.4	12.4	43.9	205.0	91.0	42.1
U.S. Totals	896.9	4.7	8.0	43.5	65.5	392.4	226.0	156.4

*Computed from Table 3—Index of Crime, United States, 1958, *Uniform Crime Reports*, 1958, 63.

TABLE II

CITY CRIME RATES BY POPULATION GROUPS

(rate per 100,000 population)*

Population Group	Murder, Non-negligent Manslaughter	Forcible Rape	Robbery	Aggravated Assault	Burglary over $100	Larceny	Auto Theft
Total Groups I-VI 3,276 cities; pop. 98,317,123	4.5	8.4	61.4	80.3	479.1	300.7	218.8
Group I 45 cities over 250,000; pop. 38,517,456	6.3	13.9	112.4	131.6	597.2	405.0	314.0
5 cities over 1,000,000; pop. 17,909,957	5.7	17.2	132.3	158.6	587.2	491.1	251.0
8 cities, 750,000 to 1,000,000; pop. 6,766,964	7.9	11.9	112.4	161.3	569.9	310.0	420.3
9 cities, 500,000 to 750,000; pop. 5,311,311	6.0	9.3	84.4	69.0	566.8	276.4	361.0
23 cities, 250,000 to 500,000; pop. 8,529,224	6.5	11.4	88.0	90.1	658.7	379.4	332.6
Group II 85 cities, 100,000 to 250,000 pop. 12,653,265	5.2	6.8	51.7	79.7	572.7	316.7	258.7
Group III 173 cities, 50,000 to 100,000; pop. 11,809,981	3.6	5.7	35.3	60.0	455.4	300.5	188.7
Group IV 361 cities, 25,000 to 50,000; pop. 12,603,836	2.8	4.0	21.7	34.1	374.0	235.2	139.4
Group V 820 cities, 10,000 to 25,000; pop. 12,934,620	2.1	3.8	17.3	32.6	322.9	169.0	107.4
Group VI 1,792 cities under 10,000; pop. 9,797,964	2.4	4.0	14.1	26.4	263.7	128.8	78.0
Rural pop. 42,035,033	6.0	7.4	12.42	43.9	205.0	91.0	42.1

*Uniform Crime Reports, Federal Bureau of Investigation, 1958, 73; rural rates computed from Table 3, page 63, same publication.

The greatest differences between rural and metropolitan rates are for crimes against property, the ratios, in favor of the metropolitan areas, being about 5 to 1 for auto theft, 3 to 1 for larceny, $2\frac{1}{3}$ to 1 for burglary, and 5 to 1 for robbery. And within area categories the metropolitan ratio between crimes against property and crimes against the person is about 11 to 1; in the rural areas the ratio is about 6 to 1. Thus, these figures support the general conclusion that crimes against property are associated more with urban areas than rural areas.

Since the mertopolitan area category is a gross one, including cities of various sizes, a comparison of the rates of cities of different sizes with the rural rate may be profitable. In Table II city crime rates as well as rural rates are shown.

For murder, it may be noted, that the rural rate is greater for all groups except group I (cities over 250,000 in population). In group I only cities over one million show a lower rate for murder. Similarly for forcible rape, the rural rate is greater than all groups except group I cities. For aggravated assault the rural rate is greater than rates for groups IV, V, and VI (cities up to 50,000 in population). And finally, for crimes against property, burglary, robbery, larceny, and auto theft, the rural rate in each case is lowest.

The general conclusion that one may draw from these comparisons is as follows: rates for all crimes against property are lowest in rural areas, and rates for crimes against the person are highest in rural areas except for the very large cities.

Over a period of years the data of the Uniform Crime Reports have exhibited much the same relationship between rural and urban crime rates. The trend, however, appears to be toward a greater uniformity between the two population areas due apparently to an increase in rural property crimes. In explaining such variations in crime the F.B.I. has offered a list of factors which they feel affect the amount of crime reported in a specific community. These factors which are probably also pertinent to an understanding of rural and urban differences are as follows:[47]

1. Population of the city and metropolitan area adjacent thereto.

2. The composition of the population with reference particularly to age, sex, and race.
3. The economic status and activities of the population.
4. Climate.
5. Educational, recreational, and religious facilities.
6. The number of police employees per unit of population.
7. The standards governing appointment to the law force.
8. The policies of the prosecuting officials and the courts.
9. The attitudes of the public toward law-enforcement problems.
10. The degree of efficiency of the local law enforcement agency.

Criminologists have usually sought an explanation of rural and urban differences in the character of rural and urban life. Generally the heterogeneity of the urban area as compared to the homogeneity of the rural area has served as a basis for this explanation. What in short has been previously said about social disorganization is applicable here as well. The relatively stable rural area with its personalized relationships, its consensus in values, and its techniques of social control such as gossip, familial pressure, and community opinion probably inhibit the expression of criminal behavior. On the other hand, the relatively unstable, highly mobile, impersonal urban area with its subcultural differences, anonymity, and its relatively ineffective techniques of social control, appears to provide a milieu in which opportunity for committing crimes is greater.[48]

Differences in crimes against the person and crimes against property, however, are only partially explained by these factors.[49] Perhaps the high rate of crimes against property in the urban area may be explained in terms of economic want, the existence of more property in the city, the greater opportunities for stealing, and the greater possibility of escaping detection. The prevalence of crimes against the person in the rural area as compared to small and medium size cities, on the other hand, may be explained by the relative isolation of the rural dweller, his self sufficiency, his greater sensitivity to personal affront, and a carry-over, perhaps, of the frontier tradition of indifference to legal authority.[50] The high rates of crimes against the person in the largest cities, however, are doubtless related to an extreme degree of social heterogeneity. Of the trend toward an increase in rural property crimes, it may be suggested that the effect of modern communication and transportation has been to erase some of the differences between urban and rural life. Perhaps it may be anticipated that as sub-cultural differences between rural and urban areas disappear as a consequence of modern technology, so also with differences in the rural-urban rates of crime.

Appraisals of rural and urban crime differences have also been concerned with rural and urban criminal behavioral systems. On the basis of an investigation of 60 rural property offenders between 17 and 30 years of age, Clinard drew the following conclusions: (1) rural offenders were highly mobile as compared to rural non-offenders (2) rural offenders participated to only a limited extent in local community affairs (3) their relationships were impersonal (4) their criminal behavior commenced relatively late in their youth (5) their criminality was largely adventitious (6) they did not generally engage in organized criminal activity (7) their knowledge of criminal techniques was limited, and (8) they did not conceive of themselves as criminals.[51] For Clinard the most important finding was that the rural offenders did not identify themselves as criminals. On the other hand, Clinard's appraisal of the characteristics of urban criminals led him to conclude that the urban criminal commenced his career in crime at an earlier age, was more familiar with techniques of crime, tended to engage in organized criminal activity, and conceived of himself as a criminal. Unlike the rural offender, the urban offender was a criminal "social type." [52]

Lentz, in a more recent investigation of rural and urban differences, studied a group of 130 rural delinquents and compared them to a group of 290 urban delinquents, all of them being committed during 1948-49 to the Wisconsin School for Boys.[53] Urban boys were characterized by considerably more versatility in their delinquencies since as compared to rural boys who committed an average of 1.7 kinds of offenses, they committed an average of 3.0. Urban delinquents were also members of delinquent gangs in much larger percentage than rural juveniles: 87 per cent compared to 22 per cent. Sixteen per cent of the urban boys had been apprehended alone whereas 52 per cent of the rural boys were so apprehended. Urban delinquents possessed considerably more skill and knowledge in the commission of offenses than did the rural delinquents. And rural youth tended to appear in court once or twice while urban youths were brought before the courts "repeatedly."

From a theoretical point of view, differential association and differential identification would appear to "explain" the contrast between rural and urban offenders.[54] But that these theories are entirely explanatory seems questionable. After all, the rural offenders were frequently alone in their crimes. And while this may be partially explained in terms of mobility, that is, contact with non-rural and criminal influences, it is likely that their alienation from their rural communities, whatever its source, was also etiologically of some considerable significance. In short, to view the development of criminality in both urban and rural areas in terms of the "normal processes" of differential association without reference to the possibility of there being a "psychological readiness" seems ill-advised.[55] This is particularly pertinent to the rural offenders who seemed inordinately, as Clinard's data revealed, detached from their home communities.

CONCLUSION

The relationship between geographical factors and crime appears to be of negligible importance. Investigations of this problem have been of dubious significance in explaining crime, although from the point of view of crime control they may be of more value. Perhaps the only relationship between geographical factors and crime of any consequence is the fairly reliable correlation between season and crime, that is, the so-called thermic law. But here too, the significance of the relationship is etiologically of questionable worth. And yet it is perhaps not sufficient, in evaluating the thermic law, to merely note the greater social contact in the summer and the increased economic distress in the winter. It would probably be desirable that further research be undertaken to appraise more specifically the relationship between season and crime.

Investigation of ecological areas and criminality have provided considerable information about the relationship between community characteristics, particularly the urban milieu, and crime. Such studies have also served as a point of departure for the development of criminological theory, empirical examinations of criminal behavioral processes, and attempts to prevent and control criminal behavior.

Differences in rural and urban can perhaps be best explained in terms of the differences between the urban and rural subcultures. The relative homogeneity of the rural area and the heterogeneity of the urban area and their respective techniques of social control, are probably explanatory of differences in property crimes. Differences in crimes against the person are similarly explainable, although the relatively greater rate for crimes against the person in rural areas can be probably understood in terms of isolation, self sufficiency, sensitivity to personal affront, and an individualistic tradition.

SELECTED BIBLIOGRAPHY

Brearley, H. C., *Homicide in the United States*, University of North Carolina Press, Chapel Hill, 1932. Chapter IX, "Seasonal Variations in Homicide," assesses the impact of season upon crime. Includes an examination of the validity of the "thermic law" particularly as it applies to homicide.

Cohen, Albert, *Delinquent Boys: The Culture of the Gang*, The Free Press, Glencoe, Illinois, 1955. A theoretical analysis of the nature of the delinquent sub-culture. Offers not only a description of gang life but seeks to explain it as well.

Cohen, Joseph, "The Geography of Crime," *The Annals of the American Academy of Political and Social Science*, 217, September, 1941, 29-37. A brief survey of historical literature concerning the "thermic law" of delinquency and an examination of Uniform Crime Reports data with respect to season and crime, and regional variations in crime.

Clinard, Marshall, "The Process of Urbanization and Criminal Behavior," *American Journal of Sociology*, 48, 1942, 202-13. A comparison of the criminal "behaviorial systems" of rural, small city, and urban offenders. The urban offender is viewed a criminal "social type" in contrast to the rural adventitious offender.

Clinard, Marshall, "Rural Criminal Offenders," *American Journal of Sociology*, 50, July, 1944, 38-45. An examination of the "behavioral system" of the rural offender. Characterized by adventitious criminality, mobility, and a limited knowledge of criminal techniques, the rural offender does not regard himself as being a criminal.

Curry, Manfred, "The Relationship of Weather Conditions, Facial Characteristics and Crime," *The Journal of Criminal Law and Criminology*, 39, July-August, 1948, 253-261. An example of what appears to be incautious speculation about the effect of the atmosphere upon homicide and suicide. Even facial characteristics and type of attire are linked to an ozone-like gas in the atmosphere.

Dexter, Edwin G., *Weather Influences*, The Macmillan Company, New York, 1904. A turn of the century exploration of meteorological phenomena and behavior. While the data are carefully gathered, the inferences drawn, based upon a theory of "reserve energy," are questionable.

Falk, Gerhard J., "The Influence of the Seasons on the Crime Rate," *The Journal of Criminal Law, Criminology and Police Science*, 43, 2, July-August, 1952, 199-213. A relatively recent survey of historical literature pertaining to the "thermic law of delinquency." The author also appraises data gathered from 10 United States cities and shows the relationship between time of day, season, and crime.

Glaser, Daniel, "Criminality Theories and Behavioral Images," *American Journal of Sociology*, 61, 5, March, 1956, 433-44. An extension and modification of the theory of "differential association." The criminal, the author feels, identifies himself as a criminal.

Hartshorne, Richard, *Perspective on the Nature of Geography*,

The Associations of American Geographers, Rand McNally and Company, Chicago, 1959. An exploration of the substance and meaning of geography with particular reference to its methodology. Includes a brief assessment of geographical determinism.

Hurvitz, Stephan, *Criminology*, George Allen and Unwin, Ltd., London, 1952. One of the few contemporary texts treating geographical phenomena and crime seriously. Significantly enough it is written by a European.

Lander Bernard, *Towards an Understanding of Juvenile Delinquency*, Columbia University Press, New York, 1954. A recent and provocative contribution to the literature dealing with the ecology of crime. Using sophisticated statistical techniques the author concludes that anomie characterizes the delinquency area.

Llewellyn, Emma C., and Hawthorn, Audry, "Human Ecology" in Gurvitch, Georges, and Moore, Wilbert E. (editors), *Twentieth Century Sociology*, Philosophical Library, New York, 1945, 466-499. An account of the development and significance of "human ecology." One of the best brief treatments of an area of sociology which has declined in importance in recent years.

Lentz, William P., "Rural Urban Differentials and Juvenile Delinquency," *The Journal of Criminal Law, Criminology and Police Science*, 47, 3, September-October, 1956, 331-339. A comparison of 130 rural and 290 urban boys committed to the Wisconsin School for Boys during 1948-49. The author recommends that in investigations of delinquency rural-urban differentials be carefully distinguished.

Reckless, Walter C., Dinitz, Simon and Murray, Ellen, "The 'Good Boy' in a High Delinquency Area," *The Journal of Criminal Law, Criminology and Police Science*, 48, 1, May-June, 1957, 18-25. The authors regard the self-image as the key to understanding why some boys in areas of high delinquency do not succumb to prevailing patterns.

Semple, Ellen C., *Influences of Geographic Enviroment*, Henry Holt and Company, New York, 1911. Based upon Ratzel's system of anthropogeography, it is an investigation of the operation of geographic factors in history as well as in contemporary life. An excellent example of how geographical factors are linked to cultural forms by geographical determinists.

Shaw, Clifford and McKay, Henry, et. al., *Juvenile Delinquency and Urban Areas*, University of Chicago Press, Chicago,

1942. A study of rates of delinquency in relation to "differential" characteristics of American cities; provides excellent characterizations of the "delinquency area."

Taylor, Griffith (editor), *Geography in the Twentieth Century,* Philosophical Library, 1951. One of the finest treatments by many specialists of the scientific and academic boundaries of geography. Contains several excellent accounts of the history of geographical determinism and the contemporary attitude toward it by professional geographers.

Vold, George B., "Crime in City and Country Areas," *The Annals of the American Academy of Political and Social Science,* 217, September, 1941, 38-45. An appraisal of urban and rural crime differences. The homogeneity of the rural area as compared to the heterogeneity of the urban area is invoked to explain these differences.

Sidney J. Kaplan (b. 1924), Associate Professor of Sociology at the University of Kentucky, attended graduate school at Boston University where he took his M.A. in sociology, and at Washington State University receiving the Ph.D in 1953. His major publications have been in criminal law and delinquency. As a member of the Juvenile Court Advisory Committee of Fayette County, Kentucky, he is currently engaged in an evaluation of the Juvenile Court's Citizenship School.

NOTES

1. Accounts of geographical determinism from both a contemporary and historical viewpoint may be found in Sorokin, Pitirim, *Contemporary Sociological Theories,* Harper and Brothers, New York, 1928, Chapter III; Taylor, Griffith (editor), *Geography in the Twentieth Century,* Philosophical Library, New York, 1951, Chapters I through VI; and Hartshorne, Richard, *Perspective on the Nature of Geography,* The Association of American Geographers, Rand McNally and Company, Chicago, 1959. See also, Hartshorne, Richard, *The Nature of Geography,* The Association of American Geographers, The Science Press Printing Company, Lancaster, Pennsylvania, 1939.

2. Buckle, Henry T., *History of Civilization in England.* D. Appleton and Company, 1910. An Appraisal of Demolins may be found in Tatham, George, "Environmentalism and Possibilism" in Taylor, Griffith, *op. cit.,* 138-143. Ratzel, Friedrich, *Anthropogeographie,* J. Engelhorn, Stuttgart, 1899. Semple,

Ellen C., *Influences of Geographic Environment*, Henry Holt and Company, New York, 1911. Huntington, Ellsworth, *Civilization and Climate*, Yale University Press, 1924.

3. Cohen, Joseph, "The Geography of Crime," *The Annals of the American Academy of Political and Social Science*, CCXVII, September, 1941, 29.

4. See De Quiros, C. Bernaldo, *Modern Theories of Criminality* (trans. by DeSalvio, Alfonso), Little, Brown, and Company, 1912, 9-10.

5. Dexter, Edwin G., *Weather Influences*, The Macmillan Company, New York, 1904.

6. In Denver homicides were more prevalent during rainy and cloudy days. For these data Dexter offered the suggestion that rain and cloudiness called up emotional instability and impulsiveness. That this explanation is contrary to the one offered for the New York crimes is evident.

7. Referred to by Hurvitz, Stephan, *Criminology*, George Allen and Unwin, Ltd., London, 1952, 246.

8. *Ibid.*, 252.

9. Falk, Gerhard J., "The Influence of The Seasons on the Crime Rate," *The Journal of Criminal Law, Criminology and Police Science*, XXXXIII, 2, July-August, 1952, 211.

10. *Ibid.*, 212.

11. Curry, Manfred, "The Relationship of Weather Conditions, Facial Characteristics and Crime," *Journal of Criminal Law and Criminology*, XXXIX, July-August, 1948, 253-261.

12. Surveys of this literature may be found in Cohen, Joseph, "The Geography of Crime," *The Annals of the American Academy of Political and Social Science*, CCXVII, September, 1941, 29-37, and Falk, Gerhard J., *op. cit.* See also, Aschaffenburg, Gustav, *Crime and Its Repression* (trans. by Albrecht, Adalbert), Little, Brown, and Company, Boston, 1913, 15-30; Lombroso, Cesare, *Crime, Its Causes and Remedies*, Little, Brown and Company, 1912; Brearley, H. C., *Homicide in the United States*, The University of North Carolina Press, Chapel Hill, 1932, 161-199; Bonger, William A., *Criminality and Economic Conditions*, Little, Brown, and Company, 1916. Von Hentig, Hans, *The Criminal and His Victim*, Yale University Press, 1948, 345, 379; Dexter, Edwin G., *op. cit.* Lottier, Stuart, "Distribution of Criminal Offenses in Sectional Regions," *Journal of Criminal Law and Criminology*, 1938, 29, 329-344; and Parmelee, Maurice, *Criminology*, The MacMillan Company, New York, 1926, 43-53.

13. Cohen, Joseph, *ibid.*, 34. In this survey only that part of the "thermic law" that concerns season will be evaluated. That is, region will not be treated.

14. Falk, Gerhard J., *op. cit.*

15. See, for example, Aschaffenburg, Gustav, *op. cit.*, 17 and 27.

16. Schmid, Calvin J., "A Study of Homicides in Seattle, 1914 to 1924," *Social Forces*, 4, June, 1926, 745-756. It is interesting to note that Schmid also relates the homicide rate to the "equable" temperature of Seattle. Critics of the thermic law have often ignored this reference to the temperature.

17. See Brearley, H. C., *op. cit.*, 179-181.

18. Dexter, Edwin G., *op. cit.*, 146.

19. *Ibid.*, 143.

20. Cohen, Joseph, *op. cit.*, 34.

21. *Ibid.*, 32-33.

22. *Ibid.*, 33.

23. Brearley, H. C., *op. cit.*, 189-190.

24. *Ibid.*, 182.

25. *Ibid.*, 184. See Table VII, December, 1928. See also, footnote 16.

26. Falk, Gerhard, *op. cit.*

27. *Ibid.*, 212-213.

28. An appraisal of ecology, its history, and its significance may be found in Llewellyn, Emma C., and Hawthorn, Audrey, "Human Ecology" in Gurvitch, Georges and Moore, Wilbert E. (editors), *Twentieth Century Sociology*, Philosophical Library, New York, 1945, 466-499.

29. Shaw, Clifford, et al., *Delinquency Areas*, University of Chicago Press, Chicago, 1929. Shaw, Clifford and McKay, Henry, et. al., *Juvenile Delinquency and Urban Areas*, University of Chicago Press, Chicago, 1942. For criticisms of this approach see Robinson, Sophia, *Can Delinquency Be Measured?* Columbia University Press, New York, 1936. See also, Jonassen, Christen, T., "A Re-evaluation and Critique of the Logic and Some Methods of Shaw and McKay," *American Sociological Review*, XIV, October, 1949, 608-17.

30. See, for example, Schmid, Calvin, "Minneapolis and St. Paul, Minnesota," in Shaw, Clifford and McKay, Henry, *ibid.*, 431.

31. Studies dealing with the ecology of crime are legion. A study worth noting because of its detailed statistical approach is Lander, Bernard, *Towards an Understanding of Juvenile Delinquency*, Columbia University Press, New York, 1954. Using factor analysis Lander concluded that delinquency was related to anomie. Many conventionally offered relationships he argued were statistically questionable.

32. See Glueck, Sheldon and Eleanor, *Unraveling Juvenile Delinquency*, The Commonwealth Fund, New York, 1950, 5.

33. See Shaw, Clifford, *The Jack-Roller: A Delinquent Boy's Own Story*, University of Chicago Press, Chicago, 1930. See also, Shaw, Clifford R., and Moore, Maurice E., *The Natural History of a Delinquent Career*, University of Chicago Press, 1931.

34. Cohen, Albert, *Delinquent Boys: The Culture of the Gang*, The Free Press, Glencoe, Illinois, 1955.

35. Cohen, Albert, *ibid.*, 24-32.

36. *Ibid.*, 135.

37. Redl, Fritz, "The Psychology of Gang Formation and The Treatment of Juvenile Delinquents," *The Psychoanalytic Study of the Child*, I, 1945, 371.

38. Clinard, Marshall, "Criminological Research" in Merton, Robert, et al., *Sociology Today*, Basic Books, Inc., New York, 1959, 515.

39. *Ibid.*

40. Reckless, Walter C., Dinitz, Simon, and Murray, Ellen, "The 'Good Boy' in a High Delinquency Area," *The Journal of Criminal Law, Criminology and Police Science*, XXXXVIII, 1, May-June, 1957, 18-25. See also, Reckless, Walter C., Dinitz, Simon, and Kay, Barbara, "The Self Component in Potential Delinquency and Potential Non-Delinquency," *American Sociological Review*, XXII, 5, October, 1957, 566-570.

41. Reckless, Walter, Dinitz, Simon, and Murray, Ellen, "Self Concept as an Insulator Against Delinquency," *American Sociological Review*, XXI, 6, December, 1956, 746.

42. Marshall Clinard also finds the self-concept useful in analysis. See Clinard, Marshall, "The Process of Urbanization and Criminal Behavior," *American Journal of Sociology*, XLVIII, September, 1942, 202-13.

43. See *Uniform Crime Reports*, Federal Bureau of Investigation, U.S. Department of Justice, 1958, 14-15.

44. *Ibid.*, 23. In 1958 area population totals were as follows: Standard Metropolitan—105,735,561; Other Cities—25,489,735; Rural—42,035,033.

45. *Ibid.*

46. Computed from Table 3—Index of Crime, United States, 1958, *Uniform Crime Reports*, 1958, 63.

47. See, for example, *Uniform Crime Reports*, Federal Bureau of Investigation, U.S. Department of Justice, XXVI, 2, 1955, 97.

48. See Vold, George B., "Crime in City and Country Areas," *The Annals of the American Academy of Political and Social Science*, CCXVII, September, 1941, 38-45. See also Clinard, Marshall, "The Process of Urbanization," *op. cit.*

49. It should be recognized that the data showing rural and urban differences may be questionable. Different techniques of reporting, incompetence, deliberate distortion, tolerance levels of different communities, and the like, probably confound the accuracy of the data.

50. See Reckless, Walter C., *The Crime Problem*, Appleton-Century-Crofts, Inc., New York, 1955, 59-60. See also, Henry, Andrew F., and Short, James F., *Suicide and Homicide*, The Free Press, Glencoe, 1954, Chapter VI.

51. Clinard, Marshall, "Rural Criminal Offenders," *American Journal of Sociology*, L, July, 1944, 38-45.

52. Clinard, Marshall, "The Process of Urbanization," *op. cit.*

53. Lentz, William P., "Rural Urban Differentials and Juvenile Delinquency," *The Journal of Criminal Law, Criminology, and Police Science*, XXXXVII, 3, September-October, 1956, 331-339. See also, Lagey, Joseph C., "The Ecology of the Small City and the Rural Hinterland, *Rural Sociology*, XXII, 3, September, 1957, 230-234.

54. See Glaser, Daniel, "Criminality Theories and Behavioral Images," *American Journal of Sociology*, LXI, 5, March, 1956, 433-44.

55. See Clinard, Marshall, "Criminological Research," *op. cit.*, 517-518.

IDEOLOGICAL ASPECTS OF CRIME

Robert M. Frumkin
State University of New York (Oswego)

INTRODUCTION

1. *Definition of Ideology.* For the purpose of this chapter, modification of Bierstedt's definition of ideology will be used. Bierstedt defined an ideology as an idea supported by a norm.[1] He stressed the fact that ideologies as such are ideas which individuals are obliged to believe if they are to remain in good standing in particular social groups. Ideologies are then sacred ideas toward which there is little tolerance of skepticism. Sociologically, according to this definition, an ideology is a part of the ideal culture, the culture its members *think* they have. Bierstedt's definition of ideology is thus a definition of an *ideal* ideology. In order to understand crime, however, we must take into account the real culture, and the *real* ideologies which govern criminal behavior. I would, therefore, like to redefine *ideology as* an *idea supported by a norm which may or may not be associated with real behavior.* A real ideology is then an idea supported by a norm and is associated with real behavior. Real ideologies are consequently distinguishable from ideal ideologies which generally are not closely associated with real behavior. As ideas, real ideologies are sacred generally in a covert way. That is, skepticism concerning them is tolerated in membership groups but not in reference groups.[2] Concerning athletics in this country, for example, there is an ideal ideology which calls for "good sportsmanship."[3] In public, in their non-athletic membership group (American society), the athletes and their coach profess

193

belief in the ideal ideology and skepticism or complete rejection of the real ideology ("poor sportsmanship"). In the dressing room, in their reference group (the team), the athletes and their coach stress winning (or sometimes losing) at all costs. The real ideology is "poor sportsmanship" and, if anything, competitive athletics supports this ideology. Following in the wake of this real ideology, as any athlete finds out sooner or later, is the fixing of athletic contests, hiring professional athletes for "non-professional" sports, brutally injuring star athletes on opposing teams, and plethora of other real behaviors supported by this real ideology.

2. *Definition of Crime.* Since we are concerned with the sociology of crime and not simply crime in the legalistic sense, crime is here defined as conduct which society at any given time considers sufficiently dangerous to its welfare to be deemed punishable by criminal, civil, or mosotic laws.[4] In terms of Horton and Leslie's classification of criminals, such a definition would include the crimes of the following types of criminals: legalistic, moralistic, psychopathic, institutional, situational, habitual, and professional.[5]

MAMMONISM AND CHRISTIANISM

An ideology in American culture is Christianism. In Christianism there is a low valuation of wealth and property which are regarded as hindrances to the religious life; an emphasis on frugality and simplicity in living; stress on mutual aid, sharing, communalism; devaluation of competition; emphasis on service without ulterior motives; and brotherhood.[6] If this were a real ideology in American culture, most of the behavior which is criminal, in the way we have defined criminal, would be anachronistic and antithetical. Criminal behavior in our society indicates without a doubt that Christianism is an ideal ideology.

According to the Federal Bureau of Investigation, during 1957, someone was criminally assaulted or killed every five minutes; a larceny was committed every 30 seconds; and almost 480 million dollars worth of property was stolen.[7] These F.B.I. reports referred only to *known* crimes.

There is a real ideology that supports these known crimes as well as the unknown crimes and tolerated "white-collar" crimes. Most clergymen and most social and behavioral scientists will admit that, perhaps, the most characteristic real ideology in America is Mammonism, the idea that wealth and possessions are the measure of the worth of a person and should be obtained by the most expedient means available.[8] The Horatio Alger legend supports Mammonism.[9] The historic tradition of capitalism supported by the Protestant ethic of Calvinism,[10] and the frontier tradition support Mammonism. Our mass media of communication certainly support it. American advertising and motivation research are based on it.[11] George Kelly's Pulitzer Prize winning play *Craig's Wife* (1925) depicted the effect of this real ideology on family life. During the recent investigations of television quiz shows, Charles Van Doren, a young college professor and the son of a famous scholar, admitted "winning" $129,000 and a $50,000-a-year NBC job as a bonus for being a party to a fraudulent series of *Twenty One* television quiz programs.[12] Both a large number of Van Doren's T.V. audience and students supported him in his criminal behavior. They thought NBC should not have fired him or Columbia University "accept his resignation." Numerous job offers have now been flooding into him, including a lucrative Hollywood motion picture contract for Van Doren to be a leading man. Van Doren has been rewarded, implicitly been praised, rather than punished for his deeds—proof that the real ideology leads to success in our society.

Many contemporary cynics often suggest that if Christ, by some miracle, were to appear in on one of our cities preaching Christianism that he would be probably thrown in jail for vagrancy and suspected of supporting Communist subversion.

For the Mammonist everyone has his price. And, as Fromm put it, man himself becomes a commodity.[13] With such a real ideology prevalent in our society it is a wonder not that there is so much crime but that there is so little. Embezzlement, fraud, forgery, counterfeiting, white-collar crimes, and many other crimes are supported by the ideology of Mammonism.[14] Mammonism mainly supports the behavior of the institutional, habitual, and professional types of criminals.

HEDONISM AND ASCETICISM

Consistent with Christianism as an ideology is the ideology of Asceticism, the idea that rigorous discipline of the self, self-denial, the avoidance of earthly pleasures help one to reach a high state of spirituality, to live and work for some higher ideal. If this were a real ideology, the billions spent on recreation in America would not be necessary. If Asceticism were a real ideology, our nation would not spend almost twice as many billions of dollars on alcoholic beverages as on education. Asceticism is obviously an ideal ideology in America.

In America, Hedonism is a real ideology.[15] Pleasure is defined as a chief good to be pursued by everyone. Happiness is defined as the amount of pleasure one is getting and has gotten out of life. Gambling, drinking, sensualism of various kinds are condoned as necessary for happiness. Some parents even excuse their son's vandalism on this basis, saying, for example: "Well, boys must have fun. Boys must be boys." *The Three Stooges* and the cartoon series *Tom and Jerry,* both strongly suggest, via motion pictures, that Americans get much pleasure in viewing aggressive and destructive acts. It is a sad but nevertheless true fact that college hazing on many campuses is justified as pleasure fraternities and sororities cannot be denied in examining prospective members or pledgees. Every year tragic deaths or "accidents" occur on American college campuses because the fraternities and sororities must have their fun. And few would deny an American's right to drive cars at death defying speeds for the pleasure it gives, in spite of the needless slaughter on our highways. What is significant about American Hedonism, however, is that it centers on Philistine and barbaric values. It is an easy step from these values to the criminal behavior of the moralistic, certain psychopathic and situational, and many professional

196

criminals. American Hedonism, like American Mammonism, supports many kinds of criminal behavior.

MOLLYCODDLISM AND INDIVIDUALISM

An almost sacrosanct ideology in American culture is Individualism[16] the idea that each individual in our society is so sturdy and hardy as to be able and willing to take the responsibility for shaping his own destiny. During the frontier days this might have been a real ideology but today it is an ideal ideology, a myth, as are Christianism and Asceticism.

Mollycoddlism, the idea that the individual is too fragile and too weak to endure hardships, must be continually pampered, coddled, reassured of his worth, is not responsible for his own acts, is surely an American real ideology of relevance to criminal behavior. We praise Individualism but we act and support Mollycoddlism. If we want Americans to be fairly autonomous, responsible, mature individuals, we cannot create them through Mollycoddlistic methods. We must be willing to be honest and critical about behavior which we regard as criminal and detrimental to our way of life. We must try to understand but not avoid letting the criminal know his behavior is not what we expect of him. We must reward those whose behavior is of a positive, non-criminal nature. We must not wink at criminal behavior and hope for improvement. We must try to get at the causes of such behavior but not fail to indicate that this behavior is undesirable, wrong, etc., and that a different kind of behavior is expected and desirable.[17] A parent who ignores his child's delinquent behavior as "growing pains" and who fails to indicate that such behavior is undesirable for fear of hurting the child's feelings helps to prepare the child for criminal behavior in adulthood. A person in a democratic society must learn to take the responsibility for most of his acts. If we must depend on force, on fear, on intimidation, on the threat of the withdrawal of love, etc., to insure responsible behavior, we must then have a society which is devoid of humanity, a society full of zombis. The essence of man, as compared to non-man, is the fact that man can, with reason, help shape his own destiny. Our schools and our colleges, and our prisons have much in common. Their alleged purpose is to make individuals mature and responsible citizens. However, the environment provided is one in which responsibility is *not* delegated to the student or the prisoner but rather to the teachers, prison guards, and administrators. Our schools of higher education are full of Mollycoddlistic practices which prevent maturity rather than foster it—for example, requiring daily attendance records, curfews, proctoring examinations, chaperoning of dances, etc. The danger of Mollycoddlism is that it conceives of man as too fragile to face reality and so prevents him from facing reality. There can be no democracy where the average individual in a society cannot face reality. Criminal behavior of almost all types seems to stem, in part, from the real ideology of Mollycoddlism. Today more than ever, we need a real ideology of responsible Individualism, of the courage to face reality.[18]

NEPOTISM AND OBJECTIVISM

In the early history of our country, Jefferson promoted the ideology of Objectivism, the idea that a free, democratic society must be based on virtue and talents and not wealth and birth, that such a society must have all its members educated to the limits of their abilities, regardless of their ascribed statuses, and must likewise be given positions on the basis of their achievements, regardless of their ascribed statuses.[19] Thus stated Jefferson, referring to a society based on Objectivism, "The natural aristocracy I consider the most precious gift of nature, for the instruction, the trusts, and government of society." [20] While Jefferson's ideology of Objectivism has become to some extent a real ideology in our society, for the most part, it remains more of an ideal ideology. A typical example of the lack of Objectivism in our society is the recent case of a well qualified scholar who, interviewed for a position at one of the nation's leading "liberal" arts colleges, was told that "We would have hired you if you were not a Jew, but we are not permitted to have Jews, Catholics, or any non-Protestants on our faculty."

There is then in America a real ideology of Nepotism, the idea that favoritism must be granted to relatives, friends, persons of particular religious, racial, ethnic, social class background, etc., without due regard for merit, whether they are qualified or not. Yet it is a basic belief in a democratic society, as we profess to be, that any qualified person can reach the highest positions regardless of his, as Jefferson put it, "artificial" background characteristics, i.e., social class position, religion, race, etc. The myth persists, for example, that anyone who is objectively qualified might become president of the U.S. It is Merton's contention that much of America's criminal and delinquent behavior is a result of this "contradiction between legitimized cultural aspirations and socially restricted opportunities." [21] He goes on to say that "Al Capone represents the triumph of amoral intelligence over morally prescribed 'failure', when the channels of vertical mobility are closed or narrowed *in a society which places a high premium on economic affluence and social ascent for all its members.*" [22] In effect, Merton suggests that anomie, sociologically speaking, in American society, is a condition in which persons are conditioned to be treated in terms of Objectivism but are in reality treated in terms of Nepotism. More specifically, states Merton, "Anomie is then conceived as a breakdown in the cultural structure, occurring particularly when there is an acute disjunction between cultural norms and goals and the socially structured capacities of members of the group to act in accord with them. In this conception, cultural values may help to produce behavior which is at odds with the mandates of the values themselves." [23] Since there is a considerable degree of frustration, due to the contradiction between Objectivism and Nepotism, and since frustration often leads to aggression and nonrational or irrational behavior, Merton also suggests that non-utilitarian destructiveness, negativism, and juvenile vandalism are some of the consequences of anomie.[24]

The Beat Generation. A discussion of the Beat Generation is included here because it is believed that this movement was created by the anomie which results from a great contradiction between Objectivism and Nepotism in an allegedly democratically oriented society.

There have been many recent commentators on "the Beat Generation" (a phrase coined by Jack Kerouac, one of the leading Beatniks). Most of these commentators, in fact, almost all, have been biased against the Beatniks.[25] Social scientists, however, can provide a more objective interpretation of this movement.

When criminal behavior is found among them, it is not widespread or as great as the popular mass media of communication would suggest. Most of their criminals have been of the "moralistic" type—specifically, narcotics and homosexuals. Yet, as recently pointed out, marihuana, which is not usually considered by investigators in the United States as a real form of narcotic addiction, is the most common form of narcotic used by the Beatniks, probably because they cannot afford the more expensive narcotics. Some experts say it is easier to quit smoking marihuana "reefers" than to quit smoking ordinary cigarettes. The predominant aim in its use seems to be the euphoria it produces. There seems also to be little homosexuality among the Beatniks or as much deviant sexual behavior as is popularly believed.[26] The only other criminal behavior occurring in the group to any extent is also of a moralistic nature, namely, that of exhibitionism (e.g., stripping to the nude at public gatherings) and the extensive, uninhibited use of obscenity in speech and writing. The Beatniks then tend to be "moralistic" criminals, according to the Horton and Leslie classification cited earlier.

I think an investigation of the backgrounds of the leading Beatniks, as well as those of the ordinary followers, provides significant clues as to the meaning of the movement. Almost invariably the Beatniks have the backgrounds of pariahs. That is, they tend to come from minority groups and social class backgrounds which prevent them from vertical mobility and the pursuit of the American Dream of wealth, success, etc. The overwhelming majority of Beatniks come from Catholic, Jewish, low socio-economic class families, and from such disprivileged ethnic groups as the Italians. It is estimated that 10 per cent of their number is Negro. At any rate, they represent groups who have been victims of Nepotism as far as vertical mobility is concerned. For that reason, I feel that their *extreme* rejection of the American high standard of living is a "sweet lemon" type rationalization, in some ways even regression. In fact some Beatniks specifically mention their desire to return to the womb. For supposedly in the womb, there is the greatest kind of euphoria; in their argot, the greatest "kick."

In a study which will be published in the near future by Dr. Francis J. Rigney, a San Francisco psychiatrist, it is estimated that about 60 per cent of the Beatniks studied were mentally ill. When reading Beatnik novels and poetry that is the first impression many persons get: the Beatniks are mentally ill, they are sick, and not simply social and cultural deviants. Like many of the mentally ill they find contentment in "catatonic" passivity, or in a primitive expression of their emotions. Far from being inarticulate, as their critics maintain, the Beatniks are eloquent in expressing the sickness and insanity of our times, both in their novels and poetry and in the style of life they lead. Beatnikism, it is maintained, is like a prominent boil on the body which is a symptom of infection not the cause of it.[27] Like 19th century Russian nihilism,[28] it will pass when the conditions producing it pass. Instead of condemning the Beatniks, we should try to understand them as a symptom of American sociopathy.[29]

MISANTHROPISM AND ALTRUISM

Consistent with the ideology of Christianism is the ideology of Altruism, the idea that we should work and devote our lives to the betterment of all persons regardless of their station in life, that we should lead unselfish lives.[30] In our society it is apparent that Altruism is an ideal ideology, since far more lip service is paid to Altruism than to altruistic behavior.

It would be more accurate to state that Misanthropism, the idea that man should be hated, disliked, and exploited because he is basically egocentric and egoistic, is a real ideology in American society and lends support to certain types of criminal behavior. The sadistic and masochistic nature of many popular forms of recreation provides us with the meaning of the real nature of this ideology. Thus boxing and football are extremely popular spectator sports in the U.S. The bloodier the battle, the more "enjoyment" both participants and spectators seem to get out of such sports. Likewise our mass media of communication—T.V., radio, movies, comics, etc.—seem to have an overabundance of misanthropic themes.[31] Even Alfred Hitchcock's ever popular and sometimes sophisticated mysteries are loaded with a sardonic and cold-blooded attitude toward human life. As Barron put it: "American culture is permeated with violence in personal relations." [32] While professional criminals take an adverse view toward unnecessary violence, the general attitude is one of Hitchcockian misanthropy.

NATIVISM AND HUMANISM

A basic ideology associated with democratically oriented societies is that of Humanism, the idea that the good life may be achieved through science, reason, through cooperative efforts of mankind living in brotherhood.[33] Objectivism and Altruism are ideologies related to Humanism. In modern America with its real ideologies of Mammonism, Hedonism, Nepotism, and Misanthropism, it is evident that Humanism is, unfortunately, an ideal ideology.

American society strongly supports a real ideology of Nativism, the idea that the good life is achieved through the patriot-warrior, through preserving sovereignty at all costs, won by the strong over the weak in the struggle for existence. Nativism supports the philosophy of Spartanism—militancy, obedience, ethnocentrism. Nativism also supports the ideologies of Nepotism and Misanthropism. While Humanism conceives of persons as ends, Nativism conceives of persons as instruments, as tools. It is essentially the thesis of Merton that Nepotism associated with Nativism is responsible for the rise of such gangsters as Al Capone. Nativism helps create a state of anomie in a heterogeneous, complex society as our own. Since Nativism attracts authoritarian personalities it can lead to Fascistic and militant tendencies which make brotherhood within our nation and with other nations very unlikely.[34] The Ku Klux Klan, a nativist organization, engages in all kinds of criminal behavior from simple vandalism to outright murder.[35] Nativism also finds a place in intergroup conflict involving criminal behavior, that is, interracial, interfaith, and interethnic gang fights and the like. While we ordinarily do not think of Nativism except in political terms, extreme orthodox religious groups often manifest a non-violent Nativism in which quasi-criminal behavior is used to keep various opposing groups in check.[36] Nativism thus supports various types of behavior which is sociologically and legally criminal behavior.

COMPETITIVISM AND COOPERATIVISM

Closely allied with the ideology of Christianism, Altruism, and Humanism is the ideology of Cooperativism, the idea that the good life might best be achieved through cooperative efforts of people working together for the benefit of all.[37] In America with its real ideologies of Mammonism, Hedonism, Nepotism, and Nativism, Cooperativism is an ideal ideology.

The sacred real ideology of America is Competitivism, the idea that the good life can be achieved only through people striving against each other. Mammonism and Nativism have made a virtue of the competitive man. As one of the mainsprings of American life, it supports much criminal behavior in our society, for its defines men not as brothers but as competitors, enemies; other people are barriers to one's personal success.[38]

ANTI-INTELLECTUALISM AND INTELLECTUALISM

It is said that with the arrival of Russia's technological advances in missile development that a new respect for the intellectual has been kindled. There seems to be, however, relatively little evidence for such optimism.[39] Intellectualism, the idea that the good life can be brought about through man's love of ideas and reason, through man's use and trust in reason and science is predominantly an ideal ideology.

More characteristic of American culture is Anti-Intellectualism, the idea that both science and reason are not as trustworthy guides to the solution of man's problems as are intuition, common sense, superstition, adherence to sacred, supernatural dogma, or habitual ways of doing things.[40] People do not trust the intellectual because he approaches life with a critical rather than a submissive attitude. If the essence of anomie is the utter confusion of ends and means, of a contradiction in cultural goals and social structural routes to such goals, social disorganization, etc., it is likely that the tradition of Anti-Intellectualism helped to make such anomie possible. The critical attitude embodied in Intellectualism is the keystone of a democratic society.

Continual examination of the status quo through reason and science makes democratic progress possible. Anti-Intellectualism, because it takes a timid, childish attitude toward the status quo (except where the status quo supports Mammonism, Nepotism, etc.) actually produces anomie and, therefore, leads to various types of criminal behavior. Could there be many legalistic, moralistic, institutional, habitual, and professional criminals if there were not a great amount of Anti-Intellectualism in this country? The essence of Intellectualism is the humanistic adjustment of means to ends through the exercise of reason and science. Can there be a very sick or delinquent society in which there is a real ideology of Intellectualism? It is alleged that much criminal behavior in American society is dependent on a strong and vigorous real ideology of Anti-Intellectualism.

IDEOLOGIES, CRIME AND ANOMIE

According to Merton, anomie occurs "particularly when there is an acute disjunction between cultural norms and goals and the socially structured capacities of members of the group to act in accord with them." [41] Frank's idea of society as the patient and Bain's concept of sociopathy are similar to the idea of anomie because they too point to the malfunctioning of society as the source of various social problems, criminal behavior among such problems.[42]

IDEOLOGIES AND COMMUNIST SUBVERSION

The danger which Communism presents to America is, for the most part, an imaginary one as long as America remains prosperous and free. Shannon and others have shown that Communism in America had its greatest appeal during the great depression and during the period when many minority groups, immigrant and native, began actively seeking a larger share of the good things America had to offer. When the depression ended and there had been a continual advancement in the status of America's minorities Communism declined. Today the American Communist Party is quite impotent.[43]

Studies of American ex-Communists seem to agree that Communists had many characteristics in common. They tended to be young people of average or better intelligence, of average or better than average education, and extremly unhappy with the status quo.[44] Many seemed to be following what Johnson has called the "I.F.D. Pattern" (where I stands for idealism, F for frustration, and D for demoralization). Maladjusted people often have ideals which are too high to be achieved, leading them consequently to frustration and demoralization.[45] Such persons are attracted to Communism because it seems to answer one of their basic needs—the need to see some of their ideals become realities. Since our society produces a good number of such unhappy people, some are bound to be attracted to the panacean ideology of Communism. During times of depression and manifest anti-democratic trends, persons from minority groups are particularly vulnerable to the appeals of Communism.

Studies of adolescents and young adults sympathetic to and members of the American Communist Party during the latter part of and the early post World War II years seem to indicate that, almost invariably, they were of the pariah type—maladjusted persons who were members of minority groups, physically and emotionally unattractive persons, and various types of deviants.[46]

It should be pointed out that these pariah types have many alternatives of action and that becoming Communists is only one of them. Since the American Communist Party, due to its impotence, is no longer attractive, except for, perhaps, the most distraught and frustrated pariahs, other movements have gained the allegiance of today's pariahs. Thus, for example, Beatniks have much in common with many ex-Communists, in terms of social background and other characteristics. Certainly the I.F.D. Pattern seems to be an etiological factor in many pariahs becoming Beatniks.

Two real ideologies seem to be of special relevance to the viability of American Communism, namely, Nepotism and Anti-Intellectualism. Nepotism, as Jefferson, among others, has pointed out is subversive to the achievement of a democratic society. Worst of all it breeds the kind of demoralization which recruiters for Communism can easily take advantage of.

One particular point seems well worth emphasizing, in this connection, about the Essex County study mentioned previously. The Communist members and sympathizers were manifestly deficient in behavioral scientific knowledge. They were at most "half-baked" intellectuals, many were pseudo-intellectuals. A mature intellectual could not be easily drawn into a movement in which some of the basic principles about human nature and society, and, more important, the basic principles governing the dynamics of American democracy were ignored, or rejected *without* valid evidence. There was abysmal ignorance among them of the Bill of Rights and American civil liberties. Recent studies have indicated that even among today's college students such ignorance is all too common.[47] If Intellectualism was a real rather than ideal ideology in America, instead of Anti-Intellectualism, such ignorance could not prevail, nor could the ideology of Communism survive the critical analysis of the scrutinizing intellectuals.

While Nepotism and Anti-Intellectualism are still with us as real ideologies, in the last decade new life has been given to Objectivism and Intellectualism. The more Objectivism and Intellectualism become dominant real ideologies the less need we fear Communism and inevitable subversion of democracy which it brings with it.[48]

SUMMARY AND CONCLUSIONS

It is the thesis of this chapter that there exist in American society real ideologies which support the kinds of behavior which we designate legally and sociologically as criminal behavior. However, there are ideal ideologies in American society which, if changed into real ideologies, could help eliminate or rather prevent most existing forms of criminal behavior. This could be done if we institutionalized these ideal ideologies, that is, provided the socially approved means by which these ideologies might be realized and rewarded, might become a part of our real culture.

An ideology is an idea supported by a norm. There are *ideal* ideologies which are a part of the ideal culture and which have little relation to real behavior. There are *real* ideologies which are a part of the real culture, and which are very closely related to real behavior.

Crime was here defined as conduct which society at any given time considers sufficiently dangerous to its welfare to be deemed punishable by criminal, civil, or mosotic laws.

It is suggested that there are real ideologies which support criminal behavior, as defined above, in our society. An attempt was made to show the relationship of some of the more important American real ideologies to criminal behavior in America:

Mammonism, Hedonism, Mollycoddlism, Nepotism, Misanthropism, Nativism, Competitivism, and Anti-Intellectualism. There were also presented antithetical ideal ideologies which, if made real, could theoretically prevent and reduce much criminal behavior in our society. These ideal ideologies were: Christianism, Asceticism, Individualism, Objectivism, Altruism, Humanism, Cooperativism, and Intellectualism.

Anomie is in large part the result of our professing ideal ideologies but supporting antithetical real ideologies by not providing the means, the institutional avenues, so to speak, by which the goals upheld by ideal ideologies might be reached. Put in simple terms, a democratically oriented society demands that some of the ideal ideologies mentioned here must become real ideologies if the democratic goals it hopes to achieve are to be more than daydreams. If, as Jefferson suggested, the democratic orientation becomes a sham, a sickening mockery of a society, then the punishment for this, among other things, is criminal behavior and other symptoms of sociopathy which make us vulnerable candidates for an authoritarian state.[49] The Beat Generation is a symptom of American hypocrisy. The Beatnik looks at other Americans and says to himself: I can't stand those "phonies" and I can't stand myself. I hate them; I hate myself. I hate this whole sick society that made me what I must be. I want to die. I want to be reborn in a sane society, a society in which I need not be ashamed to call myself a human being.[50]

SELECTED BIBLIOGRAPHY

Adorno, T. W., Frenkel-Brunswik, E., et al, *The Authoritarian Personality*, Harper, New York, 1950. An extensive study in which the ideologies of Nativism, Nepotism, Anti-Intellectualism, and Misanthropism were examined in relation to personality and prejudice.

Almond, Gabriel A., et al, *The Appeals of Communism*,

Princeton University Press, Princeton, N. J., 1954. A study of 221 former Communists to see what attracted them to Communism, and why they eventually left it.

Bain, Read, "The Concept of Sociopathy," *Sociology and Social Research*, XXXVIII, September-October, 1953, 3-6. Suggests that a serious symptom of a malfunctioning society is the occurrence of ideological inconsistencies.

Barron, Milton L., "The Delinquent: Society or the Juvenile?", *Nation*, CLXXVIII, June 5, 1954, 482-484. Indicates that certain ideologies such as Mammonism, Misanthropism, and Hedonism are responsible for much juvenile delinquency—the delinquent society is full of delinquent ideologies.

Ernst, Morris L., and Loth, David, *Report on the American Communist*, Henry Holt and Company, New York, 1952. A description of the kinds of people who become Communists, based on interviews with 300 ex-Communists.

Feldman, Gene, and Gartenberg, Max (editors), *The Beat Generation and the Angry Young Men*, Citadel Press, New York, 1958. Perhaps the best collection of Beat Generation literature available. Includes the works of such leading Beatniks as Anatole Broyard, R. V. Cassill, George Mandel, Clellon Holmes, Jack Kerouac, "William Lee" (pseudonym of William Burroughs), Carl Solomon, and Allen Ginsberg. The poem entitled "Howl" by Ginsberg received national publicity when San Francisco authorities banned its sale on the grounds that the work was "lewd and obscene." After an intense court battle, the poem was declared to be not obscene. This book is a must for anyone who hopes to gain some understanding of the Beat Generation.

Frank, Lawrence K., "Society as the Patient," *American Journal of Sociology*, XLII, November, 1936, 335-345. Presents the thesis that a sick society can only be healthy if its ideologies are healthy and supported by its social institutions.

Fromm, Erich, *Escape From Freedom*, Farrar and Rinehart, New York, 1941. One of the brilliant works on the ideology of Nativism.

Fromm, Erich, *Man For Himself*, Rinehart, New York, 1947. A classic on the ideology of Humanism.

Fromm, Erich, *The Sane Society*, Rinehart, New York, 1955. An attempt to show that many American real ideologists have given us an almost insane society. Suggests that a society with

Humanism, Individualism, Cooperativism, Altruism, and Intellectualism as real ideologies could be a sane society.

Gorer, Geoffrey, *The American People*, W. W. Norton, New York, 1948. A trenchant examination of some American ideologies by an insightful British anthropologist.

Hubben, William, *Four Prophets of Our Destiny*, Macmillan, New York, 1952. Four giant "Beatniks" of the past, Kierkegaard, Dostoevsky, Nietzsche, and Kafka, are re-examined in the light of the meaning their diagnosis of man and society yesterday have for man today.

Iversen, Robert W., *The Communists and the Schools*, Harcourt, Brace and Company, New York, 1959. Suggests that the best weapon against Communism in America is the development of a vigorous democratic Intellectualism. Anti-Intellectualism, on the other hand, allows non-democratic ideologies to spread like cancer.

Kropotkin, Peter, *Mutual Aid,* Extending Horizons Press, Boston, 1955. The significance of the ideology of Cooperativism is the subject of this classic.

Lindner, Robert, *Prescription for Rebellion*, Rinehart, New York, 1952. A devastating attack on American Nativism. Presents the thesis that adjustment to a maladjusted society is not only stupid but dangerous.

Merton, Robert K., *Social Theory and Social Structure* (revised edition), Free Press, Glencoe, Illinois, 1957, 121-194. The most lucid account of anomie and its relation to deviant behavior that might be found in sociological literature.

O'Neil, Paul, "The Only Rebellion Around," *Life*, November 30, 1959, 114 ff. This is one of the few fairly objective accounts of the Beat Generation. Includes some interesting photographs of the leading Beatniks and their style of life.

Packard, Vance, *The Hidden Persuaders*, Pocket Books, New York, 1958. Mammonism and Hedonism are the ideologies which, it is shown, are cultivated by advertising agencies in order to facilitate white collar crime in America. A very timely book in the light of the most recent investigations of white collar crime in meat markets, gas stations, drug industry, etc.

Shannon, David A., *The Decline of American Communism*, Harcourt, Brace and Company, New York, 1959. Attributes the decline of American Communism not so much to increasing

Intellectualism and Objectivism as to an increase in the American standard of living and increasing hostility between the U.S.A. and the U.S.S.R.

Sutherland, Edwin H., *White Collar Crime*, Dryden Press, New York, 1949. A classic on the type of criminal behavior sanctioned by the real ideologies of Mammonism, Hedonism, Mollycoddlism, Misanthropism, and Competitivism.

Sorokin, Pitirim, A., *Altruistic Love*, Beacon Press, Boston, 1950. One of the few studies of real ideologies of Christianism, Asceticism, Altruism, Humanism, and Cooperativism.

Veblen, Thorstein, *The Theory of the Leisure Class*, Macmillan, New York, 1899. A classic on American Mammonism and Hedonism.

Wagner, Geoffrey, *Parade of Pleasure*, Library Publishers, New York, 1955. An analysis and description of the way in which our popular mass media of communication aid in the inculcation of the real ideologies of Mammonism, Hedonism, and Misanthropism.

Warner, W. Lloyd, *American Life: Dream or Reality*, University of Chicago Press, Chicago, 1953. Some of the most significant real and ideal ideologies in America are subjected to social scientific scrutiny.

Weber, Max, *The Protestant Ethic and the Spirit of Capitalism* (translated by Talcott Parsons), Allen and Unwin, London, 1930. Suggests that Calvinism supports the real ideology of Mammonism as embodied in capitalism.

Wertham, Frederic, *Seduction of the Innocent*, Rinehart, New York, 1953. Provides convincing evidence that one of our mass media of communication, comic books, helps to inculcate a real ideology of Misanthropism in American children and, in so doing, establishes a beachhead for juvenile delinquency.

Wylie, Philip, *Generation of Vipers*, Rinehart, New York, 1955, Newly Annotated Edition. The American Library Association's choice as one of the major non-fiction works of this century, this book demolishes criminogenic ideologies, particularly Anti-Intellectualism, and makes a convincing case for the ideologies which can help prevent widespread criminal behavior.

Robert M. Frumkin as an undergraduate majored in the physical sciences at Upsala College and as a graduate majored in the behavioral sciences at the New School for Social Research and the Ohio State University. Previous professional and related work experience include service in the U.S. Navy Hospital Corps, teaching psychology and sociology at Hampton Institute and the University of Buffalo, research for the Ohio State Department of Mental Hygiene, psychiatric social work at the Buffalo State Hospital, and consultant work for the New York State Department of Health and the National League for Nursing. Currently assistant professor of social studies at the State University of New York (Oswego), research editor for the *Journal of Human Relations*, and abstracter for *Psychological Abstracts*. Author of *The Measurement of Marriage Adjustment, The Meaning of Sociology, Hospital Nursing: A Sociological Interpretation, The Patient as a Human Being*, and *The Nurse as a Human Being*. Has published articles in the following journals: *Alpha Kappa Deltan, Canadian Nurse, Educational Research Bulletin, Ethos, Jewish Teacher, Journal of Educational Research, Journal of Family Welfare, Journal of Human Relations, Journal of Negro Education, Marriage and Family Living, Nursing Outlook, Ohio Journal of Scince, Ohio State Medical Journal, Public Welfare Statistics, Rural Sociology, Sociology and Social Research,* etc. Contributed chapters on "Occupation and Major Mental Disorders" to A. M. Rose (editor), *Mental Health and Mental Disorder*, and on "Social Psychology" to J. S. Roucek (editor), *Contemporary Sociology*. Member of the following national honor societies: Alpha Kappa Delta (Sociology), Psi Chi (Psychology), and Kappa Delta Pi (Education). Biographic inclusion in *Who's Who in New York* and *Who's Who in the East*. Recipient of the John Ericsson Society of New York Fellowship in Science (1945-46).

NOTES

1. Bierstedt, Robert, *The Social Order*, McGraw-Hall, New York, 1957, 150.
2. Newcomb, Theodore M., *Social Psychology*, Dryden Press, New York, 1950, 225-227.
3. Tappan, Paul W., *Juvenile Delinquency*, McGraw-Hill, New York, 1949, 150.
4. Raab, Earl, and Selznick, Gertrude J., *Major Social Problems*, Row, Peterson, Evanston, Illinois, 1959, 137. Mosotic laws are laws which are informal, that is the mores.

5. Horton, Paul B., and Leslie, Gerald R., *The Sociology of Social Problems*, Appleton-Century-Crofts, New York, 1955, 103-112.

6. Dahlke, H. Otto, *Values and Culture in the Classroom*, Harper, New York, 1958, 63-64.

7. Federal Bureau of Investigation, *Uniform Crime Reports*, U.S. Government Printing Office, Washington, D. C., 1958.

8. See *inter alia*, Thorsten Veblen, *The Theory of the Leisure Class*, Macmillan, New York, 1899; Robert M. Frumkin, "Mammon, Shylock, and the New American Jews," *Ethos*, I, Spring, 1956, 13-14.

9. Warner, W. Lloyd, *American Life: Dream or Reality*, University of Chicago Press, Chicago, 1953.

10. Weber, Max, *The Protestant Ethic and the Spirit of Capitalism* (translated by Talcott Parsons), Allen and Unwin, London, 1930.

11. Packard, Vance, *The Hidden Persuaders*, Pocket Books, New York, 1958.

12. "Television," *Time*, November 16, 1959, 72 ff.

13. Fromm, Erich, *Man for Himself*, Rinehart, New York, 1947.

14. See *inter alia*, Edwin H. Sutherland, *White Collar Crime*, Dryden Press, New York, 1949; "Crime: The Cheaters," *Time*, November 30, 1959, 17-18.

15. See *inter alia*, Geoffrey Wagner, *Parade of Pleasure*, Library Publishers, New York, 1955; Vance Packard, *op. cit.*

16. Individualism, as used here, refers to *humanistic* and *not* rugged individualism. On humanistic individualism see Fromm's *Man For Himself*, *op. cit.*

17. It is pointed out by many criminologists that the "fix" is a prime example of American Mollycoddlism. See *inter alia*, Walter C. Reckless, *The Crime Problem*, Appleton-Century-Crofts, New York, 1950, 499.

18. For a devastating attack on Mollycoddlism see Philip Wylie, *Generation of Vipers*, Newly Annotated Edition, Rinehart, New York, 1955.

19. See Saul K. Padover (editor), *Thomas Jefferson on Democracy*, Appleton-Century-Crofts, New York, 1939, Chapter V; Dumas Malone (editor), *The Jeffersonian Heritage*, Beacon Press, Boston, 1953.

20. Padover, *op. cit.*

21. Merton, Robert K., *Social Theory and Social Structure* (revised edition), Free Press, Glencoe, Illinois, 1957, 178.

22. *Ibid.*, 146.

23. *Ibid.*, 162.

24. *Ibid.*, 178. See also the works of Robert Lindner, particularly his *Prescription for Rebellion*, Rinehart, New York, 1952.

25. There have been many biased, anti-Beatnik critics, and their works have often had the tone of intellectual snobbery. Among the most articulate writers in this anti-Beatnik class have been Brustein and Podhoretz. See Robert Brustein, "The Cult of Unthink," *Horizon*, I, September, 1958, 38-44, 134-135; Norman Podhoretz, "Where Is the Beat Generation Going?," *Esquire*, L, December, 1958, 147-150.

26. See Paul O'Neil, "The Only Rebellion Around," *Life*, November 30, 1959, 144 ff. O'Neil's article is one of the very few fairly objective accounts on the Beat Generation.

27. Frank's work suggests this hypothesis. See Lawrence K. Frank, "Society

as the Patient," *American Journal of Sociology*, XLII, November, 1936, 335-345.

28. Yarmolinsky, Avrahm, "Nihilism," in E. R. A. Seligman and Alvin Johnson (editors), *Encyclopaedia of the Social Sciences*, Macmillan, New York, 1933, XI, 377-379.

29. Bain, Read, "The Concept of Sociopathy," *Sociology and Social Research*, XXXVIII, September-October, 1953, 3-6.

30. Sorokin, Pitirim A., *Altruistic Love*, Beacon Press, Boston, 1950.

31. "Television," *Time*, October 26, 1959, 48 ff. See also, Frederic Wertham, *Seduction of the Innocent*, Rinehart, New York, 1953.

32. Barron, Milton, L., "The Delinquent: Society or the Juvenile?," *Nation*, June 5, 1954, 482-484.

33. See *inter alia*, Erich Fromm, *The Sane Society*, Rinehart, New York, 1955.

34. Adorno, T. W., Frenkel-Brunswik, E., et al, *The Authoritarian Personality*, Harper, New York, 1950; also, see Samuel H. Flowerman, "Portrait of the Authoritarian Man," The New York Times *Magazine*, April 23, 1950, 9, 28-31.

35. Lloyd, R. Grann, "The Historical Background of Super-Americanism as a Technique of Political Persuasion," *Negro Educational Review*, X, January, 1959, 17-31.

36. See *inter alia*, Paul Blanshard, *American Freedom and Catholic Power*, Beacon Press, Boston, 1953.

37. Kropotkin, Peter, *Mutual Aid*, Extending Horizons Press, Boston, 1955.

38. Ploscowe, Morris, "Crime in a Competitive Society," *Annals of the American Academy of Political and Social Sciences*, CCXVII, September, 1941, 105-111.

39. See Robert M. Frumkin and Miriam Z. Frumkin, "Education and Crime: A Study in Sociopathy," *Journal of Educational Research*, XLIX, April, 1956, 613-616; also, Robert M. Frumkin, "American Arete and Teacher Education," *Ohio Parent-Teacher*, XXXVII, January, 1959, 12-13.

40. On Anti-Intellectualism and attitudes toward science and scientists, see Robert M. Frumkin, "Science and the Jewish Ethos," *Ethos*, IV, Spring, 1959, 19-25.

41. Merton, *op. cit.*, 162.

42. See Frank, *op. cit.*, and Bain, *op. cit.*

43. Shannon, David A., *The Decline of American Communism*, Harcourt, Brace and Company, New York, 1959.

44. See *inter alia*, Morris L. Ernst and David Loth, *Report on the American Communist*, Henry Holt and Company, New York, 1952; and, Gabriel A. Almond, et al., *The Appeals of Communism*, Princeton University Press, Princeton, N. J., 1954.

45. Johnson, Wendell, *People in Quandaries*, Harper, New York, 1946.

46. Based on the writer's unpublished studies of the characteristics of Communist youth and young adults in Essex County, New Jersey, 1944-1948.

47. Mack, Raymond W., "Do We Believe in the Bill of Rights?," *Social Problems*, III, April, 1956, 264-269; also, Robert M. Frumkin, "Attitudes of American College Students toward Civil Liberties," *Il Politico*, forthcoming.

48. The tremendous progress of the Negro in American society is dramatic

214

proof for this assertion. Intellectualism is a potent force in the Negro's resistance to Communist infiltration. See *inter alia*, Joseph S. Roucek and Robert M. Frumkin, "The Relationship of Major Ideological Premises of Whites and Negroes as Manifested in Political and Social Policy Changes to the Present and Future Education of Negroes in the United States: A Social Scientific Analysis," *Negro Educational Review*, X, July-October, 1959, 141-157.

49. See Fromm's, *The Sane Society, op. cit.*

50. It is unfortunate that many stuffy and snobbish quasi-intellectuals have not taken an *objective* look at some of the leading Beatnik writers such as Kerouac and Ginsberg. Such biased critics as Brustein and Podhoretz, *op. cit.*, say that the Beatniks are inarticulate, that they do not communicate. Actually, objectively viewed, they are as articulate as the giant "Beatniks" of the past, Kierkegaard, Dostoevsky, Nietzsche, and Kafka (see in this connection the book by William Hubben, *Four Prophets of Our Destiny*, Macmillan, New York, 1952). The Beat Generation of today cries out in anguish about American anomie. Their recent attachment to Buddhism is a symbolic representation of their hope for reincarnation in a different, better world than we now have. In short, the Beatniks are a symptom of the sociopathic real ideologies that make us the sick society we are. In their own way, the Beatniks are the most articulate diagnosticians of our times.

JUVENILE DELINQUENCY AND
THE SCHOOL

I. Roger Yoshino
The University of Arizona

Well-intentioned leaders who set out to rehabilitate societal deviants in conflict with the law, and other protagonists who devote their efforts to bettering reformatories and penal institu‑‑ tions, could perhaps perform a greater service by emphasizing the preventive approach. Much law-violating behavior finds its roots in the social-psychological milieu in which the children grow up.

Considerable research has been done in an effort to determine the genesis and causes of criminal behavior. Studies show that the etiology of juvenile delinquency and adult crime is not attributable to a single source but has a multiplicity of variables. What significance does the school have as a factor in the control of juvenile delinquency, which all too often is the precursor of later crime?

By the time a child starts school, many of his attitudes and behavior patterns have already been conditioned by the family, the playgroup and the neighborhood environment. Incipient tendencies toward delinquency may well be established by the time a wayward youngster enrolls in school. Therefore, it is expecting a great deal of the schools to assume that they can overcome the negative influences of such primary forces. Moreover, even after the child is in school, teachers and administrators must contend with the continuously operating values of the home and gang which may conflict with educational objectives. In spite of such seemingly insurmountable obstacles, better schools may be the most positive influence in the lives of many children.

In support of this thesis, Robert McIver, director of the New York City Juvenile Evaluation Project, has stated that the school may be the only stable social institution which many of the children know. Where the families have been disorganized, and the churches stand still, the school is the one organization which can help the youngsters. The police and the courts are regarded as their enemy, and it is too late when the time for legal intervention has come.[1]

THE GENERAL ROLE OF THE SCHOOL

The school's general role with respect to juvenile delinquency has emerged inasmuch as it has been forced to assume a range of responsibilities and functions formerly carried on by other institutions. While the main function of the school is intellectual training and enculturation, it must also be concerned with the general problem of life adjustment, including the handling of behavioral problems. The educator's concern should be one of dealing with all its pupils in such a manner that delinquency will be minimized, and not likely result on the part of individual children.[2] Delinquent behavior encompasses all modes of conduct which deviate from the norms maintained by society and the schools. As such, deviation, or lack of conformity, runs the gamut along a continuum. Some of the norm-violating types of behavior are minor and infrequent; others are more serious offenses. Most children go to school and carry their problems, no matter how large or small. The competence with which the school can work with these youngsters will depend upon the nature and quality of relationship that characterizes its operation.[3] As one administrator has said: "What a school does is determined by what a school believes its function to be."[4]

Some of the more basic social-psychological forces which en-

217

hance crime are nurtured by the schools. Juvenile delinquents come from compulsory schools, where they supposedly have been imbued with law-abiding norms established by society and the educational institution. The fact that such indoctrination is often ineffective presents a challenge to the schools. For many maladjusted and potentially delinquent children, the teacher and the school situation often intensify frustrations generated by the parents. Often youngsters caught in these circumstances seek an outlet for their disappointments in truancy and delinquent behavior.[5]

Thus, along with the family, the gang, the church and the community, the school, as an atlantean member in the social structure, should subject itself to reexamination to see whether it is doing its part in the prevention of delinquency and latent adult crime.

The school, its administrators and its teachers are in a strategic position for dealing with the needs of the juvenile age population who engage in delinquent behavior. Since school is compulsory for all children, it has direct and continuous contact with practically all youngsters in the community, and it reaches the young at a crucial period of their growth. In comparison, with the exception of the family, most other social institutions do not exert as much control, and they are in contact with a smaller and more selected segment of the population. The juvenile age group spends more of its time in school than in any other place except the home, and in too many cases, unfortunately, more than in the home.

Opportunities for the detection of children who by defective nature or nurture show signs of potential delinquency are woven into the fabric of everyday functions of the school.[6] The observant teacher and school administrator should be able to perceive and understand the problems of the emotionally disturbed and socially maladjusted child. Many of the behavior problems may be judiciously dealt with in their early controllable stage if the school personnel could recognize the first symptoms of delinquency and if need be, contact outside professional help. William Kvaraceus, one of the foremost authorities in the area of Juvenile Delinquency and the School, tersely points out four factors which school personnel should keep in mind:[7]

- · Know your pupils
- · Seek expert help
- · Watch first symptoms
- · Keep objective

Ultimately, the school's major contribution in working with the youngsters who exhibit pre-delinquent and delinquent behavior will be most effective when the teacher's efforts are coordinated with those of the total community.

THE ROLE OF THE CLASSROOM TEACHER

Society cannot guarantee good parents or environment for every child, but it has the responsibility to provide competent teachers in every classroom. Almost every teacher faces the responsibility of dealing occasionally with children who are unruly and annoying, and who distract and create problems of discipline. Where the home environment is unsatisfactory, the teacher can help to meet the basic needs of all children for affection, for a feeling of belonging, for a sense of achievement, and for an opportunity for creative expression.[8] All too often the overworked teacher must take on the added responsibility, as the laws of many states acknowledge, of serving *in loco parentis* (in place of a parent).

The classroom teacher is in a good position to observe pre-delinquent[9] behavior, and to administer discipline with kindness and firmness. This is not to suggest that the classroom teacher should take on the role of the school guidance specialist, the psychiatrist, the probation officer or others qualified to work with the proto-delinquent.[10] A scientific way to cope with difficult discipline problems is to have a psychiatric clinic attached to the school with a psychiatrist and a staff of psychiatric social workers and clinicians to whom problems may be referred by

219

the teachers.[11] However, personnel and finance-wise, only a few of the larger and more progressive school systems can be so equipped; therefore, the greatest part of the responsibility rests with the classroom teachers in detecting the pre-delinquent early. It is important for the teacher to bear in mind that he is not doing the juvenile, the school or society a favor by resorting to such techniques as avoidance or overlooking a problem child. If the teacher has one such problem, he is apt to have two. It only takes one such case to cause more difficulty than a number of adults can handle adequately.[12]

Also, it should be recognized that there is much deviant behavior which should not be labeled "delinquent," and if the classroom teacher understands the youngster's problems, he can try to protect the child from becoming a delinquent. In the teacher's anxiety to control delinquent behavior, he may overlook the person behind the behavior. In the concern over what he does, the teacher may ignore why the youngster behaves as he does, what he is like, and how all this looks through his "colored glasses."[13] There is the danger of over-predicting the innocuous, perhaps mischievous act as delinquent behavior. Teachers frequently associate problem behavior with such aggressive tendencies as disobedience, obstinacy, boisterousness, the telling of falsehoods and looking for new experience. Teachers must be trained to recognize the real symptoms of delinquent behavior which on the surface may be misleading.

The behavior of pre-delinquents may be recognized as an expression of an inner conflict and troubled feelings. Teachers are among the first to recognize the danger in defiance of the laws and rules of conduct in school and in society. Unfortunately, in many instances, teachers crack down blindly on these youngsters in haste and alarm, trying by corporal punishment and superior strength to force them into better behavior. Unable to accept the type of punishment often administered the child tends to develop a greater indifference and contempt for his teacher and sometimes his classmates.

A teacher cannot be ambivalent in his attitudes, nor can he punish one youngster for something and then let another go for the same act. Youngsters must be taught to understand that the discipline is for his behavior and not because of himself. The discipline must be administered with understanding and kindness, but it still must be discipline. A combination of friendliness and firmness, with responsibility demanded of the juveniles should prove effective in the handling of most pre-delinquents.

While the school's personnel are dedicated to their work and are usually resourceful in their approach to juvenile problems, in some cases teachers may become guilty by dereliction of indirectly encouraging delinquent behavior. Even more disconcerting is that in many instances a teacher may aggravate a situation to the extent that frustration, rebellion, and ultimately delinquency result.[14] A brief case study may help to illustrate this point.

George B., age 15, was sent to the state reformatory last year. He is to remain there until he is 21. The chain of events which preceded this final adjudication illustrated how a teacher actually contributed to the delinquency of a minor.

The official case of George began when the Coach marched the boy into the vice-principal's office. George was a pest in the study hall the Coach supervised. He wouldn't sit quietly and took every clandestine opportunity to create a disturbance. The Coach described him in front of the other students as sneaky and a "rotten apple," in the study hall. The V.P. sent the boy back to the study hall after a stern reprimand. George promised to be good but he got into trouble frequently.

The Coach, in the teacher's lunchroom where nothing is sacred nor wholly true, described this new villain to some of his colleagues. It was not long before other teachers heretofore unaware of George's shortcomings began to find his behavior irritating. George's trouble had begun.

The V.P. knew George was average in all respects. He also knew that his behavior, although irritating, was not malicious. George's mother was consulted and it was found that he came from an adequate if economically restricted home.

As teachers put on pressure, he became more defiant. He began to be truant, running around with several other boys who had dropped from school because of failure, lack of interest or suspension. They had one thing in common—maladjustment to school. One day they all ran away, stealing a car in the process. In due time they were caught and placed on probation with the provision that they attend school regularly. It was near the end of the school year and the teachers were resentful of having these "trouble makers" forced upon them.

Next year, George returned to school. Physical Education was a required subject and the Coach taught the only period he could get into. Trouble began again. After repeated warnings, the V.P. suspended him.

Three weeks later, George and his gang, brandishing knives, tried to rob two ladies. The ladies' screams frightened the boys who ran into the arms of the law. They were all sent to the reformatory.

"I told you that boy was not good," said the Coach to the V.P. The Vice-Principal didn't reply. He just looked sadly around at the brick and mortar which held together the institution called school.[15]

Suffice it to point out that, in the above case, one can't help but wonder if the classroom teacher could not have helped the youngster with the pre-delinquent behavioral attitudes which he exhibited in the beginning.

To feel affronted or to take a youngster's misconduct personally will limit the teacher's effectiveness in the classroom, the school and in the community. When a juvenile fails to gain recognition and response through normal channels, he may resort to deviant behavior which may single him out from the rest. He begins to develop his own norms of behavior to overcome feelings of insecurity, deprivation and rejection. He seeks the association of those who are sympathetic to his situation and those who understand him. He gradually withdraws from a socially acceptable system of norms into a subculture where he can fulfill his basic needs and wishes.

It is the capable teacher who provides guidance and understanding for the youngster in need as well as for the general student body.

DETECTION OF THE POTENTIAL DELINQUENT

One of the major efforts of the school in general and of the teacher in particular should be to provide an educational milieu conducive to normal emotional and personality growth and to cope with a child's adjustment problems before they ripen into delinquency. By the time that the youngster assumes the status and role of a legal delinquent, deviant attitudes and behavior may be too firmly established for the ordinary school to deal with this juvenile successfully. Where treatment in a reform or correctional school is indicated, the public school, with its concern for the general student body, may not be able to do much for the delinquent.[16]

Preventive efforts at delinquency control may be more successful if the child who is vulnerable or exposed to the development of delinquency patterns can be identified early. Since the school receives the child relatively early and maintains a continuous contact with him for a prolonged period of time, it is in a good position for locating the potentially delinquent. A check list of eighteen factors, all perceptible within the school setting, has been compiled to estimate delinquency proneness. Since these factors are generally characteristic of delinquents when contrasted with nondelinquents, it is suggested that the school staff and especially the classroom teacher look for the following tell-tale signs:[17]

1. Generally shows dislike for school
2. Rebels against school routine
3. Verbalizes a disinterest in school progress
4. Fails in a number of subjects
5. Has repeated several grades
6. Attends a class for retarded pupils
7. Has changed schools frequently

8. Intends to drop out of school as soon as possible
9. Has nebulous academic or vocational plans
10. Shows limited academic aptitude
11. Has frequent or serious misbehavior problems
12. Destroys school property
13. Is a habitual bully
14. Exhibits extreme temper tantrums
15. Wants to quit school immediately
16. Plays truant
17. Generally isolates himself from organized extra-curricular activities
18. Doesn't feel accepted in the classroom

Early identification by the classroom teacher of children who show many of these signs may provide the precious ounce of prevention. On the basis of his extensive research, Edwin Powers reports that the majority of boys who became delinquent were anticipated ten years before by teachers as well as by the experts.[18]

On the other hand, it should be remembered that teachers' opinions and observations are not always based on objective evidence. Halo effects can prejudice the teachers in favor of or against a given youth. However, teachers skilled in observation are able to identify the inner motives, feelings, attitudes and experiences of youngsters.

The youth's pattern of differential association is another useful index. Although a child's association with a known delinquent is not by itself sufficient evidence of his own delinquency, it indicates a need for the teacher's attention. A sociogram may be quite effective in this respect. The interest survey, survey of favorite pastime activities, problem inventory and other formal or informal devices will provide further information on a predelinquent.

Sources and kinds of data are almost unlimited for a capable teacher. If conditions permit, it is desirable that the teacher personally interview the parents of the pre-delinquent. It must be kept in mind that the home is generally more influential upon the youngsters than the school. Although assistance from school psychologists, guidance teachers and administrators is helpful for the teacher in detecting and diagnosing the pre-delinquents, the key person is the classroom teacher who has daily contact with the pupils.

REMEDIAL ACTION

As soon as a child is suspected of potential delinquency, a case study should be made on the youngster. His academic records, social relationships, activities outside of the school, and other relevant factors must be studied more intensively. Psychological tests of personality, mental abilities, aptitude and achievement tests should be administered to the child. Interviews with parents and study of family conditions and personal history should prove helpful. A group conference involving members of the school staff and professional consultants, if available, will be an effective means of interpreting the child's problem.

The ultimate remedial action to be decided upon is dependent upon the nature of the potentially delinquent problem; there is no single pattern of action which is effective in all cases. The teacher's main concern should be upon the youngster's personal, academic and social adjustment. The teacher must recognize the fact that the classgroup is a social unit presided over by a teacher who represents adult authority. To the maladjusted youth, the teacher can become either a hostile, punitive authority, or a benign adult, kind, patient and understanding. The building up of mutual rapport is therefore, a *sine qua non* in any remedial action.

Another point is that the child must be made to feel secure, worthy and adequate in the school situation. The pre-delinquent youngster is usually unable to satisfy his basic needs in normal social situations; thus he develops more or less deviant patterns of behavior to compensate for the deprivation he feels. Feelings of security and adequacy are based upon the attitudes of others toward the individual as he internalizes them himself. Feelings

225

of insecurity and inferiority result when the youngster feels that he is being unfavorably evaluated by others.

The child should be given the opportunity to work with materials which are at the level of his own abilities and interest. A variety of activities should be planned so that the child will not experience repeated failures and disappointments. One of the basic goals underlying all programs of remedial instruction is that the child becomes better able to adjust by having received such instruction. Often the maladjusted child who is sent to a remedial reading program feels that he is "singled out" because he is a failure. Remedial instruction in subject matter areas should equip the youngster with new skills and abilities which increase his feelings of personal worth and competency and which make the school experience more challenging to him. The teacher should make the classroom climate more hospitable to the maladjusted child by helping other children accept him, and by giving him an opportunity to demonstrate his achievements as much as possible.

Too often parents are contacted by school authorities only after a child is involved in serious difficulty. The school and the parents can mutually benefit by exchanging relevant information on the child and by working cooperatively in helping the child meet his needs at home and at school. The teacher should recognize and come to grips with different types of parents' reactions. Some parents resent the teacher's interference in personal and family affairs. There are others who recognize their child's problems but try to pass the buck by blaming someone else. It should be remembered that the parents of maladjusted children may be abnormal themselves. The parent's behavior should give added insight to the teacher.

Several other projects for improving the school's efficiency in working with the problems of delinquent behavior are curriculum reorganization, providing in-service teacher training, improving special services, exploring the possibilities of community cooperation, re-examination of teacher qualifications and a general reappraisal of the school system. We shall now consider some of these.

RE-EXAMINATION OF THE TEACHER'S QUALIFICATIONS

Although there is a shortage of teachers in many parts of the United States, there is an even greater shortage of teachers who understand modern children, especially those with personality problems. Therefore, from time to time, a reappraisal should be made of both the educational training and socio-psychological fitness of the classroom teacher.

While the teaching profession has some negative aspects, there are many rewards in being a teacher. There are many dedicated men and women who enjoy their work and association with the schools and are suited for their calling. On the other hand, it must be realized that some students, especially co-eds, use the education major as a means toward achieving a relatively easily attainable profession. Others go into teaching for an interim period until such time as they are beckoned by the institution of marriage. Inasmuch as most colleges and departments of education are interested in building up their enrollment statistics, they are often forced into a position of compromising their standards. If such institutions feel it necessary to train marginal teachers, particularly those beset with personality problems, they should make every effort to help those students resolve their difficulties.[19] There should be a careful selection process, and some students should be discouraged from going into the profession, even though their academic records are beyond reproach.

Teaching is not infrequently in the hands of emotional misfits, or immature, inferiority-ridden men and women seeking a secure, respectable and quickly attainable higher social status.[20]

A practical question to be considered is: what are the specific personality characteristics which a good teacher ought to have? Robert J. Havighurst of the University of Chicago's Committee on Human Development has listed the following personality characteristics as the beginning of a list of qualities necessary for the good teacher capable of working with problems of delinquency.[21]

1. The teacher should be interested in people and sensitive to their feelings. He should be a reasonably outgoing person.

2. The teacher should be warmhearted and genuine. He should know how to give and take in a social situation.

3. The teacher should not be so meticulous and demanding of himself that he cannot accept others who are satisfied with lesser standards.

4. The teacher should be permissive toward the behavior of non-conformists so long as it does not clash with general moral principles. This is not to imply that the teacher should be Bohemian or Philistine himself.

5. The teacher should have moral convictions, and at the same time have a broad and sympathetic understanding of human behavior.

6. The teacher should know his own personality well enough so that he may be aware of any inclination he may have for using the children to satisfy his own needs.

7. The teacher should accentuate the positive rather than the negative and weak points of people.

A teacher as an individual must have achieved a sense of personal worth and must have a set of socially acceptable values. He must understand the growth and development processes of the juvenile age group, and in addition he must be aware of the socio-economic factors that affect the youngsters. The teacher must develop insight into the problems of personality in youth, as well as his own, or attitudes are likely to be inculcated in the youngsters with behavioral problems which may start them on the road to delinquency. As important as is the consideration of what the teacher teaches is the matter of how the teacher carries out his role.[22]

A REAPPRAISAL OF THE SCHOOL SYSTEM

Have the leaders of American communities and school superintendents kept abreast of the changing needs of the public schools? The majority of states have laws requiring compulsory school attendance from the ages of seven to sixteen.[23] Should all nonintellectuals and disinterested students be forced to stay in school just to fulfill the technicalities of the attendance laws? The opinion has been expressed that no one questions the value of universal education; in fact, universal education is accepted as an incontrovertible necessity to our democratic way of life. And yet, the schools of many metropolitan areas serve simply as custodial agents for some children who merely sit in the classroom to wait out the legal age requirements. This type of student does nothing and may be capable of doing very little; as a matter of fact, he may be a detriment to the progress of the class as a whole.[24]

Is universal education for the heterogeneous masses feasible? There are wide variations of intellectual, emotional and social maturation among children, but the schools have a program with relatively little diversity. Unfortunately, the needs and interests of many youngsters are not met.

Historically, the pattern of free and compulsory public education for all children developed in the 19th Century in keeping with the age which exalted the rights of the common man. The school stressed the principle of acquisition of knowledge for its own sake which amounted to book learning and mental discipline through memorization. However, as the schools set out to provide all children with the kind of intellectual training which had hitherto been reserved for the few going into the professions and commerce, they lost sight of the effect on the masses.

In this day of technology and the blue-collar worker, it indicates lack of foresight on the part of school authorities not to utilize more adequately the talents of the nonintellectuals. Regarding the correlation between intelligence and juvenile delinquency, we no longer accept the sententious judgment of those writers who singled out low grade mentality as the main factor in delinquent behavior. Rather, using such devices as the Wechsler-Bellevue scale the evidence seems presumptive that the delinquents are on the whole somewhat superior in those tasks pertaining to concrete realities, though they average lower in verbal intelligence. When children from the lower socio-economic classes are given "culture fair" tests or when they are viewed within the context of their own milieu, they turn out to be extremely bright.[25] This does not imply that the potential delinquent or lower class children are necessarily better than nondelinquents or upper class children in mechanical ability. However, for the nonintellectual child who wants to pursue a practical training program, every opportunity should be provided for him to realize his interests and goals. The student who is not academically inclined, and who wants to serve an apprenticeship even though he has not reached the legal age under the Child Labor Act, should be allowed the opportunity to petition to a board of examiners for a waiver of age requirements. Although such youngsters may affect the labor market in certain localities, there is the possibility that there may be a rebirth of the apprentice system which might help to alleviate the shortage of well-trained mechanics, electricians, plumbers, carpenters and other craftsmen.

Generally, the school program has not been a satisfactory one for those who exhibit delinquent behavior, and on account of a lack of interest in their studies and in school, many pupils become truants. Truancy has been called the "kindergarten of crime" for frequently enough, through association with older boys and girls, the young truant is exposed to the game of stealing and other forbidden activities during his stolen hours.[26] Many of the truants graduate into a new subcultural world and eventually into a life of crime. Unsatisfactory school experiences are in the background of the majority of delinquents. There is a preponderance of low school achievement and a high incidence of truancy, and an intense dislike for school. Leaving school early is often the culmination of a most unsatisfactory situation.[27] School has aggravated and frustrated those who find little acceptance, recognition or interest in classroom living. As a number of experts in the field of juvenile delinquency have aptly stated: while the delinquent is troublesome to the school, one should remember that the school is an even greater headache and heartache to him.

The classic works of Clifford Shaw reveal that all too often schools do not consider the importance of informal experiences.[28] Teachers need to be reminded that informal in-between-class and after-school contacts with students have much significance,[29] especially in working with the nonconformist.

The entire school staff should be continually concerned with the process of curriculum evaluation to improve the over-all educational program. The ideal is to have a rich and varied program so that all children will be interested and motivated to find experiences which will meet their individual needs as well as social responsibilities.

Most states do not provide public kindergartens for young children, the majority of whom have curious and inquiring minds. Should this seemingly natural inclination for learning be parried because the parents of lower socio-economic classes cannot afford to send their four and five-year-olds to private nursery schools? To what extent should the schools assume the responsibility of helping to develop the personalities of younger children? Inasmuch as the pre-school age is an important time in the personality development of all children, this writer suggests that the minimum age requirement for entering school be lowered to five and that kindergarten be included in the system of compulsory public education. Perhaps the experience gained in the schools at an early age can help to offset the subcultural values which persist in many lower class families and neighborhoods. It has been observed that it is the working class children who are likely to be the "problems" because of their relative lack of training in order and discipline, and their lack of reinforcement by the home in conformity with the requirements of the middle class norms of the school.[30]

Also, the schools may help in the socialization process where there has been disinclination on the part of upper class parents to take the responsibility for enculturating their children to the norms of the dominant society. With respect to younger children, standards of values and a sense of right and wrong behavior are largely those learned through imitation and osmosis from parents, neighborhood friends and teachers. A child seldom questions those standards, and therefore, the schools may be in a position to impress children with middle class values at a relatively young age.

The delinquent usually begins his norm-violating activities as a problem child. Compulsory kindergartens with a program aimed at developing the "whole child" may help such a youngster. The maladjusted child usually reaches a certain level of maturity before he becomes a legal delinquent.[31]

Special services organized for the purpose of providing direct assistance to children or to their teachers and parents in dealing with delinquency problems are necessary to supplement the instructional program of the school. The types of special services to be provided will vary according to the needs of the community, size of the school and financial ability. Many schools cannot provde even a minimum of guidance or counseling services; therefore, the key role in the prevention of delinquency falls upon the teacher and the school social worker. The potentially delinquent youngster may give trouble to the most experienced teachers. Yet, generally speaking, the teachers with the most experience will not choose to teach in schools where a sizable portion of the students are incorrigible. Therefore the less experienced and perhaps less effective teachers are often placed in schools that most need qualified teachers.

In order to make the task of working in such schools more worthwhile and challenging there should be a substantial salary differential favoring the teacher devoted to working with these children.

Every school should have a social case worker or a capable teacher with additional social work training. Such a worker can not only help the adjustment of a child who has been referred by a teacher or administrator,[32] he can serve as a valuable resource link between the school and the community. The experienced and qualified teacher should be given every opportunity to enroll in sociology, social work, psychology and anthropology courses during the summer months with pay equivalent to or better than that he would earn while working at a supplementary summer job.

There is no question that the task of curbing delinquency is the responsibility of many social institutions and agencies. However, the teacher and the school play a vital role in this task and can often exert a more desirable influence on the youngster than any other social institution. The school is in a strategic position to render aid to the potential delinquent when the home and the community have not carried out their functions adequately. Senator Robert C. Hendrickson, formerly chairman of the Senate Subcommittee investigating juvenile delinquency, maintains the thesis that the first line of defense in the prevention of delinquency is the school. Furthermore, that unless we provide the money for better schools now, we will be faced with a large expenditure in years to come for more police and more prisons.[33] Juvenile delinquents, no matter what their problems, are human beings in need of affection, recognition, security and understanding.

SELECTED BIBLIOGRAPHY

Barron, Milton L., *The Juvenile in Delinquent Society*, Knopf, New York, 1955. The provocative theme of this book is implicit in its title. Chapter X entitled "Institutional Omissions and Commissions" discusses the measurement of school experience as an etiological factor.

Bettelheim, Bruno, *Truants from Life*, The Free Press, Glencoe, Illinois, 1955. This volume contains four case-studies of emotionally disturbed children who lived in the therapeutic community of the University of Chicago's Orthogenic School, of which the author is director.

Davidoff, Eugene and Noetzel, Elinor, *The Child Guidance Approach to Juvenile Delinquency*, Child Care Publication, 1951. Deals with the structure and function of a child guidance clinic in Syracuse, New York, and shows how a clinic may be utilized in the treatment of the potentially delinquent as well as the delinquent.

Ellingston, John R., *Protecting Our Children from Criminal Careers*, Prentice-Hall, New York, 1948. A serious consideration of causation, prevention and treatment based upon the objectives and philosophy of the California Youth Authority.

Glaser, Daniel and Rice, Kent, "Crime, Age and Employment," *American Sociological Review*, XXIV, 5, October, 1959, 679-86. Appreciable evidence is presented for the hypothesis that juvenile delinquency varies inversely with unemployment while adult crime varies directly with unemployment.

Gnagney, William J., "Do Our Schools Prevent or Promote Delinquency," *Journal of Educational Research*, L, 3, November, 1956, 215-19. Data is cited which places the school in the role of an important institution for the prevention of delinquency.

Goldberg, Harriet L., *Child Offender, A Study in Diagnosis and Treatment*, Grune and Stratton, New York, 1948. The rehabilitation of delinquents in terms of application of social work concepts and procedures is presented by a lawyer assigned to the Children's Court of New York City.

Hathaway, Starke, R., and Monachesi, Elio D. (editors), *Analyzing and Predicting Juvenile Delinquency with the MMPI*, The University of Minnesota Press, Minneapolis, 1953. A report of a series of experiments in which the Minnesota Multiphasic Personality Inventory was administered to samples of delinquent and nondelinquent boys and girls.

Kahn, Alfred J., "Who Are Our Truants," *Federal Probation*, XV, 1, March, 1951, 35-40. Suggests that truancy, defined as unlawful absence from school, be regarded as one of the more significant symptoms of a child in trouble.

Kvaraceus, William C. (editor), *Delinquent Behavior: Culture and the Individual*, National Education Association, Washington, D. C., 1959. A joint report aimed at arriving at an integrated theory of delinquent behavior prepared by an educational-psychologist, a cultural-anthropologist, a sociologist, a psychiatrist, a pediatrician and a criminologist, all of whom have had experience dealing with delinquents.

Kvaraceus, William C., *Juvenile Delinquency*, National Education Association, Washington, D. C., 1958. A well-known author and professor of educational psychology at Boston University interprets various research material and makes recommendations as to what the schools can do to appraise teacher competencies in dealing with pre-delinquents and delinquents.

Kvaraceus, William C., *Juvenile Delinquency and the School*,

World Book Company, New York, 1945. A descriptive study of the school system administered by the Passaic Childrens' Bureau in New Jersey. It reviews the dynamic adjustment processes of 761 children and shows that schools and police can pool their efforts in the prevention and control of delinquency.

Merrill, Maud A., *Problems of Child Delinquency*, Houghton Mifflin, Boston, 1947. The author studied 300 delinquents and 300 nondelinquents in California primarily by means of various psychological and personality tests and an interview schedule to show how the two groups differ and how they are alike. Also contains a chapter on intelligence of delinquents based on an additional sample of 200 delinquents.

National Society for the Study of Education, *Juvenile Delinquency and the School*, Forty-Seventh Yearbook, Part I, University of Chicago Press, Chicago, 1948. The contributing authors deal with the many roles of the school in promoting remedial and preventive measures in relation to juvenile delinquency.

Powers, Edwin, "The School's Responsibility for the Early Detection of Delinquency-Prone Children," *Harvard Educational Review*, XIX, March, 1949, 80-86. Points out that the school might concern itself with the problems of all children inasmuch as many boys identified as delinquency-prone did not become delinquents.

Powers, Edwin and Witmer, Helen L., *An Experiment in the Prevention of Delinquency*, Columbia University Press, New York, 1951. A ten-year research effort known as the Cambridge-Somerville Youth Study, to find out the effectiveness of assigning counselors to two matched groups of problem boys for the purpose of preventing law-violating behavior and recidivism.

Redl, Fritz and Wineman, David, *Controls from Within*, The Free Press, Glencoe, Illinois, 1952. This report depicts techniques used in handling a small group of extremely aggressive youngsters in an experimental institution in Detroit.

Salisbury, Harrison, E., *The Shook-Up Generation*, Harper, New York, 1958. A New York Times journalist gives a firsthand report of teen-age gangs. Two chapters deal with the question of what can be done by the schools to reduce blackboard jungles.

Short, James F., Jr., and Nye, F. Ivan, "Reported Behavior as a Criterion of Deviant Behavior," *Social Problems*, V, 3, Winter, 1957-58, 207-13. The authors' research shows that deviant behavior can be studied through reported behavior in the general population. This methodology is suggested as a feasible alternative to the traditional method of obtaining data through official institutional records and clinical cases.

Shulman, Harry M., "Intelligence and Delinquency," *Journal of Criminal Law and Criminology,* XXXXI, 6, March-April, 1951, 763-81. Discusses the relationship between general, social and mechanical intelligence and delinquency, and the relationship between levels of intelligence and response to treatment.

I. Roger Yoshino, Associate Professor of Sociology, University of Arizona, was born in Seattle, Washington on September 8, 1920. He attended the University of Washington and Denver University where he was initiated into Phi Beta Kappa, and obtained his B.A. degree. Following graduation, he served as Military Intelligence Officer in the Far Eastern theater of operation. After the end of World War II, during the early phase of the Occupation, he served as Book and Magazine Censor with the United States Civil Service. Later, he worked as an Economist with the Natural Resources Section, SCAP, and was awarded a Certificate of Achievement for efficient and faithful service. Returning to school to continue his education, he obtained his M.A. degree (1951) in Political Science and International Relations, and his Ph.D. degree (1954) in Sociology from the University of Southern California. He has taught at the University of Southern California and at Washington State University, where he was advisor to Alpha Kappa Delta—the National Sociology honor society—for four years prior to joining the staff of the University of Arizona in 1958. He has had a variety of teaching and research experience, having taught, among other courses Juvenile Delinquency, Criminology, Educational Sociology, Social Problems, Ethnic Relations and Collective Behavior. In 1952, he was a Ford Foundation Fellow and lived in a rural village of Japan for a year to carry on a re-study of the late Professor John Embree's social anthropological classic, *Suye Mura.* A summary of this study is written up in the *Washington State Research Bulletin,* with a book currently in process. Dr. Yoshino has been a frequent contributor to sociological and educational journals. His main writings are "College Drop-Outs at the End of the

Freshman Year," "The Classroom Teacher and the Pre-Delinquent," and "The Stereotype of the Negro and His High Priced Car."

NOTES

*Considerably revised and expanded version of "The Classroom Teacher and the Pre-Delinquent," *The Journal of Educational Sociology*, XXXIII, 3, November, 1959, 124-30.

1. As cited in Salisbury, Harrison E., *The Shook-Up Generation*, Harpers, New York, 1958, 139.

2. Stullken, Edward H., "What Can the Home and the School Do About the Juvenile Delinquency Problem?," *National Assocation of Secondary School Principals*, XXXVIII, 202, April, 1954, 181.

3. Kvaraceus, William C., *Delinquent Behavior: Culture and the Individual*, National Education Association of the United States, Washington, D. C., 1959, 143.

4. Statement made by Sampson G. Smith, an experienced administrator, as cited by Block, Herbert A., and Flynn, Frank T., *Delinquency: The Juvenile Offender in America Today*, Random House, New York, 1956, 199.

5. Vedder, Clyde, *The Juvenile Offender*, Random House, New York, 1954, 84.

6. Sullenger, Earl T., *Social Determinants in Juvenile Delinquency*, John Wiley, London, 1936, 97.

7. Kvaraceus, William C., *Juvenile Delinquency*, National Education Association, Washington, D. C., 13.

8. Stullken, *op. cit.*, 182.

9. Pre-delinquent—one who has a tendency to display behavior which is generally characteristic of the incipient delinquent. He has emotional and psychological disturbances and possesses other etiological traits which may precede delinquency.

10. Proto-delinquent—one who has engaged in acts which are considered delinquent, but for whom no legal complaint has yet been filed.

11. Sullenger, *op. cit.*, 97.

12. Salisbury, *op. cit.*, 135-36.

13. Young, Leontine R., "Delinquency from the Child's Viewpoint," in Vedder, *op. cit.*, 62-63.

14. For example, see Ellingston, John R., *Protecting Our Children from Criminal Careers*, Prentice-Hall, New York, 1949, 277-78. The author points out that one out of five delinquents apprehended, in a New Jersey study, stated that the schools treated them more unfairly than any other individual or agency.

15. As told to the writer by Forbes Bottomly, a graduate student at Washington State University in Pullman, Washington.

16. Harris, Dale B., "Suggestions for the School from Recent Literature on Juvenile Delinquency," in National Society for the Study of Education, *Juvenile Delinquency and the Schools*, Forty-Seventh Yearbook, Part I, University of Chicago Press, Chicago, 1948, 262.

17. Kvaraceus, *Juvenile Delinquency*, 17.

18. Powers, Edwin, "The School's Responsibility for the Early Detection of Delinquency Prone Children," *Harvard Educational Review*, XLIX, March, 1949, 80-86.

19. Cain, Leo F., "Delinquency and the School," *School Life*, XXXV, 5, February, 1953, 66.

20. Barron, Milton L., *The Juvenile in Delinquent Society*, Knopf, New York, 1954, 174.

21. Havighurst, Robert J., "Preparing Teachers to Meet the Problem of Delinquency," in National Society for the Study of Education, *Juvenile Delinquency and the Schools*, Forty-seventh Yearbook, Part I, University of Chicago Press, 1948, 236.

22. Barron, *op. cit.*, 174.

23. "Schools Help Prevent Delinquency," *National Education Association Research Bulletin*, 31, 3, October, 1953, 119.

24. Salisbury, *op. cit.*, 155.

25. Kvaraceus, *Delinquent Behavior: Culture and the Individual*, 36. See also Glueck, Sheldon and Glueck, Eleanor, *Unraveling Juvenile Delinquency*, Commonwealth Fund, New York, 1950, 139. Vold, George B., *Theoretical Criminology*, Oxford University Press, New York, 1958, 88-89, provides sufficient documentation that there is no peculiarly large proportion of criminal feeble-minded or of excessively low intelligence when compared to the general population.

26. Vedder, *op. cit.*, 83-84.

27. Barron, *op. cit.*, 173.

28. Shaw, Clifford R., *Brothers in Crime*, University of Chicago Press, Chicago, 1948; *The Jack Roller*, University of Chicago Press, Chicago, 1930; and Shaw, Clifford R., and Moore, Maurice E., *Natural History of a Delinquent Career*, University of Chicago Press, Chicago, 1931.

29. Harris, *op. cit.*, 262.

30. Cohen, *op. cit.*, 115.

31. Harris, *op. cit.*, 248.

32. Volz, Horace S., "The Role of the School in the Prevention and Treatment of Delinquency and Other Abnormal Behavior," *School and Society*, LXXI, 1829, January, 1950, 22.

33. Hendrickson, Robert C., and Cook, Fred J., *Youth in Danger*, Harcourt, Brace, New York, 1956.

MASS COMMUNICATION AND CRIME

David Z. Orlow and Albert Francis
Columbia University

In this chapter we shall discuss the mass media; their characteristics, and the ways in which they can be seen to be associated with the occurrence of crime, and in general, deviant behavior. The authors feel that discussions by other writers in this area have tended too much to emphasize the differences between the media. While it is true that certain differences do exist between the media, the important basic similarities must be stressed. All of the media may be viewed as economic structures, each possessing its owners, producers, transmitters, and consumers. More important, the same basic principles of communication apply to all of them, again, with some differences expected.

With the emphasis on similarities in mind, the reader can better understand the logic of not dividing this section into the customary parts on "the press and crime," "movies and crime," and the like. The differences between the media, however, will not be overlooked, and will be stressed throughout the section.

WHAT ARE THE MASS MEDIA? WHAT ARE THEIR CHARACTERISTICS?

Any listing of the mass media, in America today, would of necessity include the movies, radio, newspapers, many magazines of the "pulp" and "slick" varieties, and, in the last decade, television. Other large scale forms of communication, such as phonograph recordings, may also be peripherally considered.

It is important to realize that these forms of communication are relatively unique both in our time and location. It wasn't until the nineteenth century, in the United States, that the first "dime novels" began to appear in abundance. Neither the radio nor the movies were common here, on any large scale, until some time after the first world war, and it has only been in the first half of this century that the great volume of comic books and magazines has emerged. Television is perhaps the most striking example of the rapid growth of the mass media, growing from its first authorized use on a commercial basis in 1941 to its present "state of indispensability" in the modern home. But, it must be remembered that even today, the vast bulk of the world's population is virtually unexposed to these media.[1] In short, the mass media can be viewed as a phenomenon of the western world, and more especially, a phenomenon of the United States.

Whereas a comparison of the mass media to forms of *interpersonal* communication reveals many similarities which may be treated under the nomenclature of "communication theory," [2] it also reveals many differences which serve to uniquely identify the two forms. These basic differences may be stated as follows:

    1) Availability
    2) Low Unit Cost
    3) Mass Acceptance
    4) Impersonality[3]

Let us now examine each of the above characteristics.

1) Availability: This trait may best be considered as a prerequisite to a mass medium. It refers to the fact that in order to be used by a mass audience, a particular medium must be readily available in the market structure of the economy. Regardless of its price or acceptance, it must at least *be there*.

2) Low Unit Cost: In 1948 the average price of a television set had been greatly decreased, and was in fact "down" to a low of $384. Today, in 1960, a television set may be purchased for under $100 new, although of course many sets are still quite expensive. There is no doubt that a "low" unit cost is another

prerequisite of the mass media. The problem of what price may be considered a low one, is a matter of the relative buying power of the consumers. Although a price of $100 may appear to us as quite low indeed, and consequently including the great mass of our population as potential consumers, consider the same unit cost in a country where $100 represents 1 or even 2 times the average yearly income. Here, indeed, the $100 represents an extremely high unit cost, approximately equivalent to $7,000 in this country.

3) Mass Acceptance: While a medium is fulfilling its prerequisites of availability and low unit cost, it must also be accepted by a "mass," that is, a large conglomeration of people from all strata of society and from all walks of life. Blumer lists four attributes of this mass; its membership coming from all classes and strata of society, anonymity of the individual members, the minimum interaction between the members of the mass, and the loose organization of the mass that does not enable it to work with the concertedness of the more organized groups such as crowds and formal organizations.[4]

4) Impersonality: Perhaps the most outstanding characteristic of the mass media is the lack of personal contact involved in the communication process. The actual communicating is accomplished with no knowledge of the individual consumers. It is not a question of the radio addressing you as a particular personality, but rather one of the radio speaking to John Doe, a member of the listening audience, or in some cases, a member of a particular subgroup of the population that is being appealed to at the time. Further, there is no direct interaction provided *between* the consumers, with the possible exception of the movies. One does not need to interact with another reader in order to read the newspaper or in order to watch television. Although interaction is not a requirement of attending the movies, movie-going has been found to be a social action, and attendance with others is the rule rather than the exception. There is also the obvious point that the actual movie goers comprise an audience at any one motion picture showing as well as a part of the mass.

THE MASS MEDIA AS ECONOMIC SYSTEMS

We have mentioned above that the mass media may be viewed as economic structures, each possessing its own owners, producers, transmitters, and consumers. Let us now examine the relationships between these economic statuses and the occurrence of crime.

Owners and Producers: In this group fall the manufacturers of the various media, including the owners of radio stations and television channels, publishing firms, newspaper syndicates, and the great concentration of movie manufacturers located in Hollywood.

The commission of criminal offenses by the owners and operators of these channels of communication may be considered to fall into the realm of "white collar" crime. The media are run, after all, by business men, and as such, they seek profit for their efforts. It was early recognized that some forms of governmental control and legislation for radio and television production were necessary to insure and safeguard the public rights in communication.

In 1927, Congress passed the Radio Act which formed the basis for the establishment of the Federal Commission (FCC) through the Communications Act of 1934. These acts granted regulatory power to the FCC in the form of licensure, that is, the FCC had the power to grant and revoke the privilege of operating a broadcasting station. Through this power the FCC is able, at least in theory, to enforce such regulations as are deemed to be in the public interest and safety.[5]

Aside from the violation of these regulations, there is also a long history of debate in the radio and television fields, over monopolistic tendencies and practices by the owners of stations and networks. Periodic Congressional investigations, reports by the FCC, and reports by the Federal Trade Commission (FTC) all attest to this problem. The first major attack on monopolistic practices by the industry was delivered in the now famous Report on Chain Broadcasting, issued in 1941, as a result of Congressional investigations into business practices in the radio in-

242

dustry. This was followed by the issuance of "Chain Broadcasting Regulations and Free Speech" by the FCC in 1942.[6] Another high water mark of concern was the issuance of "The Merger Movement. A Summary Report," by the FTC in 1948.[7]

In general, the actions of the various governmental agencies have had only an indirect effect on control of the media, which is perhaps, the better arrangement. After each large investigation, there is feed-back which results in increased demand on the part of the consumers, for the owners to "clean shop." In all fairness it must be added that the owners, themselves, have expressed great concern in this area.

Most criminal offenses in the production end of the mass media can be seen then, to fall into two types. In the case of the radio and television fields, there are the violations of the regulations of the FCC, and in all media, there are the violations of the laws relating to business practices, such as those under the jurisdiction of the FTC.

One additional note should be added at this point. According to the law, the manufacture of pornographic and obscene literature is, in itself, a crime, although the specifics of the definition vary from jurisdiction to jurisdiction. While there is some evidence that pornographic literature is produced here in the United States, there is also evidence that much of it is illicitly imported.[8]

Sponsors and Transmitters: The term sponsor refers to a person or organization which pays any given medium in exchange for the right to deliver a message to the consumers, usually consisting of the advertising of a product that the sponsor wishes to sell. This definition excludes messages delivered to the consumers of a medium as a "public service" by the owners of the medium.

Transmitters are those persons, usually hired by the medium, who actually convey or transmit the communication. In the case of radio and television they are the announcers, M.C's, and actors. In the case of newspapers and magazines, they are the editors, writers, and cartoonists.

Until the present time, there has been little or no regulatory legislation directed towards the sponsors and transmitters of the mass media. However, begining with the scandals late in 1959 and continuing at the present time, there is increased agitation for such legislation.

This concern has been stimulated by the public airing of two phenomena in the broadcasting and televising industries. First was the disclosure of the "fixed" or "rigged" quiz shows. There were charges and even open admissions that sponsors had intervened in the determination of winners by selecting contestants whom they felt would attract the largest audience and prompting them with answers to questions which were later alleged to be secret and not known beforehand. The second scandal in the communication industries has been centered around "payola," that is, the practice of secretly receiving money in return for favors granted, in a sense, a form of graft. The particular case in point in the payola scandal has been the receiving of money by disc jockeys (M.C's of shows which play popular music on the radio or television) from record manufacturers, in return for the promotion of particular recordings.

These acts of quiz show rigging and payola, at the present time, are not (or at least have not yet been judged to be) violations of existing statutes, although there is increased public sentiment that they are violations of moral and ethical codes. It appears highly likely that in the near future, legislation proposed by the FCC will be passed, making such acts into criminal offenses.[9]

Consumers: The effects of the mass media on consumer behavior in America, is perhaps one of the most widely debated topics of our time. This area of debate is replete with charges and counter-charges, value conflicts, and an endless stream of literature ranging from microscopic empirical investigations to grandiose generalizations.

Here it is good to keep in mind the following observation. When we consider the effects of the mass media on human behavior, we are looking only at a half of the process that is going on in the system. Just as the media may be presumed to be having effects on the consumers, so the consumers may be presumed to be having effects on the media. There is a two step process of communication going on at all times, consisting of the mass media which affect the consumers, and the feed-back from the consumers which affects the media.[10] With this caution in mind then, let us concentrate on the flow from production to consumption.

The idea that the mass media *can* foster criminal behavior, as well as immorality, corruption, and social disorganization is an old and deep-rooted one. Moralists, politicians, churchmen, social scientists, and informed laymen have been concerned with the possible effects of the media for some time. Consider, for instance, the following statement about writers of motion picture scripts in 1936. "They are men and women who care nothing for decency, good taste or refinement."[11] This and many similar statements[12] lead us to distinguish two aspects of the problem. First, although the moral and ethical aspects are of *vital* importance, we are interested here, primarily in the behavioral effects of the media, that is, what results from them. In the above reference, for instance, if the tastes and morals of film writers had no effect on the behavior of the consumers, it remains in the domain of the personal. If, on the other hand, there are such consequences, it is a public problem. Second, the distinction must be made between what the media *can* do, and what they actually do. It is the latter that interests us more here.

WHO ARE THE CONSUMERS?

In the cases of radio, television, films, and many of the popular magazines, it is quite obvious that their content is overwhelmingly geared toward entertainment, rather than being informative or educational. In the case of the newspapers this is also true but to a lesser extent. Anyone doubting this need only to look at any current listing of films or T.V. programs, or glance through a sampling of magazines. The charges that the press "glorifies" crime also refer to the reporting of crime in such a way as to entertain the public rather than simply to inform them.

It is therefore quite understandable that the greater part of the literature in the field concentrates on the younger portion of the population since they are the ones who most utilize the media for entertainment[13] (as well as perhaps being the most impressionable). The juveniles and young adults are, even more, the ones who listen to and watch those shows and programs which have as their content—crime, criminal life, and various aspects of deviant behavior.[14] It has also been found that people with lesser amounts of education and those in the lower socio-economic strata are more prone to watch films and programs with crime content.[15]

THE DYNAMICS OF "EFFECT"

Having briefly examined the nature of the mass media and the composition of the audiences, we may now turn our attention to the interaction process between the two. Schramm speaks of four stages in the communications process. These are: attention; sharing of common symbols between sender and receiver; the arousing of personal needs and the suggestion of ways to meet them; and the relating by the receiver, of these suggested means to his social environment.[16]

For a communication to have an effect on a consumer, he must first listen to it, watch it, or read it. At the same time there must be a common language between the sender and the receiver, both linguistically aand culturally. The consumer must understand the communication. It then must arouse in him some needs or desires which he must become motivated to satisfy. These needs can be physical, as in the case of a sex drive, emotional, as in the case of the "need" to be secure, or social, as in the case of the desire to vote. Regardless of their origin or genre, there must be in the communication, a suggestion of the ways in which to meet these needs. With the needs in mind, as well as the ways for their gratification, the consumer then acts. At this step, he will then consider such acts in the light of his social environment, and its standards of behavior and conduct.

These processes suggest an old and unanswered problem about

the mass media, a version of the chicken-or-egg dilemma. To what extent is there a self-selective process going on in the consumption of crime movies, stories, and programs? [17] To put it another way, to what extent are those people with high dispositions to commit crimes, the very ones who are seeking out the crime aspects of the mass media? Are the media "causing" crime, or are they merely serving as outlets for those who would commit crime anyway? To deal with this question, we shall have to distinguish various types of effects, rather than look at "effect" as a homogeneous phenomenon.

DIMENSIONS OF "EFFECT"

We consider here three types or dimensions of effect on human behavior. First, the effect can either be on *individuals or groups*; second, the effect may either be *temporary or long range*; and third, it may either pertain to *cognitions or evaluations*.

Individual vs. Group Effects: Individual effects are those which apply to a person regardless of their application to groups of which the person is a member. The group effects are those applying to any homogeneous (with respect to variables other than the effect itself) group of people, be they a social class, a group of age cohorts, or whatever.

Temporary vs. Long Range Effects: The dimension of time is used here to distinguish those effects of a short run or single act nature from those which are relatively permanent in either the social group or the individual.

Cognitive vs. Evaluative Effects: This dimension will serve to differentiate the effects on a person's (or group's) perceptions (with its knowledge of facts) from his evaluations of this perceived reality.

A TYPOLOGY OF EFFECT

When these three dimensions are combined, eight types of effect emerge.

247

Typology of Effects

		Temporary	Long Range
Individual	Cognitions	1	2
	Evaluations	3	4
Group	Cognitions	5	6
	Evaluations	7	8

Consider, for example, cell number 3 of the matrix, the temporary effects on the evaluations made by individuals. Newcomb[18] suggests that some forms of mass communications provide their audiences with temporary value orientations, or philosophies, although receptivity varies according to the particular traits of the receiver.

Turning now to the press, we can recall the many arguments that the "glorification" of crime on the front pages induces, at least to some extent, the commission of new crime. It is immediately clear that the treatment of crime in such a way has some effect on the readers. Certainly they learn more about crime in the short run (cells 1 & 5), but does this learning have meaningful carry-over in time, and are there any changes in the value structure of the individuals or grouped readers? In the case of individuals, there do appear examples of the effect on value changes, or to use a more appropriate term, value suspensions. These would be the individuals who, having a high disposition to commit a criminal act but yet being checked by some value orientation, are thrown over the "threshold" by their exposure to the accounts of criminal acts through the press. In general, however, empirical evidence is conspicuously lacking and we are forced to relegate the problem to the realm of the "not-yet-known."

Hovland, Lumsdaine, and Sheffield[19] have shown that there is an effect on the cognitions and evaluations of viewers of propaganda films but at the same time there is a dampening or forgetting process. This, as well as other pieces of research, highlight the difficulties in distinguishing between long range and temporary effects.

Blumer and Hauser[20] in their celebrated study of the effects of the movies on delinquency and crime, divided the types of effects into their substantive components such as the display of criminal techniques, the suggestion of questionable methods of achievement, and the arousing of intense sex desires. Their study, for the greater part, consisted of gathering personal histories from delinquents and non-delinquents. The subjects were asked to tell how they felt the movies had affected their behavior, if at all. Although their technique is methodologically questionable, their work is quite thorough. Among other things, they point to the possibility of the replacement of the primary socializing agents by the mass media as a factor in delinquency. In other words, when the primary socializing institutions, such as the family, are disorganized, the mass media may then be taken over by the juvenile as a basic source of his value orientations. The danger in this process is plain, but it is difficult to ascertain whether the danger comes from the *absence* of the primary institution or the *substitution* of the mass media.[21] This type of problem, while unanswered, can be seen to fall into the category of long range effects on the evaluations of individuals (cell #4).

The movement from the considerations of the effects of the media on individuals to the effects of the media on groups is at the same time a movement toward the more speculative. If there is a paucity of evidence on the individual level, there is complete absence on the level of the group. Merton[22] has pointed out the neglect of this aspect of media effect on long range group values and, possibly of even greater significance, on the very social structures in which the media exist. In this vein, Riesman[23] has pointed out that the mass media contain implicit social values and behavioral cues along with the more explicit entertainment content.

We can now begin to see that the initial problem of the "effect" of the mass media on crime is no longer a simple matter

249

of "yes-or-no" and "does-it-or-doesn't-it." When the different effects of the media are distinguished, different audiences found among the media, and varying environmental factors are seen to affect the issue, the problem becomes quite complex indeed.

CRIME AND THE MASS MEDIA IN PERSPECTIVE

Clinard[24] has spoken of the mass media as forms of secondary community influence. By this he means that they ". . . are largely administered or controlled by forces outside the immediate local community or neighborhood." [25] He goes on to speak of the fact that, while the secondary community influences certainly have some effects on criminal behavior, the primary influences involving more of the face-to-face relationships certainly appear to be more crucial.

In a discussion such as this on the mass media, it is important to keep in mind that there are other factors which have been demonstrated to have a greater effect on crime and delinquency than the mass media.[26]

CONCLUSIONS

In this chapter we have tried to present a model with which to examine the effects of the mass media on deviant behavior and crime. We have viewed the mass media as systems containing owners, producers, transmitters, and consumers. The dynamics of the communication process have been briefly discussed and a typology of eight different effects has been presented. This typology is based on the consideration of the dimension of; *cognition-evaluation,* *individual-group,* and *temporary-long range.*

Within these eight types, a few of the empirical studies of the effects of the media on behavior are reviewed. The shortage of such studies is seen to be acute. For the most part, the existing studies are inconclusive either by their own admission or through questionable research methods.

If we are to make an over-all assessment of the effect of the mass media on crime, it can only be that, at least according to what has been demonstrated by study, the mass media exert no *wide-spread* effects on the occurrence of crime in the short run. The effect of the mass media on our society in the long run is even more uncertain, and remains completely in the realm of speculation.

SELECTED BIBLIOGRAPHY

Adler, Mortimer J., *Art and Prudence*, Longmans, Green, and Company, New York, 1937. A fine critique of the Blumer-Hauser study of the movies.

Blumer, Herbert, and Hauser, Philip M., *Movies, Delinquency, and Crime*, Macmillan, New York, 1933. One of the best examples of empirical investigations into the effects of movies on delinquents and non-delinquents. While methodologically weak due to its case history technique, it raises some excellent points.

Bogart, Leo, *The Age of Television*, Ungar, New York, 1956. An empirical study of the viewing habits of Americans and an attempt to uncover some of the impacts of television on American life.

Clinard, Marshall B., "Secondary Community Influences and Juvenile Delinquency," *The Annals*, January 1949, 42-54. The elaboration of the mass media as indirect influences on behavior as opposed to more face-to-face types of contact.

Hayakawa, S. I., *Language in Thought and Action*, Harcourt, Brace and Company, New York, 1949. An excellent and easy to understand discussion of the nature of communication.

Lazarsfeld, Paul F., and Kendall, Patricia, *Radio Listening in America*, Prentice-Hall, New York, 1948. A highly regarded study of the attitudes and behavior of the public in regard to radio listening. It also contains some comparisons to behavior with respect to the other media.

Schramm, Wilbur (editor), *The Process and Effects of Mass Communications*, University of Illinois Press, Urbana, 1954. A fine collection of papers and essays on mass communications including some excellent papers by Berelson, Riley, Lazarsfeld, Blumer, Merton, and others.

Siepmann, Charles A., *Radio Television and Society*, Oxford University Press, New York, 1950. A review of the development of the radio and television fields along with a consideration of some of the ethical issues involved in these media.

Thrasher, Frederic, "The Comics and Delinquency: Cause or Scapegoat," *Journal of Educational Sociology*, XXIII, December, 1949, 195-205. A scholarly review of the work of Wertham on the relation of comic books to crime.

Waples, Douglas (editor), *Print, Radio and Film in a Democracy*, University of Chicago Press, Chicago, 1942. Another excellent collection of essays on the mass media including essays on the effect of print and radio on public opinion, one by Berelson and the other by Lazarsfeld. In these two may be found many of the basic ideas that have been advanced about the effect of media.

Wertham, Frederic, *Seduction of the Innocent*, Rinehart and Company, Inc., New York, 1956. Here Wertham presents his central ideas about the importance of comics in the causation of crime and delinquency.

David Z. Orlow is currently a research assistant at the Bureau of Applied Socal Research, Columbia University. He received his A.B. in Sociology from the University of Pennsylvania and is currently completing requirements for the Ph.D. in Sociology at Columbia University. In the year 1957-1958 he was a research member of the staff of the Philadelphia Youth Services Board, during which time he conducted studies in juvenile delinquency. He has, in the past, helped to conduct research in the fields of race relations and adult education. He is presently working on a study in the field of medical education.

Albert Francis, Lecturer in Sociology at Columbia University, has been working on a number of projects at the Bureau of Applied Social Research. From 1954 to 1956 he was the Director of Public Relations at Brown-Raymond-Walsh, U.S. Government prime contractor for the construction of the American Air and Naval base in Spain. Since 1957 he has been associated with the U.S. Department of State under a service contract. He also has the L. en D. (Law) degree from the University of Madrid, and

252

is the author of several publications in the fields of sociology and law, including the chapter on "Automation and Social Stratification" (with Jeri Nehnevajsa) in *Automation and Society*, edited by Howard Boone Jacobson & Joseph S. Roucek (Philosophical Library, 1959.

NOTES

1. Too often many of the reasons for the vast differences in the use of the mass media in other parts of the world are overlooked. Aside from the more obvious ones involving the differences in technology, wealth, and geography, there exist great structural barriers to communication on a mass level, such as plurality of languages, and cultural differences within a given country.

2. For more thorough discussions of communication theory, see: Bryson, Lyman (editor), *The Communication of Ideas*, Harper, New York, 1948; Hartley, Eugene L., and Hartley, Ruth E., *Fundamentals of Social Psychology*, Knopf, New York, 1952, 15-195; Hayakawa, S. I., *Language in Thought and Action*, Harcourt, Brace, New York, 1949.

3. There are, of course, as many different characterizations of the qualities of the mass media as there is literature. Frank Stanton, in an address in 1949 to the Institute of Radio Engineers entitled *Television and People*, came close to our statement when he said that ". . . I can count up to four basic characteristics which I think apply universally to them (mass media) . These are, in order, first broad appeal; second, speed; third, availability; and fourth, low unit cost. . . ."

Other writers have either modified or emphasized particular factors, but there remains a basic consensus in the field which need not be further demonstrated here.

4. Blumer, Herbert, "The Crowd, the Public, and the Mass," *New Outline of the Principles of Sociology* (edited by Alfred M. Lee, Jr.), Barnes and Noble, New York, 1946.

5. Examples of violations which may result in the suspension of an operator's license are:

    a) Willfully damaging or permitting radio apparatus or installations to be damaged.

    b) Having transmitted superfluous radio communications or signals or communications containing profane or obscene words, language, or meaning.

For a complete statement of the rules, as originally set forth, see Section 303 of the Communications Act of 1934.

6. *Chain Broadcasting Regulations and Free Speech*, Federal Communications Commission, Washington, D. C., 1942.

7. *The Merger Movement. A Summary Report*, Federal Trade Commission, Washington, D. C., July, 1948.

8. See for instance: Hendrickson, R. C., and Cook, F. J., *Youth in Danger*, Harcourt, Brace, New York, 1956, 144-164.

9. These scandals received much attention on the front pages of the popular press beginning in late 1959. For the announcement of the first

proposals by the FCC to enact legislation see: The New York *Times*, February 12, 1960, 1.

10. A fine early statement of this two way process may be found in: Berelson, B., "The Effects of Print Upon Public Opinion," *Print, Radio and Film in a Democracy* (edited by Douglas Waples), University of Chicago Press, Chicago, 1942, 41-42.

An excellent recent treatment of the effect of feed-back on the systems is: McPhee, W., *For Whom the Ratings Toll*, unpublished paper from Bureau of Applied Social Research, Columbia University, forthcoming in article form in *The Nation*.

11. Cantwell, Most Rev. John J., "The Motion Picture Industry," *The Movies on Trial* (edited by W. J. Perlman), Macmillan, New York, 1936, 21.

12. See for instance: Wertham, F., "The Comics . . . Very Funny," *Saturday Review of Literature*, May 29, 1948, 6-7.

13. Here there is a wealth of data. See for instance: Lazarsfeld, Paul F., and Kendall, Patricia, *Radio Listening in America*, Prentice-Hall, New York, 1948, 11.

14. Schramm, Wilbur, *The Process and Effects of Mass Communication*, University of Illinois Press, Urbana, 1954, 72. There are also many other examples of research which support this finding.

15. Again here there is a wealth of data. For example see: Bogart, Leo, *The Age of Television*, Ungar, New York, 1956; Schramm, Wilbur, *op. cit.*

16. Schramm, *op. cit.*, 3-26.

17. This concept of self-selection has been pointed out in many of the writings of Paul Lazarsfeld. For an early statement see: Lazarsfeld, Paul F., "The Effects of Radio on Public Opinion," *Print, Radio and Film in a Democracy* (edited by Douglas Waples), University of Chicago Press, Chicago, 1942, 68.

18. Newcomb, T. M., *Social Psychology*, Dryden Press, New York, 1950, 90-96.

19. Hovland, Lumsdaine, and Sheffield, *Studies in Social Psychology in World War II*, Vol. III, Princeton University Press, Princeton, 1949.

20. Blumer, H., and Hauser, P., *Movies, Delinquency, and Crime*, Macmillan, New York, 1933. This volume is one in the series of works sponsored by the Payne Fund in an effort to learn more about the effects of motion pictures as a then new medium.

21. Some aspects of this problem are discussed in relation to television in: Pearlin, L. I., *The Social and Psychological Setting of Communications Behavior*, Columbia University, unpublished doctoral dissertation in Sociology, 1957.

22. Merton, R. K., *Social Theory and Social Structure*, Free Press, Glencoe, Illinois, 1957, 442-446.

23. Riesman, D., *The Lonely Crowd*, Doubleday, New York, 1953.

24. Clinard, Marshall B., "Secondary Community Influences and Juvenile Delinquency," *The Annals* of the American Academy of Political and Social Science, January, 1949, 42-54.

25. Clinard, M. B., *The Annals*, *op. cit.*, 43.

26. See for instance: Cohen, Albert K., *Delinquent Boys*, Free Press, Glencoe, Illinois, 1955.

EXPERIMENTAL EFFORTS AT
TREATMENT AND "SOLUTIONS"

SOME THEORIES OF PENOLOGY

Roy G. Francis
&
Arthur L. Johnson
University of Minnesota

Strictly speaking, "penology" is an upgraded term. Despite the verbiage written about "crime and punishment," the implications of the suffix "logy" seem improper. For the most part, "penology" refers to systematic belief systems rather than a basic science. What, in the literature, passes for "theories of penology" are more properly "philosophies of punishment." There have been very few studies which proceed with any acceptable degree of rigor relating types of punishment with modifications in behavior.

We can anticipate considerable objection to the last sentence. Nonetheless, it is necessary to accept it. As Vold has indicated, studies comparing various kinds of penal institutions and recidivism can hardly be held to have tested the significance of modifications in the penal structure. The reason for this is that *convicts are not randomly assigned to the various kinds of custody;* they are pre-selected. Until a randomization procedure has been used, one will never know for certain whether it was the selection procedure or the institution or both which leads to the variation in recidivism.

Before discussing the various "functions" of custody, we must identify the position of the state in the handling of the criminal. The state may be defined as that institution which claims the sole legitimate use of violence.[1] Because of this monopoly, the state has the power to remove certain citizens from every day life, more or less permanently. How it will exercise this power—when, or against whom—is not contained in the statement of its power. Indeed, this proposes the problem of where the control over the legislature, the judiciary, and the police system actually resides.

It seems reasonable to assume that the use of this right for violence by the State varies as does the ideological climate of the State. Penal institutions, if we subscribe to a Durkheimean functionalism, are a "clue to the times." [2]

In a situation characterized by high death rates, maternity death rates and such other curtailments of life, we find growing up the tradition, "The good die young." In a crude society in which physical violence is a part of the everyday life—where, for example, the idea of surgery is a radical one and anesthesia unheard of—that the State itself could be violent ought to come as no surprise.

We can define "punishment" as the deliberate infliction of pain for the presumed purpose of achieving a change in someone's behavior. Our preceding paragraph simply states that that which constitutes "pain" varies culturally. It is possible that pain is associated with things that one holds dear. When life itself is relatively short, then the State's worst punishment is to claim the criminal's life. But when freedom and liberty are man's most precious possessions, then the worst punishment that can be meted out is a deprivation of personal liberty. It is not surprising, then, that a democracy forces its convicted criminals to live in what is essentially a fascist state.

In some sense, punishments involve a conception of the criminal and/or the crime. In general, major differences center around whether the criminal is held responsible for his actions. Those who hold to a strict determinism frequently argue that the criminal is not responsible for his actions; and therefore, punishment makes no sense. This point of view overlooks the possibility of a people being trained to act as if they were responsible.[3] It is not always clear what those who feel the criminal is responsible actually appeal to. Frequently it will be a rationalistic idea that a responsible person will avoid pain.

INSTRUMENTAL "FUNCTIONS" OF FORMAL PUNISHMENT

Whether explicitly argued, or only implicit, punishment rests upon what it is supposed to do for society. It is possible to conceive of a situation in which means having been elevated to ends, punishment becomes a thing desired in its own right. Clearly, this would be abhorrent behavior in most societies. If formal punishment brutalizes the custodian—making him the prisoner of his prisoners—we might observe instances of punishment being pursued for its own sake. In such situations, brutality could be tolerated on the grounds that "the hound needs to mangle some foxes or he's ruined"—that the SS trooper had to give vent to his urges for brutality or become less effective. For the most part, however, we can ignore punishment as an end, and regard it as some sort of instrument. Below, we shall discuss a number of the most commonly held images of the functions of punishment.

REVENGE

Society's sense of right has been impaired, and it is necessary to "get even." Like the thesis of Hamlet, this requires the assumption that criminal violence having thrown Nature off her steady course, an act of violence is required to restore order. An appeal is sometimes made to "instinct" as a justification for a revengeful attitude.

It is easy to criticize this sentiment on moral grounds. At best, it can be held, revenge is a child-like attitude. At worst, it spreads a sentiment of hatred which does more harm than good. It is also argued that this sentiment offends the Christian teaching to "turn the other cheek," that "vengeance is mine, sayeth the Lord." Yet, however crude it might be, the sentiment of revenge invokes a sentiment of justice. Some idea of "restoring things" is inherent in it. And it is understandable that those who have been injured would desire to retaliate. Whether retaliation must be in kind is the question.

IDENTIFICATION OF VALUES

On the premise that punishment is a clue to the times, we can argue that punishment involves the assertion of a people that certain values are not to be violated. A current debate regarding the traffic deaths of youthful pedestrians sometimes points out that the State evokes a greater penalty for slaying a deer out of season than for the death of a child. The more prized a value is, the logical argument would be to be consistent, the greater the punishment for its violation.

It is not likely that any society has in legislative assembly attempted to catalog its values and to assign penalties according to some such scheme. On the other hand, one can assess differences in punishments for various crimes from just this point of view. In some localities rape caries a death penalty; in others, the same act involves less than ten years' incarceration. Appealing to a principle of the sort explicated here allows us to "explain" such differences.

Life doesn't work out in such a simple way. The definition of an act as a felony may so dismay law enforcement officers that they refuse to uphold the law; subsequent redefinition to make the act a lesser crime—a misdemeanor—frequently brings about stricter enforcement.

DETERRENCE

Insofar as man is presumed to be rational, punishment will "deter" man from committing an act of a certain sort. It is quite likely that this is frequently true in many unrecorded instances. Absence of a survey showing its existence has led many criminologists to hold against it. Recently, however, I was in a conversation with a business leader who was discussing Bernard Goldfine's indictment for having evaded some $800,000.00 in income taxes. The businessman said that he was surprised to find Goldfine in such a fix. With the income-tax laws giving informants half of what is recovered in a suit to recover past taxes, the man should have assumed that someone would be willing to turn him in for the reward. And, my friend continued, a man in high places must presume that he has a number of enemies who would be willing to turn him in. Who can say that my friend had not either seriously or otherwise calculated the risk of success and failure? Who can say that he had not been deterred?

Yet, it must be admitted many criminal acts are not the results of rational action. Moreover, not all people are capable of rational behavior; lack of knowledge, lack of training and factors of an immediate situation are all involved in the criminal's behavior.

Moreover many criminals are quite rational in assessing their chances of success. And despite their full knowledge of the law, and a fairly realistic appraisal of their chances of getting caught, go ahead and pull the job. The most emotionally laden argument against "deterrence" is that, the act of criminal violence culminating a moment action, personal injury cases cannot possibly be deterred by severe punishments. In addition, pickpockets have been known to work crowds gathered to see the hanging of a pickpocket. I suppose pride in one's craft requires the surviving ones *to* feel that they won't get caught.

CUSTODIAL

At least during the length of incarceration this particular criminal cannot prey on society—except through the cost via taxation for the penal institution. This is in one sense literally true. Unfortunately, the fact of custody has certain unpleasant side effects:

Whatever other purpose a jail might have, its primary one is that of custody. The jailer has a number of bodies which he, by law, must account for. We saw earlier that the jail is essentially a fascist state; the individual has a minimum of freedoms. Except for those who will die or be executed, the criminal will at some time be released. He may become perfectly adjusted to the prison routine. He may need to have someone define his every action. This could become quite a source of personal security for him. He may be completely at a loss when thrust again on his own resources.

It is also possible that there are those who could never again be trusted outside the walls. There may be some who, by the time a formal agency has graduated them from boys' reform schools to the Big House, are incapable of any other kind of management. It is possible that there are some who could never be "reformed," that either execution or continuous custody is society's only safeguards from them. In short, custody will always be a part of our penal system. But the consequences of mere custody will have to be carefully considered. It could be damaging.

PENITENCE

There are those who feel that every man must have the chance to repent. Repentance requires a contrite heart, a facing up to the responsibility for having been evil. Accordingly, the criminal should be given a chance to become penitent. After all, the worst punishment is that which man metes out to himself; and unless the criminal accepts as just his incarceration, he is not likely to learn to modify his behavior.

It is possible that we will continue to read stories of men who "found themselves" in a prison or "penitentiary." The name for the institution was deliberately chosen to designate a place where man could be penitent. Just who becomes penitent and reforms himself inside the high gray walls is not known. Nor is it clear how many we have to waste in order to save the few who do succeed.

RATIONALISTIC

The "deterrence" argument has its counterpart from the criminal point of view. If all crimes could be coded in terms of the severity of punishment and this code were uniformly adopted,

262

the criminal could sensibly order his life. He could compute his risks, estimate his gains and losses. He could actually determine whether at any point in his career he was ahead or behind the game. Thus, the criminal whose arrest record shows a smaller percent than the national average, whose conviction record is also smaller than the national average, and whose average take is greater than the national average, would have a basis for feeling proud of his perverse response to the Protestant ethic. Today, those who would be rationalistic have to insert another variable: how much time it cost them per conviction.

REHABILITATION

Because almost every man who enters prison will someday be released, the argument runs, the man should be better when he leaves than when he enters. He must be "rehabilitated." If his deficiencies are of a personality sort, the services of a psychiatrist should be made available. Of course, psychiatric help requires the willingness and desire on the part of the subject. It is not always likely that they (the personality-warped criminals) desire to "go straight." Some do; and the prison term may be a good experience for them.

At one time, the common explanation for crime was "education," or its lack. Accordingly, prisoners were to learn a trade—some useful occupation. And a number of men have learned some skills which put them in good stead. Some became barbers, plumbers, carpenters, farm helpers and the like. For most of the men, the jobs were not the sort they were likely to get on the outside. The jobs available were for the tasks necessary for the maintenance of the institution itself. The chance to teach really needed trades has never succeeded in our penal system.

This is because prison labor (free, or a modicum of wages) competes with "free" labor. Both business and labor reject the idea of competing with prison-made goods. At one time, prison goods were to be labelled as such—to warn people not to buy. The tendency has been to permit the prison to engage in non-competitive manufacturing: the manufacture of license plates, for example. However laudable this may be in saving the State money it means that few men can learn a trade immediately useful on the outside.

Moreover, jobs were not always given to those who needed to learn a trade. Work breaks prison routine. Certain jobs became rewards within the prison system: to convicts for stool-pigeon work, to the top of the power structure, to the friends of the custodial personnel, to those with political contacts. In addition, there never were enough jobs for the number of men who could be accommodated. Hence, a system of "boondoggling" was built into the scheme of prison labor.

It is not clear that prison labor has been a strong factor in rehabilitation; it is not so much the skills which the ordinary prisoner needs to learn. It is an attitude towards work. He must learn the sense of responsibility that goes with a gainful occupation. He needs if anything, the Protestant Work Ethic. And, so far, at least, the prison is simply no place to learn that.

The idea of rehabilitation goes much further. Currently, it involves an assessment of likelihood of success based upon current attitudes, past record, and the like. Under this argument, various types of prisons are needed. From those requiring little custodial work for the prisoners most likely to succeed, to the institutions requiring a maximum of custodial work for those least likely to succeed.

The sentiment of attempting to enable the prisoner to re-enter the adult social world is fundamental to the spirit of rehabilitation. Currently, there is a tremendous amount of research—some excellent, some rather badly designed, to determine which of many alternative ways are the most likely to maximize successful adjustment to civil life. It is remarkable that a society will spend millions of dollars for the research needed in a disease that touches less than 10,000 persons a year and yet will spend practically nothing on research involving hundreds of thousands of criminals who are now not able to be productive members of society. It is as though the experts have arrived at the station called "Rehabilitation," while the mass of society is content with "custody"—out of sight, out of mind—priding itself on how civilized it is not to demand revenge.

CAPITAL PUNISHMENT

Custody is a temporary removal of an individual from social life. Capital punishment is a permanent one. And therein lies the difficulty.

As in all acts of man, there are two possible errors: one can do something he ought not to have done, or he can refrain from doing something he ought to have done. In this case the State can either execute an innocent man (Type I error), or it may release a man who later murders one or more other victims (presumably Type II error). We label the latter "presumably Type II error" on the supposition that the life of an innocent victim is more to be preferred than the life of a murderer. Few people like to regard capital punishment in these terms, particular those who oppose capital punishment. They prefer to see only the criminal; they are willing to estimate high probabilities for the Type I error and essentially deny the possibility of estimating the probabilities for Type II error. In this way they can present a rigorous argument.

THE CASE AGAINST CAPITAL PUNISHMENT

First, the State can make an irrevocable error. An innocent man may be executed, and history has given a number of names of men so destroyed by a righteous society. Second, a so-called "Christian society" has no right to take a man's life unless the situation is so desperate as to require immediate action. This latter condition justifies taking lives in war and in a gun-battle with a criminal in action. Third, though the man might be guilty of the crime—say, murder—he may have repented and actually be "cured." He may be a perfect risk. Even the hardened criminal whose victims are "things" rather than persons known and socially related to the killer, he may have "changed his ways" and would sin no more. Fourth, there is good in every man. Under proper guidance, he can be a productive agent of society. Why waste all the training that has been poured into him? Fifth, killing the murderer does no real good. It must have a bad effect on the executioners. It is hardly good mental health for a public to desire the death of anyone. And taking the murderer's life will certainly not restore the life of the one who has been destroyed. Sixth, "Vengeance is mine, sayeth the Lord"; and "Judge not, lest ye be judged." The implication is that a judgment of this kind ought best be left to the Deity. Seventh, death is too good for the really wicked: Make them suffer a long time cooped up in a jail, living with their consciences.

A CASE FOR CAPITAL PUNISHMENT

First, the State has simply a finite amount of money at its disposal. Since the likelihood of a criminal's actually becoming a productive member of society is very small, why spend all the money needed to sustain his life for some thirty or forty years? Why not put that money into the training of the kind of scholars and scientists we need? To destroy some unknown's genius for the sake of a known murderer is a poor exchange. Second, the likelihood of Type II error is as easily computed as Type I error. As long as it is the smaller of the two possibilities, the total saving of worthwhile lives will be maximized. Third, even if Type I error has been committed, if there is a righteous God, He will rectify the wrong. Do not presume to commend a man to Hell simply because he has been executed by man. Fourth, the human life is so precious that we ought to reaffirm its value by being extremely drastic to those who violate it. The death penalty is simply a re-affirmation of basic human values. To do away with the death penalty equates a human life with a loaf of bread. Fifth, the argument that ours is a "Christian society" is erroneous. No society, no state, can be Christian. There are no theological grounds for supposing a "life eternal" for a state or a society. One

266

must "give unto Caesar that which is Caesar's"; and since the State is an impersonal thing, the idea that it is "wrong" for a State to take a life is meaningless. It is wrong for people, as individuals, to take the life of another human being.

Other arguments, pro and con, can be easily devised. It should be completely clear that the argument cannot be resolved by *science*. Whether or not there *ought* to be capital punishment is not a *scientific* question. It is a *moral* problem. It is not a matter of fact, but a question of one's philosophy and, if you will, his theology.

ANOTHER SORT OF PROBLEM

Since the State has claimed a monopoly on the use of violence, it alone has the authority and the power to settle disputes. As this has prevented the destruction accompanying the vendetta and the feud, society has indeed benefited.

It may seem strange to consider that the State claims to have been injured in a criminal case—not the victim. To be sure, some jurisdictions permit civil suits to grow out of criminal cases, but this is scarcely worthwhile from an economic point of view. When a penniless psychopath burns down one's house, a suit for damages hardly settles anything. For the most part, the State presumes to be the victim. This came about as far as the United States was concerned, at the time of the Revolution.

When the states were faced with developing their own laws, they mostly copied the English tradition (Louisiana being a notable exception, adhering to French law). Where the English law had put the Crown as the injured party, the new states simply put the "State" itself. If the Crown could do no wrong, neither could the State: it must grant permission to be sued.

Where, before, the problem of "justice" was significant, the new relationship of combat between the State and the accused tended to destroy "justice" as a problem. What is the law—not "what is just"—became the issue: for the truly injured party was only an interested bystander. Suppose that a man had been accused of rape: the victim was wrung through the ordeal of a public trial where the defense attorney could destroy her reputation if that would at all help his client's case.

Criminology became centered around the criminal. The victim was presumed to be randomly related to the violator: because he was a "random variable," he needed no explanation.[4] Our attention was drawn elsewhere. In our concern for "punishment," we neglected to consider the victim, or even define him. In the case of rape, who is the victim? Surely, the girl; but what of her parents? Were they "damaged"? What of her friends?

This raises the question, what is the relation of the State to the victim of a criminal act. Up to now, most jurisdictions simply let the victim fend for himself. Because of our attitudes, mostly maudlin about the criminal being the product of a bad society, many people act as though society had a debt to pay to the criminal. So the convict gets medical and psychiatric help. But his victim? Heavens, no! That would be an invasion of private enterprise!

Suppose an arsonist burned a man's house down. The victim gets no help at all from the State, even though he is essentially unable to do anything to help himself. He cannot even get the pitiful satisfaction of revenge. His loss is complete.

It would seem that if the State must assert that it is the real victim, it has a responsibility to those directly injured. It should then replace the home burned by the arsonist, assist the family whose breadwinner has been destroyed by a murder. It should give medical and psychiatric help free to the victim, regardless of ability to pay. Perhaps if the crime load were distributed generally throughout society, its cost would be more generally felt and the attention this problem deserves would be forthcoming.

SELECTED BIBLIOGRAPHY

American Prison Association, *Manual of Standards for a State Correctional System*, The Association, New York, 1954.
American Prison Association, Committee on Riots, *Statements*

Concerning Causes, Preventive Measures and Methods of Controlling Riots and Disturbances, The Association, New York, 1953.

Bates, Sanford, *Prisons and Beyond,* The Macmillan Co., New York, 1936. By a well known authority in this field.

Dressler David, *Practice and Theory of Probation and Parole,* Columbia University Press, New York, 1959. The best up-to-date introduction to this field.

Lawes, Lewis E., *Twenty Thousand Years in Sing Sing,* Long and Smith, New York, 1932. A well-known story by a liberally minded warden.

McKelvey, Blake, *American Prisons: a Study in American Social History Prior to 1915.* University of Chicago Press, 1936. Useful as an introduction to a rather neglected field.

Osborne, Thomas Matt, *Prisons and Common,* Lippincott, Philadelphia, 1924. Outdated, but suggestive.

Scudder, Kennyon D., *Prisoners are People,* Doubleday, Garden City, New York, 1952. a humanitarian approach.

Sellin, Thorsten, (editor), "Prisons in Transformation," *Annals of the American Academy of Political and Social Science,* CCXCIII, 1954. Invaluable for its varied points of view and summaries.

Tappan, Paul W., *Contemporary Correction,* McGraw-Hill, New York, 1951. A systematic survey.

United Nations, Department of Social Affairs, *Parole and After Care,* UN, 1954.

Roy G. Francis, Associate Professor in the University of Minnesota, received his B. A. (Magna Cum Laude) from Infield College, M.A. (with honors from University of Oregon), and Ph.D. from University of Wisconsin (1950). Taught at the University of Oregon, Wisconsin, and Tulane Universities. In addition to *An Introduction to Social Research* (with Doby and others) and *Service and Procedure in a Bureaucracy* (with Robert Stone), has published numerous articles in the field of logic, scientific procedure, prediction and other methodological problems.

Arthur L. Johnson, Ph.D., is Associate Professor of Sociology at the University of Minnesota. His special teaching and research interests are social problems and social control and the family.

269

He is an Associate Member of the Family Study Center at the University of Minnesota and has participated in a number of projects and conferences related to social problems and their control.

NOTES

1. Gerth, Hans H. and Mills, C. Wright (translators and editors), *From Max Weber: Essays in Sociology*, Oxford University Press, New York, 1946, 334.

2. Francis, Roy G., *Seventeenth Century Background of Individualism*, University of Oregon Library, Eugene, (unpublished M.A. thesis, 1947).

3. MacIver, Robert, *Social Causation*, Ginn and Co., Boston, 1942, especially Chapter 8, "Cause as Responsible Agent," 225-250.

4. An exception is the recent research which indicated that in many murders the issue was frequently "Who will strike first?"

RECENT EFFORTS TO HANDLE JUVENILE DELINQUENCY

By Rose C. Thomas
Howard University

Juvenile delinquency is one of our most serious domestic problems and efforts to handle it have challenged the knowledge, skill and imagination of a variety of specialists in the field of human relations. Social researchers are responding to current demands, ofttimes conflicting demands, to provide the public with useful knowledge; practitioners are challenged to discover more effective techniques of study, diagnosis and treatment; institutions serving young offenders are asked to isolate and/or reduce the threat of increased violence by youth, and the public in turn is pressed to provide an ever-increasing source of funds to perform a staggering social task.

When we speak of delinquency, it becomes necessary to look beyond acts of a delinquent nature as defined by society to those conditions which create and foster a social climate conducive to and giving rise to such acts. Internalized problems which lead to acts such as running away from home, truancy from school or incorrigibility should be placed in juxtaposition to changes in expectations and standards of living of the American family which now require employment of both parents, lengthened compulsory school laws and similar external forces which weaken primary parental controls upon the child. However, when society fulfills its obligation to children whose parents have failed them through services offered in the child's own home,[1] these programs "rarely single out individual children because of their supposed proneness to delinquency." On the other hand, externalized problems such as auto thefts (in 1956, 54% of those thefts were perpetrated by youths under 21) should require closer scrutiny of the role of the automobile in American society.[2]

Juvenile delinquency or "Norm-violating behavior which brings the non-adult to the attention of official authority or agency,"[3] reflects culturally determined attitudes and values in conflict with legal restraints as many researchers have shown. Since methods of handling problems of juvenile delinquency imply methods used in dealing with cases coming to the attention of courts, the magnitude of the problem is difficult to estimate when, as we know, a child's appearance before a court is determined in part by attitudes of the parents and of the community. Nevertheless, an estimate of the size of the problem is needed against which to assess success or failure of modern society.

Statistics on file in the Children's Bureau of the U. S. Department of Health, Education and Welfare reveal that in 1957 more than 600,000 cases of delinquency were referred to juvenile courts.

Perlman states that the problem is greater than the figures of any one year indicate; and a more accurate picture is obtained "by estimating the percentage of all children who will become involved in at least one court delinquency case during their adolescence."[4] It can be assumed also, that the increase in child population in the United States is likely to mean a proportionate rise in the number of delinquents.

The incidence of juvenile delinquency in other highly "civilized" countries is comparable to that which exists in the United States as the files of the United Nations will show. These latter provide shocking evidence that improved living conditions in most countries of the world have not lessened the rise or seriousness of the problem. Lopez-Rey states that juvenile delinquency is increasing rapidly in many countries, especially in the United States, the United Kingdom and Sweden, notwithstanding an increase in social services and the number of social workers employed to administer social services in these highly developed countries. In an effort to explain this social paradox experts have advanced theories, among them international tensions and some effects of war, yet the theories fail to account for variations and differences in the extent of tensions felt by different groups in the same country, or, why it is that the delinquency rate is higher in the United States than in a country like Spain when the former experienced none of the destruction and devastation experienced by the latter.

Study of the problem of juvenile delinquency reveals four characteristics according to Lopez-Rey: 1) steadily and insidiously it is reaching every group and every aspect of the community in many countries; 2) it is increasing in gravity; 3) it is not restricted any more to the urban populations and finally it is no longer confined to poverty areas of certain populations or regions.[5] Looked at from these view-points it is understandable why this country is presently seeking solutions to the problem through efforts directed toward bringing about changes in individuals and changes in the environment conducive to the promotion of acceptable standards of conduct of youth. Special services now being used and extended to provide opportunities for legitimate success for delinquents include:

Research studies of individuals, groups and communities financed by the Federal Government, experiments focused on individuals, groups, neighborhoods, community-agency resources, residential treatment centers, area projects and special services in schools. In the remainder of this paper illustrations will be given to highlight some current attempts to turn back the tide of juvenile delinquency.

Before turning attention to newer methods of approaching the problem of delinquency, mention should be made of facilities long associated with and well known to the general public as resources used to deal with the problem of delinquency such as, police departments, detention facilities and probation departments of juvenile courts, and training schools. As the problem of aggressive behavior of youth looms larger and national concern about young law-violators heightens, it may be assumed that these aforementioned traditional institutional services have been ineffective unless consideration is also given to the adequacy of their facilities and services, qualitatively and quantitatively.

POLICE DEPARTMENTS, DETENTION FACILITIES, JUVENILE COURTS, TRAINING SCHOOLS

Experts in the field of juvenile delinquency agree that the youth who violates the law for the first time needs sound police handling in order to avoid more serious anti-social acts subsequently. To achieve proper handling of delinquents communities need special juvenile police units, especially to deal with youth whose acts of an anti-social nature are more damaging to themselves than to members of society. Youth behavior such as running away, incorrigibility and truancy falls within the purview of juvenile courts and therefore requires evaluation by police officers who can distinguish appropriately between those cases in need of referral to other community resources, the court, or can be dealt with within the home. Effective police handling at so crucial a point in a youngster's life is a responsibility of every community if youthful offenders are to be rehabilitated and citizens protected against their aggression.

Juvenile units of police departments usually serve to interpret policies affecting delinquents and to make dispositions based on knowledge and understanding of the individual youth. In the District of Columbia, for example, the Youth Aid Division handles cases of a non-arrest nature when further legal redress is deemed unnecessary. Although juvenile bureaus are designed for individualized study of children they are not always equipped with competent staff, and further, it has been estimated that 50% of the cities with a population over 100,000 have no special juvenile police officers.[6]

Detention facilities for the temporary care of children awaiting court hearings should be adequate to meet the need, if while in the arms of the law, minors are to be protected from exposure to adult offenders. Nevertheless, fewer than 200 detention homes are available to some 2,500 courts which require detention services. To meet the need more adequately in sparsely settled areas the National Probation and Parole Association proposed a plan to construct and operate detention facilities on a regional basis according to Kahn.[7] More important than building costs, the same writer observed that the program should be geared to communicate to the offender that society disapproves his act, not the offender to whom help is offered. To make the distinction between the youth and his act, to study, guide and redirect him requires skillful handling which as yet is not available in detention facilities, not to mention the unsegregated incarceration of 100,000 youths with adults annually.

A quick glance at the primary resource for the youthful offender, the juvenile court, reveals that of the one-third million adjudicated delinquents, only three states, Connecticut, Rhode Island and Utah, provide separate children's courts to deal exclusively with their problems. In varying degrees, however, all states have statutes which incorporate juvenile court philosophy. Nevertheless, of the 3,000 or more counties of the United States, only 40 have special judges who devote their time exclusively, and only 40 more counties have judges devoting a part of their time to children's cases. The effectiveness of this primary resource in meeting the needs of delinquents can hardly be measured when the overwhelming majority of the delinquents in the United States have their fate determined within the framework of adult courts unequipped to meet their special needs.

Qualitative probation services are the vitality of juvenile courts in which children receive justice and individualized treatment. Yet the appalling fact is, half the counties of the United States are completely without juvenile probation services, and where these services do exist, staffs are poorly qualified to make sound recommendations to the court on the basis of adequate psychosocial study. Gradually, courts in larger cities are strengthening probation services by employing professional social workers and/ or creating opportunities for employed staff to study in schools of social work. The courts of the District of Columbia, and Baltimore, Maryland, reflect this trend; the former, through the employment of professional social workers, the latter through provision of educational opportunities for employed staff.

Training schools in most instances represent a last resort in handling delinquents after other methods of dealing with them have failed to yield results. Most training schools are overcrowded and frequently insufficiently and poorly staffed. Here as elsewhere, inadequate personnel cannot be expected to offer remedial, educational, psychosocial and other forms of therapeutic treatment which are at the present time the core of rehabilitative methodology.

New and re-newed attempts to deal with problems of juvenile delinquency are occasioned in part by the ever-increasing size of the problem, failure in dealing with the problem adequately, fragmentary knowledge of the subject and failure to use on a broader scale knowledge already accumulated. Here and there studies and special projects offered a glimmer of hope but when curtailed or terminated for a variety of reasons these efforts failed to provide sustained, systematic findings useful for theory-building and within which, newer methods could be developed to handle problems of delinquency. That is why in recent years leadership by the Federal Government has been welcomed by individuals, groups and localities who were enmeshed in the struggle to meet the nation's problem of youth.

ROLE OF FEDERAL AGENCIES

In a general way, every division of the Department of Health, Education and Welfare touches upon the problem of juvenile delinquency in the sense that the Department is interested in the well-being of all children especially those who live in particularly disadvantaged environments. Specific responsibility for services centers within the Children's Bureau, which has as one of its functions mobilization of the home, the school and the community to improve family life. Tufts[8] describes the method used by the Children's Bureau in securing advice from many experts and involving them for the purpose of juvenile delinquency prevention.

276

Although the Bureau's services are action-centered it has a continuous program designed to discover effective measures to prevent and reduce delinquency. Chief among these measures are research programs conducted by trained staff equipped to coordinate programs on the state and local level, and development and distribution of knowledge and information to public and private agencies. For example, from 1952-1955, the Bureau sponsored the Special Juvenile Delinquency Project, a project which emphasized programs designed for the control of delinquency. The Congress of the United States was influenced by the success of the venture to appropriate in 1954, funds for the establishment of a Division of Juvenile Delinquency Services in the Children's Bureau. Nation-wide the Children's Bureau has become known as "one Federal source to which community, State and national individuals and groups can turn for knowledge about acceptable standards of service to delinquent youth, and for means to make their services more useful to the children who are vulnerable to delinquent behavior." [9]

The Division of Juvenile Delinquency Services does not encompass the Children's Bureau's total program for the prevention and reduction of delinquency. Its Division of Social Services is concerned with all child welfare services; the Division of Research makes a substantial contribution in reporting statistical findings from legal sources and conducts research on various phases of juvenile delinquency.

The U.S. Senate's Sub-Committee to Investigate Juvenile Delinquency. The dilemma over delinquency was catapulted to a number-one position and spot-lighted as a problem of national concern when in 1953, the Committee of the Judiciary of the United States Senate formed the Sub-Committee to Investigate Juvenile Delinquency. Its personnel included specialists in law, sociology, education, criminology, social research and social work, who were charged with the responsibility of providing the Committee with facts in regard to causes, methods and adequacy of facilities, and, the efficacy of Federal laws dealing with juvenile delinquency. One of the objectives of the Sub-Committee was to recommend on the bases of findings, "such measures and action as the sub-committee may determine to be needed to prevent juvenile delinquency and the commission of criminal offenses by youths, and to rehabilitate those children and youths who have already embarked upon delinquent or criminal careers . . ." [10] In addition to study and investigation of state, local and voluntary agencies, the Sub-Committee has taken a broad-view of Federal responsibility to assist with the problem of delinquency. It was responsible for the establishment of an Advisory Council on Juvenile Delinquency to the Secretary of Health, Education and Welfare; it recommended federal funds to assist states with educational programs for staff, program expansion and research; it authorized grants for additional research at the National Institute of Mental Health, and introduced legislation to expand the services of the Children's Bureau and the Office of Education, of Health, Education and Welfare. The latter contributes to delinquency prevention through its activities to improve services of guidance and counseling in school programs of the kind to be mentioned later.

JUVENILE DELINQUENCY PROGRAM OF THE NATIONAL INSTITUTE OF MENTAL HEALTH

The most far-reaching and comprehensive attempt to handle juvenile delinquency was begun when the House Appropriations Committee of the 86th Congress directed the National Institute of Mental Health to make "a most useful and thoughtful study of what can and should be done in future years in the field of juvenile delinquency." [11] Later, the Senate Appropriations Committee ordered the inclusion of the Children's Bureau in the undertaking. These two units of the Department of Health, Education and Welfare made their first legislative and fiscal proposals for juvenile delinquency research to the 87th Congress in January, 1960.

The National Institute of Mental Health regards delinquency as a major area of deviant behavior among youth but its research programs are broad and cover a wide range of activities related to children.

Specific to the problem under discussion it conducts a program of training, research and consultation in the mental health aspects of delinquency. The cost of projects now underway totals $1,113,000 with $5,600,000 having been granted these projects thus far. Three research projects are underway in three different locations with foci on delinquency as follows:

1. The project at the South Shore Courts Clinic, Quincy, Massachusetts, is an attempt "to classify into treatment categories a sample of all delinquents coming to the juvenile court. Evidence accumulated previously revealed that plans for delinquents, nation-wide, had been determined by untrained persons." From the pilot phase of the study it is estimated that 50% of all delinquents coming to the court need intensive mental health or social work treatment, and it is hoped that findings from the project will aid present court staffs in applying treatment classification procedures.

2. A second demonstration project undertaken at New York University was to test the conviction of many specialists, "that the provision of adequate treatment and prevention services in a high-delinquency area will now reduce the problem within tolerable limits."

3. The project at the University of Michigan seems to strike at the core of the problem and may point to a more scientific and effective method of dealing with delinquents. This community study focuses on social and psychological factors and the study subjects are drawn from middle and lower social-class-status groups. It will culminate in an experimental delinquency prevention and treatment program.

Tentative findings from the study regarding the development of delinquent behavior of children include:

a. Employment of the mother may or may not be a factor in child-rearing only insofar as it reflects a woman's attitudes and behavior in the role of mother.

b. Working mothers living in poorer neighborhoods are not increasing the likelihood of their sons becoming problems more than the sons of their non-working neighbors.

c. Employment of the mother from better neighborhoods may be a factor in the development of patterns of delinquency of their sons.

d. A high, positive self-evaluation of the boy seems to be very difficult without perceived high esteem from the father.

e. The junior high school years are the most critical for the boy and should be the period for intensive remedial help for the boy headed toward a pattern of delinquency.

Other research related to juvenile delinquency in progress at the National Institute of Mental Health are of two varieties: Those with a direct and immediate application to the delinquency problem; and those which are of a more basic nature but which contribute significantly to knowledge in the field of juvenile delinquency.[12]

Eighty-four different grants classified within eleven categories make possible a diversified program which has both direct and indirect bearing on the problem of delinquency. These include six long-term follow-up studies: Three of these follow as many as 15,000 children, the ninth grade population of a whole county over a period of 10 years; two studies are concerned with the social fate of children designated as delinquent and will follow the subjects for as long as thirty years; the sixth study compares delinquents with non-delinquents to highlight the role of environmental factors in producing delinquent behavior. Other groupings of studies include: Treatment methods, 14 studies; family structure and attitudes, 14 studies; peer group processes, 4 studies; delinquency and the school, 7 studies; special communities, 5 studies.

It can be seen therefore that the citizens of America through their elected representatives in Congress recognize the gravity of the problem of delinquency and are making long-range plans to deal with it constructively. Accordingly, more than 80% of the funds appropriated by Congress for projects in delinquency under the auspices of the National Institute of Mental Health is for research grants; some with direct bearing on the delinquency problem and some to be used for more basic research of indirect importance to the understanding and treatment of delinquents. Other funds in the form of training grants have been allocated to the Judge Baker Guidance Center in Boston to develop training methodology for personnel in the area of delinquency prevention. This five year program at the Judge Baker Foundation nearing its completion, offers training to personnel working in many areas of human behavior: juvenile police work, probation, school guidance, remedial education, theology, sociology, psychiatry, clinical psychology and psychiatric social work.

In their attempt to prevent juvenile delinquency federal agencies as described are making many indirect approaches to the problem. They are helping to improve the quality of services at the state and local level to children in trouble; and they are trying to offset the development of delinquency patterns through study and treatment of the delinquency-prone youth.

What are some programs not sponsored by the Federal Government designed to reduce juvenile delinquency? These can be divided into two broad classifications: Programs designed to effect change through direct treatment of the individual, and those designed to effect change through improvement of the environment.

Studies such as the Cambridge-Somerville Youth Study, the Street Corner Groups of Boston and Chicago, the Englewood Experiment involving police and social-agency cooperation and the Highfields Experiment are examples of approaches to the problem of delinquency through focusing treatment on the individual. Examples of efforts to promote growth through changes in the environment are: All Day Neighborhood Schools, Coordinating Community Councils and the Chicago and District of Columbia Area Projects. Brief references to these projects may illustrate some progress made in recent years as a result of increased knowledge about human behavior and motivation, used to combat juvenile delinquency.

THE CAMBRIDGE SOMERVILLE STUDY

This study,[13] though initiated fifteen years ago has an important bearing on more recent studies because it was the first extensive attempt to provide early treatment and intensive contact with study subjects as a means of crime prevention. Also, a follow-up report on the results of the study provides knowledge of the impact of this carefully planned project on work now in progress in the interest of troubled children.

Three hundred twenty-five youths were selected for treatment and matched against an equal number of boys in a control group, both from two densely populated factory cities, Cambridge and Somerville, Massachusetts. For a period of five years, the best known methods and techniques of psychosocial study and treatment (family guidance, medical and academic assistance, coordination of community agencies and supplementary entertainment of the boys) were utilized, but without having demonstrated an appreciable difference in the behavior of the treated boys in comparison with the untreated boys. Moreover, three years after the conclusion of the project researchers reported as many crimes of as serious a nature had been committed by boys from each of the two groups. A follow-up study made recently[14] traced into adulthood 253 of the matched mates and concluded that "whatever benefits the treated boys received were not reflected in their criminal rates." Despite this negative conclusion, and even in its failure, the program was a "magnificent experiment" which produced a fund of information "invaluable to future studies of the causation and prevention of crime." [15]

STREET CORNER GROUPS: THE BOSTON DELINQUENCY PROJECT

The corner-group-worker program reported by Miller[16] was designed to test the hypothesis that between the ages of twelve and nineteen "the dominant set of influences on the behavior of members of lower-class adolescent groups derive from the group's conception of prestige-conferring behavior and valued objectives." The principal target of the Project was the value-system of the group and the primary device used to alter the group's value-system was to restructure the group into a formal organized club. To bring about change through this process, there must be available to the group, law-abiding avenues tc valued ends present in the group's own cultural milieu if prestige values are to shift from law-violating to law-abiding behavioi. Miller found that worker-activity had a measurable impact on patterns of group behavior especially during early phases of contact with the worker. However, the Project's goal of in-hibiting community delinquency was limited—in part because of factors such as time, insufficient personnel and inefficient execution of planned procedures.

THE HYDE PARK YOUTH PROJECT, CHICAGO

The experiment at Hyde Park had as its aim the development of a coordinated community-centered juvenile delinquency pre-vention and control program.[17] Group work with pre-delinquents was attempted outside of building-centered programs and fol-lowed the general pattern used in work with delinquent gangs. Intensive service for periods of six to eighteen months was pro-vided to delinquency-prone groups by workers who served as liaisons between them, the block clubs and individual adults for the purpose of achieving understanding and respect between them. The Project demonstrated that "work with street clubs, or other groupings of youth with a high delinquency potential, is an effective approach to the prevention of delinquency . . . (and) can be done within the framework of existing community agencies." Also, findings of the Project suggest that group work and recreation agencies should consider extending their services to meet a greater community need by giving more staff time to youths not yet adjusted to building-centered programs.[18]

THE ENGLEWOOD PROJECT

Another effort to curb delinquency through direct work with individuals was an experiment in police-social agency cooperation conducted in the City of Chicago, and covered the period 1954-1957.[19] This undertaking focused attention on children identified by police as delinquency-prone but not yet in need of referral to court. It had as its goals: Determination of the feasibility of police and social-agency cooperation in the prevention of delinquency; utilization of casework skills to develop a method of working with the police on voluntary referrals to the Project and, integration of community resources to achieve more effective restraint and resocialization of children with developing patterns of delinquent behavior. The goals of the study were verified by the findings. That is, police-social agency cooperation was found to be both feasible and essential in lowering the rate of delinquency in an area like Englewood where caseloads, "gave grim evidence of the extent to which the continuous grind of extreme poverty corrodes family morale . . ." Further, approximately 50% of the subjects and their families were helped through a casework relationship. Moreover, it was found that some children who could not be helped in their own homes could be helped in residential treatment centers.

As a result of this experiment, recommendations were made to establish in congested areas treatment centers staffed by trained caseworkers in order to provide a resource other than the court for children who may be in the process of becoming behavior problems or delinquent; and to expand and strengthen the Police Juvenile Bureau, since it is likely that the presence of a juvenile officer in a neighborhood is a deterrent to delinquent activity.

RESIDENTIAL TREATMENT CENTERS

The residential treatment center is another method used in offering direct help to the delinquent. Although residential treatment centers cannot at any one time serve but a small number of individuals, the work of the treatment center is significant in that it helps to provide answers to questions in regard to the delinquent's treatability via comprehensive milieu therapy. The Highfields Experiment is illustrative.

Highfields was established in 1950 on recommendation of New Jersey's Director of Correction and Parole. He wished to test methods which he believed would be effective in working with offenders between the ages of 16-18 years.

Highfields[20] is unique among projects in the treatment of delinquency. Its story is an interesting account of the philosophy, organization and operation of a correctional institution. A therapeutic atmosphere was created in an environment almost free of rules and restrictive measures for the purpose of undermining faulty self-concepts and attitudes of 24 youths, and substituting for them self-conceptions favorable to reformation. Sessions on "guided group-interaction," a method which employs psychiatric and social approaches to the control of human behavior, were utilized to achieve the goal of law-abiding behavior.

Highfields has been a scientific experiment. After five years of operation, funds from the Astor Foundation made it possible to conduct a carefully controlled study of 50 subjects in comparison with a control group from the Annandale, New Jersey State Training School. In contrast to findings from such well-known studies as the Gluecks' in Massachusetts, and Shaw and his associates in Illinois, recidivism occurred much less frequently among boys with three to four months Highfields experience than of the boys with 12 or more months residence at Annandale Training School.

The Highfields experiment makes an important contribution to the growing body of knowledge on methods of handling juvenile delinquency; it illustrates that an informal atmosphere can be achieved in a residential treatment center; and that a treatment center can be operated successfully by a small staff without the usual precautionary measures employed in large custodial-type reformatories.

ENVIRONMENTAL APPROACHES

For those who believe that juvenile delinquency is the result of social learning primarily, attempts are made to enrich the environment through provision of youth centers for residents of the immediate area; and frequently, adults from the area are employed to help give redirection and training opportunities to the delinquent child.

The Chicago Area Project directed by the late Clifford R. Shaw brought to the investigation of delinquency the ecological and socio-psychological points of view. The first was concerned with the epidemiology of delinquency in the large city; the second with the social experience of the delinquent in his immediate environment.[21] The theory on which the Project is based is that delinquency in a large city is "principally a product of the breakdown of the machinery of spontaneous social control."[22]

In his assessment of the Chicago Area Project 25 years after its beginning, Kobrin calls attention to its historically unique character among delinquency prevention programs. Shaw's image of the youngster as a human being likely to engage in violative activity if he is neglected, despised or ignored, and his notion of the purposiveness of behavior established the practice of centering the activity in the delinquency-producing area, including among workers persons already involved in the youth's living experiences, and according to the troubled youngster individual dignity and respect. Kobrin suggests that the Chicago Area Project discovered an effective pattern of operation which no doubt contributed to the reduction of delinquency in the program areas; but its "distinctive contribution to delinquency prevention as a field of practice and technique will be seen in its development of a method designed to keep prevention work focused upon its proper object, the delinquent as a person in his milieu."[23]

THE WASHINGTON, D. C. AREA PROJECT

Perhaps the action taken by the Federal Government in 1953 set in motion the machinery which led to the organization of the Commissioner's Youth Council in the same year. Unlike the Chicago Project, the Washington Council was assigned the

286

responsibility of dealing with the *total* problem of juvenile delinquency. Its objective is to extend the interest of residents of a given block to the larger community. Also, the Youth Council's professional staff is used to supplement services normally rendered by established community resources. Key city officials are included on the 25-member board, and the professional staff has been enlarged from two to nine social workers. In February, 1960, 25 area boards spanned the city with a membership of 600 civic leaders.

The Youth Council works cooperatively with the Police Youth Aid Division and the District of Columbia Recreation Department's Roving Leaders who have a similar interest in discouraging delinquency. It created the Odd Jobs Pools which gave employment to 6,000 boys in 1959, and organized forty Carrier Boys Clubs which serve local supermarkets. Although delinquency increased 3.6 per cent in 1959, for the years 1954-1958, the rate decreased 33.5%, thus, the Council has been a successful venture in the Nation's Capital where anti-social and criminal behavior has been a baffling problem.

In summary, area projects emphasize a higher level of cooperation and coordination of organized social agencies. Under these programs, projects may be set-up independently but are usually attached to neighborhood centers. Communities make funds available in the belief that financial responsibility facilitates effective services. Thus, the community outlines its objectives, formulates policies and finances area projects to correct the social disorder of delinquency areas.

YOUTH BOARDS

Youth agencies now exist in seventeen states and eleven metropolitan areas of the United States. The New York State Youth Commission, established in 1945, receives an annual appropriation of nearly $4,000,000, sufficient to conduct a "total push" type of program within reach of local communities in need of services and funds. By legislative act, cities, counties or townships may develop youth serving organizations by appropriating 50% of the funds required for a project, to be matched by funds from the State Commission. Locally, the work of the New York City Youth Board is well known for its multiple-type approaches to combat delinquency in the steaming metropolis. Counseling services to individuals and in groups, guidance clinics centered in schools, special youth employment services, subsidies and assistance to recreational agencies, councils and settlement houses attest to the Board's wide-spread activity. Perhaps the New York Youth Board is best known for its "detached-worker program" introduced in 1945, which aims at destruction of gang activity for which New York is so well-known. Omitting the feature of matching-grants to local governing bodies, five state youth commissions adopted the design of New York State.[24]

Within a different conceptual framework under the Model Youth Authority Act, six other states[25] set up programs with which to battle their juvenile problems. The theoretical base of youth authority programs is, that the judicial function should be separated from the treatment function because judges, untrained in the behavioral sciences may be less well qualified to render decisions appropriate for the *treatment* of offenders. Thus, offenders under 18 years of age within the legal limits of the Model Youth Authority Act are usually detained on commitment by the Youth Authority.

The development of forestry camps, including camps following the design of Scout camps brought wide publicity to the California Youth Authority. Forestry camp programs reach many youthful offenders through a combined treatment, recreational and work program in a physical environment with appeal for most youths. On a lesser scale, other states operating under the Youth Authority Act have followed California's lead and are rapidly expanding this form of treatment with considerable success.

Other unique attempts to rescue troubled youths too numerous to mention are catching hold in all sections of the United States. California has its "Town Meetings" on youth problems, Illinois is strengthening its playground and camp programs, Minnesota is attempting a better coordination of existing services, Maryland controls three forestry camps for boys over sixteen released from training schools, and the State of Washington now operates a reception-diagnostic center and maintains on a state-wide basis, child guidance centers where parents may receive advice on child-rearing.

THE ROLE OF THE SCHOOL

The school plays a vital role in the lives of most children and in the case of the delinquent child, pupil personnel services furnish diagnostic data which shed light on his needs and in some instances services are available to meet those needs.

Pupil personnel services usually consist of pupil accounting, attendance department services, guidance functions, psychological study of maladjusted pupils with special classes for the handicapped. Psychiatric and social work services are more limited though no less needed. It is the work of the team of specialists to coordinate their functions to meet the identifiable needs of the school child. A serious limitation in most localities where these services do exist is availability of services to children at the high school level only.

In her research to assess the extent and content of special services embraced in a selected group of public school systems, Hypps[26] sent questionnaires to 80 public school systems in 29 states and the District of Columbia from whom 51 replies were received. With one exception the questionnaires revealed that these schools limit guidance and counseling services to secondary schools almost wholly, and in addition provide attendance services. Forty-nine of the fifty-one school systems provide special classes for handicapped children and four-fifths of the respondents said special services included social work services. However, only in eleven cities are pupil personnel services available to all pupils. Dr. Hypps proposed more special services for schools "to help establish, develop, and supervise programs in counseling, psychological study, therapy of all kinds, and related social services." Services such as the aforementioned would help to identify, and to a lesser degree offer treatment to children including delinquents. Nevertheless, Dr. Hypps endorsed Beck's assertion in regard to the school and control of delinquency:

> "The emphasis in the school program needs to be on developing teacher potential rather than on a proliferation of adjunctive services." [27]

VOCATIONAL TRAINING FOR PROBATIONERS

While the Hypps investigation pointed up needs and gaps with reference to special personnel services in schools and about which communities need to bestir themselves, Ghastin[28] reports on the results of an interagency vocational program carried out for probationers 17-21 years old in Macomb County, Michigan.

In the Summer of 1956, the heavily populated county of Macomb adjacent to the industrial city of Detroit, initiated a program to increase the employment prospects of young probationers. Through the cooperation of a battery of public services (School, Probation Department, Corrections Department, Office of Vocational Education, Michigan Employment Security Commission) the program subsequently known as PREP (Pioneer Readiness for Employment Program) was launched.

Special criteria were used to select "qualified" probationers who were able to support themselves for the seven week period needed for training in machine shop, drafting and retail merchandising. Twenty-four students were selected, nineteen enrolled and fourteen received certificates on completion of the 240 hour course. Twenty-five students enrolled in 1957 of whom thirteen completed the course. Fifty per cent of the men received employment as a direct result of their training. Of the twenty-seven men who completed the course in the two different years, only two were cited as violators at the time the report was written. In an evaluation of the program, the staff psychologist underscored the significance of personality growth, changed attitudes and realistic thinking of the men presumably because of group membership and group discussions. These traits were revealed in more wholesome attitudes toward males, increased verbal communication and in general a more wholesome social orientation.

The goal of this unusual project-preparation for employment, was achieved substantially, but more important than learned skills was, "something of equal or greater value, acceptance of self and others through group counseling, and greater feelings of self worth." [29] Ghastin expressed the same conviction as Beck and Hypps when he said, "Good teaching is the key to this program."

Does the Macomb experiment provide a valuable clue for further experimentation in working with delinquents? Since many delinquents are school drop-outs the methods used in this experiment may be used to stimulate other young men to re-enter school or take special courses to increase their employability. There may be merit in Ghastin's proposal that we "shift school programs around until areas can be found where the students can achieve and find an experience of competency and adequacy."

THE MAXIMUM BENEFITS PROGRAM, WASHINGTON, D. C.

Efforts have been made to off-set or control delinquency at the elementary school level. In the District of Columbia a Maximum Benefit Program, named to describe the intent of providing maximum benefits to children during the school period, was another experiment designed to forestall delinquency. In addition to services and identification of pre-delinquents the Project hoped to demonstrate some advantages of additional professional services to the school and its pupils. To test the hypothesis that maximum benefits in a slum area may forestall delinquent behavior the Project was located in two schools in Washington's police precinct with the highest crime rate. The subjects of the study represented the city's most deprived children, economically, socially, culturally. To pierce these deprivations services in all appropriate specialities were provided through joint planning of city and voluntary officials. Follow-up studies on the 179 families who had "benefited" by every service provided to meet identifiable needs revealed negligible results from the point of view of the school and the court. And in the case of the latter a slightly larger number of treated children had come to the attention of the court than the untreated matched mates of the study. From the point of view of handling or controlling delinquency, this experiment at the elementary school level did not yield results in terms of forestalling delinquency of children or increasing the social functioning of their parents.

ALL DAY NEIGHBORHOOD SCHOOLS

A novel attempt to augment the work of youth-serving agencies is being made by the New York City Board of Education. Nine All Day Neighborhood Schools have been set-up in elementary schools to determine to what extent the extended school day with additional help for teachers can help to meet the needs of children living in impoverished environments.

Within the school setting, combined techniques of social work, sociology, education, and recreation are used to involve parents and citizens for the improvement of the social structure of the immediate neighborhood where the school is located. The extended school day supplements for inadequacies of the home by engaging parents in a program with their children which should develop some feelings of self-worth.

All Day Neighborhood Schools of New York City were not planned to combat juvenile delinquency, but to extend the period of care for children of working mothers who without restraint may be in danger of becoming delinquent.

In summary, in the past few years we have witnessed the development of a multitude of programs and services the result

292

of imaginative thinking, planning and experimentation on which we pin our hopes to rescue troubled youth. The Federal Government, individual cities and states, voluntary organizations, and foundations, have individually or jointly attempted to meet the problem of delinquency by dispensing services to juveniles and their families, in their homes or other treatment centers; in neighborhoods, schools and camps.

Recent efforts to reduce juvenile delinquency have not been dramatic although researchers in the behavioral sciences have acquired a wealth of information about aggressive children and juvenile delinquents with which to make slow but steady progress.

A developing body of evidence reveals that researchers see the problem of juvenile delinquency as one symptom of disruptive family life. To heal it requires analysis of the changes in our social institutions and their changing functions as these are reflected in social values, and in the general pattern of American life, particularly, the family.

In our emphasis on the family in its traditional sense we have given insufficient recognition to the impact of evolutionary social, economic and political influences on social values and customs. Until recently we continue to hold to the same expectations of the family and its functions but treated the delinquent as a person outside of family influences.

The unresolved and conflicting images and expectations parents have of themselves may be associated with social, economic and political changes of the last 30 years, among them, functions and responsibilities shifted from the family to governmental authority, residual effects of a world war, increased employment of women in industry and the need to become emotionally adjusted to a cold war of international scope. These and other factors are to be understood and placed in proper perspective when consideration is given to the social milieu of the juvenile delinquent for his violative behavior reflects these and other changes.

The problem of curbing or curing delinquency is a torturous one, not only because enough is not known but because we seem

293

to be reluctant to use the knowledge we have with certainty. We have in the past limited our attention to the drama and pathos of the needy, disadvantaged and disfranchised who manage to eke out the means of subsistence, but little more, in our great land of plenty. Possibly Lewis' cogent comment will help to point the way to new horizons. In a recent review he said:

> The bulk of research and most control and treatment programs are geared to theories and beliefs about lower-class and minority (primarily Negro) life conditions and imperatives and urban areas of high delinquency . . . in popular shorthand "the milieu of the delinquent" . . . In practice, however, identifying, understanding and changing the really important elements of the milieu is an extremely difficult task because they ramify every aspect of society—not just the high delinquency area or the segregated Negro community.[30]

To develop a general theory of delinquency prevention it is perhaps imperative that we broaden our scope to include study of the *total* family and the *total* society of which we are a part.

SELECTED BIBLIOGRAPHY

The Annals of the American Academy of Political and Social Science, CCCXXII, March 1959. Entire volume devoted to "Prevention of Juvenile Delinquency" consisting of 16 papers by different authors, edited by Helen L. Witmer, Ph.D. Published bi-monthly.

Delinquent Behavior: Culture and the Individual, Washington, D. C.: National Education Association, 1959, 147 pp. A report prepared by the National Education Association Juvenile Delinquency Project by an inter-disciplinary team of specialists from a variety of disciplines in the field of human relations. The title is descriptive.

Federal Probation, edited by the Federal Probation System, Washington, D. C. and is published quarterly by the Administrative Office of the U.S. Courts and the Bureau of Prisons of the U.S. Department of Justice. Deals with all phases of preventive and correctional activities in delinquency and crime. September, 1958, December, 1958 and June, 1959.

The Journal of Negro Education, "A Quarterly Review of Problems Incident to the Education of Negroes." Published for the Bureau of Educational Research, by the Howard University Press, Howard University, Washington 1, D. C., XXVIII, #3, Summer 1959. Entire volume devoted to "Juvenile Delinquency Among Negroes in the United States," Charles H. Thompson, Ph.D. (editor). Seventeen papers by different authors including a critical summary.

Juvenile Courts Statistics. Children's Bureau Statistical Series Number 52, 1957. U.S. Department of Health, Education and Welfare, Social Security Administration, Washington, D. C., 1959, 17 pp. A statistical report on the extent of delinquency in the United States in 1957.

Juvenile Delinquency. Report of the Senate Sub-Committee on Juvenile Delinquency, Report #137, March 1959. U.S. Government Printing Office, Washington, D. C. report on delinquency in the schools, and a proposed study of the role of institutions in the treatment and rehabilitation of juvenile delinquents; also legislation introduced by members of the sub-committee.

McCorkle, Lloyd W., Elias, Albert, and Bixby, Lovell S., *The Highfields Story,* Henry Holt and Company, New York, 1958, 182 pp. The work is a description and evaluation of New Jersey's group treatment center for youthful probationers written by the people who conceived the idea and developed the program. It is valuable because it reveals a departure from the usual American way of dealing with offenders. The authors seemed to have been influenced by the Austrian pioneer August Aichorn's *Wayward Youth.*

Powers, Edwin, and Witmer, Helen, *An Experiment in the Prevention of Delinquency: The Cambridge-Somerville Youth Study,* Columbia University Press, New York, 1951, 792 pp. One of the most extensive attempts in the study and prevention of juvenile delinquency. To test the hypothesis that many delinquent or delinquency-prone boys would develop into stable youths if they were provided with wise counsel and friendship and use of community resources, 325 boys were selected to receive preventive treatment and carefully matched with a control group of equal number. The exhaustive study describes in detail, the purpose, methods, scope, findings and conclusions based on five years of study and treatment via the use of prevalent methods in use by welfare agencies at that time.

Social Legislation Information Service, Issue #30, Washington, D. C., August 10, 1959. A weekly publication which reports impartially on Federal legislation.

Rose C. Thomas was born July 11, 1909 at Florence, South Carolina, reared and received her early education in Richmond, Virginia. She received the Bachelor of Arts degree from Virginia Union University, June 1929, the Master of Social Work degree from the New York School of Social Work, June 1944, and the Doctor of Social Work degree from the Catholic University of America in June 1955, the first woman to be awarded the doctoral degree from the University's School of Social Work. Subsequently, she has held positions of caseworker, supervisor in the New York Children's Aid Society and as psychiatric social worker in the Neurological Institute, Presbyterian Medical Center of New York City. In the District of Columbia she has served as Superintendent of the National Training School for Girls, Psychiatric Social Worker in the Howard University School of Medicine and Research Social Worker for the architectural Study Project of the American Psychiatric Association before joining the faculty of the Howard University School of Social Work where she is now Associate Professor and Chairman of Admissions. Dr. Thomas is the author of Mother-Daughter Relationships and Social Behavior and has published several articles in professional journals. Since 1957 she has served as a book review editor for the American Catholic Sociological Review. Dr. Thomas' professional memberships include the National and International Conferences of Social Welfare, The Council on Social Work Education and the National Association of Inter-Group Relations Officials. In January 1961 she will be one of several American social workers to direct Study Tours around the world following the International Conference at Rome, Italy. She will also serve as a resource consultant for the 1960 White House Conference on children and youth.

296

NOTES

1. Thomas, Rose C., "Family and Children's Agencies and Juvenile Delinquency Prevention," *Journal of Negro Education*, XXIII, Summer, 1959, 307.

2. Bloch, Herbert A., "They are not Born Criminals," *Federal Probation*, September 1958, 16.

3. "Delinquent Behavior: Culture and the Individual," *National Education Association Report*, 1959.

4. Perlman, I. Richard, "Delinquency Prevention: The Size of the Problem," *The Annals*, The American Academy of Political and Social Science, March 1953, 3.

5. Lopez-Rey, Manuel, "Present Approaches to the Problem of Juvenile Delinquency," *Federal Probation*, June 1959, 24.

6. *Ibid.*, p. 25.

7. Kahn, Alfred J., "The Untried Weapon Against Delinquency," *Federal Probation*, September 1958, 13.

8. Tufts, Edith M., "The Role of the Children's Bureau and other Federal Agencies in Juvenile Delinquent Prevention," *Journal of Negro Education*, Summer 1959, 329-338.

9. *Ibid.*, 332.

10. *Juvenile Delinquency*, Interim Report of the Committee on the Judiciary, U.S. Senate, 83rd Congress, Second Session, Report 61, Washington: Government Printing Office, 1955, 3.

11. *Social Legislation Information Service, Issue #30*, Washington, D. C., August 10, 1959, 181.

12. *Ibid.*, 183.

13. Powers, Edwin & Helen Witmer, *An Experiment in the Prevention of Delinquency*, New York: Columbia University Press, 1950.

14. McCord, Joan & William, "A Follow-Up Report on the Cambridge-Somerville Youth Study," *The Annals*, American Academy of Political and Social Science, CCCXXII, March 1959, 89-96.

15. *Ibid.*, 96.

16. Miller, Walter B., "Preventive Work with Street Corner Groups: Boston Delinquency Project," *The Annals*, American Academy of Political and Social Science, CCCXXII, March, 1959, 97-106.

17. Gandy, John M., "Preventive Work with Street-Corner Groups: Hyde Park Youth Project, Chicago," *The Annals*, American Academy of Political and Social Science, CCCXXII, March 1959, 107-116.

18. *Ibid.*, 116.

19. Penner, G. Lewis, "An Experiment in Police and Social Agency Co-operation," *The Annals*, American Academy of Political and Social Science, CCCXXII, March, 1959, 79-88.

20. McCorkle, Elias & Bixby, *The Highfields Story*, New York: Henry Holt and Company, 1958.

21. Kobrin, Solomon, "The Chicago Area Project: A 25 Year Assessment," *The Annals*, American Academy of Political and Social Science, CCCXXII, March, 1959, 19-29.

22. *Ibid.*, 22.

23. *Ibid.*, 29.

24. Tennessee, New Mexico, Florida, Louisiana and Mississippi.

25. California, Minnesota, Massachusetts, Illinois, Delaware and Texas.

26. Hypps, Irene C., "The Role of the School in Delinquency Prevention," *Journal of Negro Education*, Howard University Press, XXVIII, #3, Summer 1959, 327.

27. Beck, Bertram M., "The School and Delinquency Control," *The Annals*, American Academy of Political and Social Science, CCLXVII, November 1955, 65.

28. Ghastin, James F., "A Public School Offers Special Courses for Young Probationers," *Federal Probation*, December 1958, 37-4.

29. *Ibid.*, 41.

30. Lewis, Hylan, "Juvenile Delinquency Among Negroes: A Critical Summary," *Journal of Negro Education*, Vol. XXVIII, Number 3, 386.

SOME SOCIOLOGICAL ASPECTS OF THE CONFINEMENT

Theodore M. Zink
Board of Corrections
State of Delaware

The normal prison society is one composed of a complex of cultural, racial and intellectual backgrounds forcibly thrust together in an environment of persistent psychological pressure. It has often been suggested that the required associations of prison life are analogous to those encountered in the service. While superficial similarities are present, the overall pattern of the two experiences is characterized by basic differences. First, membership in the armed forces is related in the public and individual mind with the ideal of patriotism, service to one's country. A prison sentence, on the other hand, bears with it a completely negative societal implication. In this situation, the individual is not buoyed by the knowledge that he is fighting to protect society from a common enemy; he is rather harassed by the fact that he is the 'enemy'. This psychological effect is heightened by the zoo-like appearance that is typical of the majority of prisons today. From the ever-present handcuffs to the row on row of barred steel cages the degrading concept of societal disinheritance is emphasized. Second, membership in the Army, Navy, etc., while sometimes humorously equated with possession of a warm body and the ability to see, is based upon a reasonably rigid selection process. The prison population is limited by no such selection. Misfits of every description are squeezed into a single facility. Most men who commit crimes are beset with deep emotional problems. They are "out of whack" with society. These men possessed of already serious troubles are housed with the mentally incompetent, the physically unfit, the infirm, the aged, the psychopath, the pre-psychotic, the homosexual, the racist, the addict, the 'jitterbug', the alcoholic, and innumerable others. The myriad streams of personality widely separated in community cultural life funnel into the artificial prison society creating a potential maelstrom of pent-up conflict.

That such a society differs widely from the average service society, as well as from any other normal societal segment, can be readily seen.

THE INVERTED SOCIETY

In whatever situation people are they are normally social beings. When they go to prison they do not cease to exist. Interaction must occur among the varied types of offenders housed there. It would be encouraging to suppose that the offenders of circumstance (murderers without prior history, traffic violators, and those with minor criminal backgrounds who have not deep-seated anti-social tendencies) might exercise a positive influence for good upon the chronic offenders. Logic dictates the reverse. Society has rejected men convicted of crime; has said in effect, "You are dangerous as wild beasts are dangerous, therefore you must be locked away as wild beasts are." Within this society which has been labeled anti-social, status is frequently a function of the degree of anti-sociality displayed. In this setting the most serious and consistent offender becomes a sort of elder statesman. The first or casual offender has not status on this basis. Thus the young impressionable incarcerate must emulate the hardened recidivist if he aspires to peer group status. This is the pattern. The prison environment enhances tendencies toward 'bad' behavior far more than it influences men toward 'good' behavior.

The prison population is the one group that tolerates and accepts anti-social behavior. Mores and values are askew, topsy-turvy in terms of the 'normal' societal view. Psychologically fundamental human needs are love and acceptance. Many men sentenced to servitude have never had either. Since all are in the same boat, i.e., socially rejected, it is quite natural that their common cause of difficulty should not serve as a source for intergroup rejection. It is often the case that men find acceptance in the prison society for the first time.

Perhaps as an indirect result of this, the myth about 'honor among thieves' has been maintained. There is certainly a 'bond' among thieves which would appear to be the outgrowth of a fraternal acceptance bred from society's almost complete rejection. For this reason, the convict group while accepting behavior against society at large will not tolerate violations of trust against its own individual members. The violent castigation of 'rats' and 'squealers' luridly publicized in Hollywood films is in a less dramatic sense a very real characteristic of the convict culture. This dichotomy is a major source of difficulty to the released, paroled or probated offender. Warned to eschew evil companions, he finds that to do so results in his having no companions, since to law-abiding members of the community he is himself an evil person. The courts ask him to refuse to mingle with the only group which will accept him and are outraged when he cannot comply.

Within the prison a strange social hierarchy exists. All 'honest' criminals are accepted. The only persons found unacceptable here are the 'rats' and 'stool-pigeons' who collaborate with prison officials, and several types of unusual offenders, i.e., the baby-beater, the child-molester, the incestuous father. The convict group will welcome a vicious gunman, and may make him a leader, while turning in disgust from one whose offense they consider unmanly. Men in prison conform to social standards generally alien to those found in the community. There is without question a criminal code of decency. It is however such a warped and twisted thing that it defies practical description.

The author had played basketball in the large prison yard of the New Castle Correctional Institution in Wilmington, Delaware. Upon leaving, he discovered the loss of a pack of cigarettes and a lighter. Since there was no means of tracing the lost articles, it was something of a surprise to have a Negro inmate return both articles intact. When asked why he had bothered, the boy retorted with some asperity "Man, I never rob my friends!" This may be contrasted with the response noted when the writer asked a former prison regular how he had managed to remain free for over a year. He said, "Well you know I was never bad. I never went in for no violence. It was always just fighting and a little cutting that used to get me in trouble." This remarkable moral judgment is thrown into strong relief by the case of the courteous boxer. Several years ago the local prison boxing team in Delaware was captained by an astute lightweight, who not only boxed well enough to whip two local professionals but displayed exceptional natural humanity and consideration for others. Though he asked no quarter, he invariably stepped away when an opponent slipped and in all other aspects of this, as well as other athletic endeavors, showed genuine natural sportsmanship. Within weeks of his release from prison he had bilked members of a service organization who had offered him acceptance and friendship; he had clubbed and robbed a man who had offered him employment.

And so it goes. There are as many different ethical responses as there are experiences to recount. For each example of honor among thieves, there are balancing cases of criminals informing on brothers and friends. One thing seems clear in this melange. The inmate social hierarchy is constant in its divergence from norms maintained in the free society. Inverted value systems dictate acceptance, and the reward of class status, for those who behave in socially unacceptable ways. Yet we postulate the absurdity that the offender can learn adjustment to democratic social mores in this inverted society.

We persist in asserting the fiction that the purpose of prison in this modern era is preparation of the offender for successful return to society in spite of the fact that the contacts made, attitudes engendered, and the overall psychological setting dictate an opposite effect.

James V. Bennett, Director of the Federal Bureau of Prisons, has stated the paradox of prisons: "On the one hand, prisons are expected to punish; on the other, they are supposed to reform. They are expected to discipline rigorously at the same time that they teach self-reliance. They are built to be operated like vast impersonal machines, yet they are expected to fit men to live normal community lives. They operate in accordance with a strict autocratic routine, yet they are expected to develop individual initiative. All too frequently restrictive laws force prisoners into idleness despite the fact that one of their primary objectives is to teach men how to earn an honest living. They refuse a prisoner a voice in self-government, but they expect him to become a thinking citizen in a democratic society. To some, prisons are nothing but "country clubs" catering to the whims and fancies of inmates. To others the prison atmosphere seems charged only with bitterness, rancor and an all-pervading sense of defeat. And so the whole paradoxical scheme continues, because our ideas and views regarding the function of correctional institutions in our society are confused, fuzzy, and nebulous." [1]

It will be the purpose of this chapter to attempt to identify some sociological factors that contribute to modern penal problems and to evaluate briefly present procedures designed to ease those problems.

SOCIOLOGICAL FACTORS CONTRIBUTING TO PRISON PROBLEMS

Sentencing and Detention Practices. Unfortunate court practices often magnify the pressures seething within the prison's caldrons. Professor Teeters, the noted criminologist, has estimated that 50 percent of a prison's population at any given time is unconvicted. Sixty-two percent of this untried group are eventually discharged without conviction. These citizens will have served prison terms ranging from a few weeks to six months, two years, and even more. Thus our democratic society tacitly condones a practice which results in vast numbers of legally innocent persons spending long periods in unmerited confinement. This is by no means the most astonishing situation fostered by tardy, inept court practices. In the case of the unconvicted prisoner, it is at least of minor comfort to know that persons so held are suspected of some crime. In most jurisdictions, on the other hand, material witnesses in major crimes have bail bonds set as guarantees of court appearance. This means that the economically handicapped citizen unfortunate enough to be a witness to an infraction of the law may well be summarily remanded to prison until the court trial date arrives. Thus he, as well as the untried prisoner, is subjected to much of the same stigma attached to actual conviction and sentencing. The reason for being in jail is far less significant to society at large than the fact. Jobs are lost, society ostracizes, families suffer as though guilt had been established. Obviously, in the area of courts and prisons the ideal of functional Democracy exists primarily for those who can afford it.

Inequitable, crazy-quilt sentencing laws provide constant irritations within the confined society. Sentences vary for similar offenses unbelievably in different areas.

A study of sex statutes, for example, reveals that penalties for conviction of rape vary from a $2000 fine with no imprisonment in Vermont to death in 18 states. Most states using the death penalties have established minimum sentences extending all the way down to one year. In Rhode Island, the maximum penalty for rape, however heinous the circumstances, is five years. In Louisiana, the minimum sentence is death.[2]

The problems inherent in a legal structure founded on confusion and lack of uniformity are discussed in detail elsewhere. The above sample is sufficient to suggest that our sex laws are incomplete and unrealistic. This is typical of the total field of American jurisprudence.

Additionally, individual judges, magistrates, justices of the peace of the various courts and jurisdictions move from pole to pole in applying the diverse criminal laws. As a result even relatively stable local laws tempered with the human variable become tools of inequity. 'Hanging' judges have largely disappeared but the individual tendencies toward stern or merciful treatment remain. Thus judges become known as harsh taskmasters in certain criminal areas; others gain reputations for leniency. Consequently, a violator convicted of robbery may arrive at the prison with a five, ten, or twenty year sentence to find others convicted under similar circumstances serving six months or a year, while yet others under the same charge remain in the community on probation. Obviously circumstances alter cases. Offenders with extensive previous criminal histories must be dealt with more sternly than first offenders. Unfortunately, the disparate sentences listed above are daily administered to offenders with identical backgrounds. This is one reason that the accused through their legal representatives will leave no stone unturned in seeking delays, transfers, continuances, in the hope of standing trial before a sympathetic judge.

Men serving excessively long terms develop attitudes of hopeless desperation and contribute greatly to the unrest within the prison community. The point at which a prison sentence becomes oppressive and foments rebellion is an individual thing. No specific rules can be drawn. Yet it must be recognized that as the length of sentence increases the potential threat to safekeeping also increases. It is not surprising then that administrative problems are multiplied in states where life sentences with no possibility of parole are employed.[3]

The effects upon men in prison of inequities between treatment of the rich and poor, haphazard sentencing procedures, and unjust detention are profound. Deep bitterness develops, primarily represented in the lower socio-economic class, toward all people in more comfortable or authoritative circumstances. This resentment often takes the form of overt aggressive behavior or smoldering hatred toward other inmates possessing more favorable cultural or financial backgrounds. Additionally, it almost invariably serves to enhance already well established anti-social attitudes.

Cultural Differences. The tremendous diversity of cultural backgrounds flung together in the restrictive society gives rise to many problems based on the individual differences involved. Racial bigotry, often encountered primarily at the conversation level in the free world, becomes an immediate daily problem in a situation requiring direct contact between people of all races. Discriminatory feelings tend to heighten, or at least are less well masked, as position on the social ladder descends. In addition, the strong tendencies toward greater intolerance at the lower cultural levels are magnified by the tremendous tensions and constant frustrations of prison life.

Other factors exert considerable influence upon the social interaction. The depth of effect of these factors is dependent very often on the cultural background of individuals involved. It has been well established psychologically that perceptions of a stable object will differ widely among any group of people in terms of past experience and biological heredity. An extension of this idea is seen in the present consideration. Prison conditions which appear squalid and sub-human to the person from upper societal levels, will seem very satisfactory to the son of migratory farm parents. Obviously the frame of reference is of utmost importance.

For persons of any moderate cultural background, a prison sentence can be a deeply traumatic experience. The effect of usual commitment procedures tends to heighten the emotional shock concomitant with sentencing. Sentenced prisoners are handcuffed together or separately, herded into prison or police vans, and carted off to jail. Once at the institution the group is stripped, searched, washed, photographed, and subjected to a routine roughly reminiscent of that used in de-ticking cattle. Processed and clothed in ill-fitting prison garb, inmates are remanded to isolation cells for the period of days necessary to receive results of blood tests and the like. During this crucial period when individual shock is greatest, regular rehabilitative and activity programs are not available to the new arrivals. They sit alone and brood.

To a reasonably intelligent, reasonably sensitive human being, the effects of having one's hands cuffed or legs shackled can be demoralizing and degrading beyond belief. The idea is forcibly projected that he is so dangerous to the interests of decent society that he must be chained and barred away from them. Unquestionably a minority of cases, cited above, involve persons representing the threat inferred. For this small minority, the bar and chain is the only course of action now available. What of the traffic violators and the non-supporters, however; does deep personal humiliation serve any useful function toward furthering ultimate ends of readjustment and rehabilitation for them? The lessons of history answer resoundingly—no! Public humiliation of exquisite and often fatal ingenuity has been resorted to since earliest recorded time. In America, the Puritans supplemented use of the famous scarlet letter A with other initials symbolizing different crimes branded on hand, cheek, or forehead. The stocks and pillory were other well-known implements of public disgrace.[4] Flogging, mutilation, the duckingstool, cage wagons, and the dame's bridle were other means of attempting to force rehabilitation through exposure of the culprit to public scorn.

This concept that shame and fear hold the key to individual reform has been in all manifestations at all levels a sensational failure. Public degradation as official practice has fallen into disuse as a result. The policy nonetheless still flourishes by indirection in our prisons. Commitment practices cited above, in league with early confinement 'cold storage' detention, provide strong deterrents to adequate social adjustments in prisons. We espouse the ideals of rehabilitation and reform while our prisons remain as the perfect reflection of our continuing insistence upon punishment as the central function of incarceration.

We commonly hear of the hardships and misery wrought on long suffering families by the criminal ways of errant husband, wife, son, or brother. The material aspects of such problems can be appreciated with relative ease in terms of restriction of ordinary societal standards of living. Considerably less is known of the socio-emotional impact of incarceration upon the offender and his family.

The relationship between the incarcerate, the family group and society at large does not vanish with imprisonment. It does undergo a tremendous change however. In case of the family relationship, the nature of the change is conditioned by the perceptions, attitudes, and values of the individuals involved.

Generally speaking, family disruption at the lower cultural levels is not so severe. This is partially due to the fact that moral personal ties are less rigid among these groups. Multiple common-law relationships and unstable paternal groups are familiar criteria of the lower class. These less substantial, less socially restrictive family bonds break rather easily, accompanied by less emotional trauma than would occur at a higher cultural stratum.

As the standard of living or social position of the offender rises, the degree of family and societal disruption tends to increase in direct proportion. This hypothesis would require qualification under closer study. Research has indicated that social groups at the middle class levels are least tolerant of wide deviations from accepted norms. At these levels social pressure toward rejection of the offender might be expected to be greatest. Since the stigma is greater the individual emotional stress, as well as the strain on the family relationship, tends to be more severe.

The average offender from the slum districts sentenced to imprisonment encounters little ostracism from the society he knows. Crime rates are high thus crime is, to an extent, accepted. He adjusts well to the prison society since the majority of its members come from a similar social environment. The low living standard characteristic of institutions is not intolerable. It often differs little from that to which he has been accustomed, if indeed, it is not superior.

The average middle class offender, in contrast, finds his conduct castigated by those in his social milieu. Crime is not accepted, the offender is not accepted. Once sentenced, he encounters an alien society within the walls. Background, experience, attitudes differ. There is a strong sense of not belonging accompanied by a conflicting drive to shun membership. Sub-standard living conditions plus coarse treatment compound the conflicts. In the final analysis, the more cultured offender stands to lose much more simply because he has much more to lose, and he feels more strongly about the losses involved. To him job, home, family, friends, in short, social class membership, are primary. Prison threatens some if not all these symbols.

Homosexuality. The presence of the homosexual in a penal setting is a source of constant major problems to administrative and custodial personnel alike. A deputy warden in a large Pennsylvania prison has characterized this as the most disruptive influence in that institution. That homosexuality should be so serious a bar to institutional calm is less than surprising when one considers the anomaly of incarcerating a group of human beings possessing female drives with a population of men starved for female companionship. Of all abnormalities inherent in the prison society, perhaps the greatest is that of the male or female group shut away from contact with the opposite sex for long periods of years. Basic sexual needs and desires in such an environment are magnified beyond reason. When outlets for these drives are found in this artificial situation they must, by definition, be beyond the pale of societal acceptance, thus abnormal, homosexual, deviate. The wonder is not that perversion is rampant in our prisons but that a reasonable percentage of our inmates successfully resist the pressure.

Our reform schools, reformatories, and penal institutions do, in fact, create functional homosexuals through stupid classification procedures, inadequate facilities for segregation, and the like. Young boys dumped in with hardened regulars are fair game. Once labeled, the pattern is set and very difficult to crack. Perfectly normal individuals are swept up in the system and indulge in casual homosexual acts usually returning to accepted norms upon release. Too often, however, the establishment of perverted sex patterns in prison may preclude the return to heterosexual behavior.

While the male population succumbs unwillingly but in great numbers to this unfortunate substitute for normal outlets, the true homosexual lives in a restricted paradise. Naturally (or unnaturally, depending on point of reference) directed toward male relationships he has them here in abundance. Others vie for 'his' favor; they argue, fight, occasionally die over the blushing prize.

The depth of this problem is not known. Kinsey reported the prevalence of true homosexuality in six percent of the male population of America. Donald Clemmer, Director of the District of Columbia Dept. of Corrections conducted a study indicating that over thirty percent of the inmates in one unnamed institution engaged in homosexual acts. This research while limited and, in the author's words, raising "as many questions as it answers", represents the first definitive attempt to evaluate problems in this delicate area.[5] The only work available then suggests that more than five times as many men in prison engage in perverted sexual activity as do men in free society. Yet there is no reason to assume that a greater percentage of criminals is naturally homosexual. An unpublished study by Ulrich on this point indicates no more than average incidence of latent homosexual drives among the population in the New Castle Correctional Institution in Delaware.[6]

It would appear that the nature of our penological structure has largely created and continues to nurture the problem of homosexuality. It is a serious and permanent condition, tacitly accepted and thoroughly misunderstood by most administrators.

The true homosexual, one of the six percent discovered by Kinsey, presents a severe custodial problem in the institution setting. He requires individual, restrictive attention at all times. He must work under the nose of a guard, bunk near a guard station, and engage in all activities on a segregated basis. Such measures are not very successful. They are wasteful of personnel, time, and money, and they fail to achieve their avowed purpose, isolation of the deviate from the normal population.

The discussion thus far has overlooked an important correlate of this problem. The nature of homosexuality is but poorly understood since the causes are nebulous and complex. They may stem from glandular defects, inborn aberration or other biological factors; or from abnormal environmental conditions such as absence of sex training, perverted parental views or actions, traumatic experiences, and the like. Professional diagnosis is often a question mark; effective treatment is lacking even in ideal settings. The prison setting is not ideal. Prisons are practical places. Psychological and psychiatric services are nominally available in most modern facilities. Treatment and psychotherapy programs however are, to all intents and purposes, non-existent since the limited time and professional staff available must be devoted to diagnosing and, when possible, removing aggressive, violently insane inmates from the prison routine. The homosexual does not ordinarily display the wild, disturbing characteristics necessary to qualify him for psychiatric referral. Thus the sensitive job of diagnosis often falls by default to some ranking member of the custodial staff to whom a high-pitched voice, an unfortunate wiggle, or a vicious rumor may represent the requisite tools of accurate prediction. The individual social and emotional damage possible under such circumstances is incalculable.

Troublemakers. A primary source of unsettling interaction within the prison society results from the presence of potential and actual troublemakers. Institutional troublemakers split roughly into two groups. First, those who are problems as a result of external factors and second, those who are problems as a result of internal personality disorders.

Among the externally oriented factors promoting the growth of trouble in correctional institutions are sentencing and detention practices, homosexuality, inmate idleness, monotony; in short, all those sociological factors discussed elsewhere in the chapter. Amid the strange anomalies created by the pressurized diversities of racial and cultural background, it is perhaps surprising that a far greater proportion of inmates do not become active troublemakers in prison. What causes this group, made up of men who could not adjust successfully in free society, to interact acceptably in a closed society? The answer to this question, as to most others associated with the problems of crime and punishment, is not simple, nor is it fully available. Fragmentary research has been done but not nearly enough to provide a basis for definitive conclusions.

One aspect of the question has been explored in a study by Zink[7] who attempted to isolate cultural factors peculiar to those who became troublemakers in prison. He discovered three areas of significant difference between troublemakers and non-troublemakers. The non-troublemakers were as a group: (a) Serving far longer sentences (11 yrs. to 3.5 years); (b) Older at the time of latest sentencing (30.5 yrs. to 24.2 yrs.); and (c) Older at the time of first arrest (21.4 yrs. to 15.4 yrs.).

In a corollary investigation to determine the source of these differences, it was discovered that a great majority of life-term criminals of passion (murder, rape) were encompassed in the non-troublemaking group. Elimination of this segment from the study left the troublemakers and non-troublemakers with no differences that approached significant levels.

A further comparison of the criminals of passion with the remainder of the sample studied revealed that criminals of passion were about the same age as the others (28 mean, 27 mean) when sentenced, yet they had served significantly fewer previous sentences, (1.3 to 3.5) and had been in far less trouble while in prison. There appeared to be a basic difference in criminality between the group comprising murderers and rapists and the group lumping other offenses. Generalizations from this study would be extremely risky in light of the limited sampling (number in study, 100) available.

A larger study of a similar nature (N-1762) was done by Alfred C. Schnur.[8] After analyzing behavioral and cultural characteristics he concluded that murderers have the worst conduct records of all offenders although they have as a group less previous criminal history and a better than average chance of not committing new crimes. Thus, while on the one hand, conclusions concerning conduct of murderers reached in Zink's study were completely reversed, the basic thesis that these offenders were less criminally inclined than other groups was supported. Schnur's results further indicated that age is a key factor in predicting prison conduct. The older a man is when he comes to prison the less likely is he to misbehave in prison, he concluded.

Daniel Glaser[9] supported this contention, attributing the phenomenon to older men's learning "how to do time"; becoming "prison wise." Little subsequent research has been done to validate the conclusion cited above. The ultimate basis for behavior in prison remain a mystery. Informed people in the field don't know why some inmates get into trouble, and, conversely, they don't know why others stay out of trouble. The significance of conduct records in terms of predicting future activity is uncertain at best. Yet, these records provide the primary consideration for administrative decisions relative to inmate release dates and often parole.

These men who are potential troublemakers in prison as the result of internal maladjustments (psychosis, neurosis, *et al.*) usually require the presence of none of the seething external pressures of the caged environment to make them into first-rate administrative and custodial problems. Unfortunately, all these pressures are brought to bear on the unbalanced prisoners who in turn react in erratic, unpredictable ways tending to increase overall tensions. There is no satisfactory body of authoritative evidence on the extent to which serious emotional disturbances are present in our prisons. The difficulties of definition of the varied terms of insanity, along with the absence of adequate numbers of psychologists and psychiatrists for diagnosis,[10] has caused knowledge in this area to remain in the shadows. Dr. Winfred Overholser contended that three to eight per cent of 5000 defendants examined in Massachusetts were insane and fifteen per cent mentally abnormal. The Medical Director of the Federal Bureau of Prisons, on the other hand, estimated that only fifteen per cent of the inmates of any adult prison can be considered fully normal mentally.[11]

Whatever the actual rate, it is clear that a high incidence of mental and emotional abnormality exists in American prisons. Token psychological-psychiatric services permit removal of the most obvious cases. The vast majority of the unbalanced and the abnormal remain in the prison community, contributing immeasurably to the eternal unrest and turmoil; usually becoming the central figures in any projected escape, riot, or other disturbance.

Inmate Idleness. A state senator in Delaware noted recently that the best means of teaching criminals a lesson might be to make them work so hard that they would never want to return. The chairman of the State Board of Corrections piously concurred in this pronouncement. Both these gentlemen would probably be startled to find that the vast majority of the inmates in our institutions would like nothing better than to do real work. Idleness is a primary trouble source for men in jail. It has been estimated that between 60 and 80 per cent of all those incarcerated spend their time in idleness or pseudo labor.

The United States Dept. of Labor Statistics for 1940 revealed that of 191,776 prisoners under sentence, on the average during the year, only 83,515 were productively employed. There is no reason to believe that the percentage of employment has increased appreciably since that time. Even the distressing figures cited are suspect since the definition of productive employment is arbitrary. Often 15 or 20 men are assigned full time to keeping the institution rotunda or center clean, a job that would normally take ten men about 45 minutes per day. Hundreds of men are assigned to tier or gallery duty, a janitorial service requiring 15 or 20 minutes labor (?) daily. These are men who are considered productively employed in some institutions. A huge minority have not even these "made" jobs to occupy them. They remain in their cells, thinking, brooding, eventually plotting. Where security is slipshod, the unemployed inmate wanders about the institution, becomes involved with others, finally succumbs to the stifling boredom and violates prison rules.

A request most frequently heard by classification boards is, "Please give me something to do so I can do my time, and keep my nose clean." Unfortunately the work is not available. Conflicts of interest with labor groups have prevented widespread passage of state-use laws which require state agencies to use products of prison labor whenever feasible. Maryland is among the notable exceptions to this trend. State-use legislation there has permitted development of a multi-million dollar industrial products program with the attendant sharp decrease in idleness in the state's prisons. The dreary majority of our national institutions continue to proclaim full-scale, on-the-job vocational training programs which involve in reality nothing more than the employment of five or ten skilled craftsmen as maintenance men in their respective trades. The rest of the so-called vocational programs usually involve training men to sew, sand,

314

scrape furniture, cane chairs, make brooms, sweep floors and the like. These are skills with a limited if not non-existent market in society. Certainly such routine, pointless labor can do little to promote healthy, cooperative work attitudes in the individual. Nor can it be expected to provide an outlet for the tensions and pressures built up in the artificial society. Rather it supplies idle time for men to focus and magnify problems.

The dearth of meaningful work programs in prisons is a contributing factor to another major problem inherent in the nature of prisons themselves. The restrictive, regimented existence chains the offender in deadly monotony. Initiative, ambition, the very soul's vitality are sapped. In the vast grey blank of institutional life, time is oppressive. Minor worries are intensified and become the basis for set neuroses. Social interaction creates tensions that should be relieved by means of such interaction. Misunderstandings arise over meaningless incidents. Accumulated trivia result in suspicions, enmities, feuds, hatred, and eventually serious trouble. Inmates without suitable outlets for their physical and emotional energies build frustration upon frustration until they 'blow-up' individually or as a group.

When serious disturbances are reported in the press, inmate demands usually appear minor and often ridiculous. Majority public reaction very often suggests that, "If we'd stop coddling those criminals and give 'em a little taste of good old-fashioned discipline they'd stop trying to run the prisons." It is necessary in understanding the fallacy in this view that we realize that almost without exception prison riots are not the outgrowth of a list of grievances; grievances are born of riots. In reality that very "old-fashioned discipline" exhorted by the layman has been a basic cause of a large percentage of prison problems.

Prison administrators are thus trapped in a tightening circle. The repressive, regimented nature of the prison ensures monotony, boredom, idleness, finally trouble. Public demands result in 'firmer' administration in the form of more repression, sterner regimentation. The source of the first riot becomes the seed for the next.

Prison Guards and Administrators. Sociologic complexities are multiplied by two administrative aspects. First, the presence of guard forces nearly approximating the inmate population in heterogeneity; second, the eternal conflict between rehabilitation and custody as primary motivating philosophies.

Custodial personnel are universally under-paid. The problem is not nearly so serious in the more progressive systems of California, New York, and the Federal Bureau of Prisons where reasonable wage scales permit some standardization of personnel. In the vast majority of jurisdictions, however, pay levels are far too low to permit effective merit, psychological, or aptitude screening. Institutions must take what they can get. Since they cannot compete with either industry or labor markets in terms of money, working hours or risk involved, prison officials often wind up with a band of misfits—unqualified, untrained, uninterested. Psychopaths, sadists, occasionally active psychotics may be employed under the hit or miss employment programs most prisons follow. In the absence of top-flight dedicated personnel at the administrative levels, where similar monetary problems prevail, incompetents often drift into positions of command through the simple process of compiling years of service. Thus we have stupidity compounded. Alert, competent officers frequently are mired in such systems. Their intelligence is feared and envied. Promotion is not forthcoming and they quietly leave.

Beginning then with sub-standard types as a result of the low wage scales and the generally unpleasant nature of the work, we must consider the further deterioration elicited by the job itself. Prison guards have none of the esprit de corps of the state police. They lack status in the public eye, and the job becomes one of dull routine. Work in prison is inevitably degrading and brutalizing to a degree. Dedicated professionals often become 'institutionalized' despite possession of knowledge and understanding of the basic problems of penology. The guard, lacking such understanding, has little chance to avoid the moral stagnation implemented by the deadly monotony of prison employment.

Wardens retain prison posts if they successfully avoid escape or scandal. The safest way to accomplish this is to rely on rigid tenets of discipline and regimentation. This reliance on coercion results in the smashing of the natural bonds of sympathy and understanding that might normally grow between the guards and inmates, often people of similar cultural backgrounds. The guard must not be the inmates' friend. To be so invites charges of coddling, favoritism, even corruption. He must succumb to the dehumanizing weight of prison convention or leave. Thus those most needed are often weeded out.

Lacking societal prestige, the correctional employee seeks and finds status within the walls. He may eat after the dog at home, but on the job he is 'lord of the wing, king of the tier'.

It is natural that the existence of these conditions exercises a a strong impact upon the lives of members of the inmate society. There are innumerable complexities involved in the concept of large unstable groups of humanity forcibly confined under the control of stable, dedicated custodians. It is infinitely more disturbing to imagine that unstable group controlled by a similarly unstable band of custodians. Yet this is the rule rather than the exception in American prisons today.

It is to be expected that custodial personnel, equipped with generally low intellectual and educational levels, should differ widely in basic penal philosophy from professionally trained prison employees. The custodial view holds that criminals are in jail for punishment and that detention provides security for society at large. The rehabilitative view maintains that the primary function of the prison should be to bring about changes in the attitudes and value systems of prisoners in order that they might successfully adjust to acceptable societal life.

Both philosophies are in a sense unrealistic. The custodial, because it ignores the well-known fact that over 95% of those incarcerated at a given time will reenter the community eventually. The rehabilitative, because it pretends to cure social diseases, the causes of which have never been isolated. The presence of this deep cleft between the goals of the two groups has resulted in continual conflicts of interest and struggles for control.

Invariably custody is the winner. This is a foregone conclusion. It is dictated by the stern reality that the American public, while paying lip-service to the idea of rehabilitation, humane treatment, *et al.* becomes, when the chips go down, custodial centered in great predominance.

Causal factors may be explored in greater depth elsewhere. The effects of the basic disagreement between custodians and penologists upon men in prison concern us here. They are serious. Guards may ridicule men attending school, forget to open gates, refuse to let men get books, lose passes, and otherwise interfere with the various treatment programs in the endless ways available to them. Rehabilitative personnel may help inmates bypass rules that seem to have no meaning, criticize prison practices before inmates, carp about employees, provide special privileges for favored inmates, curry positions of favor with the administration, and generally help to widen the gulf. The continuous sniping of both factions causes severe tensions among the populations caught between the two fires.

Classification Practices—Physical Facilities. Existing methods of classifying levels of crime contribute to the sociologic conflicts within the walls. Institutional placement is based almost exclusively upon custodial considerations. Within the limits prescribed by security requirements, progressive authorities do whatever is possible to allow for individual differences. This is unfortunately often very little.

The Federal Bureau of Prisons has estimated that less than one-third of all those in prisons today require maximum security custody for the protection of society. Barnes and Teeters place the figure nearer 20 per cent and other professional estimates range even lower. Public outrage would, of course, follow any attempt to act in keeping with these estimates. The fact remains that there are basic differences among the degrees of criminality inherent in various anti-social acts which are not reflected in our sentence hierarchies. Penal authorities know that the first offender serving life for murder or rape is usually a far better risk in society than the third offender serving 18 months for breaking and entering. Institutional placement, however, will very often imply the opposite, since the lifer will languish behind the heavy barred gates of maximum security while the confirmed thief wins medium or minimum security transfer.

Serious physical liabilities increase the classification problems of the prison society. The heterogeneous admixture of humanity is squeezed into obsolete, antiquated facilities built long ago to hold far fewer. Overcrowding adds immeasurably to the complexity of social interaction occurring in our institutions. It vitiates classification and assignment procedures which under favorable circumstances might implement partial separation of the dangerously diverse elements. Most states have institutional placement programs designed to provide some relief from the difficulties arising when mentally and emotionally disturbed inmates are thrust in with others of varying degrees of abnormality. As population figures bubble out over listed capacities, idealistic plans are scrapped and various installations gradually become dumping grounds for all manner of mankind. The vast majority of penal institutions in the United States are operating beyond reasonable capacity.

California, generally conceded to have one of the finest prison systems extant, recently released figures indicating that seven of the eight adult institutions in the state are housing population in excess of capacity. The State Prison at San Quentin, built to hold 3050 men, registered an average population of 4821 in 1958. The single institution not hampered by overcrowding was the Institution for Women at Corona. It is interesting to note that this facility with a normal capacity of 680 housed an average of 678 women during the year. The highly regarded prison system in New York had eleven of its sixteen adult facilities peopled in excess of listed capacity. The Federal Prison System, the pinnacle of current correctional enlightenment, controls nineteen major rehabilitative installations for adult offenders. Thirteen of these were over-populated in 1958. These serious defects in the best of American prisons offer convincing data on the sorry condition of our country's detention facilities at large. The facts are distressing even if we assume that the crowded facilities referred to are modern structures reflecting modern correctional philosophy. Unfortunately this is not the case. Over one-third of California's mature inmate population in 1958 was confined in two state prisons at Folsom and San Quentin, built in 1880 and 1854 respectively. Like California, New York has constructed modern institutions whenever possible yet remains saddled with penal monstrosities in the Auburn, Clinton, and Sing Sing prisons built in 1817, 1845, and 1825, and still confining over one-fourth of the state's adult inmate population. The most forward looking programs for classification and treatment of offenders can realize but a small fraction of their potential in ancient, overcrowded relics of an outmoded philosophy.

REHABILITATIVE SERVICES AS MEANS OF EASING PRISON PROBLEMS

Important in any consideration of forces exerted in prison toward release of tensions is the understanding of the limitations inherent in modern concepts of penology.

Programs and activities that may be considered as contributing to the release of social and emotional tensions within the prison milieu are by and large the same programs and activities whose primary purpose is publicly proclaimed to be rehabilitation. In point of fact prison rehabilitative programs have for the most part flourished as public relations gambits. It has become penologically fashionable to have psychological, psychiatric services, educational, recreational, vocational services, and more recently group therapy and social education programs. There has never been established any consistent body of research systematically validating the claims for the various rehabilitative activities. This may be traced to two causes. First, research in the overall field of corrections has been so woefully scant and piecemeal that it would be difficult to statistically prove any hypothesis. Second, the complexities of accurately controlling the measurement of attitudinal and behavioral change have not been satisfactorily standardized.

By definition a man is rehabilitated only if from the time he leaves prison until the time he dies he does not commit another crime. Most studies purporting to measure rehabilitation of offenders are based upon set periods following release ranging from three months to ten years. Under such circumstances an offender may complete the time period of the study without violating the law. The next day he may commit a series of crimes, yet he stands forth in the statistics as a successfully rehabilitated person. The same statistical non-entity will result if the released offender commits one or fifty crimes during the study period and avoids detection. Until crime detection approaches perfection and rehabilitative studies can span lifetimes, knowledge of the forces fostering change will be incomplete.

The anomaly of penology does not end here. It has been made clear earlier that the factors creating criminality are complex, interactive, and very obscure. We don't know yet why people act as they do. To attempt to treat a social disease whose origins are unknown is absurd, yet this is what is being done in corrections. We postulate treatment programs yet remain unable to adequately identify that which we treat.

The picture is not one of complete confusion. The experiences of the past with corporal punishment, inhumane treatment, public humiliation, and the like have provided proof of the inadequacy of concepts founded upon external fear or force. In addition, the modicum of intelligent research completed in the field has indicated the importance of internal individual change as a factor in rehabilitation. As one outgrowth of such research experimental prison programs have been inaugurated in Seagoville, Texas (Federal), Chino, California, and Wallkill, New York. These facilities are minimum security, 'open' institutions lacking the wretched cage concept of the traditional prison. They are based on the thesis that rehabilitation must grow and develop from within; that a man must be permitted to exercise responsibility while incarcerated if he is to be expected to behave in a socially responsible manner when released.

Results obtained at these facilities are most encouraging. Prior to completion of long-range statistical analyses of released offenders, conclusions concerning absolute rehabilitative value of these foresighted programs remain somewhat conjectural.

321

There are, however, tangible benefits accruing from the use of treatment programs encompassing education, recreation, psychological, psychiatric and casework services. The presence of specialized programs whether good, bad, or indifferent provides opportunity for the release of emotional tensions, for momentary relief from the overpowering monotony of the shackled life.

Hobby shops, school classes, baseball games, psychological tests and interviews all provide breaks in the dull vacuum of institution routine. This is crucial since it has been well established that repressive, degrading monotomy is the trigger for most major disturbances. It is axiomatic in the field of penology that the inmates 'down on the prison farm' don't cause trouble. This is true partly because men on the farms have relatively shorter sentences. Many long-termers are assigned to these minimum security sections, however, and the overall difference in terms is not great enough to explain the truism. The single major variable between the prison and the farm is the freedom from deadening restriction and routine typical of the latter. It is in supplying relief from this anathema that rehabilitative services are an established boon.

A more substantial psychological value may be inferred for treatment programs. The research series entitled the Hawthorne Studies was designed to determine the effects of various distractive stimuli upon performance of office workers. The single significant conclusion of this ponderous study was that performance and attitude were uniformly improved by the presence of someone who was genuinely interested in the employee and her work. An analogous situation is encountered in corrections. The absolute value of a given program may be slight. The important thing for many men in jail is to learn that someone in the vast, impersonal world has an interest in them; in what they are doing and can do. The institution classification board is usually hampered, as we have seen, by extremely limited selections of jobs and facilities to which men may be assigned. Specialized, vocationally useful jobs are at a premium, institutions are overcrowded, and the board is often thought of administratively as merely a necessary nuisance for assuaging occasional public concern. Under these circumstances most classification committees contribute little of a significant material nature to prison operation. For the man in prison, however, their value may be far greater. The paramount factor for him is that someone is concerned with him as a person, as a human being. The effect may be momentary, characterized by the lessening of bitterness and frustrations, or it may signify the start of permanent change.

The significance of the effect postulated has not been measured, perhaps cannot be measured. We do know that acceptance is a basic human need. Rejection is the trait that best characterizes the criminal's relations with society at large. Any activity that permits mitigation of convict feelings of futility and rejection must eventually foster attitudes of individual dignity and worth.

Informed penologists hope that present day treatment and rehabilitative programs are successfully rehabilitating men in our prisons today. They know that these services are acting as invaluable "safety valves" for the pressure-cookers we anomalously label correctional institutions.

SUMMARY

Prisons have often in the past been characterized as melting pots of humanity. In this era of pseudo-enlightenment, the appelation is still unfortunately apt. Prisons today are a far cry from either the effective rehabilitative workshops professional penologists envision or the strict disciplinary-custodial facilities tacitly endorsed by a considerable body of public sentiment.

Prison provides an artificial, tension laden environment wherein a social hierarchy exists which, in terms of normal free societal mores, tends toward inversion. Behavior contrary to societal norms is acceptable, but behavior in violation of individual trust is not tolerated.

It is essentially a 'cage culture' stifling to the ambitions and initiative of inmates and employees alike. It is made up of a grossly heterogeneous group characterized by general instability and a low cultural level. The difficulties intrinsic to dwelling in a restrictive environment with a widely diverse assortment of persons, are multiplied by the absence of meaningful labor within the walls and unstandardized dilatory court practices. Antiquated, overcrowded buildings, underpaid, unqualified custodial and administrative personnel compound the problems and symbolize the futility of much that is attempted in penology today.

The problems of men in prison have been and are being studied piecemeal by dedicated organizations and individuals. The research being done is woefully scant and must remain so until a concerted voice is raised in behalf of the public. Without deep popular concern, funds necessary for comprehensive study of prison problems will never be forthcoming. Without money, solutions can't be found, let alone implemented.

Several years ago a prominent member of the national movement toward improved mental health deplored the fact that the United States government had expended in the neighborhood of 40 million dollars for agricultural research during the preceding year, while only 12 million dollars had been designated for study of the problems of mental health. It is interesting to note that during the year in question, not one nickel was appropriated for use in studying the problems of criminality.

Until the public at large recognizes that the expenditures necessary to procure intelligent, enlightened penal practice will be incidental compared to the immense annual cost of crime in terms of both money and human suffering, the major function performed by the vast majority of our prisons must be to 'hold the line' to maintain the 'status quo'.

SELECTED BIBLIOGRAPHY

Barnes, Harry E., Teeters, Negley K., *New Horizons in Criminology*, Prentice Hall, Englewood Cliffs, 1955. The best reference book currently available in the field of criminology.

Beck, Bertram M., *Youth Within Walls*, Community Service Society of New York, New York, June 1950. A professional appraisal of the reformatories in New York State.

Clemmer, Donald, *The Prison Community*, Rinehart, New York, 1958. A detailed study of the organization of an American penitentiary; designed to provide insight concerning the social structure of typical prisons.

Duffy, Clinton, and Jennings, Dean, *The San Quentin Story*, Doubleday, New York, 1950. An absorbing history of Warden Duffy's life at the famed California prison.

Fenton, Norman, *Introduction to Classification and Treatment in State Correctional Service*, California State Dept. of Corrections, 1953. A concise, clearly written resume of treatment procedures used as a training text for correctional employes in California.

Fishman, Joseph F., *Crucibles of Crime*, Cosmopolitan Press, New York, 1923. A famous critique of deficiencies in small prisons and jails.

Gillin, John L., *The Wisconsin Prisoner*, University of Wisconsin Press, Madison, Wisconsin, 1947. A statistical and historical study of inmates of Wisconsin prisons designed to provide insight into origins of various criminal types.

Grunhut, Max, *Penal Reform: A Comparative Study*, XV, Oxford, 1948. A synthesis of past efforts to improve prison structure and function with a plan for future reform.

Haynes, Fred E., *Criminology*, McGraw, New York, 1935. A sociological approach to the study of criminology.

Lindner, Robert, *Prescription for Rebellion*, Rinehart, New York, 1952.

Martin, John B., *Break Down the Walls*, Ballantine Books, New York, 1954. A remarkably exciting description of the forces combining to cause the Jackson, Michigan prison riots, accompanied by an incisive, factual condemnation of the American prison system.

Nelson, Victor, *Prison Days and Nights*, Little Brown, Boston, 1932. A documented picture of prison life in the 1930's.

Ohlin, Lloyd E., *Sociology and the Field of Corrections*, Russell-Sage, Social Science Series, 1956. A brief overview of sociological aspects of the correctional field.

Proceedings of the 88th Annual Congress of Correction of the

American Correctional Association, New York, 1958. An annual publication of proceedings of Correctional Assn. meetings. It provides good coverage in the area of current happenings in the field of corrections.

Roucek, Joseph S., "Social Attitudes of the Prison Warden," *Sociology and Social Research,* XXI, 2, November-December, 1936, 170-4. A study of environmental and empirical factors affecting the warden's function in modern society.

Roucek, Joseph S., "Sociological Aspects of Prison Mentality," *Journal of Human Relations,* VII, 3, Spring 1959, 307-311. A study of interrelationships between the mental processes of the inmate and the prison environment.

Vold, George B., *Theoretical Criminology,* Oxford University Press, New York, 1958. This text provides good general coverage of the field with substantiating research.

Weinberg, S. Kirston, "Aspects of the Prison's Social Structure," *American Journal of Sociology,* March, 1942, 717-726. An interesting inspection of attitudes of prison officials and inmates, derived from person interviews.

Wines, Frederick H., *Punishment and Reformation,* Crowell, New York, 1895. An excellent historical outline of the rise of the reformatory movement written by an enlightened criminologist of another era. It reveals a startlingly modern viewpoint.

Zilboorg, Gregory, *The Psychology of the Criminal Act and Punishment,* Harcourt Brace, New York, 1954. A general discussion of psychological aspects of all those associated with the criminal act—defendant, judge, jailer, etc.

Theodore M. Zink, Director of Education and Recreation, Board of Corrections, State of Delaware, was born in 1926. He attended the University of Delaware, receiving a Bachelor of Science degree in 1949 with a Master of Science in 1956. He is presently completing requirements for a Doctorate in Education at Temple University. Following graduation he became an English instructor and athletic coach at Asheville High School in Asheville, North Carolina. While there he was named the outstanding basketball player in Asheville in 1951, and a member of the All Tournament Basketball team at the Southern Regional A.A.U. Elimination in 1952. He entered the field of correction in that year with his appointment as Director of Education and

Recreation at the New Castle County Workhouse in Wilmington, Delaware. When the legislature consolidated the county prisons under a single state authority, he was named Director of Education and Recreation for the state system, the position he presently holds. In 1957 he acted as professional consultant to the Delaware Welfare Council Committee on Services for Juvenile Delinquents. In 1959 he was employed as an Instructor in Education, in the Extension Division of the University of Delaware. In April 1960 he served as a round table discussant on prison educational-custodial problems at the Middle Atlantic Conference of Corrections in Baltimore, Maryland. He is a member of the American Correctional Association, the Correctional Educational Association, the Delaware Association of Correction and Rehabilitation, and the Delaware Association of Chiefs of Police. He has written professional articles for the *Journal of Criminal Law, Criminology and Police Science*, and *The Journal of Correctional Education*.

NOTES

1. Bennett, James V., "A Report of the Work of the Federal Bureau of Prisons," *Federal Prisons*, 1948, 3.

2. Bensing, Robert C., "A Comparative Study of American Sex Statutes," *Journal of Criminal Law, Criminology, and Police Science of Northwestern University*, XLII, 1, May-June 1951, 57-72.

3. The life sentence in practice is not nearly so final as it sounds. It has been estimated that the average length of time served on a life term is 10 years. This is due to the existence of several avenues of relief for a man under sentence. He may apply to an executive body of state or federal government for a pardon, or a commutation of sentence (a shortening of the original term). He may apply for parole (release under supervision) ofter serving a locally specified length of time. In Florida, a life-termer may be paroled after serving 6 months; in Georgia he may apply after 7 years; New Jersey, 16 years and 8 months; Arkansas at any time; New York, 13 years and 4 months.

The true life sentence exists largely as a result of application of the habitual criminal laws. These statutes passed in almost all the states provide generally that men convicted of a felony for the third or fourth time shall be committed to prison for a mandatory life sentence or a long term of years without recourse to parole. Such terms are often referred to as "natural" life. Extreme sentences of 99, 199 years or more often meted out in sensational cases have much the same effect as 'natural life' terms.

4. In Delaware, the pillory was still approved by law as recently as 1905.

The whipping post, though unused since 1952, remains on the books and in 1959 legislative attempts were made to make its use mandatory in several types of criminal activity.

5. Clemmer, Donald, "Some Aspects of Sexual Behavior in the Prison Community," *Proceedings of the Eighty-Eighth Annual Congress of Corrections of the American Correctional Association*, 1958, 377-385.

6. Of 272 inmates studied by means of the Minnesota Multiphasic Personality Inventory (MMPI), 5.14 per cent registered significant homosexual tendencies. This figure, it will be noted, is slightly below Kinsey's national estimate above.

7. Zink, Theodore M., "Are Prison Troublemakers Different?" *Journal of Criminal Law, Criminology and Police Science*, XLVIII, November-December, 1957, 433-34.

8. Schnur, Alfred C., "Prison Conduct and Recidivism," *Journal of Criminal Law, Criminology of Northwestern University*, XL, 1, May-June, 1949, 36-41.

9. Glaser, Daniel A., "A Reformation and Testing of Parole Prediction Factors," *American Sociological Review*, June, 1954, 335-41.

10. Gilbert, Raymond, "A Psychologist Looks at Classification and Education," *Journal of Correctional Education*, XII, 1, January, 1960, 13.

11. Barnes, Harry E., Teeters, Negley K., *New Horizons in Criminology*, Prentice Hall, Englewood Cliffs, 1955.

THE SOCIOLOGY OF THE POLICE

THE SOCIOLOGY OF THE POLICE

C. Ray Jeffery

Arizona State University

The purpose of this chapter is to relate the growth and development of police systems to changing sociological conditions. The police systems we know today in Europe and America are a result of historical changes in our society associated with urbanization and industrialization. Centralization and specialization of police systems have occurred as a result of these basic changes in social organization.

The relationship of police powers to the legal structure of society is examined, as well as the role of the police in the treatment and prevention of crime and delinquency. The influence of politics upon police administration is discussed.

THE HISTORY OF POLICE SYSTEMS

Police in Primitive and Archaic Societies. In primitive societies there were no special agencies or officials responsible for offering to the community police protection. A man with the aid of his kin and friends resorted to self-help. There was no strong centralized state system to protect him or his property. The kinship unit was responsible for the blood-feud. Gradually the payment of compensation came to be the preferred and established method for settling injuries and the use of self-help was forbidden. Society developed other ways than the feud for handling injuries, and special officials emerged to settle disputes and enforce the peace of the community. Among the Cheyenne Indians special military societies existed which were responsible for law and order during the buffalo hunts.[1]

Early English Police Systems. In England the disintegration of the tribal system between 600 and 1200 A.D. left the people without strong kinship units to enforce law and order. As a result other substitute groupings were made responsible for the peace of the community. A tithing was an artificial grouping of ten men which was responsible for the conduct of its members. It acted as a surety for the individual members of the tithing, and in case an individual committed a crime the tithing paid his fine or compensation. The frankpledge functioned in much the same way as the tithing. Every man had to have a lord, and if he did not have a lord he had to find a surety or leave the county. A lordless man was a threat to the peace of the community.[2]

The Normans introduced into England the rule of Englishry. If a man was found murdered the county or hundred in which he was murdered had to pay the murder-fine unless they could establish that the murdered man was of English ancestry. In this way the Normans required the county to pay a fine for any Frenchman killed in England.[3]

The Statute of Westminster of 1285 stated that the hundred had to raise the hue and cry and pursue any lawbreakers within its boundaries. If the hundred failed to produce the criminal within forty days it had to pay a fine to the victim of the crime. In this way kings attempted to make local units responsible for any crimes committed within their districts. Police protection was regarded as a local and a private matter.[4]

The Development of King's Justice. Between 1200 and 1800 a centralized state system under the domination of the Crown emerged in England. The king placed in the counties several officials who extended the judicial power of the king at the local level. The king's justices visited the counties administering the common law of the land. The shire's reeve or king's reeve was common in the eleven and twelfth centuries. The reeve was a member of the local landed gentry. The shire's reeve or sheriff watched over the king's financial interests in the county, and performed various judicial functions for the king's court. He received writs, summoned juries, executed judicial judgments, and was the presiding officer at the county court.[5]

From 1285 to 1829 each parish had a constable who acted as a police official. By Edward I's time each hundred was under the command of a constable. He was in charge of the *posse comitatus* or county militia. With the aid of the armed citizenry he raised the hue and cry and pursued law violators. He also collected taxes and supervised highways.[6]

The coroner was originally the *corona* or representative of the Crown in the county. He represented the king in the county to see that the sheriff was living up to his financial obligations to the king. In felony cases the felon's property was confiscated for the king's treasury, and the coroner was there to see that the prosecution was carried out. Since criminal law suits were initiated by private appeal the individual might settle the case for compensation, in which case the defendant's property did not go to the king. The coroner in time came to be interested in unlawful deaths since the king might have a financial interest in the case.[7]

Justices of the peace, who were responsible for the preservation of the king's peace in the counties, emerged during the thirteenth century. These justices took over many of the functions of the coroner, sheriff, and constable from the thirteenth to the nineteenth centuries. They gained control over the police system at this time. The justices were unsalaried and worked for fees, a system which led to many abuses of their powers. They were appointed by the king but were a member of the local landed gentry, so that local self government was preserved in England along with some degree of centralization under the direction of the Crown. The justices tried criminal cases and performed general police duties. In 1865 the justices were stripped of their police functions when paid police magistrates appeared. The justices were left to act as presiding magistrates at preliminary hearings, to fix bail and issue warrants, and exercise limited jurisdiction over misdemeanors.[8]

During the period from 1300 to 1900 there was no strong centralized police force in England. Crimes were common and there was no adequate way of meeting the problem. During the sixteenth and seventeenth centuries the Enclosure Acts and the Industrial Revolution created widespread poverty and unemployment. Many villeins left the manors and moved to the new urban centers in order to find employment in the factories. Crowded slum areas were characterized by high rates of crime and delinquency, prostitution, drunkenness, vagrancy, and theft. The Statute of Labourers of 1349 ordered men to remain in their townships and on the jobs which they occupied. This was an attempt to keep men from moving from one county to another. The Elizabethan Poor Laws of 1598 and 1601 attempted to provide relief for the poor. Workhouses and houses of correction were established, the one to provide work for the unemployed, the other to provide punishment for those who would not work; however, the two were never clearly distinguished. The Settlement Act of 1662 made each parish responsible only for those legally residing there, which meant residence by birth. This act was another attempt to control mass migrations from one county to another. A number of criminal laws aimed at controlling vagrancy and poverty were passed during the seventeenth and eighteenth centuries.[9]

The most common form of punishment at this time was capital punishment. Over two hundred offenses were capital crimes. Because of the severity and injustice of capital punishment several methods for acquitting the accused were made a prominent part of criminal procedure. Benefit of clergy, whereby clergy were not tried in the king's court, was extended to all who could read, while at the same time benefit of clergy was removed from over one hundred and fifty offenses by Parliamentary action. Judges, juries, and prosecutors refused to convict the guilty of crimes for which they could be executed.[10] Most of the convicted were executed at this time for crimes against property which were numerous because of social and economic conditions.

Few criminals were apprehended and convicted because of the

poor police organization that existed. Because few criminals were apprehended punishment had to be made severe. Certainty of punishment was lacking, so severity of punishment was used in its place. A weak police system at this time in history led to the use of severe penal methods.

The Classical School of penology, led by Beccaria, Bentham, and Romilly, advocated a system of punishment which was more certain and less severe and arbitrary. Certainty of punishment is a more influential deterrent than is severity. Though Beccaria believed in the need for certainty of punishment he did not feel that adequate police protection and investigation were important aspects of the penal program. On the other hand Bentham advocated a strong police system. He called for dividing England into districts as France was divided, with a centralized agency or Ministry of Justice controlling the activities of each district. Many Englishmen opposed the French system because it created a national police system with the danger of a police state.[11]

There were many advocates of police reform during the eighteenth century in England. Police work was still on a local level and was a private matter. Rewards were offered for information leading to the arrest and conviction of criminals. Advertisements of these rewards were carried in *Hue and Cry* and the *Police Gazette*. Informers were common at this time and bribery and corruption of police officials was widespread. John and Henry Fielding and Patrick Colquhoun led a movement for a centralized police system in England. Colquhoun wanted the police force separated from the control of the local justices of peace. Public opinion still favored police protection at the local level. John Fielding was a magistrate in London who established the famous Bow Street Runners, an efficient group of policemen attached to the Bow Street Station in London.[12] A few years later, in 1829, Sir Robert Peel established the Metropolitan Police Force in London which was under the jurisdiction of the Home Office and not local magistrates. This was the first attempt to establish a centralized police force in England.

Introduction. Police systems are now organized along three different lines. In Europe police units are highly centralized under a Ministry of Justice. The national government is in charge of police operations. In England there is local administration of police systems plus a degree of centralization under the Home Office. In the United States there exist independent local, county, state, and federal police agencies, each with a high degree of autonomy and independence. Complete decentralization of police agencies is characteristic of American police units, with the result that there is little coordination or cooperation between the various police systems. Duplication of services, conflicting jurisdictions, and poorly organized police systems are aspects of decentralization.[13] The reason for decentralization is the fear of a strong national state system under a national police system. J. Edgar Hoover is opposed to centralization of law enforcement agencies and regards a national police force as unnecessary.[14]

Roscoe Pound has analyzed the administration of criminal justice in terms of rapid urbanization and industrialization. The older forms of social control, such as group disapproval, religion, and the family were weakened by urbanization, and as a result criminal law came to be an important agency for social control. Pound notes that over half of the people arrested in Chicago in 1912 were arrested for offenses which did not exist twenty-five years before.[15] He argues that we are still attempting to meet the problems of criminal justice on a local level whereas they can best be met at the state level. Pound does not feel that we need federal police units for successful law enforcement. He notes that there is opposition to centralized police systems in this country and concludes: "If we fear centralization, we must learn to bring about cooperation." [16]

Urban Police Systems. The heart of police protection in the United States is the urban or city police force. Though a few unincorporated townships and villages still maintain constables or marshals, most cities now have professional police units. The

Chief of Police or Commissioner is usually a political appointee and as such has very limited tenure in office. The police force itself is now usually under civil service or some type of merit system. There is some stability in the personnel of the city force, and it is now possible to have a career as a professional police officer.

The men selected as policemen are often required to be residents of the city, a practice which encourages favoritism and political influence. In London a policeman cannot be a resident of that city and is always a man brought in from Liverpool, Bristol, or Southampton.

The city police force is responsible for traffic control, criminal investigations, foot or motor patrols, vice control, crime prevention, maintenance of the city jail and police property, and maintenance of police records. In large urban centers the police force is divided into special units or divisions which specialize in homicide, robbery, auto theft, or some other aspect of police work.[17]

County Police Units. During the colonial period fear of the Crown motivated the colonists to remove the sheriff from the control of the king, and they placed him under the control of the local citizenry by means of popular elections. As in England his main duty in the United States is as an official of the court. He maintains the county jail, feeds the prisoners, serves legal papers such as warrants, summons and subpoenas, and conducts sales of delinquent properties. He often receives fees rather than a salary. The Western sheriff was active in law enforcement and is often a symbol of the law enforcement officer; however a sheriff seldom takes part in law enforcement today. Deputies occasionally are used to patrol county roads. The sheriff system has collapsed in most areas.[18]

The overlapping jurisdiction of city and county police units has created many administrative headaches. In a recent case in Chicago involving the murder of several boys the city police and the county police competed with one another for evidence, witnesses, and publicity. As a result the investigation was interferred with in many respects. Often informal agreements between city and county units are entered into as to assignment of patrol cars and other related matters. Because the sheriff is an elected official he is very much a part of local politics. There has been less professionalization of the sheriff's office than other police agencies for this reason. County personnel are often changed after every local election.

State Police Units. In the latter part of the nineteenth century and the early part of the twentieth century several states, notably Texas, Pennsylvania, Massachusetts, New York, and New Jersey, established state police systems. In some of the states, and in Pennylvania in particular, state police were used as strike breakers in the fight against organized labor. Though this phase of state police development has passed, many labor organizers still are fearful of state police systems and oppose any attempt to centralize police control in the several states.[19]

State police are assigned the task of patrolling the state and federal highways within their respective states. In a few states such as Pennsylvania, New Jersey, and New York, state police have general jurisdiction over the enforcement of the criminal laws of the state. However, in most states the state police do not interfere with local law enforcement unless asked to do so by city or county officials.[20] For this reason one often finds conflict between the state police and the sheriff's departments. Often there exists in counties beyond the jurisdiction of the city police illegal gambling operations which operate under the protection of the county police. Interference with these establishments by the state police is opposed by county officials in some states.

The state police sometimes operate a state crime laboratory, which is helpful to the smaller departments within the state which do not maintain their own laboratory facilities. State police also perform many quasi-police functions such as riot control, giving aid and relief during a disaster such as a flood or tornado, and so forth.[21]

Federal Police Agencies. There are eight major federal police agencies located in three major departments—Justice, Treasury, and Post Office. These agencies are: The Intelligence Unit of

338

the Bureau of Internal Revenue, the Enforcement Division of the Tobacco and Alcohol Tax Unit, the Bureau of Customs, the Secret Service Division, the Bureau of Narcotics, the Office of the Chief Inspector of the Post Office Department, the Immigration Border Patrol, and the Federal Bureau of Investigation.

Due to the increased complexity and interstate nature of crime, which is related to new and rapid means of communication and transportation with the use of automobiles in crimes today, many federal laws related to crimes have been passed in the past thirty years. The Mann Act covers interstate transportation of women for immoral purposes, the Harrison Act regulates the use of narcotics, the Dyer Act makes the interstate transportation of automobiles a federal offense, and the Lindbergh Law covers kidnapping. Besides these laws, most local and state banks now carry federal deposits and/or are insured by federal agencies, so that most bank robberies are now under federal jurisdiction.

The activities of the special police agencies of the federal government involve such crimes as counterfeiting, smuggling, tax evasion, illegal entry into the country, and violations of laws regulating the sending and delivery of mail.

Agents of the Federal Bureau of Investigation are either lawyers or accountants. The Federal Bureau of Investigation maintains a central identification bureau, a technical laboratory, and a training program which are used by local and state police systems. Also the Federal Bureau publishes the *Uniform Crime Reports* which represent the sole attempt in this country to gather and classify crime statistics on a national scale.[22]

LEGAL LIMITATIONS ON POLICE POWERS

The legal sources of the power of the police come from (1) the Federal Constitution, federal statutes, and court decisions, (2) state constitutions, statutes, and decisions, and (3) municipal charters and ordinances. Police powers not delegated to the federal authorities are reserved for the states. In 1857 the State of New York created a state-controlled metropolitan police force for New York City and Brooklyn. This was also carried out in most other states with large municipal police departments. In practice the organization and administration of police departments is left to city officials. Police departments in Boston, St. Louis, Baltimore, and Providence are under state control. Municipal police agencies are usually under the control of a mayor, city council, or board of commissioners. Cities change their administrative set-up quite frequently, due to the influence of politics and political patronage upon police units.[23]

Law of Arrest. The law of arrest is an outgrowth of the system described above whereby a private citizen had the general power of police action. Recently the powers of the police have been differentiated from those of the private citizen, but they are still similar. The law of arrest with a warrant differs from arrest without a warrant. The warrant is secured from a magistrate by a complainant who swears to an alleged offense. The warrant names the person to be arrested or describes him with some degree of accuracy. A warrant for arrest is usually executed by a police officer and not a private citizen.

If the arrest is made without a warrant both a police officer and a private citizen may arrest the person for a misdemeanor committed in their presence, though in some states statutes limit the right of a private person to make an arrest under such circumstances. In a majority of states an arrest may not be made for a misdemeanor not committed in the presence of the arresting person, though in a few states police officers are given such rights if they have good reason to believe the person arrested did commit the misdemeanor.[24]

If the arrest without a warrant is for a felony the powers of a police officer are generally broader than those of a private citizen. A police officer may make an arrest for a felony not committed in his presence if he has reasonable grounds for believing a felony has been committed and that the person arrested committed the felony. A private person may make an arrest for an act not committed in his presence if a felony has actually been committed and he has reasonable grounds for believing that the person arrested committed the felony.[25]

340

Although the law varies from state to state, the general rule is that the amount of force used in making an arrest must be reasonable and not more than is necessary to protect life. Deadly force may be used to protect life or to meet a deadly attack upon one's person; however, in many jurisdictions the use of deadly force to prevent an escape is not sanctioned, especially if the escapee is a misdemeanant. Once a person is arrested he must be arraigned before a magistrate within a reasonable period of time.[26]

Search and Seizure. The Fourth Amendment of the Constitution protects a citizen from unreasonable searches and seizures. A search is reasonable if it is incident to a lawful arrest, when it is made under a valid search warrant, or when there are reasonable grounds for believing that evidence of a crime will be revealed by the search.[27] A search is unreasonable if it is exploratory in nature, if it goes beyond the authorization of the warrant, or if the arrest grows out of the search and not the search out of the arrest. A person when arrested may be searched in order to determine if he is carrying concealed weapons or evidence of the crime for which he is arrested. The search may be extended to the car in which he is found or the room in which the arrest is made. The search may not be extended to other rooms in the house however.[28]

In the case of *Rochin v California*[29] the defendant swallowed a capsule of narcotics and in order to recover the evidence the state police administered an emetic to him without his consent. The Supreme Court held that this was a coerced confession. In *Weeks v United States*[30] the Supreme Court held that evidence illegally gained by police could not be introduced in a federal court. The Court held in *Wolf v Colorado*[31] that the *Weeks* case was not binding on state courts. In *Irvine v California*[32] evidence gained by wire tapping was admitted into the trial, and the Supreme Court affirmed the conviction on the authority of the *Wolf* case. Most states today follow the *Wolf* doctrine and do not use the exclusionary rule of the federal courts, that is, they will admit illegally-gained evidence. These decisions encourage police officers to gain evidence illegally, and the easiest way to discourage such practices is to adopt the exclusionary rule in state courts.

It should be noted that most illegal search and seizure cases involve narcotics, alcohol, gambling, prostitution, illegal sex activities, internal security measures, or labor union activities.

Confessions voluntarily given are admissible in court; however coerced confessions are not admissible. This rule follows the doctrine of the Fifth Amendment that a man shall not be forced to testify against himself, and it serves as a control on the part of the court over third degree methods used by the police to gain confessions. What is a coerced confession has bothered courts a great deal. In *McNabb v United States*[33] the Supreme Court invalidated a confession obtained when a defendant was not promptly arraigned before a magistrate. The judiciary thus acts as an important check on the activities of police officers. The judiciary has an important function to play in safeguarding the rights of citizens as opposed to the police power of the state.

The police often use informers to gain evidence, which creates an unfavorable public opinion of police investigations. Informers are especially useful in cases dealing with the enforcement of laws dealing with alcohol, narcotics, gambling, prostitution, illegal sex activities, and internal security measures.

Puttkammer suggests that one answer to police illegality and brutality is to change our legal system so that it follows the Continental system.[34] On the Continent under the inquisitorial procedure magistrates and police officers are given wide discretionary powers to question defendants and suspects. The problem in the United States is that our police have no legal ways in which they can question suspects, so naturally they use illegal ones.

One of the sources of law enforcement abuses is the fact that 90 per cent of those arrested and convicted are from the lower socio-economic class. They cannot afford to hire a lawyer and 90 per cent of them plead guilty to the charge or to a reduced charge. Prosecutors encourage this practice by accepting pleas of guilty to lesser charges. The fact that most defendants are lower class encourages illegal police activities because the police know the individual will not complain or if he complains he is not influential enough to be heard. The flagrant violations of civil rights involve minority groups such as Negroes or Puerto Ricans.

In recent years the Federal Bureau of Investigation has been involved in enforcing a security and loyalty program as an aspect of the new atomic era and the cold war with Russia. In carrying on this work the Bureau has used paid informers and wire tapping to gain evidence, for which it has been criticized. The stand one takes on these issues depends upon one's political philosophy. If one feels that national security is more important than individual rights, then one will commend the actions of the Bureau; if one feels that individual rights are more important than national security then these practices will be viewed with alarm.

Many prosecuting attorneys and policemen are critical of judges, especially the Justices of the United States Supreme Court, for decisions which limit the scope of police investigations. They argue that such decisions allow guilty men to go free after the police and prosecutor have worked hard to gain a conviction. There is little respect for "mere legal technicalities" in such situations. For this reason there is often a tug of war between the police and the prosecutor on one hand and the judiciary on the other hand. The law assumes that no man is guilty until proven in court to be so, and the procedure used to determine guilt must be one conforming to standards of due process.

There is also tension between the police and the prosecutor. The police will gather evidence which the prosecutor cannot use or which he feels does not justify a prosecution of the case. The police feel that their efforts are undermined by the arbitrary actions of prosecutors. Often judges will release criminals on probation or a jury will acquit a man whom the police feel is guilty, and such actions are viewed as unfair by the police.

Throughout the history of criminal procedure the pendulum has swung from protection of the rights of individuals to the increased police power of the state. If we wish efficient police work greater freedom will be allowed the police in carrying on their criminal investigations; if we wish to protect the civil

343

rights of citizens we will limit the manner in which the police carry on their investigations.

POLICE AND THE COMMUNITY

Police and Politics. A perpetual problem in police administration is police corruption. The recurring shakeups of city police departments, such as those in Chicago, are examples of the problems faced by many departments today in the United States. The fact that police departments are dominated by politics and political machines make such influence possible. If we could somehow remove our police systems from politics it would be a big step in the direction of doing away with corruption.[35]

The heart of police corruption is the vice squad of a police department. This squad enforces laws dealing with gambling, alcohol, narcotics, prostitution, and illegal sex practices. Police protection is sought and found by the operators of these activities. Criminal syndicates in our major urban areas pay thousands of dollars a day for police protection. The public demands the availability of these services, and people are willing to pay for them. It has been suggested that if these various activities were regarded as private affairs and not as crimes then they could be handled in other ways than by criminal laws. We have legalized the sale of alcohol, and to some extent legalized certain types of gambling operations, but there is opposition to legalizing homosexuality, prostitution, and the sale of drugs to addicts. There is not the time in this chapter to discuss the many aspects of such proposals, but it can be noted that the criminal law is a most ineffective way to deal with what are essentially standards of private morality. Other methods of social control are more effective.

Treatment and Prevention. Most police work involves traffic control, criminal investigation and identification, and uniformed patrols. In recent years there has been increased emphasis on the role of the police in the prevention and treatment of delinquency. Police athletic leagues were established in New York

City and elsewhere in an attempt to combat juvenile delinquency. This type of police activity is not as popular today as thirty years ago, perhaps because of the failure of recreational centers to reduce the rate of delinquency in an area.

Many urban police units have a juvenile section or division. The juvenile officer has initial contact with the offender, and about 80 per cent of these cases are handled by the officer without referral to a judge or probation officer. Often the delinquent is told to report to the juvenile officer, a type of "unofficial probation." [36]

It is felt that juvenile officers should have training in delinquency prevention and control. In order to offer such training to police and probation officers the University of Southern California several years ago established the Delinquency Control Institute. Today two other universities have such institutes—Arizona State University at Tempe and Florida State University.

Whether or not police officers should be doing social work is a debatable point. It is pointed out that the best service the officer can provide is adequate patrol work in an area which will discourage delinquency. The juvenile officer can also make referrals to existing community agencies and thus perform a very important function. Police ought not to be probation officers, and recreation is not a task for a police department.[37] It can be said that the job of the policeman is to protect life and property. It can also be argued that since the juvenile officer has initial contact with the delinquent he is in a position to play a vital role in delinquency prevention and treatment. Training in sociology, psychology, criminology, and corrections is not going to hurt the police officer if he recognizes the limitations of the service he is able to offer.

Though there is a movement to use police as agents for preventing and treating crime and delinquency, the main orientation of police officials has been an anti-reform attitude. Police officers have advocated a "get-tough" policy for criminals in place of treatment and reform. One of the major sources of opposition to attempts to abolish capital punishment in this country has come from the police. They argue that capital pun-

345

ishment is necessary in order to protect the police from every deranged psychopath who wants to make a reputation for himself by "gunning down" a policeman in the manner of the gunslinger of the Old West.

Racial Factors and the Police. A survey of the Philadelphia Police Department[38] revealed that 10 per cent of the police commanders are proud of their Negro policemen and feel they are competent; 15 per cent feel that Negroes are inferior as policemen; 75 per cent feel that skin color has nothing to do with police efficiency. There is little rapport between Negro community leaders and police commanders. Negro policemen feel that they are handled fairly in assignments except in patrol car assignments. Negroes are usually assigned to foot or motorcycle patrol rather than car patrol. Most white policemen do not object to having a Negro as a companion except in a patrol car assignment. The white policeman who has contact with Negroes has opinions more favorable to Negroes than do those without such contacts, thus reaffirming the results of the Stouffer study of the American soldier.

The white community accepts Negro patrolmen. Few Negroes are promoted to ranks above patrolman. Race prejudice is a factor in police promotions. Negro policemen are more indignant about Negro criminals than are white policemen. Both groups agree that Negro offenders are treated more harshly than are white offenders, and it is generally agreed that Negro policemen are more severe with Negro offenders than are white policemen.

SELECTED BIBLIOGRAPHY

Crump, Irving, *Our State Police*, Dodd, Mead, and Co., New York, 1955. Crump describes the history, organization, personnel, and functions of the various state police agencies in the United States.

Encyclopedia of the Social Sciences. This standard reference work contains articles on the "Sheriff" by Theodore F. T. Plucknett, "Justice, Administration of," by William Seagle, "Law Enforcement," by Thurman Arnold, "Justice of Peace," by Chester H. Smith, and "Police," by Bruce Smith.

Kephart, William M., *Racial Factors and Urban Law Enforcement*, University of Pennsylvania Press, Philadelphia, 1957. Kephart discusses here his survey of racial factors in law enforcement in the City of Philadelphia. The role of the Negro in the community and on the police force is discussed along with promotions, assignments, and Negro personnel on the police force.

Leonard, V. A., *Police Organization and Management*, Foundation Press, Brooklyn, 1951. An experienced police officer discusses police organization, personnel selection and management, police records, patrol, strategy and tactics.

"New Goals in Police Management," *Annals*, 291, January, 1954. This issue of the *Annals* is devoted to police administration. The police challenge in urban areas, small cities, and rural areas is discussed, along with such topics as sound law enforcement, patrol methods, criminal investigation, traffic control, juvenile delinquency, merit systems, police training, and crime reporting.

Orfield, Lester B., *Criminal Procedure from Arrest to Appeal*, New York University Press, New York, 1947. This is a standard textbook on criminal procedure by a professor of law. The legal limitations on police actions in making arrests and search and search and seizures are discussed.

Pike, Luke O., *A History of Crime in England*, Smith, Elder, and Co., 1873, two volumes. This is a historic survey of social and economic conditions in England during the Middle Ages and the crime conditions which resulted from vagrancy, poverty, and alcoholism. The role of the police in crime control at that time is presented.

Police Service for Juveniles, United States Department of Health, Education, and Welfare, Washington, D. C., 1954. This government publication discusses the role of the police in delinquency prevention and control, the availability of police services for juveniles, offenses by adults against juveniles, organization and training of police for work with juveniles, and police relations with other social agencies in the community.

Pound, Roscoe, *Criminal Justice in America*, Harvard University Press, Cambridge, 1945. This book by the former dean of the Harvard Law School and the father of sociological jurisprudence was first published in 1930 and still stands as one of the great classics in the field. Pound analyzes criminal justice in terms of the transition from rural to urban in our society, with the accompanying stress placed upon criminal law as a means of social control. He discusses the need for centralization and specialization of police forces in the light of these social changes. A historical treatment of some topics related to criminal law is presented.

Puttkammer, Ernest W., *Administration of Criminal Law*, University of Chicago Press, Chicago, 1953. Another classic in the field is this book by the former professor of criminal law at the University of Chicago. Puttkammer discusses in his book the purpose of criminal law, police organization, law of arrest, legal limits of police investigations, preliminary hearings, role of the coroner in criminal justice, indictments and informations, arraignment, criminal trials, post-trial motions, sentencing, and paroles.

Radzinowicz, Leon, *A History of English Criminal Law*, Stevens and Sons, London, 1948. Three volumes of this historic work by an English professor have been published. Volume III deals with "The Reform of the Police" in England during the eighteenth and nineteenth centuries. The various sources of support and opposition to a centralized police system in England are presented in this volume.

Smith, Bruce, *Police Systems in the United States*, Harper and Brothers, New York, 1949. One of America's outstanding scholars of police administration discusses the police problem, crime problems, traffic control, rural and suburban police, state and federal police, police control and organization, and police services.

Stephen, Sir James F., *A History of the Criminal Law of England*, Macmillan and Co., London, 1883, 3 vols. Stephen's work is one of the standard reference works on the history of criminal law. He discusses the development of criminal law in England in response to social and economic conditions. The historical development of police systems in England is presented.

Vollmer, August, Peper, John, and Boolsen, Frank, *Police Organization and Administration*, California State Department of Education, Sacramento, 1951. This is a compilation of mimeographed materials issued by the State of California for its law enforcement officials. In it are discussed such topics as the legal sources of police power, police organization, administrative organization, public relations, and police supervision and control.

Wilson, O. W., *Police Planning*, Charles C. Thomas, Springfield, 2nd ed., 1958. In this volume a veteran police officer and former dean of the School of Criminology at the University of California, now Superintendent of Police for the City of Chicago, discusses planning, gathering data, organization, police patrol, detective units, vice control, delinquency control, traffic control, records, equipment, personnel, and public relations.

Wilson, O. W., *Police Administration*, McGraw-Hill Book Company, New York, 1950. In this book Wilson is concerned with police organization, command, planning, and control; patrol, investigation, traffic enforcement, vice control, crime prevention, juvenile delinquency, police records, communication, police equipment, district stations, personnel selection, training, promotions, and public relations.

(*Clarence*) *Ray Jeffery* was born May 14, 1921, in Pocatello, Idaho. His father was a prosecuting attorney in Idaho for many years. After graduation from the Pocatello school system his studies at the University of Idaho were interrupted by service in World War II. He transferred to Indiana University after discharge where he received his A.B. degree in 1949 and his Ph.D. degree in sociology in 1954. While at Indiana he worked with Edwin H. Sutherland in criminology and Jerome Hall in criminal law. He has taught at Colby College in Maine and at Southern Illinois University, and is now associate professor of sociology at Arizona State University at Tempe. In 1958-59 he was a Senior Fellow in the Law and Behavioral Sciences Program at the University of Chicago Law School. During the summer of 1960 he attended the Institute for the Administration of Criminal Justice at the University of Wisconsin as a Social Science Research Council Fellow. The following articles of his have appeared in the *Journal of Criminal Law, Criminology, and Police Science*: "The Structure of American Criminological Thinking," "Crime, Law and Social Structure," "The Development of Crime in Early English Society," "An Integrated Theory of Criminal Behavior," and "The Historical Development of Criminology." He is a co-author, with F. James Davis, Henry H. Foster, Jr., and E. Eugene Davis, of a book on sociology of law entitled *Law in Context* published in 1960.

349

NOTES

1. Hoebel, E. Adamson, *The Law of Primitive Man*, Harvard University Press, Cambridge, 1954; Seagle, William, *The History of Law*, Tudor Publishing Co., New York, 1946; Malinowski, Bronislaw, *Crime and Custom in Savage Society*, Kegan, Paul, Trench, Trubner, and Co., London, 1926; Llewellyn, Karl N., and Hoebel, E. Adamson, *The Cheyenne Way*, The University of Oklahoma Press, Norman, 1941; Radcliffe-Brown, A.R., "Law, Primitive," *Encyclopedia of the Social Sciences*, IX, 202 ff.

2. Pollock, Frederick W., and Maitland, Frederic W., *The History of English Law*, University Press, Cambridge, II, 516-530; Pike, Luke O., *A History of Crime in England*, Smith, Elder and Co., 1873, I, 57-58.

3. Pike, *op. cit.*, 137; Holdsworth, W. S., *A History of English Law*, Little, Brown and Co., Boston, 1923, II, 150.

4. Pollock and Maitland, *op. cit.*, II, 578; Pike, *op. cit.*, I, 220.

5. Stubbs, William, *The Constitutional History of England*, Clarendon Press, Oxford, 1891, I, 649-652; Plucknett, Theodore F. T., "Sheriff," *Encyclopedia of the Social Sciences*, XIV, 20-22.

6. Stephen, Sir James F., A History of the Criminal Law of England, Macmillan and Co., London, 1883, I, 190-194; Smith, Bruce, *Police Systems in the United States*, Harper and Bros., New York, 1940, 75-80.

7. Puttkammer, Ernest W., *Administration of Criminal Law*, University of Chicago Press, Chicago, 1953, 108 ff.

8. Smith, *op. cit.*, 75-80; Smith, Chester H., "Justices of Peace," *Encyclopedia of the Social Sciences*, VIII, 524-526.

9. Pike, *op. cit.*, I, 144 ff., 322 ff.; Radzinowicz, Leon, *A History of English Criminal Law*, Stevens and Sons, London, 1948, II, 1-20.

10. Holdsworth, *op. cit.*, III, 293-301; Hall, Jerome, *Theft, Law and Society*, (second edition), Bobbs-Merrill Co., Indianapolis, 1952, 110 ff.

11. Radzinowicz, *op. cit.*, III, 417 ff.

12. *Ibid.*, II, 57 ff., III, 108 ff.

13. Smith, Bruce, "Police," *Encyclopedia of the Social Sciences*, XII, 183-188.

14. Hoover, J. Edgar, "The Basis of Sound Law Enforcement," *Annals*, 291, January, 1954, 39 ff.

15. Pound, Roscoe, *Criminal Justice in America*, Harvard University Press, Cambridge, 1945, 23.

16. *Ibid.*, 179.

17. Parker, William H., "The Police Challenge in Our Great Cities," *Annals*, 291, January, 1954, 5-13; Wilson, O. W., *Police Administration*, McGraw-Hill Book Co., New York, 1950; Vollmer, August, Peper, John, and Boolsen, Frank, *Police Organization and Administration*, California State Department of Education, Sacramento, 1951.

18. Smith, *Police Systems*, op. cit., 80 ff.

19. Puttkammer, *op. cit.*, 43-46; Hickey, Edward J., "Trends in Rural Police Protection," *Annals*, 291, January, 1954, 22-30.

20. Puttkammer, *op. cit.*, 43 ff.

21. Crump, Irving, *Our State Police*, Dodd, Mead, and Co., New York, 1955.

22. Vollmer, Peper, and Boolsen, *op. cit.*, 2 ff.; Caldwell, Robert G., *Criminology*, Ronald Press Co., New York, 1956, 274 ff.

23. Vollmer, Peper, and Boolsen, *op. cit.*, 1-16.

24. Orfield, Lester B., *Criminal Procedure from Arrest to Appeal*, New York University Press, New York, 1947, 14 ff.

25. *Ibid.*, 15 ff.

26. *Ibid.*, 26 ff.

27. Caldwell, *op. cit.*, 303-304.

28. Orfield, *op. cit.*, 42-43.

29. 342 U.S. 165 (1952).

30. 232 U.S. 383 (1914).

31. 338 U.S. 25 (1949).

32. 347 U.S. 128 (1954).

33. 318 U.S. 332 (1943).

34. Puttkammer, *op. cit.*, 78.

35. Smith, *Police Systems, op cit.*, 4-10.

36. Bloch, Herbert A., and Flynn, Frank T., *Delinquency*, Random House, New York, 1956, 251 ff.; *Police Services for Juveniles*, United States Department of Health, Education, and Welfare, 1954.

37. Rinck, Jane E., "Supervising the Juvenile Delinquent," *Annals*, 291, January, 1954, 78-86.

38. Kephart, William M., *Racial Factors and Urban Law Enforcement*, University of Pennsylvania Press, Philadelphia, 1957.

TRENDS IN POLICE TRAINING

Paul H. Ashenhust
Inspector, *Dallas Police Department* (Texas)

We have had law and the teaching of law since the time of Moses. Tribal chieftains, rulers by whatever name they were known, issued their proclamations. So when the leader or leaders announced that certain things must be done or that other certain things must not be done, such announcement had the force of law. Certainly it would have been foolish to proclaim the law without some means of enforcing it. So common sense tells us that someone had to enforce the decrees or laws pronounced by the governing authority.

The persons charged with the duty of enforcing the edicts of the sovereign authority were law enforcement officers. As early states and nations were organized from tribes, submitting to one authority, this powerful monarch set up law enforcement throughout his realm. Regardless of what those law men were called at various stages, or in various parts of the world, their qualifications were about the same. The men assigned the law enforcement task were men of:

(1) Loyalty
(2) Courage
(3) Ability
(4) Physical Strength

Their duties, too, were much the same, in ancient Greece, in Rome, or elsewhere.

(1) Guard the Emperor and his family
(2) Guard his property and vast estates

(3) Quell disturbances

(4) Keep the peace

(5) Enforce the rules laid down by the ruler

So we have had law enforcement from ancient times. The Medes and Persians, the Greeks and Romans, the Spartans were subject to law and knew law enforcers. Back through the history of the centuries we can trace the plain path of this profession.

What of the future? And more specifically, what of the future of the municipal police in the cities of America?

PROFESSIONAL ASPECTS

There may be some doubt in the mind of the reader as to whether or not police work is a profession. But there should be no doubt as to whether or not we have many professional policemen. For the evidence is at hand showing without any doubt that many police officers, as individuals, meet all the demands of a proposed police profession.

Today these professional policemen are engaged in a mighty effort to bring this dream of a great profession to reality. This is "The Goal; A Police Profession"[1] —and there is suddenly the possibility of success within the foreseeable future.

What remains to be done to make of this once disdained job a profession? As a basic requirement we have "an organized body of knowledge." Like the other professions the apprentice, the student, the novice, the cadet in the police field must be drilled in the skills of the job. These (would be) officers must know the law, they must know the methods and techniques, the procedures necessary to conduct investigations where a crime has been committed. They must develop skill in interrogation and a vast array of talents necessary for ferreting out and identifying the culprit. They must recognize evidence, know how to preserve it and how to use it.

Law they must know and police science, public relations and public speaking. They must know crime prevention and traffic direction. Much more they must know.

So we need training.

But training alone will not make a profession. There must be certain requirements for entrance into this profession and certain standards to be met. There must be a license issued by competent authority attesting to the fact that the individual is a member of the profession. And there must be an authority capable of ridding the profession of an undesirable member by suspending his license.

ETHICS

Finally we must have a professional code of ethics. This code must be subscribed to by all members of the profession. Whenever a member is charged with violating the code an investigation must be made. The offender's license must be suspended or other appropriate action taken if he is found guilty. "The early professions were built about philosophical or ethical codes. The common feature of these codes was some form of service to mankind. Although rigorous asceticism was seldom required, doctors, lawyers and clergymen demonstrated enough selflessness down through the years to earn general respect." [2]

When these things, training, a license, and the code of ethics, have been adopted throughout all of our country we will have a real police profession.

These requirements differ little, if at all, from the requirements of the other recognized professions. Doctors, teachers, architects, engineers, lawyers, all have such requirements.

We have a code of ethics, "The Law Enforcement Code of Ethics," rapidly being recognized as the professional code of ethics for police. Many of the largest and best known law enforcement organizations in the nation have adopted this code.

LICENSING

The license for police is on the way. Movements taking place in all sections of the country are a certain indication that the

354

various states will adopt some plan leading to the licensing of police.

As early as 1934 Donald Leonard, then Captain in the Michigan State Police, made such a proposal. While this proposal did not specify licensing it did provide for certain standards of training, and is definitely a forerunner of today's proposals for licensing.

"It is necessary for the states to assume their proper burden of police control. To accomplish this legislation should be passed in the individual states which would provide for the following:

"1. . . .   2. . .   3. . . .
4. The training of all police officers in schools organized by the state, or in local departments having training schools which comply with the standard requirements formulated by the state, with provision that no officer could be employed as such anywhere in the state who has not received such training."[3]

"It is hoped that this movement will gain momentum. With the increase in crime and particularly the increase in cost of crime, plus the trend for centralization of government in the Nation's Capital, a long delay in bringing our police forces, large and small, up to professional standards might cost us local law enforcement.

"Proposals are now being advanced to set up a federal system for licensing police. This is one more step down the short road leading to the loss of our liberty. The police license must and will come. If our cities will not provide a workable system and continue to assume the "dog in the manger" attitude when we talk of a state license, you can be sure that the efforts now being made to federalize your police will be accelerated.

"J. Edgar Hoover has told us year in and year out, and then repeated his warning, not to set up federal police in the United States. He has told us to keep our local police under local jurisdiction. We should heed his warning. We can have local police with a state license, but who is so naive as to believe that our police department can be kept out of politics and under local control when the black day comes and we have federal licensing of local police." [4]

If it is left up to the law enforcement officers of the Nation, and their professional associations this dire prediction will not come to pass.

All of these objectives of the police are being advanced on a broad front. None is without ardent proponents who engage in continuous efforts in its behalf. Standard requirements to include educational qualifications, physical fitness and a wholesome background, are being urged before police professional groups and city and state governing bodies. The Law Enforcement Code of Ethics has been adopted by hundreds of municipal and county police departments. Entrance requirements are being strongly urged before various State Legislatures.

So now we come to training, the requirement which has received the most attention for the longest period of time.

THE TRAINING

How are policemen trained? Can police training be made available to all law enforcement agencies?

Police training today is widespread. Training is carried on principally by means of

(1) Police training academies
(2) Police training offered by colleges and universities
(3) Correspondence schools home study courses.

Of the three, police academies carry the main burden. In fact, until just a few years ago they carried just about all of it. Police academies are operated by municipalities, counties, states and the Federal Government.

"Most city and state police have their own training staff. The small city which does not have such a staff should and can develop one.

"When there is no training in the Department, the Chief can

choose any one of several ways to secure it. He can arrange with a neighboring city for one or two men at a time to attend their police academy. Perhaps the state police have regular training courses to which he can send a man or two. Or, many times, the Chief can arrange with the Department in the larger city or the state police to lend him one or two instructors to help him set up a training school and even to assist in conducting it.

"A solution to the problem can be worked out by one of the methods mentioned, or by a combination of such methods. And, in addition to those mentioned, there is one method which cannot fail. The Chief of Police can write to the Federal Bureau of Investigation and request that they send an instructor to survey his department, determine its training needs, prepare a schedule and, if necessary, give the instruction." [5]

These are the methods now in use in the cities and towns of our nation. We have some regional schools where several towns set up a centrally located school and all furnish instructors and students or the instructors come from the State Police or the Federal Bureau of Investigation.

There is no pattern. Each school differs from the others. They differ in many ways including number of hours, subjects taught, and quality of instruction.

And yet, even though a quick look at the entire field of police training would bring a picture of confusion or even chaos, much good is being accomplished. In our more advanced police departments our training has paced the general improvement.

"The emergence of Police Education into a significant and distinct aspect in the total framework of law enforcement has been a comparatively recent achievement. Perhaps it is difficult for someone embarking on a career in law enforcement to realize that not so long ago a new police officer was issued a badge, a gun and a club and was ordered to go out and enforce the law. His police education was confined to observing what the other officers did." [6]

With rare exceptions modern police training began with state police organizations. Among the first was the Pennsylvania State Police. New York, New Jersey and Michigan were among the early States adopting police training. Today our state police training facilities rank with the best in the world.

Police education of the highest degree is none too good for the complex job of the American police. For the job is indeed complex today. Recruits selected must have the ability to master the subjects taught. Although standards differ throughout the country and educational requirements range from the ability to read and write upward, more and more towns and cities list a high school education as an entrance requirement. Metropolitan departments generally require high school graduation. Many members of such departments have one or more years college. But high school and college training are not of themselves sufficient for the modern police officer. He must have a police education. And he will not get that except in a police school. Certainly as our expanding population reaches higher educational levels, police departments too will show a higher percentage of college trained men.

"Because of the demand for adequate police protection, the tendency to place more responsibility on the peace officer, the scientific approach to criminal identification and investigation, the demand of administrators, and the desire of law enforcement officers generally to improve themselves, organized training in the law enforcement service is receiving more and more attention. Therefore, in recent years there has been a growing number of training programs in two-year and four-year collegiate institutions. This growth of occupational education has been brought about by long-term changes in law enforcement as previously described, and in society as a whole. Today crime is one of the foremost social problems confronting the country." [7]

As the demands of modern society upon our police continue to multiply training must be given top billing by the police administrator. We cannot expect these young men, many of them immature and inexperienced, to give satisfactory police performance without increased emphasis on police training. Many police recruits are but a little way from school. Few have had experience in meeting the public. The only experience of some is that derived from a short tour of duty in the armed services. Others come from the ranks of the farmer, mechanic, postal clerk, machinist, laborer or other occupation. Their ideas about the police service are very sketchy indeed.

THE FBI TRAINING

The unquestioned leader in police training in the United States is the Federal Bureau of Investigation. This great organization under the leadership of J. Edgar Hoover has blazed the way for others to follow. Law enforcement agencies of every type have been encouraged to provide training for their employees.

The one thing which had perhaps the greatest impact on police training was the establishment of the FBI National Academy in 1935.

As this is being written early in 1960 more than 3800 men have graduated from the National Academy. These men come from all levels of law enforcement, city, county, state and national. They are selected men. The arduous training they receive is aimed at making them adminstrators and training officers for their local agencies. A typical class will be composed of men from city, county and state law enforcement levels. Every section of the country will be represented. Some men in the class will come from the metropolitan centers of our country, others the small towns.

The graduates of this academy, the training material which has come from it, the millions of words which have been written and spoken about it have all combined to give a great impetus to training everywhere.

FBI Agents conduct or participate in hundreds of police schools annually. When we realize that few small departments have a training staff of their own the service here rendered by the FBI is readily discernible.

COLLEGE TRAINING

Of recent years, as mentioned earlier, colleges and universities have begun to make available certain training to benefit the

359

law enforcement officer. Some of the institutions contributing to law enforcement by means of special courses for the police officer are Northwestern, Yale, Harvard, Texas A & M, Indiana, Michigan State, Southern Methodist, Purdue, Louisville, Southern California and Western Reserve—there are many others. Another decade will witness a great increase in this type of training.

But college or university training courses are not available to all men. Distance, cost, the time element and other considerations prevent most law enforcement officers from attending special schools. The top schools, the FBI National Academy for example, can take but a limited number. The Academy has but two sessions each year. If a department was fortunate enough to send a man to every session it could send 40 men in twenty years. In a department with 1,000 men if only 40 or less were selected to attend the academy in 20 years, very few members of the department would stand a chance of obtaining that excellent training.

And if approximately 200 men per year from all law enforcement agencies throughout the country attend the academy, which is the case at present, there is little chance for the average officer in either the small or large department to attend.

With the advance all along the line in the police profession in recent years we have witnessed the publication of many police books. Like other professions several excellent professional magazines are available. So the ambitious officer, anxious to keep abreast of modern advances, may take advantage of professional books and journals for that purpose.

If he wishes to study a general police course or to specialize in some phase of police work he may take advantage of the opportunity to enroll in a good police correspondence school. Several, which are both reliable and inexpensive, are available. The Race Relations Course offered by The Academy of Police Training in Dallas fills a special need for instruction in a course not readily available elsewhere.

So looking over the field we find that training has made worthwhile advances from a beginning just a few years ago. We have courses available in colleges and universities and "police education by correspondence" as noted earlier. The major part of the training is carried out in police schools operated by state and municipal departments. Here the bulk of the training is done.

What does training need? Training needs to know where it is going! It needs a recognized standard. A good police officer, or each member of a good police department, in order to do an acceptable job of law enforcement must have training of such kind that he is completely familiar with the highly specialized techniques in use today.

Police science, crime prevention, police public relations are but a few of the subjects he must know. He must know much criminal law, including criminal statutes, laws of arrest and evidence. He must know when he can legally make an arrest and when he can legally make a search. He must be a trained police officer.

But the status of the individual or of the single department will remain as it is, lacking in public confidence and respect, if other police all over the country and all over the state are far below standard. Oh, the public or a part of it will recognize that this is a good department and that it is ably administered and highly trained. But the members of that department will not be recognized generally as professional people and the job of the police will not be recognized as a profession until all police or at least the overwhelming majority meet the requirements of professionalization.

We need a law, a state law, and we will have it. We will have it in each of the fifty states in time. It may differ in some respects but it must provide several major things—(1) high standards (2) minimum police training (3) enforcement methods for the

Law Enforcement Code of Ethics, and a license based on certain requirements.

Legislation of this kind can be passed. In fact it has already been passed in at least one state, New York. The Municipal Police Training Council Act passed by the Senate and Assembly of the State of New York became effective July 1, 1959.

This Act provides for a Municipal Police Training Council consisting of eight members, three of which are appointed by the governor, two from a list of six incumbent sheriffs submitted by the State Sheriff's Association and two from a list of six chiefs of police submitted by the New York State Association of Chiefs of Police, and one shall be the Commissioner of Police of the City of New York.

The governor also appoints an Executive Director with the advice and consent of the senate.

The council may recommend to the governor rules and regulations with respect to the approval or revocation of municipal police schools, also minimum courses of study, attendance requirements, and equipment and facilities to be required at approved municipal training schools.

It may also recommend to the governor regulations governing the requirements of minimum basic training which must be completed by probationary officers before they may receive a permanent appointment.

Additional duties of the council, the action by the governor and the functions, powers and duties of the executive director provide for the approval of certain training schools and the issuance of certificates of approval for such schools, the certification of qualified instructors and the certification of officers who have satisfactorily completed basic training programs and the issuance of a license to them.

And the provision that will have far reaching effect on police standards everywhere in the state "No person shall, after July 1, 1960, receive an original appointment on a permanent basis as a police officer of any county, city, town, village or police district unless such person has previously been awarded a certificate by the executive director of the municipal police training council."

Now we have required training in New York State, we have a license requirement and we have a Code of Ethics which has been adopted by at least a part of the law enforcement organizations of the state.

PUBLIC RELATIONS ASPECTS

When he is truly a professional will the general public recognize him as such? After all a "cop" is a "cop". His job is little understood by business or professional people. We have fifty years behind us in which every medium available pictured the police officer in the worst possible light. He was a clown, for a laugh, a villain when the part required it and a fool always. He had little or no ability in his own field and certainly none in any other field. He was a sadist and a grafter to the public because he was so pictured. The people were fortunate to have a good "cop" on their particular beat but they knew they must be cautious of those others throughout the city, who lurked in back rooms accepting pay offs and worked in dark basements inflicting police brutality.

These ideas were not the property of the illiterate or ignorant alone. They were the ideas of the bankers, the law makers, the teachers and others. Any old time policeman can quote a dozen incidents going to prove that policemen were considered dumb and the police job one to be taken as a last resort.

A desk sergeant in a college town received a call from an official at the university regarding a theft at a fraternity house. He was at quite a loss in his struggle for simple words to explain to the sergeant that these strange words making up the name of the fraternity were actually Greek letters. When the sergeant told the learned gentleman that the letters were familiar to him coming as they did from the Greek Alphabet beginning "Alpha, Beta, Gamma," etc., and continued his recitation right through to Omega the caller had little more to say.

This is not an isolated instance. There are hundreds like it. The educated gentleman was no doubt disturbed as he realized he had met up with a Greek scholar. Others perhaps do not realize it and continue in their own little world without recognizing that other worlds are also important.

The police officer whose book had just been published replied only with a quiet smile to the inane remark of the university professor who was so surprised that he remarked, "This ought to be reported to Ripley's Believe it or Not. Remarkable—a police officer writing a book."

It will take years and a lot of doing to overcome such ideas as those of the father who said, "I gave my son a good education. I hate to see him waste all of that by becoming a policeman." Or perhaps we should consider the remark of the secretary who said to the young officer, "You should have let your friends know. Surely some of us could have found you a job."

Thus we find a peculiarly unhealthy attitude as we examine the public's feeling toward the law enforcement officer. The police officer walks into a small store or office to pay a bill, ask a question or deliver a message, a bright office worker throws up his hands in surrender or calls out, "Look out Joe, here they come!" Why? Is it out of the ordinary for him to see a policeman? He sees one or more of them every day. If a doctor comes in he does not grasp his abdomen or his head and play act a little scene. He does not play post office when the postman comes in. He does not think he is a cow when he sees a milkman. But hundreds of times a day the little scene is played—the cue the entrance of the officer—a look of horror, hands extended for the handcuffs in token of surrender or thrust high in the air as the denial is uttered in shaken tones, "It wasn't me, officer."

The officer made a courteous approach to the traffic violator. He was hardly prepared for the vigor of the words with which she sprang to the attack. Finally he was able to say, "But, after all, this is a violation of the law." "Violation of the law," she cried, "you are not dealing with a fool. Some silly little rule made up by a bunch of dumb cops is not the law."

Perhaps she was not a fool. But the silly little "police" rule was an act of the legislature and a state law. This lady ranked with the one who said in anger, "You cannot expect much from a cop, after all if you had any education you wouldn't be a cop." The officer's smiling reply probably threw her a little off balance, "I enjoy my work. Please give your husband my regards —we were in college together."

And so it goes. The public demands better police performance, less crime, more clearances. The officer needs the support of the public if he is to do a better job. But prejudices, class pride, funny papers, and distorted pictures of the officer in stories, moving pictures and television have built up a public attitude which is hard to overcome.

The police officer is not blameless. He, too, has had a part in bringing about this unhealthy attitude. There is a dirty phrase "police brutality." This term denotes something which is almost entirely non-existent today. With the improvement in personnel standards in the past two decades police departments have very few "Keystone clowns" on their rolls.

As a professional man the police officer must not accept gratuities or favors of any kind. If he wishes to see police work a profession he must act like a member of a respected profession. He must belong to his professional associations. He must read his professional journals. He must own a professional library. He must read and study. He must take part in civic activities, belong to clubs and organizations. He must be an active citizen. He must be a good citizen.

At the risk of repetition let us consider what is being done to obtain personnel who will measure up to the standards required by the paragraph above.

In the modern departments we find (1) higher standards are being set. (2) Training is being improved.

Let us look at a police academy which has earned an enviable reputation. It was set up in the tables of organization with full time personnel 15 years ago. The Departmental Instructor was a Captain and his assistant a Sergeant. The training period for the Recruit Class was six weeks. Emphasis was placed on Criminal Law, First Aid, Firearms Training and some phases of patrol procedure.

As the years passed it was felt that it was necessary to give much added instruction on Traffic subjects. So the session was lengthened to eight weeks with most of the additional time being used for the Traffic subjects. Every recruit entering the department went through the academy, which was rapidly gaining prestige. The Departmental Instructor's rank was raised to that of Inspector and the Assistant Instructor became a Captain.

Every effort was made, and with much success, to teach the young officers attending the recruit sessions, how to shoot and how to render first aid. They were taught patrol procedures and procedures for handling traffic. Good instructors worked earnestly at the task of teaching these young men the skills of the police officer.

Public relations and allied subjects were covered by a two hour lecture on courtesy.

But the school continued to advance to keep abreast of the new ideas, new methods. So additional equipment was added, new techniques put into practice and additional hours allowed. The recruit training school became a ten week course, then a twelve week course.

Law, First Aid and Firearms are still taught. Traffic Control and Patrol Procedure receive as much attention as before. The two hours allotted to "courtesy" has been dropped in favor of some twenty four hours on such subjects as Human Relations, Public Relations, Employee Relations, Press Relations and Race Relations. Subjects like Police Ethics, Use of the Police Library and Public Speaking are now taught.

Methods, techniques, procedures are still taught. But something has been added. The emphasis no longer rests only on doing an efficient job, whether it be handling a traffic assignment or making an investigation. The job must be done efficiently, but it must be done in a manner acceptable to the public. Recruits are taught to make friends, to deserve the respect and confidence of the people and to gain them by their appearance, their actions, their words.

So we see here a trend in police training. The Recruit School is not a finishing school, nor is it a charm school. It teaches the fundamentals of police work. But a little investigation will disclose that seminars, police institutes, conferences and training sessions of all kinds usually include the subject of Public Relations on the program.

Police training in California deserves a great deal of study.

"The California Program for Peace Officers' Training" was initiated in 1935 through the joint efforts of the Peace Officers Association of the State of California and the California State Department of Education. Since that time this training program has been offered as part of the California Plan for Trade and Industrial Education. Law Enforcement training has developed as a result of the cooperative efforts of the various governmental agencies, schools and colleges, and individuals who are sincerely interested in the pre-service and in-service training of law enforcement officers." [8]

As early as 1917 some thought was given to organized training for peace officers. At that time, under the statute by which the State Bureau of Criminal Identification and Investigation was created, the Attorney General had been authorized to organize police schools to train police officers in their powers and duties, use of equipment and methods of detection, identification and apprehension of criminals. But no money was provided to conduct this training and no action was taken.

In 1935 a committee was appointed for the purpose of setting up a training program for peace officers. The committee consisted of representatives from law enforcement associations including the California Peace Officers Association and the Sheriff's Association. They came up with a plan which provided for a cooperative program which would provide for training for law enforcement officers throughout the State of California.

"The California State Department of Education has advanced furthest of any of the states in providing instructors and instructors' schools for local departments and regions. All instructors have teaching certificates and the instructors' schools are limited to training in techniques of instruction rather than in subject matter. Other states have potentially similar, but less extensive programs, and some are frankly waiting for urging by the cities before attempting to organize extensive local training. Vocational education funds can be used for both instructor training and the preparation of teaching materials, through local school boards or a state agency." [9]

An extensive program is carried out by the Bureau of Industrial Education, California State Department of Education. Several types of organization with the mission of making good training available to the police officers of the state warrant mention. In addition to this program some of the larger cities in the state have their own police academies.

Among these we find the well known police academy of the Los Angeles Police Department. Various courses are conducted at this academy. Their recruit class is a 12 weeks course, and their curriculum consists of training in government, law, social relations, patrol functions, detective functions, detention and rehabilitation, technical and staff services, administration, physical and firearms training, traffic functions, field trips, field assignments and problems, personnel policies and procedures and allied subjects.[10]

Other courses of police training given at the Los Angeles Academy include a course for police women, motorcycle riding, detective school, pre-Sergeants training course, Lieutenant's School, Staff and Command School, and other specialist schools.

Other programs include Departmental schools operating under the re-imbursable program, zone schools and basic training schools.

California has been divided into a number of zones. Small departments and agencies employing but a few men have in the zone school a real training operation.

The basic training schools are recruit schools. One is located in the Northern part of the state and one in the Southern part. Students are officers with less than three years service employed in full time law enforcement work. This program is conducted twice each year. The Northern California Peace Officers' Training Center is located at Contra Costa College and is operated by the college in cooperation with state, regional and local groups concerned with law enforcement.

The Southern California Peace Officers' Training Center is operated by Riverside College in cooperation with state, regional and local groups concerned with law enforcement. College credit may be granted for work satisfactorily completed at either school.

The Technical Institute of Peace Officers' Training is an advanced school. The Southern Institute is held at the University of California, Los Angeles and the Northern at the University of California, Berkeley.

And for those in administrative jobs, there is a 3 day institute, the Peace Officers Administrative Institute.

In this brief space it is not possible to go into details regarding the courses offered, the source of instructors, and other phases of the training program in California. Professional police associations have combined their efforts with state agencies and have provided a statewide program of training for California law enforcement officers.

Any police department can have a police library. And none should be without the best library it is possible to assemble. Not everyone can go to all of the good police schools. We cannot travel across the country to talk to the experts in Homicide, Traffic, Interrogation or Forgery. But we can learn from these experts. They have organized their knowledge and have carefully and painstakingly written it down. Page after page is filled with the lifetime experience of great officers. The law enforcement officer should have his own police library. The books can be added one at a time.

"No department should overlook the training possibilities of a departmental library since a very modest appropriation will suffice to establish an up to date collection of fundamental police books." [11]

So we see a definite trend in police training. With civil service in many jurisdictions, examinations must be mastered for promotion. Young officers are taught scientific crime detection, crime prevention and human relations. Efforts are made to remove underlying causes of juvenile crime. Officers attend classes on their own time in nearby colleges and universities. Here they study psychology, sociology, government and English.

Three or four decades back an officer had no professional magazine or journal. Only two or three books had been written for the police. Today police officers have books and time to read, courses available and time to study.

"Police officers are no longer strangers on the campus. By the hundreds they form an important part of college and university life. No longer is the college-trained police officer looked on with suspicion or as a "screwball" by his fellow officers. They are often college-trained themselves." [12]

SELECTED BIBLIOGRAPHY

Academy of Police Training—Outline of Courses, P. O. Box 13584; Dallas 24, Texas—"Police education by correspondence."

Alexander, Myrl E., *Jail Administration*, Charles C. Thomas, Springfield, Ill., 1957. An outstanding penologist treats of many problems in the operation of a jail including training.

Ashenhust, Paul H., *Police and the People,* Charles C. Thomas, Springfield, Ill., 1956. Practical human and public relations for the individual officer and the department.

Boolsen, Frank M. and Peper, John P., *Law Enforcement Training*, California State Department of Education, Sacramento, 1959. Comprehensive coverage of police training in California.

Clift, Raymond, *A Guide to Modern Police Thinking*, The H. W. Anderson Co., Cincinnati, Ohio, 1956. A good book with list of questions following each chapter and excellent bibliography.

Cooper, R. Weldon, *Municipal Police Administration in Texas*, Bureau of Municipal Research, University of Texas, Austin, 1938. A new edition should take the place of this valuable reference book.

Ellington, John R., *Protecting Our Children from Criminal Careers*, Prentice-Hall, Englewood Cliffs, N. J., 1948.

Germann, A. C., *Police Personnel Management*, Charles C. Thomas, Springfield, Ill., 1958. A stimulating book, well organized, interesting and challenging.

Gilston, David H. and Podell, Lawrence, *The Practical Patrolman*, Charles C. Thomas, Springfield, Ill., 1959. Not designed to substitute for recruit training but to supplement it.

International City Managers Association, *Municipal Police*

Administration (4th edition), 1954. Especially adaptable to administrative training.

Kenney, John P., *Police Management Planning*, Charles C. Thomas, Springfield, Ill., 1959. Police business is big business and needs to be run accordingly.

Kenney, John P. and Pursuit, Dan D., *Police Work with Juveniles*, (2nd edition), Charles C. Thomas, Springfield, Ill., 1959. In this book we find a good program from training through operations.

Kooken, Don L., *Ethics in the Police Service*, Charles C. Thomas, Springfield, Ill., 1957. "The failure of one police officer reflects against the department and the failure of one department is of vital concern to every police department in the United States." This is the theme of this book.

McCandless, David A., "Police Training in Colleges and Universities," *The Police Yearbook*, International Association of Chiefs of Police, 1956. An article giving a true picture of college level training for policeman.

Millett, John D., *Management in the Public Service*, McGraw-Hill Book Company, New York, 1954. The author does not confine himself to one field of public management but deals with problems common to all in the public service.

Neustatter, W. Lindesay, *Psychological Disorder and Crime*, Philosophical Library, New York, 1957. Dr. Neustatter has written a book from which the lay reader can gain a better understanding of psychological disorders and their relation to crime.

Newman, Charles L., *Sourcebook of Probation, Parole and Pardons*, Charles C. Thomas, Springfield, Ill., 1958. Advocates, as minimum requirement for probation officers, a Bachelor's Degree.

Peper, John P., *Police Supervisory Control*, California State Department of Education, Sacramento, 1957. The author believes and proves that police departments should be directed by professionally trained people.

Peper, John P., *A Recruit Asks Some Questions*, Charles C. Thomas, Springfield, Ill., 1954. "Must" reading for the police instructor.

Perkins, Rollin M., *Elements of Police Science*, Foundation Press, Brooklyn, N. Y., 1942. A standard text, comprehensive and worthwhile.

Vedder, Clyde B., *The Juvenile Offender*, Doubleday and Company, Garden City, N. Y., 1954. "This book makes available in one place a number of carefully selected writings by specialists in juvenile delinquency."

Inspector Paul H. Ashenhust has been a member of the Dallas Police Department for thirty-four years and for the last six years has served as Departmental Instructor. He is a graduate of the FBI National Academy and is Secretary-Treasurer of the FBI National Academy Associates of Texas and also of the Texas Police Association. His book "Police and The People" was published by Charles C. Thomas. He is associate editor of the Texas Police Journal, a contributor to many professional magazines, and a guest instructor at the Institute of Law Enforcement at Southern Methodist University. Inspector Ashenhust is associated with the Academy of Police Training, a correspondence school, as Director. Born in Denison, Texas, December 11, 1898, Ashenhust served in both World War I and World War II. As an Infantry Officer he graduated from the army's two major training institutions, Fort Benning's Commanders and Staff Officers School and the Command and General Staff College at Fort Leavenworth. While in the military service his book "The Militia Marches," a volume of poetry, was published. The author was released from active military service in January, 1946, and was retired as a Lieutenant Colonel January 1, 1959. Inspector Ashenhust wears the Police Commendation Bar of the Dallas Police Department, and has received the FBI National Academy of Texas award for distinguished service to the police profession in the field of public relations.

NOTES

1. Ashenhust, Paul H., "The Goal: A Police Profession," *Journal of Criminal Law, Criminology and Police Science*, XLIX, No. 6, March-April 1959, 605-607.
2. Roddenburg, E. W., "Achieving Professionalism," *Journal of Criminal Law, Criminology and Police Science*, XLIV, May-June, 1953, 109-115.
3. Leonard, Donald, "State Police," an address—Proceedings of the Attorney General Conference on Crime, 1934, 400.
4. Ashenhust, Paul H., "The Goal: A Police Profession," *Journal of Crimi-*

nal Law, Criminology and Police Science, XXXXIX, No. 6, March-April 1959, 607.

5. Ashenhust, Paul H., *Police and the People*, Charles C. Thomas, Springfield, Ill., 1956, 11.

6. Frost, Thomas M., *A Forward Look in Police Education*, Charles C. Thomas. Springfield, Ill., 1959, 3.

7. Boolsen, Frank M. and Peper, John P., *Law Enforcement Training in California*, California State Department of Education, Sacramento, 1959, 43.

8. Boolsen, Frank M. and Peper, John P., *Law Enforcement Training in California*, California State Department of Education, 1959, v.

9. *Municipal Police Administration* (4th edition), International City Managers Association, 1954, 213.

10. Boolsen, Frank M and Peper, John P., *Law Enforcement Training in California*, California State Department of Education, Sacramento, 1959, 148.

11. *Municipal Police Administration* (4th edition). International City Managers Association, 1954, 204.

12. McCandless, David A., "Police Training in Colleges and Universities," *The Police Yearbook*, The International Association of Chiefs of Police, 1956, 173-177.

SELECTED GLOBAL ASPECTS

CRIME AND CRIMINOLOGY IN ENGLAND

Pauline Callard
University of Exeter

OFFICIAL PROVISION FOR RESEARCH

The creation of a Research Unit in the Home Office, for the study of and co-ordination of research into the causes of crime and the treatment of criminals, is a major milestone in the development of English provision for research into these subjects. The Unit will still rely on investigations being carried out by the universities and the Tavistock Institute of Human Relations, and similar bodies and foundations, sometimes even aiding them financially. It will add to the activities and material accumulated, since its foundation in 1932, of the Institute for the Study and Treatment of Delinquency, and will supplement its rather psychiatric emphasis.

Shortly after that step was announced[1] came another—the foundation of an Institute of Criminology in Cambridge, and the creation there of a Chair and a Readership (or Lectureship) in Criminology.[2] Funds for this purpose will come partly from the Isaac Wolfson Foundation, and partly from a three-year state grant. The Institute will seek to encourage interest and provide teaching in criminology, thereby increasing the supply of young research workers in this field.

RECENT TRENDS IN CRIME

This burst of attention to criminological research is partly explicable, as the House of Lords Debate showed, by public concern at recent trends in crime. Figures indicating the contemporary situation relative to the pre-war picture are given below. Allowance should, of course, be made for the incompleteness of all criminal statistics, as only crimes "known to the police" appear in official records, and also for some variation from time to time in both public and police policy in reporting and acting on knowledge of criminal behavior whose existence is recognized by all.[3] Nevertheless, clear trends of the increasing incidence of recorded crime are evident in this period.

TABLE I

Crimes (Indictable Offenses) Known to the Police in England and Wales (per million of population over eight years of age)

| | Annual Average | | | Year |
Crime	1930-39	1940-49	1950-54	1958
Murder	3.6	4.4	3.7	(a) 3.4
Attempt, threats or conspiracy to murder	2.6	4.4	5.2	6.2
Manslaughter, infanticide, etc.	5.3	5.0	5.3	(a) 13.0
Wounding	46.1	77.2	152.2	270.0
Other offenses of violence	8.0	14.0	12.9	12.5
Burglary and attempts, etc.	25.8	59.4	139.7	137.6
Rape and other offenses against females	77.1	139.0	240.7	299.3
Bigamy	9.0	24.2	12.1	7.9
Burglary, housebreaking, etc.	1,085.5	2,208.0	2,356.8	3,296.9
Robbery and blackmail	9.0	23.9	26.8	46.7
Aggravated larcenies	446.8	1,013.0	1,098.7	1,152.1
Other larcenies	3,993.8	6,832.9	6,214.8	9,140.8
Obtaining by false pretenses	342.4	338.3	477.5	476.2
Other frauds	89.6	71.9	223.4	263.3
Receiving stolen goods	82.7	223.7	212.8	251.5
Malicious injuries to property	13.1	55.1	130.9	90.7
Forgery, coining, etc.	42.9	111.1	109.0	135.2
Suicide (attempting to commit)	89.1	85.0	121.9	127.2
Other indictable offenses	18.1	15.9	25.3	21.2
TOTAL	6,390.5	11,306.4	12,569.7	15,751.7

(a) The figures for 1958 are not directly comparable with those for earlier years because, as the result of the Homicide Act, 1957, they exclude some cases which would previously have been classified as murder but are not now so classified.

TABLE II

Persons Proceeded against for Minor (Non-indictable)
Offenses in England and Wales
(per million of population over eight years of age)

| Crime | Annual Average | | | Year |
	1930-39	1940-49	1950-54	1958
Assaults	555.9	483.6	496.3	436.1
Brothel keeping, living on prostitutes earnings & importuning by males	12.2	19.5	21.9	24.2
Offenses of prostitutes	67.0	88.3	247.8	499.4
Cruelty to children	24.5	33.9	26.4	17.2
Indecent exposure	45.4	44.5	69.7	59.6
Malicious damage	297.2	315.6	247.5	359.3
Offenses against Prevention of Crimes Act	4.5	1.4	4.5	41.0
Unlawful possession	14.7	34.9	24.4	13.9
Frequenting, found in enclosed premises	124.0	57.8	81.2	98.8
Betting and gaming	366.4	210.8	287.3	319.0
Offenses against Highways Act	10,380.0	5,909.4	10,060.6	15,105.6
Offenses against Intoxicating Liquor Laws	1,481.1	861.5	1,423.0	1,756.5
Breaches of Local and other Regulations	1,187.2	567.5	667.3	666.8
Offenses against Revenue Laws	904.9	661.0	572.3	617.1
Sunday trading, etc.	600.6	2.6	4.5	8.5
Other offenses	1,649.2	1,584.8	1,944.6	2,077.7
TOTAL	18,062.7	11,036.4	16,321.9	22,223.3

The increases in 1958, compared with 1930-39, in the field of indictable crime are greatest in sexual offenses (three to five times), and violence against the person (two to three times), though malicious injuries to property stand out as showing an even higher increase. The latter offenses reached a peak in 1950-54 of almost ten times their pre-war incidence, but have declined to some six times that level by 1958. Expressed as percentage of the 1930-39 level, crimes against the person in 1950-54 were 260, and in 1958 were 329. Crimes against property rose in that

TABLE III

Juvenile Crime in England and Wales (Number of Young People eight to seventeen years found guilty of Indictable Offenses per 100,000 of the population of the age group)

Age in Years	BOYS			GIRLS		
	1938	1954	1958	1938	1954	1958
8	220	291	293	9	12	13
9	451	599	632	27	47	35
10	703	854	962	37	58	67
11	931	1090	1161	62	88	95
12	1111	1411	1793	66	133	161
13	1315	1794	2314	73	177	217
14	1141	1975	2671	84	197	235
15	1145	1404	2014	97	179	218
16	1110	1271	2096	91	188	225
17	867	1179	2331	99	185	265

Source of all tables—Criminal Statistics, England & Wales, 1958, Cmnd. 803— Home Office, Her Majesty's Stationery Office, 1959.

period from 100 to 194 in 1950-54, and to 243 in 1958. Larcenies and fraud have shown a somewhat similar rate of growth to that of indictable offenses as a whole. The murder rate has generally remained steady at its low level of about 3.5 per million, except for the war decade, though that of attempts, threats and conspiracy to murder has about doubled. The rate of murders has dropped a little with the more restrictive definition given by the Homicide Act, 1957, while the rate for manslaughter, infanticide, etc., has more than doubled. This increase may be due to more killings, now that certain methods of murder are not capital, and it may indicate a greater willingness to prosecute when some alternative to the death sentence may follow a finding of guilt; in part it is swollen by the diversion to this heading of cases now regarded as manslaughter on grounds of "diminished responsibility."

The total of non-indictable offenses is mostly affected by its major component—offenses against Highway Acts. Though naturally much reduced (nearly to half the 1930-39 level) in the war decade, their incidence was nearly back to that level in 1950-54, and in 1958 was fifty percent higher. The other figure which has increased sharply is that of offenses connected with prostitution. This may be largely a "statistical increase", due to more police activity in dealing with this type of offense, but the rise of over seven hundred percent since the average of the 1930's can hardly all be explained in those terms. The multiplication by ten of Offenses against the Prevention of Crimes Acts in 1958 is mainly due to new legislation and stricter enforcement regarding the prohibition of carrying offensive weapons—the flick knife in particular. Apart from these changes, the movements are not spectacular if the restrictions of the war decade are considered, for instance, on the availability of vehicles and intoxicants.

Serious concern about the increase in juvenile delinquency is explained by the statistics of its growth. Below the age of thirteen for boys and twelve for girls the incidence of indictable offenses has mostly risen from one quarter to one half. Above those ages it shows increases of over three quarters to two (i.e. from 175 to 300 of its 1938 level expressed as 100). The extreme expansion is at the ages of twelve, thirteen and fourteen for girls though the incidence relative to their numbers is still slightly higher at seventeen. The proportionate growth for boys is greatest for seventeen-year-olds, but is also high at the main peak of incidence—at fourteen years. At the age of 14 one boy in forty appears before the court for an offense legally treated as serious. For girls, indictable convictions occur only about one-tenth as often. Larceny forms nearly sixty percent, and breaking and entering thirty percent, of the cases of male juvenile crime, while larceny constitutes over eighty percent of the offenses of girls. Non-indictable offenses of the under seventeens are mainly traffic offenses, railway offenses, and cases of malicious damage, but the juvenile increase has been roughly parallel to the spread of these crimes among the total population.

These are the facts against which recent trends in criminal research should be seen.

DEFINITION OF CRIME

Though East's working definition of crime "as an act or omission forbidden by law under pain of punishment" [4] may be accepted throughout this chapter, weighty evidence is available to show how relative is the application of this concept in different societies. Mannheim has followed Sellin's and Sutherland's lead in regarding as proper material for criminology many actions clearly antisocial which are not illegal in English legal code, such as its attitude to suicide, tax avoidance, and strikes.[5] Some observations on another aspect, the sociology of the criminal law, are made by Wootton[6] who has indicated the social class bias evinced, for instance, in the relative toleration towards serious motoring offenses, causing personal injury and death, compared with the attitude towards minor property offenses. She shows the difficulty of establishing an objective definition of deviancy which society cannot tolerate, so often equated with mental disease, and seeks to by-pass definitions which undermine the concept of responsibility by concentrating attention on effective means of correcting the deviation.

AETIOLOGY OF CRIME

In the study of crime, its causes and cures, there has been much international cross-fertilization, making it impossible to disentangle the contribution of one country alone. Nevertheless, certain significant hypotheses have been formulated, or corrected, by particular criminologists.

Goring's examination of three thousand English convicts, together with controls from the general population,[7] for instance, successfully refuted Lombroso's theory of physically degenerated criminal types. Yet Goring, in his turn, postulated physiologically inferior characteristics to be typical of recidivists and others convicted of serious crimes. Later writers have, however, turned against the theory of inborn physical inferiority, Burt[8] having shown no marked line of abnormality or physical defectiveness to distinguish delinquents from others. Yet more ill-health and defect were found among his delinquents than among the non-delinquent children, drawn from the same population. The same was true of Trenaman's young servicemen.[9] Ferguson's sample showed convictions to be considerably higher among the mentally handicapped cases, and slightly greater among physically handicapped cases, compared with ordinary boys.[10] The difference was even more striking for reconviction rates, so that some effects of treatments given, and perhaps of the varying probabilities of detection, may be reflected in these divergences. Physically, as mentally, some inferiority relative to the average seems more likely to predispose to crime than major defect. On the whole, English material points to more ill-health among delinquents, but that it arises more from underlying social factors than from inherited physical inferiority.

The incidence of crime is also clearly affected by age, associated as it is with physiological and psychological maturity.[11] Far more offend during adolescence than in later years, although Roper,[12] Spencer,[13] and Morris[14] among others, show that one third or more of recidivists had no criminal record before they were eighteen. Wootton has trenchantly analyzed and condemned as circular argument the maturation thesis of the Gluecks,[15] but she ignores the fact that immaturity, on their definition, is shown in more than delinquent behavior alone. It is truer to argue, as Mannheim,[16] Roper, Ferguson and Morris do, that "the more intractible the criminal the earlier, as a rule, he will begin his operations," [17] though even this hypothesis is still without precise and extensive confirmation.

The same tendency to see environmental factors as hampering and conditioning the exercise of innate potential has affected the role accorded today to intelligence as a criminogenic element. Though it is recognized that the more intelligent may more often avoid detection, the intelligence range of proved offenders is wide. Mental handicap rather than defect is associated with crime,[18] and Ferguson[19] found theft and sex crimes more common among adolescents of lower intelligence than housebreaking. More clear-cut is the association between delinquency and poor educational achievement,[20] as found by Ferguson, Trenaman, Morris, Burt, Mannheim and Bagot.[21] The use of teachers' assessments of achievements make many of these reports imprecise, so that bias may be presnt. But the widespread agreement over divergent criminal groups lends weight to the hypothesis that inability to achieve success at school is more frequent among delinquents than among non-delinquents, whether due to lack of innate endowment or of educational opportunities or their use. The close correlation found between truanting from school and delinquency[22] is obviously relevant here.

The existing personality of offenders, though partly dependent on inborn characteristics, is currently attributed largely to upbringing, especially to home discipline and the emotional relationships with parents. Bowlby[23] holds the view that six months or more maternal deprivation in the first five years of life is the foremost cause of delinquent character development, particularly of the "affectionless" type. Lewis[24] has produced data which cast doubt upon this view, because nearly one third of her sample of children who had been separated from their mothers even before two years of age behaved satisfactorily, and she and several others have drawn attention to the father's contribution to a child's security. Holman's findings[25] suggested that it is the combination of a series of deprivations which is more criminogenic. Closely allied to this approach is the hypothesis of Stott[26] that denial of emotional satisfactions and psychological security leads to the search for substitutes through anti-social actions, in what Stott calls, for instance, avoidance-excitement and inferiority-compensation. He links "unsatisfactory discipline" with the equally vague phrase "the unsatisfactory characters" of parents. Similarly, in other works, the terms "emotional disturbance" and "maladjustment" of delinquents themselves are open to the same criticism.[27] This lack of precision also attaches to the concept "broken home," which is so variously defined in different investigations as to render comparison nearly impossible.[28] Most investigations show a higher percentage of delinquents than of controls drawn from homes broken by death, divorce, separation or desertion, though Burt includes these cases in "defective family relationships," [29] and Bagot[30] links with them households in which the father is "unemployable," where the child is illegitimate, or the mother is "out working." During wartime, Mannheim was surely justified in including homes where the father was absent in the Services, too. Only two studies, those of Ferguson and Gibbs,[31] show little more delinquency (and none during schooldays) where one parent is absent. More precise data is therefore desirable to establish the connection between the nature of family relationships in early years and in later life and delinquency, especially as such a high proportion of delinquents come from complete families.

Another significant element in the role of the family relates to the norms they uphold. Ferguson suggests that evidence supports the view that "The presence of a bad parent in the home is less to be preferred than his absence from it." [32] The presence in the family of other offenders also appears highly correlated with early crime, and its persistence.[33]

Similar emphasis is laid on the norms of the social environment by studies of the locality and the social group of offenders. Shaw[34] first pioneered the examination of the relationships between local circumstances and the frequency of crime, indicating how poor living conditions and the prevalence of adverse social practices in an area coincided with a heavy crime incidence, though this fact had been suggested by Booth before 1900.[35] Ecological studies of limited areas of particular cities have increased since the war.[36] In some areas, such as the slum district of Liverpool, it is observed that delinquency in youth may be the norm rather than the exception.[37] Improved housing conditions on new estates do not necessarily change this,[38] although delinquency has been found closely correlated with over-crowding [39] even when family size, consistently found to vary directly with delinquency, was held constant.

It is clear that many social factors typical of low economic status form a syndrome, which constantly accompanies delinquency, which, if motoring offenses be excluded, may itself be regarded as a low status group phenomenon.[40] Poor physical health, large family, overcrowding, poverty, unskilled employment of father, and often employment of mother outside the home[41] are characteristics which occur frequently together, and are likely to denote poor intelligence and socialization of parents. It is not improbable that children from such backgrounds will not achieve success at school, will take up unskilled jobs, and seek relief from monotony by frequent changes of employment.[42] They may also be exposed to the influence of anti-social habits such as drink, drug-addiction, gambling, and promiscuity.[43] Perhaps, therefore, the most constructive line which future research could take would be the pursuit of positive factors which explain why there are so many non-delinquent children subject to these same adverse conditions of heredity and environment.

At present, the hypothesis of Carr-Saunders, Mannheim and Rhodes[44] stands, that crime occurs in some cases exposed to its influence in the same way that only some persons exposed to physical infection succumb to it. Cohen carried this idea further in his profound sociological study of social status implications, by indicating certain personal factors which predispose boys of low social status groups to remain law-abiding, and boys of higher economic groups to delinquency. Morris[45] attempts to list some reasons why all working class children exposed to certain stresses and delinquent norms are not convicted, bearing in mind Mays' finding that about four-fifths of slum youths of even the more socially-motivated type commit offenses, sometimes undetected.[46]

He distinguishes between "social delinquency," largely a reflection of environmental norms, and "psychiatric delinquency", whose root lies in individual emotional disturbance, and is associated with long-term criminality. An approach of this kind weighs the contribution of both personal disposition and social opportunities and frustrations, which always exist, in criminal or in accepted behavior. For it is truer to conclude that "the anti-social behavior of one social circle takes one form, while the members of other circles both behave and misbehave differently" [47] than most of us like to admit.

THE NATURE OF PUNISHMENT

Theories about the objectives of punishment have been modified by experience of different methods, and by growing knowledge of factors associated with criminal behavior. In particular, psychological research has severely amended the view of unqualified individual responsibility for all offenses. Some writers have adopted a determinist position, and many have accepted degrees of "diminished responsibility", varying with circumstances. The philosophical consideration of older theories of expiation, restitution, deterrence or prevention, retribution, and reformation has been dwarfed by this issue. An escape from this dilemma is sometimes sought by aiming only at "the protection of the public." Arguments, however, have not all run in the same direction; such experts as Mannheim have shown misgivings at the trend to remove moral considerations entirely from the idea of punishment.[48] Others have suggested that there is danger in weakening any power within the offender to improve by encouraging him to attribute all his activities to circumstances.[49] If the fully determinist theory is adopted, making moral considerations irrelevant and the retributive argument untenable, society must accept the conclusion that the term "punishment" (as implying responsibility) and penal measures of any kind should be eliminated from its code, as the very meaning of these concepts implies unpalatable action by society as a consequence of the offense.[50] On the other hand, painful experience is usually held by psychologists to be an effective conditioning process, of course.

PENAL POLICY

This change of attitude to punishment developed first in practice with juvenile offenders. Here full responsibility has rarely been expected, and pleas for education and training rather than punishment proper resulted in the nineteenth century growth of industrial schools and reformatories, and the beginning of distinct treatment of juveniles by the reservation of Parkhurst Prison for young offenders alone in 1838. Much international exchange of ideas has also been evident in penology, and the influence of the American Reformatories on the English system was marked, as well as that of Continental experiments like those by Wichern near Hamburg, and at Mettrai by Demetz. The major English pioneer contribution was projected by the outstanding penological publication of the last hundred years—the Report of the Departmental Committee on Prisons, under Herbert Gladstone, completed in 1895. The proposal was first implemented at Borstal by Sir Evelyn Ruggles-Brise in 1902, and the regime of reformative training for adolescents proved so effective that it was incorporated into the penal system by the Prevention of Crime Act, 1908.[51]

More clearly indicative of the new attitude of pity rather than punishment was the introduction of Juvenile Courts by the Children's Act of 1908.[52] Discussion of their purpose and operation since then has focused largely upon the conflict between their status as criminal courts, requiring all the safeguards of rights of the accused, and their avowed objective—the pursuit of the offender's welfare, including especially his education and training. No longer penal in intent, should they not become purely civil courts, with the State assuming legally the role of guardian in its attempt to re-educate the offender?[53]

Another sign of less punitive measures is given by the increased use of probation in this century, evoking considerable interest in its practice. Formally constituted in England by the creation of the Probation Service by the 1907 Probation of Offenders Act, its conditions are now regulated by the 1948 Criminal Justice Act. Its wider use is mainly in the percentage of Magistrates Court cases of indictable offenses so treated, a figure which is now roughly forty percent for juveniles, and twelve percent for adults—a large increase over the twenty-five percent for juveniles in 1910. But for both groups the percentages were nearly ten percent higher still between 1925 and 1938 (though very many fewer in actual numbers). Investigations into the records of cases so treated[54] shows encouraging results for both adult and juvenile first offenders—seventy-five percent free of reconviction for the next three years, and even over seventy percent success for recidivists. Women and girls in both cases produce higher proportions of successes than do men and boys. Success seems to depend primarily upon the selection of suitable subjects, but they are not easy to distinguish in all cases, and little refined analysis of relevant prediction factors for this purpose has so far been carried out.

A movement away from the more purely reformative and re-educational forms of punishment, however, is indicated by the provision, under the 1948 Criminal Justice Act, of attendance centers and detention centers for juveniles. The first provide a course of non-residential training to be undergone in the offender's spare time and the second afford residence for a period of six months, as an alternative to prison. Both regimes are intended to be rigorous and to prove equally deterrent as educational. Though the detention center was designed primarily as a severe shock treatment for first offenders, the courts are apparently at present using it for more serious and hardened cases. Probably something more fundamentally reformative, and longer, is required for such offenders. But detention centers provide a useful alternative to remand homes, which may now be used, as intended, mainly for observation and reporting.

Approved Schools afford considerable variety of institutional treatment for juveniles in disciplinary regime, religious affiliation, training opportunity, and age-groups. The work of classifying schools, providing a short period of observation before each juvenile is allotted to a school, is essential to the effective use of this system.[55]

The effectiveness of certain traditional forms of deterrence in reducing crime has been questioned in the reports of two official bodies. The Report of the Departmental Committee on Corporal Punishment (Cmd. 5604, 1938) quoted evidence which showed corporal punishment of offenders to be unconstructive in the individual's case. The record of those flogged contained proportionately more subsequent offenses, especially those involving violence, than did other similar earlier records. The retention of flogging as a form of punishment in prison alone was recommended, where it was thought necessary as a final resort, perhaps rather for the morale of prison staffs than as an effective contribution to the treatment of prisoners. Similarly, the Report of the Royal Commission on Capital Punishment (1953), in its appendices, showed that statistical evidence for a strongly deterrent effect of the death penalty was non-existent.

The pressure of specialist opinion, and the activity of Prison Commissioners like Alexander Patterson, have modified the conditions of institutional treatment compared with those of the nineteenth century. The Gladstone Committee Report condemned the deterrent practices of solitary confinement and unproductive work, recommended instead the incentives of privileges as means to "maintain, stimulate and awaken the higher susceptibilities of prisoners", and proposed individualisation of treatment. Means to this end include the use of Wakefield Prison as a training center since 1922,[56] and its progress has encouraged the development of a new type of sentence, that of Corrective Training,[57] which was formally adopted by the Criminal Justice Act of 1948. Regional Training Prisons have been organised for this purpose on Wakefield lines with more constructive programmes than are possible in local prisons. Also experiments with open prisons developed in 1933 from the open Borstals, and these multiplied after the war in order to accommodate the vastly enlarged prison population. Careful selection of prisoners for open conditions has made possible more natural relations between officers and men, and training conditions approximating more closely to the normal life for which offenders must be fitted.[58]

Habitual criminals, the hard-core of the prison stage-army, were also considered by the Gladstone Report, and by many authors and administrators since.[59] A special form of prison sentence, Preventive Detention, was introduced in the 1908 Prevention of Crime Act which would remove them from society for long periods under less strenuous conditions than the ordinary prisoner. (This shows that normal prison conditions are intended to be partly deterrent.) Some modifications were made by the 1948 Act,[60] which focused policy instead on a progressive stage sentence, and introduced an element of indeterminacy by tying the timing of promotion at each stage to the detainee's progress. Success has crowned the experiment of an intermediate arrangement for the last few months of such sentences, too, which allows the licensee to engage in normal employment in the city, to live in a small hostel supervised by a prison officer, and to pay his own way.

Among this group are many needing specialised treatment as mentally abnormal cases. The writings of East[61] have shown the need for separate provision and regimes for the treatment of "difficult" and psychopathic prisoners, some of whom may be susceptible to psychiatric treatment, either individually or by group therapy. A specialized institution for this purpose is now under construction in Buckinghamshire.

Recently attention has been given to sexual offenses and treatment of such offenders, including changes in the law concerning them.[62] Traditional measures are being rejected in favor of more frequent use of probation, combined with medical treatment. Reconvictions occur only about once in five cases, being more frequent for homosexuals and those recidivating by committing other types of offense.

Inquiries into success rates after different forms of treatment have been negligible in England until recent years. The researches of the Cambridge Department of Criminal Science (English Studies in Criminal Science Series) have made the major contributions, apart from mostly rather limited investigations.[63] Another important field only recently surveyed concerns the marked variation in court sentencing practice,[64] which is largely due to the untrained, voluntary nature of the English magistracy. Advocates of Treatment Tribunals have much evidence in their favor.[65]

The annual reports, published by the Home Office, of the Prison Commissioners and of Criminal Statistics give current evidence of numbers and treatment of offenders.

Post-treatment careers were little recorded in England until recently, though several follow-up studies had been made.[66] Rose first analyzed factors correlating with success after Borstal treatment, on the lines of the Glueck study "Five Hundred Criminal Careers." The major advance in method, however, was made by Mannheim & Wilkins with their male Borstal sample, in which they classified cases into groups with stated "decision risks."[67] This line of research promises most towards improving criminal policy at present, provided equal success can be achieved with regard to predicting the results of other forms of punishment, and even of the prospects of first offenders.

SELECTED BIBLIGRAPHY

Bowlby, J., *Forty-Four Juvenile Thieves*, Bailliere, Tindall & Cox, London, 1944. An investigation of criminogenic factors in young thieves, concluding that prolonged separation of the child from his mother before the age of five is a principal cause of the development of the "affectionless character." One of the first important studies on this aspect.

Burt, Sir Cyril, *The Young Delinquent*, University of London Press, London, 1925. An analysis of the social and psychological factors present in two hundred cases of delinquent boys and girls referred for psychological examination, others drawn from an educational survey in a London borough, and others seen in remand homes or industrial schools. These cases were compared with four hundred non-delinquents similar in social class, area of residence and school. The general findings have been elaborated rather than fundamentally changed by later, more sophisticated, enquiries.

Carr-Saunders, Sir A. M., Mannheim, H., & Rhodes, E. C., *Young Offenders*, Cambridge University Press, London, 1942. Summarizes previous investigations into juvenile delinquency and examines trends in offenses from the beginning of the century. Presents the results of a survey in London and various provincial cities of social and environmental conditions of one thousand juvenile delinquents and matched non-delinquents. Found all influences were common both to some delinquents and some non-delinquents, and that delinquency was associated with many different conditions, such as broken homes and abnormal home discipline and atmosphere, poor school attendance and achievement. Though excellent in method, the classifications used are rather less refined than later studies have been able to achieve. It was recognized as incomplete without the psychological enquiry planned to accompany it, but not carried out because of the war.

Elkin, W. A., *English Juvenile Courts*, Kegan Paul, London, 1938. A very thorough discussion of the methods used and purposes pursued by English Juvenile Courts, and their sentences. It also covers the mehods of treatment, available for juvenile cases, and the uses made of them in the 1930's. The main critical work available on this subject.

Radcinowicz, L. & Turner, J. W. C. (editors), *English Studies in Criminal Science* (2nd edition), Vol. I, *Penal Reform in England*, Macmillan, London, 1946. A series of essays on the diverse elements of the penal system—criminal legislation, administration of justice, police system, juvenile courts, probation system, approved schools, borstal system, and prison system. Briefly reviews the main features of each element, with some historical perspective, providing a concise but thorough survey of the whole.

Vol. II, *Mental Abnormality & Crime*, Macmillan, London, 1944. Reviews the main psychopathic states and their contribution to criminal behavior. One of the most comprehensive accounts of the role of mental abnormality in producing crime.

Vol. VII, *Detention in Remand Homes*, Macmillan, London, 1952. An investigation into the type and history of cases committed to Remand Homes in Birmingham, London, Liverpool and Manchester, and the treatment given there. These findings are related to the after-conduct of the offenders, in an attempt to assess the value of this form of treatment. It considers thoroughly the variety of policy pursued by various courts, and the differing results obtained, and provides a critical judgment of the present use made of Remand Homes by these courts.

Vol. IX, *Sexual Offences*, Macmillan, London, 1957. The most comprehensive compact review of trends and incidence of all types of sexual offenses in the post-war period, compared with 1937-8. Also surveys the characteristics of offenders and their victims, the punishments meted out, and their after-conduct. Concludes with an examination of existing legal provisions and recommendations for their amendment. Some comparisons with legislation concerning sexual offenses in Sweden, Norway, Belgium and the United States are included.

Vol. X, *The Results of Probation*, Macmillan, London, 1958. Reviews the conditions under which probation orders have been made for adult and juvenile offenders, and seeks to assess their effectiveness. Provides a detailed and systematic factual account.

Fox, Sir L. W., *English Prison & Borstal Systems*, Routledge & Kegan Paul, London, 1952. The most authoritative existing survey of the organization and administration of prisons and types of prisoners. Also covers the provisions, by the Borstal system, of treatment for young offenders.

Friedlander, K., *The Psycho-analytical Approach to Juvenile Delinquency*, Kegan Paul, London, 1947. Examines the necessary psychological processes for social adaptation, and the way in which failures occur. Indicates possible methods of treatment, both psychological and environmental. The most useful brief account of this approach.

Grünhut, M., *Penal Reform*, Clarendon Press, Oxford, 1948. Traces the history of the English penal system up to the present. Selects for thorough review specific problems of classifications, prison labor, the potentialities of the personal approach, types of discipline, and forms of non-institutional treatment. Then turns to the treatment of particular types of offenders—juveniles, habitual criminals, women, and mentally abnormal persons. A thorough and exhaustive account.

Jones, H., *Crime & The Penal System*, University Tutorial Press, London, 1956. An excellent review of the whole field of the aetiology of crime, the treatment of criminals, and the history of both criminology and penology in England. A full and adequate coverage of the subject-matter of this chapter, to which it is much indebted.

Le Mesurier, L. (editor), *A Handbook on Probation*, National Association of Probation Officers, 1935. Surveys the history of the probation idea, the development of the probation system, and the duties of probation officers. Reviews the work possible among juveniles and adults, and presents suggestions for improvement in administration.

Mannheim, H., *Social Aspects of Crime Between the Wars*, Allen and Unwin, London, 1940. Provides a valuable account and interpretation of English criminal statistics of the first third of the twentieth century. The main part of the book reviews the most significant sociological phenomena associated with crime —unemployment, and strikes; alcoholism; methods of business administration, and gambling; and considers prostitution, juvenile delinquency and recidivism. The only study of these correlations and associations of this quality.

Mannheim, H., *Juvenile Delinquency in an English Middletown*, Kegan Paul, London, 1948. A report of a local investigation the incidence and causes of juvenile delinquency, and various forms of treatment prescribed for it, in Cambridge in war-time. A pioneer study of the interaction between local conditions and policies and their connection with types of juvenile crime.

Mannheim, H., & Wilkins, L. T., *Prediction Methods in Relation to Borstal Training*, Home Office, H.M.S.O., 1955. An examination of the characteristics and records of ex-Borstal boys in order to reveal prediction factors and demonstrate the effectiveness of prediction tables. A few modifications of the Glueck methods are introduced, chiefly by way of weighting in such a way as to eliminate overlap in the factors used, and the employment of additional factors to indicate some discrimination between cases in the borderline group. Though intended as a methodological exercise rather than a fact-finding study, it shows greater effectiveness in avoiding further convictions for boys trained in open Borstals than closed, even when allowance has been made for different classes of offenders sent to each.

Mays, J. B., *Growing Up in the City*, University Press of Liverpool, 1954. Examines the influences at work in a community (a district of Liverpool) which encourage or evoke delinquent tendencies, and their impact upon eighty members of a boys' club. A useful account, though limited and somewhat superficial, of urban slum conditions and their contribution to delinquency.

Morris, T., *The Criminal Area*, Routledge & Kegan Paul,

London, 1958. Discusses the applicability of ecological concepts to surveys of delinquency, and critically reviews earlier studies using this approach. Data of more serious crime and of juvenile delinquency in the borough of Croydon, London, in 1952 are then examined in relation to the detailed local environment, and variations in both fields are considered. Case histories of juvenile offenders are analyzed in terms of twenty-one factors of physical, psychological and environmental origin, paying special attention to the situation concerning the immediate family relationships. The interaction of social influences, generating "social" delinquency, and personality factors, leading to what is termed "psychiatric" delinquency, is examined. Conclusions are drawn relating to the coincidence of crime and social class characteristics, and the divergent operation of social controls in different social strata. The effects of certain features of housing policy in this connection are indicated and measures to counteract them are proposed.

Wootton, Lady, of Abinger, *Social Science & Social Pathology*, Allen & Unwin, London, 1959. A stimulating review of current theories on criminogenesis, arguing that many of them have little established and incontrovertible evidence to support them at present. Summarizes, for this purpose, the findings of the major studies in Britain and the United States regarding causes of crime, and gives detail impossible in this brief chapter. Argues that views of what constitutes crime are largely culturally determined, and are class-biased. Makes an attempt to define social pathology with reference to clinical terms alone, though value judgments involved in doing so are less clearly perceived.

Pauline Callard was born in Devon, England, in May, 1917; educated locally and at Queenswood School, Hertfordshire. After six months in France, studied for B.Com. (London) degree at University College of the South-west, Exeter. After graduation, worked as assistant to the Economic Advisor of the National Savings Committee in London two years towards the beginning of the war, and then in the Office of the Minister of Reconstruction until 1944. Joined U.N.R.R.A. London Headquarters staff, Industrial Rehabilitation Division, for two years before being appointed as Chief Statistician, U.N.R.R.A. Mission to Austria. When this organization was withdrawn, began lecturing in 1947 in Statistics at the University College, Exeter, but soon transferred to the growing Sub-Department of Sociology. In 1949 became Warden of a small Hall of Residence for women students of the College, a post held in addition to that of Lecturer at Exeter. The College became a University in 1955, from which an "ad eundem" degree in the Faculty of Social Studies was received. In 1959 published two articles, "Punishment and the State—Its Motives and Form," in the *British Journal of Delinquency*, X, I; and "The Church and Older People," in *Social Service Quarterly*, XXXIII, 3.

NOTES

1. *"Penal Practice in a Changing Society,"* Home Office, Her Majesty's Stationery Office, Command 645 (1959).

2. House of Lords Debate, 8th April, 1959.

3. Considerations relevant to the interpretation of English Criminal Statistics are reviewed in Part I of Mannheim H., *Social Aspects of Crime in England Between the Wars*, Allen & Unwin, London, 1940.

4. East, Sir W. Norwood, *Society & The Criminal*, H.M.S.O., London, 1949, 4.

5. Mannheim, H., *Criminal Justice & Social Reconstruction*, Routledge & Kegan Paul, London, 1946.

6. Wootton, Lady, of Abinger, *Social Science & Social Pathology*, Allen & Unwin, London, 1959.

7. Goring, C., *The English Convict* (Home Office), Wyman, London, 1913.

8. Burt, Sir C., *The Young Delinquent*, University of London Press, London, 1925, 603.

9. Trenaman, J., *Out of Step*, Methuen, London, 1952, 44-45.

10. Ferguson, T., *The Young Delinquent in His Social Setting*, Oxford University Press, London, 1952, 111-112.

11. East, Sir W. Norwood, Stocks, P., & Young, H. T. P., *The Adolescent Criminal*, Churchill, London, 1942, 201.

12. Roper, W. F., "A Comparative Survey of the Wakefield Prison Population in 1948 & 1949," *British Journal of Delinquency*, I, 1 and 3, July 1950 & April 1951.

13. Spencer, J. C., *Crime & The Services*, Routledge & Kegan Paul, London, 1954, 142.

14. Morris, N., *The Habitual Criminal*, Longmans, Green, London, 1951, 339.

15. Wootton, *op. cit.*, 161-5.

16. Mannheim, H., *Group Problems in Crime & Punishment*, Routledge & Kegan Paul, London, 1955, 139.

17. Roper, *op. cit.*, 21.

18. Burt, *op. cit.*, 607; Mannheim, H., *Juvenile Delinquency in an English Middletown*, Kegan Paul, London, 1948, 54.

19. Ferguson, *op. cit.*, 113-114; for sexual crimes, see East, *op cit.*, 65 & Mannheim, *op. cit.* (1948), 53.

20. Wootton, *op. cit.*, 128-134; Ferguson, *op. cit.*, 29, & 119-122.

21. Ferguson, *op. cit.*, 55; Trenaman, *op. cit.*, 64-66; Morris, T., *The Criminal Area*, Routledge & Kegan Paul, London, 1958, 147; Burt, *op. cit.*, 335-355; Mannheim, *op. cit.* (1948), 46; Bagot, J. H., *Juvenile Delinquency*, Cape, London, 1941, 50-53; and *Punitive Detention*, Cape, London, 1944, 39-40.

22. Ferguson, *op. cit.*, 30; *Burt*, op. cit., 455; & East, *op. cit.*, 140.

23. Bowlby, J., *Maternal Care & Mental Health* (2nd edition), Geneva, W.H.O., 1952, 33-34.

24. Lewis, H., *Deprived Children*, Oxford University Press, London, 1954, 122.

25. Holman, P., "Some Factors in the Aetiology of Maladjustment in Children," *Journal of Mental Science*, October, 1953, 685.

26. Stott, D. H., *Delinquency & Human Nature*, Carnegie United Kingdom Trust, Dunfermline, 1950.

27. Morris, T., *op. cit.*, 137-138.

28. Wootton, *op. cit.*, 118-123.

29. Burt, *op. cit.*, 93-95.

30. Bagot, *op. cit.* (1941), 83, & *op cit.* (1944), 49.

31. Ferguson, *op. cit.*, 22, though this factor was more important among the mentally handicapped boys, 91; Gibbs, D. N., *Some Differentiating Characteristics of Delinquent and Non-Delinquent National Servicemen in the British Army*, 1955. (Unpublished Ph.D. Thesis, London.)

32. Ferguson, *op. cit.*, 146.

33. *Ibid.*, 58-62, & 136-137; Morris, T., *op. cit.*, 144; Mannheim, *op. cit.* (1948), 25; East, Stocks & Young, *op. cit.*, 64; Bagot, *op. cit.* (1941), 74-76, & (1944), 46-47.

34. Shaw, C. R., *Delinquency Areas*, & Shaw, C. R., & McKay, H. D., *Juvenile Delinquency & Urban Areas*.

35. Booth, C., *Life & Labour of the People in London*, Macmillan, London, 1892-1902.

36. London: Carr-Saunders, Sir A. M., Mannheim, H., & Rhodes, E. C., *Young Offenders*, Cambridge University Press, 1942; Liverpool: Bagot, *op. cit.* (1941 & 1944); *Youthful Lawbreakers*, Liverpool Council of Social Service, 1948; & Mays, J. B., *Growing Up in the City*, University of Liverpool Press, 1954; Bradford: Henshaw, E. M., *Report on Juvenile Delinquency*, Bradford Education Committee, 1942; Cambridge: Mannheim, *op. cit.* (1948); Glasgow: Ferguson, *op. cit.*; Croydon: Morris, T., *op. cit.*

37. Mays, *op. cit.*, 82, & 147-148.

38. Mannheim, *op. cit.* (1948), 32; Bagot, *op. cit.* (1941), 69-70; & Ferguson, *op cit.*, 17-18.

39. Ferguson, *op. cit.*, 19-22.

40. Cohen, A. K., *Delinquent Boys*, 37-44.

41. Shown by evidence summarized by Wootton to have little association with delinquency, *op. cit.*, 113-116.

42. Ferguson, *op. cit.*, 42, 129-136. The use of maximum duration of jobs

as a prediction factor by Mannheim & Wilkins for post-Borstal behavior is further evidence; Mannheim, H. & Wilkins, L. T., *Prediction Methods in Relation to Borstal Training*, Home Office, H.M.S.O., 1955, 145.

43. Mannheim, *op. cit.* (1940), reviews the impact of alcoholism (Ch. 6), gambling (Ch. 8) and prostitution (Ch. 11).

44. Mannheim & Rhodes, *op. cit.*, 153-155.

45. Morris, T., *op. cit.*, 174-181.

46. Mays, *op. cit.*, 82.

47. Wootton, *op. cit.*, 70.

48. Mannheim, H., *The Dilemma of Penal Reform*, Allen & Unwin, London, 1939, 21.

49. Goodheart, A. L., *English Law and the Moral Law*, Stephens, London, 1953, Ch. 1; East, Sir W. Norwood, *Society & The Criminal*, H.M.S.O., 1949, 5.

50. Benn, S. I., "An Approach to the Problems of Punishment," *Philosophy*, XXXIII, October, 1958, 331.

51. Fox, Sir L. W., *English Prison & Borstal Systems*, Routledge & Kegan Paul, London, 1952.

52. Elkin, W. A., *English Juvenile Courts*, Kegan Paul, London, 1938, Ch. II & III.

53. Mannheim, *op. cit.* (1939), 178-200; & Elkin, *op. cit.*, 36-49.

54. Vol. X of *English Studies in Criminal Science* (see bibliography).

55. Gittins, J., *Approved School Boys*, Home Office, H.M.S.O., 1952, & (Simmons, M. M.) *Making Citizens*, Home Office, H.M.S.O., 1946.

56. Reports of the Commissioners of Prisons—for the year 1923-4, Cmd. 2307, 1925, 16,—for the year 1935, Cmd. 5430, 1937, 27-29, Home Office, H.M.S.O.

57. Corrective Training may be imposed on any person of twenty-one or over convicted of an offense punishable by at least two years' imprisonment, who has been convicted on two previous occasions of equally serious offenses since he was seventeen. A report from the Prison Commissioners on suitability for training must have been received. The sentence may then range between two and four years.

58. Fox, *op. cit.* (1952), 152-153; & Leitch, A., "The Open Prison," *British Journal of Delinquency*, II, 1, July, 1951, 25.

59. Morris, N., *The Habitual Criminal*, Longmans, London, 1952; & *Report of the Departmental Committee on Persistent Offenders*, Cmd. 4090, Home Office, H.M.S.O., 1932, reprinted 1947.

60. The new form of Preventive Detention sentence may be for any period between five and fourteen years. It may be passed on anyone of thirty years or more who is convicted of an offense punishable by imprisonment for at least two years, and who has had at least three similar convictions since the age of seventeen. The court must be satisfied that such a sentence is "expedient for the protection of the public."

61. With Hubert, W. H. de B., *Psychological Treatment of Crime*, Churchill, 1939; with Stocks, P., & Young, H. T. P., *The Adolescent Criminal*, Churchill, 1942; & *Society & The Criminal*, Churchill, 1949.

62. *Report of the (Wolfenden) Committee on Homosexual Offenses &*

Prostitution, Cmnd. 247, H.M.S.O. 1957; & Vol. IX of English Studies in Criminal Science, (see bibliography) .

63. Home Office, *Probation Service*, H.M.S.O., 1938, 13; Mannheim, *op. cit.* (1940) , Ch. 10, (1948) , 81-92; Bagot, *op cit.* (1944) ; Grünhut, M., "Juvenile Delinquents under Preventive Detention," *British Journal of Delinquency,* V. 3, January, 1955; Rose, A. G., *Five Hundred Borstal Boys,* Blackwell, Oxford, 1954.

64. Mannheim, *op. cit.* (1948), Ch. 3; Grünhut, M., *Juvenile Offenders Before the Courts,* Clarendon, Oxford, 1956; & Mannheim, H., Spencer, J., & Lynch, G., "Magisterial Policy in the London Courts," *British Journal of Delinquency,* VIII, 1 & 2, July & October, 1957.

65. Fry, S. M., *Future Treatment of the Adult Offender,* Gollancz, London, 1944, 21-25; Mannheim, *op. cit.* (1939) , 201-211, (1946) , 223-237; Grünhut, M., *Penal Reform,* Clarendon, Oxford, 1948, 458-463; Mullins, C., *Fifteen Years Hard Labour,* Gollancz, London, 1949, Ch. 12.

66. For a bibliography of such material, cf. Rose, *op. cit.,* Ch. I.

67. Mannheim & Wilkins, *op. cit.* The methodological advances made in this study are detailed in the bibliography at the end of this chapter.

CRIMINOLOGY AND CORRECTIONS IN WESTERN EUROPE

Vernon Fox
Florida State University

Criminology and correctional procedures in Western Europe have been influenced more readily than elsewhere by the development of the major theories of human behavior. This could well be because the major theories of human behavior were developed in Western Europe and the influence of the scholars in countries geographically small would be felt more immediately by practitioners in the field of ameliorating and controlling abnormal and criminal behavior, whether directly or indirectly. The early demonological and theological theories of behavior were so well developed in medieval Europe that such case-finding techniques and judicial dispositions as those found in the Inquisition throughout Europe, and especially Spain, in the thirteenth century were rationally justified. The harshness of these supernatural approaches to criminal behavior is attested by the reported revulsion of visitors to old Denmark and Scandinavia who reported seeing the remains of offenders still dangling from the wheel at the gates of the cities, sometimes tenuously attributed to the harsh climate and rigorous life of the Viking Norsemen.

The contract writers of the Renaissance, Hobbes, Locke, Rousseau, and others, including the English noblemen who extracted the Magna Charta from King John in 1215, considered government to be at the consent of the governed. The introduction of "natural rights" into the theological milieu tended to lessen the

401

harshness of the criminal dispositions. Labor on the galleys was furnished by prisoners prior to the invention of the steam engine and transportation beyond the seas became more frequent with the breakdown of the feudal system. As gunpowder reduced the medieval castles and private strongholds of the nobles and as commerce, industry, and capitalism liberated the serf from the soil, the need for centralized and public correctional systems in Europe became manifest. The famous workhouses and houses of correction were erected in the sixteenth and seventeenth centuries in Western Europe to replace the old castle's private dungeon, the ecclesiastical prison, and the more harsh practices of mutilation and death.

Biology reached some degree of maturity as a science in the nineteenth century in Europe, the term having been first introduced in 1837 by Treviranus at Gottingen. Popularized by de Lamarck of France, the term, "biology," and the science flourished through the contributions of French, German, Dutch, and other European scholars. Northern European psychologists, such as Wundt at Leipzig, von Helmholtz at Danzig, Wertheimer, and other German students by the beginning of the twentieth century had developed a rigorous experimental approach to human behavior with a clear biological influence. Southern European scholars, such as Lombroso of Italy, were impressed with the biological and anthropological determinants of human behavior. In France, Switzerland, and Austria, the clinical approaches to human behavior developed in the late nineteenth century. Charcot and Janet of Paris contributed heavily to the clinical approaches, while Freud, Breuer, and Adler of Vienna and Jung of Zurich were developing psychoanalysis. It becomes obvious that Western Europe led the world in the formulation of theories of human behavior, normal and abnormal, by the beginning of the twentieth century.

Simultaneously, Western Europe was contributing to the study of group behavior and society. Immediately after the French Revolution, Saint-Simon presented plans for social reorganization. The term, "sociology," was first used by Comte of France in 1837. Karl Marx, Max Weber, and Ferdinand Tönnies of Germany, Bonger of Holland, Emile Durkheim and Gabriel Tarde of France, and Vilfredo Pareto of Italy are only a few of the pioneering contributors to sociology from Western Europe.

The rigid and individualistic philosophical contributions of Hegel, Kant, and Nietzsche in Germany seemed congruent with the rigid experimental method of the northern European psychologists and the harshness of their punishments. The contributions of Montesquieu, Voltaire, and Quetelet of France somewhat approximate in tone the clinical approach to human behavior and their improved understanding of abnormal behavior which they translated into action best in treatment of the mentally ill. The religious temper of Italy, incorporated into the lasting philosophy of Spinoza of Spain, manifests itself in the treatment of abnormal behavior. It is apparent that criminology and corrections in any area is part of the general social organization, social philosophy, and method of interpreting individual human behavior found in the region. Rather than being a separate unit of social endeavor, criminology and corrections in Western Europe is a congruent part of the total social structure.

Placed in a setting where sociology, psychology, biology, and physical anthropology were being developed most rapidly and in most advanced form, it would seem reasonable to anticipate that criminology and corrections in Western Europe would be the most progressive and effective in the world. That the erudition of the scholars did not unreservedly permeate through to application by the practitioners in this field must be answered in terms of social organization. It is against this background of leadership in the knowledge of individual and social behavior that is set the criminology and corrections of Western Europe.

CONCEPTS OF CRIMINOLOGY AND CORRECTIONS

Concepts of good penal practice in Western Europe in the late eighteenth century can be extracted from the writings of John Howard in reporting his visits to European prisons. As high sheriff of Bedford in England, Howard visited his jail and became interested in the state of prisons generally. In 1775, he visited prisons in France, the Low Countries, and Germany. He was impressed with the low crime rate in Holland and attributed it to the industrial and reformatory approach taken by the workhouses and prisons at Amsterdam and elsewhere. He was revulsed by the traces of torture he found in Germany. In 1778, he visited prisons in Prussia, Saxony, Bohemia, Austria, and Italy. He visited prisons in Denmark, Sweden, and Russia in 1781 and in Spain and Portugal in 1783. Howard's recommendations that were placed into practice were that arrested persons not formally accused within a reasonable time, sometimes going into months, should be released; that prisons should be whitewashed yearly; the rooms should be clean and well ventilated; infirmaries and medical care should be provided; naked prisoners should be given clothing; that underground dungeons should be used as little as possible; and an effort should be made to preserve the health of prisoners. The concept appeared to be formulating that if the community did not eliminate the offenders, it should protect itself by taking care of those kept in the prisons and who might eventually be released again to the community.

Beginning specialization of institutions and programs appeared to be based on this concept of protecting the community by not worsening the condition of the prisoners eventually to be released. The ecclesiastical prison was popular in Latin Europe, the For-l'Evêque being built in Paris in 1611, for example, to handle prisoners who had committed crimes against the church. The separation of youthful offenders from adult offenders began in France in 1568. Special educational programs were substituted for chastisements in 1791 according to a French governmental decree. Separation of the sexes was considered to be desirable, and the women were given quarters separate from the men in 1519 in Spain.

In the late eighteenth century, there was a general movement toward the concept that the punishment should fit the offense. Beccaria in Italy and Blackstone and Bentham in England influenced the field of criminology and corrections to concentrate on the offense, rather than on the community. The Classical school of criminology was espoused by Beccaria in 1764, in which offenders were to be treated or disposed of in accordance with the seriousness of their offenses. The offenders were to "pay their debt to society" in accordance with the damage done to society. This concept has persisted to the present day with some modifications. Various countries established institutions designed to hold persons who have committed offenses of varying degrees of seriousness. Present-day France has the departmental prisons, the central houses, and institutions or colonies for young offenders, where persons are sent according to the seriousness of the offenses. By the end of the eighteenth century, Italy and Spain still used the galley system for serious offenders. In the nineteenth century, Spain began placing persons in correctional detention for two years or less, other more serious offenders in peninsular prisons for from two to eight years, and some in the African prisons for more than eight years, according to the seriousness of the offenses. With much the same system, Portugal uses preventive detention in the departmental prisons, imprisonment in the central prisons, and reclusion in maximum custody units of the central prisons, with habitual offenders sent to special institutions or out of the country. Germany has the Gefaengnis or reformatory for lesser offenders and the Zuchthaus for more serious offenders. Each canton in Switzerland has a penitentiary, district prisons, a reformatory, correctional establishments for juveniles, and some have other institutions as well, their use being dependent upon the seriousness of the offenses.

During the eighteenth and nineteenth centuries, there were trends toward (1) developing a series of specialized institutions dealing with offenders who had committed crimes of various seriousness, (2) separating youthful offenders and juveniles from adult offenders, (3) development of better classification methods, (4) reduction of political and ecclesiastical prisoners and concentration on conventional criminals, (5) emergence of probation or some form of treatment without institutionalization, and (6) development of parole in some manner, frequently through incarceration by stages or grades leading to conditional release. For example, France provided in 1885 for "relegation" or transportation to a penal colony those persons who were considered to be beyond reform, while retaining in France the more reformable offenders.

With the shifting toward specialized institutions based on offense came a realization that there was a general though loose association between the seriousness of the offense and the seriousness of personality problems. When Lombroso of Italy presented his views in 1889 that criminal behavior was the result of factors involving physical anthropology, mutations, and atavism, he founded the Positivistic school of criminology. The century between Beccaria and Lombroso had been a significant period in which natural rights and reason had given way to biology and the social sciences of economics and sociology as determinants of human behavior. Lombroso had swung the emphasis of criminology from the offense to the offender, as Beccaria a century before had swung the emphasis from the community to the offense. The concept of the offender as central to criminology and the correctional process has remained until the present day in corrections in Western Europe. Lombroso and his students, Ferri and Garofalo, emphasized biological and anthropological factors, but incorporated the social factors as well, in their interpretations of the causes of criminal behavior. Change of behavior might be achieved through the introduction of rigid controls that might outweigh the inherent difficulties through learning and social re-education. Consequently, te Italian correctional system, responding to the biologically oriented Positivistic school, became rigid and suppressive for purposes of counteracting antisocial hereditary factors.

The concept of moral contamination among offenders, a seemingly logical combination of theological, social, and positivistic thinking, became an important concept in Western Europe during the nineteenth century, and it remains strong today. Following through this concept in practice, the American Pennsylvania system of solitary confinement for rigid separation of offenders, instituted in Philadelphia in 1790, had greater acceptance in Western Europe than anywhere else, including America. Italy had always been concerned with the individual treatment of offenders according to their individual needs. Belgium introduced the system in 1838, complete with face-masks and cell-feeding, and did not even discard the face-mask until 1920. France adopted the system in 1875, although the expense of changing from congregate imprisonment to individual cells prevented a complete adoption. Holland inaugurated the Pennsylvania system in 1851, Sweden in 1840, and Denmark in 1846. Norway accepted in in 1851 and it was adopted in Prussia and some of the other German states following 1834. The modern penal code of Austria goes back to 1852, when the Pennsylvania system was incorporated. Switzerland incorporated the system in their cantonal prisons in the 1830's.

During the late nineteenth century, at the height of the biological emphasis, the beginnings of psychoanalysis and the clinical approach were being developed in western Europe. Janet and Charcot from France were placing emphasis upon abnormal human behavior, with specific reference to insanity and psychosis. The French approach included concern for the acting-out disorders among juveniles. Houses for correctional education of dependent, neglected, and delinquent children were built in Paris in 1827, and in 1839, at Bordeaux and Mettray. In 1899 the French prohibited corporal punishment for children, as well as the use of handcuffs, and developed humane principles of education and a clinical approach to the treatment of delinquents.[1]

The most recent development in Western Europe is the concept of social defense.[2] Social defense has emerged as a social movement to combine the philosophy of law enforcement and corrections into a single discipline, integrated into the total social and political organization of society. Social defense embodies (1) criminology and the study of the individual personality for the purpose of rehabilitation, (2) penal law and finding the optimum balance between the mental health of the individual personality and the welfare of the total group, and (3) the science and art of manipulation of the environment for the greatest benefit of

407

all, relieving unnecessary stresses and giving direction to legislators and administrators so that laws and their implementation will be mutually conducive to the mental health of the individual and the general welfare of all. Social security programs, mental hygiene clinics, and similar socialized programs would be a part of the preventive phase of the concept of social defense. Psychiatric and psychological services in the institutions designed for rehabilitation would be the correctional phase of social defense. The "new" social defense began after World War II, although it had its beginnings in the writings of Beccaria, Servan, Lombroso, Ferri, Garofalo, Bonger, and others. The United Nations created a Section of Social Defense in 1948. An International Society on Social Defense was organized in 1949. The concept on which Western European criminology and corrections is attempting to function today is one of social defense in the broad sense.

TRENDS IN THE CRIME RATES

Trends in crime rates or the crime rates at any given time are most difficult to obtain in the international level.[3] The definitions of offenses, alertness of law enforcement, accuracy of the statistics collected, method of their analysis, and the legal elements on which the statistics are based all tend to leave considerable question as to the reliability and validity of international criminal statistics. Based on known trends, it can be rather safely concluded that war has had the greatest single effect on the crime rates as they are reported in Europe. The rates tend to go up during periods of social disorganization and, depending upon the extent to which governmental services are interrupted, there tends to be less reporting. This means that there is no way of knowing exactly how intensely the effect of social disorganization is manifest in crime rates.

Political shifts of extreme nature and the resulting political prisoners have an effect on the crime rate as reported. In Spain, for example, the official number of prisoners in 1933 was reported as 19,574. When Franco's forces won the Spanish Civil War, the rate went up considerably. Some were political prisoners held for the safety of Spain. By 1939, there were 100,000 prisoners in Spain. By 1940, there were 270,719; there were 233,328 in 1941; 159,392 in 1942; and by 1943, there were 93,000 prisoners, of whom 49,000 were political prisoners. The social disorganization resulting from Civil War and the political situation in which a tenuous control had to be protected by drastic measures demonstrated in Spain what similar situations have shown in other countries of Europe at different times.

Crime in Italy and Germany rose disproportionately after World War II as compared with the 1939 level. While crimes of violence have always been high in Italy, the largest increase here was in the area of personal violence. There were 153,813 crimes of personal violence in Italy in 1948 and 167,891 in 1949, as compared with 119,037 in 1939. Theft in Italy rose less sharply, with 369,891 in 1948 and 312,481 in 1949, as compared with 230,80 in 1939. Similar trends were observable in Germany, with less rise in offenses of personal violence. Juvenile delinquency in Germany was much higher after World War II than it was in 1939. By 1952, however, delinquency had dropped below the 1939 rates.

As soon as World War II was over in Belgium, the collaborators with the Nazi regime swelled the prison population from 5,000 to 50,000, in 1945, and on up to 70,000 within a short time. By 1946, 26,000 collaborators were still being held, but they had dropped to 600 by 1954. These persons had outnumbered by far the conventional criminals usually held in Belgium.

Some of the northern countries have experienced a consistent drop in conventional crime. Belgium, for example, has shown a drop in convictions from 1,188 per 10,000 per year at the beginning of the twentieth century to 52 per 10,000 in 1950. There were 35,480 convictions in 1949 in Belgium with a population of 6,709,879. Luxembourg has a constant prison population between 300 and 400 for a population of 300,000. In 1950, Sweden brought about 170,000 to justice for offenses, or about 32 per 1,000 persons over fifteen years of age. With a total prison population of 3,001 persons in Swedish prisons, there were 7,043 new admissions in 1952, of which 173 were women, which suggests relatively short sentences.

The crime rates, including a criminal index computed on the basis of the number of crimes per thousand population, for countries representing various areas of Europe are shown in Table 1 for 1901, 1911, 1921, 1931, 1941, and 1951, with 1936 and 1946 inserted to show the impact of World War II and the political tensions and social disorganization leading to it.

Juvenile delinquency follows the same general trend as adult offenses. The number of youngsters declared delinquent in representative European countries is shown in Table 2. It should be noted that the significant drops in delinquency rates in Germany in 1931 and in France in 1951 were due to the introduction of new legislation that changed the definitions.

It is apparent that something besides an absolute definition of criminal behavior is at work. Definitions vary, concepts of criminal behavior and the limitations to be placed on it apparently differ, and law enforcement policy must alter with national and sub-national cultures and situations within a culture. Compared with similar crime indices in the United States of 8.3 in 1936, 9.0 in 1941, 11.8 in 1946, and 12.7 in 1951, the rates of Italy, France, Germany, and England are not grossly different, suggesting that definitions and enforcement policies may be coming closer together with improved modern communication and the activity of international organizations fostering better uniformity. Even so, the best that can be expected of crime rates on an international basis is a rough estimate of gross criminal activity. Statistics may reveal shifts in types and intensity of delinquency and crime according to the temper of the times that influence and are influenced by many social factors and indices. The relationship between authority, social control, economics, political factions, war, and social trends as they relate to crime and delinquency become apparent when reviewing the literature.[4]

410

TABLE 1

Criminal Indices For Selected European Countries For the First Half of the Twentieth Century[10]
(in thousands)

Country	Rates	1901	1911	1921	1931	1936	1941	1946	1951
England	Population	38,700	42,700	44,400	46,100	47,000	48,200	49,200	50,600
	Crimes	82	98	105	290	283	358	472	524
	Criminal Index	2.1	2.3	2.3	6.2	6.0	7.4	9.5	10.3
France	Population	38,900	39,600	39,200	41,800	41,900	38,800	40,500	42,100
	Crimes	202	240	254	255	238	385	355	254
	Criminal Index	5.1	6.1	6.4	6.1	5.6	9.9	8.7	6.0
Germany	Population	56,367	64,900	59,170	63,000	65,200	70,200	43,900	48,100
	Crimes	579	693	797	680	(not available)	292	538	466
	Criminal Index	10.2	10.6	13.4				12.2	9.7
Italy	Population	32,400	34,600	38,000	41,200	43,200	43,900	44,900	46,200
	Crimes	510	542	654	511	506	624	1,042	658
	Criminal Index	15.7	15.7	17.2	12.4	11.7	14.2	23.2	14.2
Sweden	Population	5,100	5,500	5,900	6,100	6,270	6,380	6,700	7,070
	Crimes	15	14	9	12	12	15	18	20
	Criminal Index	2.8	2.5	1.6	1.9	1.9	2.3	2.7	2.8

411

TABLE 2

Juvenile Delinquents in Europe From 1911 to 1951[10]
(in thousands)

Country	1911	1921	1931	1936	1941	1946	1951
England	44	43	74	46	64	71	85
France	40	43	35	24	42	31	15
Germany	51	77	23	..*	21	28	30
Italy	16	15	12	..*	..*	24	20
Sweden	..*	..*	..*	1	2	2	2

* Not available

THEORIES AND PRACTICES IN CORRECTIONS

Practices in corrections can be surveyed to observe how well the concepts of good corrections are implemented. The theories of criminology, of course, are the rationale behind concepts of good correctional practice and the actual implementation of it. Too frequently, the gaps are wide between the concepts, the theories, and the practice. While this is also true of Western European corrections, the correlations between concepts, theories, and practice are discernible. For example, the concept of moral contamination and the theory that separation of criminals will prevent it led to the practice of solitary confinement in the Pennsylvania system so universally adopted in Western Europe.

The influence of French penal law can be seen in Greece, Portugal, Belgium, Holland, Luxembourg, and Switzerland. The use of decentralized or loosely centralized administrative techniques, education, and concentration on conventional prisoners rather than political prisoners manifests itself in all these countries. While all prison systems in Europe are now centralized, it has been a long time coming. Switzerland, for example, provided in 1942 that by 1962, certain improvements in cantonal prisons shall be made when the loose federation is to exercise more real control than ever before. Holland has now become quite centralized in correctional administration.

The Nazis centralized the administration of justice in Germany and imposed it on Austria. The Allies continued the centralization during the occupation. West Germany and Austria still maintain a centralized administration. Most of the correctional programs in Europe are the responsibility of the Ministry of Justice. While the Ministry of Justice operates the prisons in Spain, the directors of the individual prisons gained near autonomy in 1948. The French penitentiary system includes central jails in the metropolitan areas and houses of correction. Central penitentiaries have been built since World War II. A loose organization under the Ministry of Justice implements the concept of social defense through a small commission. Regional commissions of ten persons each concern themselves with correctional practices in its area in France. In Portugal, a judicial tribunal appoints a director of the prisons.

The working philosophy of prison practice integrates well the concepts, the theories, and the manner of implementation in a society. In southern Europe, where Italian anthropological influence is heavy, treatment has not developed to an advanced degree. Italy and Greece base much of their correctional thinking on biology, genetics, endocrinology, and anthropology. The correctional view is that the abnormal factors that dispose an offender toward antisocial behavior are strong and inherent. In some cases, however, these biological factors can be offset by segregation and treatment before environmental stresses cause the inherent factors to culminate in crime or delinquency. If it does not work early, then it is not going to be effective at all. Consequently, Greece begins with a study of the individual offender and conditional release, but after the third offense, the harsh habitual laws take effect. In the Scandinavian countries, some reliance is placed on biological factors in some crimes. Finland, Iceland, Denmark, Norway, and Sweden have castration laws for sexual offenders.[6] Between July, 1944, and January,

413

1952, Sweden castrated 181 men, including several exhibitionists. The Danish operation includes the use of glass prostheses to preserve the shape of the scrotum.

Institutions in Europe are small and diversified. A decree of 1936 limits prisons in Portugal to 500 and institutions for misdemeanants to 200. Sweden's prisons range in size from ten inmates to 186, with the majority between twenty five and fifty prisoners. With a prison population of 3,753 in 1957-1958, Holland's largest prison had 169 inmates. At the same time, Switzerland had a prison population of 2,100, and the largest Swiss prison was 400 inmates. Denmark's prison population of 2,837 included 327 in the largest prison. Finland's prison population of 6,108 included a prison with 658 inmates. West Germany had a prison population of 39,403, and its largest prison housed 1,496, but it reported overcrowding.

These small prisons are specialized. Belgium, where the first "prison" was built at Ghent in 1771, best demonstrates the specialization of institutions. Diagnostic centers for the scientific approach to corrections, institutions for youthful offenders, special programs for psychopaths and other abnormal cases, and similar specialization appears in Belgium, Sweden, and several other European countries. Classification procedures resulted from this specialization. While Europe had classification in the old sense as early as 1804 in Spain, modern classification techniques received impetus in Belgium in 1919. This classification system culminated from the influences of the English Borstal idea, beginning in 1908, the Italian anthropological school, the American sociological contributions, and developments in Belgium. In 1930, the concept of social defense was incorporated into Belgium's law, including psychiatric evaluation and treatment and the concept of *anomalie mentale*. The trend toward specialization of small institutions continued and spread throughout Europe. Spain has special institutions for men over age sixty years, men aged thirty-two to sixty, men aged twenty-five to thirty-two, and men aged seventeen to twenty-five. Other countries have adopted to some extent this type of age separation. Most countries make use of open institutions, and Belgium,

Sweden, Holland, Portugal, and Italy have advanced quite far in their use. Portugal, Italy, and Switzerland also maintain penal colonies.

Treatment in Europe has a clinical approach, particularly in Belgium, Sweden, France, Germany, and other countries. Most of the countries of Europe have programs of some sort for the treatment of the abnormal offender. Institutions for the psychopathic offender appear in several countries. Sweden tends to let the abnormal offender have more freedom and work in the open. Sweden has a special institution at Roxtuna for offenders who have reached the age of eighteen but have not reached twenty one. Finland requires a mental examination for everyone and has a classification committee in every prison.

Belgium and the Scandinavian countries have the same type of state-use labor system as the United States. Other countries emphasize individual crafts and production, though all have some state-use labor. Compensation to prisoners for work done appears to be rather high as compared to American standards. The compensation is generally controlled in its disposition, however. Italy deducts from the prisoners' wages the sums due as payment for damages, expenses for maintenance during the sentence, and court costs. Portugal uses the compensation to defray cost of maintenance of the prisoner, to pay indemnity for the crime, to assist dependents, and to build up a reserve toward his release. Italy has social insurance to cover inmates injured in accidents. In May, 1956, a crisis occurred in France when guards refused to let the inmates out of 115 French prisons because the prisoners were making more money selling handicraft articles than the guards were for guarding.

The use of probation services varies from practically nothing to fairly elaborate supervision systems. Belgium was the first country in Europe to have probation, having developed it in 1888. While Portugal had an incipient form as early as 1852, realistic probation did not come until considerably later. France had probation as early as 1891. Spain began probation in 1908, but the system remains quite rudimentary. Probation has been traditionally weak in the Scandinavian countries, but Sweden is now making some advances in its use. Holland has extended the fine to keep people out of prison, but probation is not used much. Holland places about 9 per cent of its convicted offenders on probation, as compared with 47 per cent in West Germany, 53 per cent in Switzerland, 30 per cent in Denmark, and 30 per cent in Finland.

Parole in Europe has been carried on primarily by private or quasi-public organizations. In Belgium, for example, a Committee of Patronage and an Office of Readaptation, both quasi-public organizations, supervise discharged and conditionally released persons. France has societies of patronage who function similarly. Italy has a public Council of Patronage, which is made up of *ex officio* public officials. The Italians do not use private associations, and considerable power is given to the "surveillance judge," who inspects all correctional institutions and determines conditional release for all inmates. Portugal has an Association of Patronage on a quasi-public basis for discharges, but the Minister of Justice is responsible for the conditionally released prisoners. Switzerland has had conditional release on a decentralized basis since 1868, but it is not particularly effective. Parole in Norway, Sweden, and Denmark is rudimentary. Of all the inmates released from prison, only 15 per cent are paroled in West Germany, 36 per cent are paroled in Switzerland, and 52 per cent are paroled in Denmark. On the other hand, 100 per cent are paroled in Finland and 70 per cent are paroled in Holland.

Juveniles in Europe have special treatment. Several countries use the same court and judge for juveniles as hear adult cases, but different laws are in effect. Laws regarding juveniles are generally for the protection of the child. Separate juvenile courts exist in Austria, Belgium, France, Greece, Italy, Luxembourg, Holland, and several Swiss cantons.

Europe is experimenting to find new methods of treatment that are more effective. Using anthropological and castration techniques, they also use sociological, psychological, and environment-manipulating techniques. Education and clinical diagnosis and treatment are being tried. France is looking for solu-

416

tions for the recidivism problem different from the traditional Anglo-Saxon long-term imprisonment. The Italian Chamber of Deputies became convinced that half the prisoners in Italy did not need imprisonment and, in 1953, voted to release approximately 25,000 inmates. France is experimenting with leaves of absence for prisoners, passes for walks, and a system of semi-freedom was introduced in 1945, in which prisoners go to "homes" or "hostels" for a period of time prior to release.

Correctional treatment is becoming less and less harsh. Spain eliminated corporal punishment in the eighteenth century and Holland eliminated it in 1854. Capital punishment was eliminated in Spain in 1932, in Holland in 1870, in Sweden in 1921, in West Germany in 1949, and in Italy in 1877 and again in 1948 after the Fascists had restored it in 1926. Switzerland eliminated capital punishment in 1942. Denmark, Finland, and several other European countries have no capital punishment. The trend in Europe is away from harsh and vengeful punishments and toward clinical, psychiatric, and rehabilitative methods.

Personnel in France, Belgium, and several other countries are expected to be fairly well trained and to participate in in-service training. While special instruction was provided prison personnel in Spain in 1873, and Criminology was included in the curriculum at the Law School at the University of Madrid in 1945, Spain has no guard training nor training for prison personnel at present. Portugal and Sweden have institutes of criminology, but they are primarily research and diagnostic in nature. An Institute of Criminal Science was established at the University of Copenhagen in 1957. A School of Criminology was established at the University of Vienna in 1932. The University of Rome has long had a school of criminal anthropology and penal law. Many European universities have subjects in criminology, usually in the school of law or in legal medicine. The United Nations has offered and is currently offering scholarships and fellowships in the field of social defense, and many Western European countries are taking advantage of them. The European concept of social defense, backed by scientific theory and practical application, appears to be growing more professional and effective.

EVALUATION

From its ancient demonological and theological interpretation of abnormal behavior and its harsh capital punishments and banishments, Western Europe has proceeded through the development of "natural rights" concepts, moral contamination, and biological determinism, to social and psychiatric interpretations. The correctional systems manifest the translation of these concepts into action, supported by adequate theoretical rationale. Northern Europe's harsh punishments have abated. Southern Europe's biological, anthropological, and religious approaches have come to recognize social and psychological factors. France, Switzerland, and Austria developed the clinical and psychoanalytic approaches to abnormal behavior, and Belgium has taken a lead in some instances in their application. Besides its own contributions to corrections, Western Europe has incorporated the American Pennsylvania system, the English Borstal system, the contributions of the American sociologists, and have implemented them with a series of many small and specialized correctional institutions, some for psychopathic offenders, some for young adults, some for alcoholics, and for other special groups of offenders.

In addition, the many international societies and groups in Western Europe dedicated to the betterment of all society in a program of social defense has assisted in communication and exchange of information. Holland, Belgium, and Luxembourg have, in fact, established in 1950 a Benelux Prison Commission for the common training of staff, collection of information, study of special problems in criminology, organization of prison labor for the common good, and exchange of documentation relating to prison questions. This type of interchange of information and informal and formal organizing for the exchange of experience and research suggests that Western European corrections may well be experiencing a renaissance in which major contributions in administrative techniques and treatment methods in the field of juvenile and adult corrections might well be expected.

SELECTED BIBLIOGRAPHY

Amilon, Clas, *Swedish Penal Institutions*, April 1, 1960, and *Swedish Institutions for Juvenile Delinquents and Adult Offenders*, November 1, 1959, Department of Justice, Stockholm, 1959-1960. This is a listing of all the juvenile and adult institutions for correction in Sweden, together with a description of their programs.

Ancel, Marc, *La Défense Sociale Nouvelle*, Editions Cujas, Paris, 1954. A review of the new concept of social defense, in which law enforcement, treatment of offenders, and social betterment are combined for the reduction of delinquent and criminal behavior.

Ancel, Marc, "Observations on the International Comparison of Criminal Statistics," *International Review of Criminal Policy*, United Nations, No. 1, January, 1952, 41-48. This is a review of the status of criminal statistics on the international level. So many problems interfere with the collection of comparable statistics that the presentation of statistics at the present time can mean only indices of estimate.

Ancel, Marc, and the Comité de Legislation Étrangère et de Droit International; *Les Codes Pénaux Européens*, Tomes I, II, et III, Centre Français de Droit Comparé, Paris, 1956-1958. This is a compilation of the penal codes of Europe. It is a revealing encyclopedia of the philosophies of crime as practiced in the various European countries.

Bernstein, Karen, and Christiansen, Karl O., "The Resocialization of Short-Term Offenders," *International Review of Criminal Policy*, United Nations, No. 6, July 1954, 25-39. This is a report of the socio-psychological investigations of 126 persons in 1952-3 who were rehabilitated as a result of short-term unconditional sentences, which the authors favor.

Costa, Jean-Louis, "Statut des jeunes delinquants en Europe Occidentale," *Revue de Science Criminelle et de Droit Pénal Comparé*, Paris, No. 3, Juillet-Septembre, 1953, 395-417. This is a survey of the treatment of juvenile delinquency in Western Europe, indicating an emphasis on protection and scientific approaches to treatment despite some contradictory elements with traces of punishment.

Cornil, Paul, "Prison Reform in Belgium Since the War";

Germain, Charles, "Post War Prison Reform in France"; and Eriksson, Torsten, "Post-War Prison Reform in Sweden," all in *The Annals of the American Academy of Political and Social Science*, CCXCIII, "Prisons in Transition," May, 1954 130-162. This volume of the *Annals* is devoted to prisons. The three articles mentioned and one devoted to England are the only ones in the section on prison reform abroad.

Gillin, John Lewis, *Taming the Criminal: Adventures in Penology*, Macmillan, New York, 1931, 165-215. This is a review of prison systems of the world. It is a cursory review of Prof. Gillin's observations as he visited the prisons.

Hugueney, Louis, de Vabres, H. Donnedieu, and Ancel, Marc, *Les Grands Systèmes Pénitentiaires Actuels*, Recueil, Paris, 1950. This is an excellent compilation developed by the University of Paris which includes major contributions describing the correctional systems of 19 countries in the world.

"Indices Criminels Comparés," *Revue de Science Criminelle et de Droit Pénal Comparé*, No. 1, Paris, Janvier-Mars, 1959, 97-105. This is a summary of crime rates of Europe since 1901 in different countries in comparison with some other rates of social breakdown, such as divorce and suicide.

Kellerhals, Hans, "L'intégration du travail pénitentiaire dans l'economie nationale," *International Review of Criminal Policy*, United Nations, No. 14, April, 1959, 13-20. A review of the manner in which prison labor and production is integrated with the total national economy in several countries of Europe. The use of open camps for work in Holland and Italy receive special attention.

Krebs, Albert, "Strafvollzugsfragen im Jugendgerichtsgesetz vom 4. August 1953," *Zeitschrift für Strafvollzug*, No. 2, 1955, 88-89. This is a review of the clinical approach being taken in juvenile cases in Germany since the revision of the juvenile court act and procedures in 1953. The work of the psychiatrist is emphasized.

Kühler, Hans, "Neue Wege des Strafvollzugs in Holland," *Zeitschrift für Strafvollzug*, I Teil in No. 3 and II Teil in No. 4/5, 1954, 213-218. This is an explanation of the new approach to corrections in Holland, with special attention to the psychiatric condition of the offenders. The psychopath receives special consideration.

Mavrommati, Marie, "Le problème de l'enfance délinquante en Grèce," *Revue de Science Criminelle et de Droit Pénal Comparé*, Paris, No. 3, Juillet-Septembre, 1953, 465-470. A review of the problem of juvenile delinquency and the treatment in Greece. The three institutions for minors are described, as are procedures in the juvenile court.

Middendorff, Wolf, "Federal Juvenile Courts Act of 1953," *International Review of Criminal Policy*, United Nations, No. 5, January, 1954, 120-122. This is an explanation of the new juvenile court act of 1953 in Germany. The juveniles are handled by the same judges who handle adult cases, but the court is set up as juvenile court independent of the adult court while juvenile cases are heard.

Racine, Aimee, *La Delinquance Juvenile en Belgique de 1939, à 1957*, Centre d'Etude de la Delinquance Juvenile, Bruxelles, 1959. An evaluation of the delinquency rates in Belgium from 1939 through 1957. This is the introductory issue of a planned annual statistical report on juvenile delinquency in Belgium.

Sellin, Thorsten, *Pioneering in Penology*, University of Pennsylvania Press, Philadelphia, 1944. This is a description and history of the Amsterdam houses of correction in the 16th and 17th centuries.

Sellin, Thorsten, *Recent Penal Legislation in Sweden*, Stockholm, 1947. This volume reviews the new acts, effective July 1, 1946, regarding correctional programs in Sweden.

Siméon, Jacques, *La Protection Judiciaire de l'Enfance Délinquante ou en Danger en France*, Centre Français de Droit Comparé, Paris, 1957. A summary of the laws covering juvenile delinquents in France and the juvenile court practices by which they are implemented. The objective is obviously toward protection of the child.

Sturup, Georg K., "Sexual Offenders and Their Treatment in Denmark and Other Scandanavian Countries," *International Review of Criminal Policy*, United Nations, No. 4, July, 1953, 1-19. The Scandanavian countries use castration as a method of treating the sexual offenders. The castrated offender develops finer skin, less hair, and has lessened sexual urges. The author was optimistic regarding the success of this treatment.

Teeters, Negley, *World Penal Systems*, Pennsylvania Prison Society, Philadelphia, 1944. This is a rather comprehensive survey of the major prison systems of the world, with attention to England, Europe, Russia, the United States, the Far East, and Latin America.

Vernon Fox (1916–), Chairman, Criminology and Corrections, School of Social Welfare, The Florida State University, received his B.A. from Michigan State University (1940), a certificate in Social Work (1941), M.A. degree (1943) and Ph.D. (1949) from the same institution. Between 1941-2 he was Case Work Director and Athletic Coach, Starr Commonwealth for Boys, Albion Michigan; 1942-6 (with the exception of 2 years in the United States Army) Psychologist at the State Prison of Southern Michigan; 1946-49, Psychologist and Director of Classification, Cassidy Lake Teaching School, Michigan Department of Corrections (Chelsea, Michigan; 1949-52, Deputy Warden in charge of Individual Treatment at State Prison of Southern Michigan and Director of Individual Treatment for the Michigan Department of Corrections; and from 1952– Professor and Chairman, Criminology and Corrections, Florida State University (Tallahassee). He is currently a member of the Florida Advisory Council on Adult Corrections and Prison Industries (a statutory body appointed by the Governor and his cabinet to advise the Governor and the Director of Corrections) and represents the United States of America on the International Board of Editors of *Excerpta Crimilologica* (Amsterdam, The Netherlands). Among his publications are: "How I Broke the Michigan Prison Riot," *Collier's*, July 12, 1952; "Blueprint for the Progressive Prison," *Federal Probation*, July, 1956; *Violence Behind Bars*, Vantage Press, New York, 1956; "The Effect of Counseling in Prison," *Social Forces*, March, 1954; etc.

NOTES

1. For additional information on this historical background, see such works as: Alexander, Franz, & Healy, William, *Roots of Crime*, Knopf, New York, 1935; Aquinas, Thomas, *Summa Theologica*, II-II, qq. 164-165; Becarri, Cesare B., *An Essay on Crimes and Punishment*, London, 1767; Bentham, Jeremy, *An Introduction to the Principles of Morals and Legislation*, several editions; Davis, John, D., *Phrenology, Fad and Science*, Yale University Press, New Haven, 1956; Ferri, Enrico, *Criminal Sociology*, trans., Appleton, New York, 1896; Garofalo, Raffaele, *Criminology*. trans., Little, Brown, Boston,

1914; Hooton, E. A., *Crime and the Man* Harvard University Press, Cambridge, 1930; Lombroso, Caesare, *Crime, Its Causes and Remedies*, Little, Brown, Boston, 1912; Lombroso, Caesare, & Ferraro, William, *The Female Offender*, Little, Brown, Boston, 1895; Rhodes, Henry T. F., *Alphonse Bertillon: Father of Scientific Detection*, Abelard-Schuman, New York, 1956; Vedder, Clyde B., Koenig, Samuel, & Clark, Robert E., *Criminology, A Book of Readings*, Dryden Press, New York, 1953; etc.

2. Ancel, Marc, *La Défense Sociale Nouvelle*, Editions Cujas, Paris, 1954.

3. Ancel, Marc, "Observations on the International Comparison of Criminal Statistics," *International Review of Criminal Policy*, United Nations, No. 1, January, 1952, 41-48.

4. Racine, Aimee, *La Delinquance Juvenile en Belgique de 1939 à 1957*, Centre d'étude de la Delinquance Juvenile, Bruxelles, 1959.

5. "Indices Criminels Comparés," *Revue de Science Criminelle et de Droit Pénal Comparé*, No. 1, Paris, Janvier-Mars, 1959, 97-105.

6. Sturup, George K., "Sexual Offenders and Their Treatment in Denmark and Other Scandinavian Countries," *International Review of Criminal Policy*, United Nations, No. 4, July, 1953, 1-19.

THE USSR AND THE EUROPEAN SATELLITES

Joseph S. Roucek
University of Bridgeport

Chapter I

JUVENILE DELINQUENCY AND CRIME IN THE SOVIET BLOC

That crime and juvenile delinquency exist in the Soviet area is a curious phenomenon, since, in the Marx-Lenin-Stalin theory, there can be no crime under the socialistic regime; and if there are any such symptoms, then they are the result of the capitalistic environment: "The Soviet social and political regime comprises no elements which bring out any vicious tendencies. Thieves and rogues are remnants of the distant past, still existing as a result of the capitalist environment and its ideology which is alien to the socialist manner of life." [1] Or, "Under conditions of bourgeois society crime is inevitable . . . The victory of socialism signifies the liquidation of the main source of crime, private capital ownership . . ." [2]

The communist explanations of the criminal and juvenile delinquency tendencies are based on the survival of bourgeois influences, and on the influences from abroad. It is impossible, however, to judge the extent of juvenile delinquency in the Soviet area beyond the fact that all the communist governments there report that the situation is bad enough to require systematic exposure in the press. The technique is to refer to delinquent children from wealthy families, and the discussions indicate an undertone of anxiety lest this anti-social behavior become a model for youths in all strata. Especially since Stalin's death, much has been written in the Soviet press about the rise of a class of juvenile delinquents from wealthy homes, whose behavior resembles that of the spoiled rich children in the West; riding

427

around in flashy cars, drinking heavily, night clubbing, and amusing themselves with intermittent seductions. Note also that the younger generation, brought up under communism as "perfect" citizens, used to be described in idyllic terms; but articles about this group now focus around such terms as "hooliganism," "bikinism," "zoot-suit boys," and "potapkyism," ("potapky," in Czech, are gaudily dressed young men with long hair and trousers worn well above the ankle).

Reports of unrest among the younger generation in the USSR are heard not only from travelers but also from the utterances of Soviet leaders, the growing frequency of complaints in the Party newspapers, and from the Party reports and discussions.[8] This crisis is quite important since in the Communist theory the Party embodies those progressive and forward-looking tendencies which claim that its appeal to the young is easy. This could be expected, anyhow, after four decades of the Soviet rule.

Prior to the de-Stalinization campaign, discontent had taken two distinct forms: (1) political opposition among small circles of students, culminating in arrests in 1951-52 at Leningrad University and elsewhere; and (2) the gradual spread in the late '40's of various curious fashions of dress and demeanor (known as "Stilyagi," or "Zoot-suiters," "Teddy-boys," in the West). In the Soviet environment this came to be regarded as something more than a passing moral problem.

Then, above these unconscious forms of resistance to political education, there was noted a growing apathy among the young, "a mood perhaps more dangerous than overt resistance."

After Stalin's death (1953), and especially since the Hungarian and Polish revolts, these "various tendencies appear to have coalesced into something like a consistent rejection of the prescribed mores of behavior, standards of thought, and even political loyalties."[4]

There has been, especially, a constant stream of complaints in the Soviet press about such post-war phenomena as "hooliganism" and the emergence of a spoiled and parasitic "jeunesse dorée." Hooliganism is clearly conceived as the most serious problem, since it influences large numbers of working-class youngsters. (In December, 1956, the Presidium of the Supreme Soviet issued a new decree on cases of "minor hooliganism," showing the seriousness of the situation; under its terms, offenders are to be held in prison and can no longer be freed before coming into court). The press complains about youthful delinquency, drunken orgies, the existence of gangs and gang warfare, the terrorizing of whole streets or districts by youthful hoodlums, and decreasing discipline in schools and factories. There have also been reports about murders in secondary schools.

But how can communist ideology explain such phenomena? The usual answer is that either the parents or the collective (school or factory) are at fault. "The question whether youthful lawlessness—from the harmless antics of the *stilyagi* with their craze for 'decadent' jazz, to the murderous activities of drunken hooligans—may not be rooted in the prevailing social conditions is naturally not raised." [5]

By attaching foreign labels to the shenanigans of their own youth, Communists aim to convince people at home—and abroad —that present difficulties are a result of foreign influence. But the outsiders must be aware about the indoctrination program the Communist children are subjected to almost from birth. Is it possible that a stray broadcast or modern rock 'n' roll and jazz tunes, heard over the usually jammed Voice of America or Free Europe, have been so effective that they have undone Communism's spadework and produced a wave of hooliganism?

In Soviet Russia, although "bourgeois manifestations" should have disappeared long ago, the "good" Communist families have been also worried about the slavish copying of foreign dress, the rock 'n' rolling at wild parties, the drinking, the mugging and stealing on the part of young people—who have known only Soviet society.[6]

In 1959, Belgrade newspapers, for instance, started pressing for heavier punishment for teen-age delinquents following a new outbreak and vandalism by the city's "dead-end kids." [7] Officials were worried about a series of incidents, including street-corner fights, rape attacks and late-night ambushes of innocent citizens by teen-age gangs in the suburbs.

These juvenile gangs appear to have made a comeback after about 2 years of relative calm. Although the problem is not as serious as it is in some other cities of both West and East, Yugoslav officials want to stamp it out before it gets worse. Newspaper appeals for rigorous action followed one of the worst incidents: a mass fight involving about 300 persons in broad daylight on one of Belgrade's main streets. The delinquents here differ in several ways from most of Europe's teen-age gangs. They rarely bother to dress up, they drink more and they are generally more violent—bottles and brass knuckles are often used. They think that the "stylish" clothes and long hair affected by many youngsters in Western Europe and in the USSR are effeminate, and their only concession to fashion uniformity seems to be an unexplained craze for jet-black trousers and blue, fleece-lined windbreakers. Usually the fights start after sessions of drinking powerful Serbian plum brandy in backstreet cafes. The teen-age toughs are called "silezdije," which means "the violent ones." They usually are between 16 and 24 years of age.

Many Communists contend that the "silezdije" try to ape what they see in American gangster or western movies, which always have been popular here.

"ROCK 'N' ROLL" AND JAZZ

Much has been said by the spokesmen of the Communist regime about the foreign influences, especially by the official line which has been persistently lumping rock 'n' roll with abstract art and other aspects of Western culture which, according to the Soviet line, debase human beings to the point where they become impotent cogs in the capitalists' machine. The most primitive assaults simply dismiss it as "decadent and vulgar." But such heavy artillery as the famous composer Dimitri Shostakovich has been brought up to the attack. "Alien primitivism—an enemy of art," he roared at rock 'n' roll. In fact, a report on Russia states: "Never in the history of cultural warfare has so much ammunition been spent on an enemy so little seen or heard as on rock 'n' roll (in Moscow). Elvis Presley probably could get one of the large popular halls if he were to call his act "Tennessee Folk Songs." But let him confess that it really is rock 'n' roll and the Young Communist League would run him out of town as one of those depraved *nekulturny*—barbarians." [8]

How offensive rock 'n' roll is to the Soviet officials was recently demonstrated by the smashing of one of the largest Soviet black-market rings specializing in rock 'n' roll music recorded on disks of exposed X-ray film. [9]

It appears that the teen-age ringleaders who produced the recordings in home studios and sold them through agents in Siberia, the Ukraine and the Far North were jailed. But the authorities remain disturbed "because the music merchants served a large and enthusiastic clientele." The "banal" music, the police reported, had found its way into dance halls and clubhouses, and members of the Young Communist League were some of its active promoters and salesmen.

The story of the destroyed partnership of Dmitri Pavlov, 20 years old, of the village of Kurkovo (near Moscow) and Victor Krupin of Novosibirsk (who headed the Siberian outlet) provided a poignant parable for the Communist Party's latest decree which ordered a massive new indoctrination program, aimed primarily at shirkers who shrink from socially useful labor and must counter "alien and bourgeois" influences from the West.

The story became public when a police major, Yefim Popok presented it in *Sovietskaya Kultura*. The major skipped over many criminal details, and did not touch on subsidiary rings that must have existed to keep the studio supplied with X-ray film, bearing pictures of ribs, thighs and other bones, from which the youths had made their records; he also did not estimate the total profits nor touch upon competing operations. But he admitted that such records had been sold illegally for years, with the public's knowledge; especially lively trade had been conducted in the Black Sea vacation resorts.

While rock 'n' roll was especially featured as being objectionable, boogie woogie, swing jazz and dance tunes were also available; so were songs of popular Russian crooners of the twenties and thirties. On occasion, even modern Russian songs and movie music turned up on "bones" records when the regular recording studios failed to meet the demand.

The thin, seven-inch disks were designed to play on one side at 78 revolutions a minute. With careful use they could be made to last for months. Some bore labels, some of which correctly identified the record's tune. Supplies were regular but prices fluctuated sharply— a distinct contrast with regular record sales at government stores. Some tunes sold for 10 rubles, twice the price of a similar, but two-sided record in the stores. The price of 15 to 20 rubles for the black-market records was not unusual. (A ruble is worth 25 cents at the official rate of exchange, but 10 cents at the more realistic tourist rate.)

Interesting is the background of the "producers." Pavlov, after failing the entrance examinations for Moscow University in 1959, was taught the record business by Yevgeni Golopuzenko, a Moscow operator with a record of seven convictions for minor speculation. The instruction completed, Golopuzenko raised the capital needed to launch Pavlov in business. The sales were rapid. Pavlov peddled his recordings, probably copies of music recorded from foreign short-wave radio programs and disks purchased from tourists, in the music department of G.U.M., the huge state department store in Moscow. Established customers outside Moscow could count on mail order service.

Pavlov and Krupin were each sentenced to two years in jail. Golopuzenko received a year at hard labor and all the other participants received "other punishment."

In November, 1959, fifteen enthusiastic Elvis Presley fans were given prison terms ranging from 6 months to 4½ years in Communist East Germany. It was reported that the youths had marched through Leipzig shouting derogatory remarks about East German music and the Communist party boss, Walter Ulbricht. The youths had also shouted "Long live Elvis Presley." [10]

Around 1959, youngsters resembling United States or French beatniks made their appearance in Prague. According to Handler, "Some have picture-frame beards that came originally from

North Africa via Paris. Others are long-haired or short-cropped. Carefully sloppy dress provides a note of elegance. "This manifestation of individualism in a collectivized society is a puzzling phenomenon." [11]

Another puzzling manifestation was, to Handler, "the extent to which jazz flourished (in Prague). Congresses of musicians pledged to oppose artistic deviation come and go, but jazz continues to be heard in public places." In fact, "the jazz specialists of Prague have developed a remarkable familiarity with jazz styles merely by listening to recordings. They are acquainted even with the styles of performers who are only at the beginning of their careers." But, "the cultural directors of the Communist party have apparently decided to come to terms with jazz because they seem unable to discourage its growth in the younger generation."

Yet, the craze for rock 'n' roll seems to have been tapering off lately. The popularity of that music remains strong among the more energetic youths, but "even their enthusiasm is cooling to the point where they are ready for something new." [12] This has been due to the fact that jazz and rock 'n' roll, around 1959, found the Polish youths plunged into a frenetic attempt to be as Western as they could. "But when it became clear that there was no real connection between dance tunes and social system, rock 'n' roll was allowed to become a matter of personal taste." [13]

WHAT IS "HOOLIGANISM"?

We are here confronted with the difficulty of defining the term "hooliganism," as used by the Communist spokesmen; it might refer to real misdemeanor and crime, but it can also mean simply young teen-agers who have adopted the jeans and jacket and other casual dress forms fashionable among such youngsters in Western states; or it is also used to designate the teen-agers' reluctance to assimilate or content themselves with stereotyped and limited Communist education. Obviously, in the countries controlled by Moscow, hooliganism refers to any juvenile tendency to stray away from the set pattern of Communist "morals,"

433

and what the current formula of the Politbureau states is good for youth.

ALCOHOLISM

But behind the thin façade of this propaganda, the Communists also admit that there is an ever growing tendency to juvenile waywardness, marked especially by drunkenness.

Excessive alcohol consumption within the Soviet bloc has reached the dimensions of a major social problem actually in all levels of the social structure.[14] Although heavy drinking in the region has been reported, "unofficially," as rising for several years, it has been only since the reports of the 20th Congress that the authorities have been admitting the seriousness of the problem and the need to handle it.

Measured in absolute quantities, the consumption in the area is about equal to that in the rest of Europe. But the main source of concern is the sharp rise in consumption of hard liquor: vodka, rum (made from sugar-beet) and brandy (while the beer consumption has continued on an equal level). Even more important has been the evidence of the use of alcohol by youngsters, and the use of alcohol by a small proportion of the population in the industrial centers. Uncontrolled drinking, the communist press reports, has been a factor in hooliganism, crime, disease and accidents, as well as a prime cause of workers' absenteeism and inefficiency resulting in production losses.

The official concern has been most evident in the case of Poland and Czechoslovakia (the relatively most industrialized states in the Soviet bloc). On August 9, 1957, *Radio Warsaw* proclaimed that drunkenness was so prevalent that there is now a saying: "Perhaps there is no Polish road to Socialism, but there is a Polish road to alcoholism." A conference of teachers, doctors and social workers, held in April, 1956, disclosed that there had been a considerable increase in teen-age drinking in students' hostels. Teachers reported that scholarship money, granted directly to students, is often spent on vodka, and that young people are prone to spend their earnings from scrap collections on liquor.[15]

These youngsters, filled with vodka, usually roam the city in groups of six to a dozen. They do not appear to be organized in regular street gangs, and "their brawls are largely spontaneous: an argument over a girl, a shove in a crowd trying to scramble onto a street car can set off a fight." [16]

In Czechoslovakia, between 1949 and 1955, the consumption of all alcoholic beverages rose 16% (and of hard liquor—chiefly rum—25%). On January 17, 1956, LUD (Bratislava), wrote: "Today in Slovakia, a considerable number of people start work 'bolstered' by alcohol. Daily, young and older people end up before the divorce courts because of alcohol . . . For many years we have been underestimating this serious danger which has grown into a social menace." According to *Lidová Demokracie*, August 31, 1931, one out of seven crimes in Czechoslovakia is committed under the influence of alcohol.

Visitors to Slovakia, for instance, are surprised at the excessive drinking of the ordinary people. One visitor of Slovakia claims: "I visited five communities . . . but the drinking problem is the same in all of them, and, I suppose, in all of Slovakia." [17] It appears that "the people there are trying to drink their hapless lot away. But the stuff they are drinking . . . is terrible stuff, poison that most people themselves make clandestinely. Perhaps it is worse than the worst moonshine ever made in America. The clergy are doing their best to convince the people not to drink, but to little avail . . ."

In Hungary the trouble had begun long before the 1956 revolution. Although the press has been publishing no figures, it has been carrying numerous articles on alcoholism, mainly in the form of individual case histories (real or hypothetical). Since the revolution, the rise of drinking has been noted.

In fact, Hungary's communist press has been loud in regard to its complaints; the Budapest trade union newspaper *Nepakarat* asserted: [18] "The children are learning that the words of the party and the newspaper are often not to be taken seriously, that words and deeds do not match . . . Only recently it was a favorite theme of the Hungarian press to print statistics about youth crime in the Western countries. It would not have harmed us then to pay more attention to our own doorsteps . . . prematurely aged children . . . Now we see in our country twelve-year-old prostitutes, teen-age bandits. These are subjects about which we were silent for fourteen long years but which we must speak about now, however painful it is." [19]

In Romania, the regime has also been complaining that heavy drinking has been spreading through all sections of all community, including youth.

Even in Yugoslavia, where youth has more freedom and more normal channels to spend their energies and the Communist regime has shown more tolerance and comprehension of youthful exuberance, the increase of the more violent forms of "teddy boyism" and juvenile banditry arising from alcohol has been causing much concern.[20]

THEFT

Next to teen-age alcoholism and drunkenness, the "Iron Curtain" has been confronted with a special kind of crime that plagues the whole area: theft of state property. By their own accounts, Communist governments have found theft of state property—from the pilfering of plant parts to plain shoplifting —a problem of growing seriousness and scope. (But statistics are unimportant in the story; almost all property—except farmland —is state-owned in Central-Eastern Europe and the Communists could probably show statistically that there were cases brought against thieves and swindlers in the West). The regimes have made it plain that they are concerned about "economic crimes" not just as economic problems but as a threat to internal discipline and morale. (The whole problem has been discussed—and is still being discussed—in Party meetings in virtually every country in the area). What bothers the communist officials is the attitude behind such crimes—the attitude that swindling of the state is part of everyday life, and that it is carried on on juvenile as well as adult levels. "Pilfering in some factories has become so common that it has almost achieved the respectability of custom,

. . . Millions of Eastern Europeans who consider themselves perfectly lawabiding and honest find that they can exist only with after-hour jobs—often with state tools and materials—that they would not dream of reporting for income tax purposes." The real worry of the government is "the feeling among a great many ordinary people that it is not immoral to cheat the state." [21]

Most frequently reported cases of "economic crimes" have been reaching us from Poland. In 1958, state inspectors found 20,000 cases of embezzlement, short-changing, over-pricing and short-weighing in 31,776 Polish shops, according to the official communist newspaper *Trybuna Ludu*.[22] The report was that 2,000 cases had been sent to the courts for prosecution, 1,000 employees had been dismissed and 100 private trading licenses revoked. On February 19, 1959, Poland's top government body called on the courts, the prosecutors, and the police to get tough faster with "economic criminals." [23]

The Council of State, which is a sort of collective Presidency, demanded swifter investigations by the police, a quicker follow-up by the prosecutors and harsher sentences by the courts (particularly in regard to "economic crimes": theft of state property, bribery, illegal foreign-exchange deals and pilfering from government-owned factories). The Council's formal statement was spread over the front page of *Trybuna Ludu* as the lead story of the day. The Council gave no statistics but it was estimated officially that about 100,000 cases of economic crimes were brought before the courts in 1958 and that about 10% were listed as "serious crimes." In 1958, the Council pointed out, the *Sejm* adopted laws authorizing tougher sentences for "economic criminals"; but the Council complained that the courts had not been taking advantage of the law and were passing lighter sentences than the law permitted. It was also suggested that greater use be made of "temporary detention" of "racketeers, bribers and embezzlers." In serious cases, the Council asked that proceedings be speeded up and use made of "summary procedure." At the same time, the Council claimed that there had been an improvement in the fight against "hooliganism." Special quick-justice courts have been set up in nine Polish cities.

A similar situation has been developing in Czechoslovakia. At its meeting on January 9, 1959, the Czechoslovak Ministerial Council complained that the criminal code designed to combat the pilfering of socialist property was not being stringently applied. It was stressed that in cases where the "criminals" were "class enemies," it was necessary to apply the provisions of the code requiring the confiscation of the wrong-doer's property.[24]

Romania was not far behind these efforts to combat theft and embezzlement of so-called "People's Property." In 1958, the Bucharest government created the "Judgment Councils" in all "enterprises and establishments" to try workers whose thefts did not exceed 200 Lei.[25]

Apparently these councils did not work too effectively. Another measure to curtail "economic crimes" was the formation of "inspection teams," composed of housewives and workers, who report on any abuses committed by managers and employers of state-owned shops.[26] Seven hundred such teams had been formed in Bucharest alone by the end of 1958. To dramatize the severity of the courts in dealing with these crimes, *România Libera* (on January 9, 1959) announced sentences ranging from 5 to 20 years imprisonment for half a dozen embezzlers.

In fact, Romania and Bulgaria have approved the use of the death sentence to fight these crimes.[27]

"EXPLANATIONS" AND CAUSES

As is usual with the explanations offered by the communist dialecticians, the main cause of all these troubles is always the same: the "negative influences" from the West—the theme, for instance, used by President Tito at the Youth Congress in 1958. As auxiliary factors are introduced, we learn, for instance, from Czechoslovakia, that the youth problem is due in large degree to a decline of parents' morals. The officials also accuse young Communists of "not giving a sufficiently good example for the remainder of the youth" and claim that "reactionary elements misuse our youth." [28] *Nepszabadság,* Hungarian government

Party organ, observed: "Our youth no longer want to believe anything, refuse to let themselves be convinced. . . . They reject the old slogans, often scorn all the doctrines of Marxism and sometimes call everything just a fake"; they blamed the "effects of the October counterrevolution" on children caught hiding guns and grenades, and on others playing shooting and hanging games.

The less politically-minded officials of the region, and especially social workers, attribute the evils of juvenile delinquency not only to the upheavals and demoralization and broken families of war occupation, but also to the totalitarian rule which induces the youth to break out in anti-social ways, to the general dissatisfaction with life. (Interestingly enough, the Youth leader of Yugoslavia, Mike Tripalo, observed, at the Youth Congress of 1958, that extravagances of behavior, dressing and dancing were symptoms of passing bad taste rather than the essence of the youth problem and wanted to create an understanding on both sides by considering what the youth wanted and what the state might be able to afford to grant).

Obviously, one of the reasons why hooliganism is sweeping through the satellite countries is that it is a revolt against the merciless communist system. And one of the most glaring but insoluble problems is that related to the communist concept of the family. By the mid-1930's, the communist rulers decided to rely primarily on the family as the agency for inculcating the moral standards, though it was to be supplemented by the school, the Pioneers, and the Comsomol. This commitment to the family has been strengthened by one to personal private property (including real estate). But, evidently, the Communist regimes have been unable to avoid the consequences of a certain proportion of spoiled children, since, speaking in generalities, many parents under the pro-Soviet systems have been unable to discipline their children, aiming to spare the younger generation from facing the harsh realities of the system.

At the same time, there has been a growing resistance to the Communist youth organizations and the policies of which they are the tool. These organizations are hoping to appeal to the group consciousness of young people of the satellites, while trying, at the same time, to suppress their equally strong urges for independence and self-expression; basically, this is a conflict between individualism and totalitarian regimentation, and many of the attitudes involved in so-called hooliganism "are simply adolescent revolt against coercion and domination." [29]

Sheer boredom with endless political and ideological lectures appears to be common among the younger generation in the Soviet orbit—as exemplified by the successful campaign of the Polish students for a drastic reduction in compulsory "Diamet" at college, and the unsuccessful efforts of their East German and Czechoslovak colleagues to achieve the same goal.

But the main trouble here is apparently the shattering discovery, on the part of the students, after graduation, between the proclaimed ideology of social justice and fellowship in society and the actual performance (the immense gap between promise and performance). The result has been cynicism, especially for those whose parents had reached some standing in the official hierarchy. Most comments heard about this phenomenon have been focused on the term "beloruchki"—those with white hand, i.e., shirkers who refuse to do their patriotic duty in connection with the officially sponsored drives for settling new territories, (since students are sent to outlying territories after graduation), or the young people from relatively well-to-do families who are unwilling to soil their hands by working.

The unrest which was started by the 20th Congress is periodically described in the press as lack of discipline, a tendency to contradict one's elders and betters; all this indicates the existence of one factor: dissatisfaction with Soviet life.

ATTEMPTED SOLUTIONS OF JUVENILE DELINQUENCY

As everywhere throughout the world, and as in the Soviet zone, there have been numerous suggestions and experiments with measures, which might solve, or at least reduce, the currently rising delinquency rate.[30]

440

Bulgaria. An attempt to keep the youngsters occupied has been introduced in Bulgaria recently, with the decision of the government to resort to labor mobilization. (The same applies to Yugoslavia). Bulgaria has, in fact, reported, officially, on its efforts to handle juvenile delinquency by segregating the convicted youngsters in the Makarenko colony (established in 1955 and named after the famous Soviet reformer of homeless children, who applied the principle of giving the children the maximum of self-management and responsibility).[31] It appears also that Sofia has plans to establish similar "more easy-going colonies under the administration of the Ministry of Education and Culture, for delinquents who have committed trivial offenses" (while the Makarenko colony is under the Ministry of Justice).

The colony consists of four buildings, sports grounds, a large artificial fish-pond, and kitchen gardens, surrounded by a barbed wire fence, 5 to 6 feet high, which is designed to hold some 200 delinquents. The minorities of Bulgaria, especially Gypsies and Turks, offer higher proportions than their general proportion in the population. (We learn that: "The minorities are more backward and poorer, and are thus naturally more prone to steal. Special provision is of course made for them in the school, both to meet their backward education and to allow for the use of their own languages"). There are regular classrooms and a library, with one-quarter being "Marx-Lenin-Stalin books." Industrial training is featured. No alcohol, cards, or smoking is allowed, and "ordinary pocket knives are not forbidden." The law prohibits "remission" of sentences, but the whole or part of the sentences can be granted by the Presidium of the National Assembly on the recommendation of a Commission (of which the Director of the colony is a member). Punishments for misbehavior are: deprivation of visits or parcels for a short period, a public reprimand before a general meeting of the colony inmates ("collective denunciation"), isolation in a room for a defined period, and the transfer to an ordinary prison "on the basis that the delinquent has shown himself to be unsuitable for treatment in a colony." There is only one "non-delinquent employed as as guard."

The unofficial reports show, however, that the government has been forced to use more radical measures. In 1957 and 1958, after several demonstrations of students in Sofia, the Bulgarian police deported thousands of "hooligans" from Sofia and other cities, sending them to state farms and other institutions.[32] The police were instructed to rid Sofia, Plovdiv, Burgas and Varna of "hooligans and youths with no fixed place of work who carry on immoral modes of life and tend to fall under the influence of hooligans." Minors were to receive lower-school education, and laws are in preparation creating special "educational institutions" for this purpose. (The campaign was launched after an incident in which a young worker stabbed another to death on a Sofia streetcar for no apparent reason and then left the car without interference by any of the car's passengers).

Czechoslovakia. Youth work brigades, a characteristic of the captive states in Central-Eastern Europe in the first years after World War II, reappeared in Czechoslovakia in 1959.[33] As in several neighboring states that also had resumed this activity, the move was aimed at combating passivism and the "anti-social" tendencies among the younger generation. The campaign has had multiple objectives: (1) To check political revolt among the youth by hard work mixed with ideological training; (2) To curb drinking and other waywardness; and (3) To step up production.[34]

At the same time, the communist states have been copying the Soviet plan to make children attend school and work part time at farms or factories. To catch the older ones, from 18 to 26, these countries have reestablished the youth work brigades to speed up reconstruction and to install Communist control.

The Czechs organized their first youth brigades in 1945 to aid in the rebuilding of the country and to help expand its industrial potential. At one time, as many as 77,000 youths were laboring without pay to build new factories and foundries in Ostrava (the big steel center near the Polish border). The brigades were disbanded in 1950 after the government had decided that their work was no longer necessary for the success of the nation's development plans.

442

Then came the 1956 armed revolt in Hungary and political upheaval in Poland. With Soviet Army support, swift reprisals were taken against the rebellious youth of Hungary. Briefly won Polish freedoms were also trimmed. In Czechoslovakia, Romania, and Bulgaria, the Communist rulers acted swiftly to prevent their youth from joining any sympathy revolts with Hungary and Poland. This required a massive reappraisal of youth-control policies; widespread drinking and delinquency also required attention. The work brigades appear to have been decided upon as the cure; enrollment is called voluntary but that does not deceive anybody.

In Czechoslovakia, early in 1958, the brigades were reorganized and set to work anew. There were about 2,000 youths living and working at five big construction sites, while thousands more were devoting time on the week-ends to local and district projects which they can reach from their homes.

Members of the brigades range from 18 to 26 years of age. They are supposed to volunteer for a period of from one to three months, for which they receive their food, shelter and clothing, but no pay. Students who take part in brigade work continue to receive their state allowances just as if they were studying and factories paid any employee who signed up, his wages during his period of service. The chief value of the brigade work, according to the Communist spokesmen, is that it gives the youths a sense of responsibility for the economic future of the country; another advantage is that it takes them away from home and enables them to experience different living conditions. The arrangement also gives a Communist regime a prepared audience for the lectures and ideological entertainment that goes with brigade life.

Poland. In Poland, for instance, where moral decay, with teenage prostitution and drunkenness, long a shocking feature of Polish life under communism, we now find the Roman Catholic Church and the Gomulka regime cooperating in trying to remedy the mess. In Warsaw, the Town Council drew up a standard of approved behavior for young people, in the fall of 1958, together with the school board regulations.[35] They call upon all youngsters to show "cultured and subdued behavior in public places." All young persons will be expected to give up smoking and drinking; they are to surrender their seats in trolleys and busses to the elderly and to the sick. Children up to the age of 14 are to be off the streets and out of public places by 9 P.M. in the summer and 8 P.M. in the winter. Youngsters aged from 14 to 19 will be expected to be at home by 10 P.M. If any youngster misbehaves, an "authorized" person will be empowered to take away his school identification card.

There is, however, some debate about how many persons are to be "authorized" and just what to do about a burly young man of 18 or 19 who is not in the mood to give up his school card. Another problem is how to deal with youngsters who have finished their elementary schooling at the age of 14, who are not going on to higher schools and who do not have jobs. This problem is serious in Poland. The rapidly rising population not only has crowded the schools but has increased the number of youngsters with time on their hands. (This was one of the reasons behind the government's decision to extend the period of schooling, combining the last two years with vocational training).

In 1959, Warsaw Radio announced that 14,000 Polish youth volunteer workers were being called up for construction jobs especially in the territories taken from Germany. They will be directed by 200 Communist activists bearing such titles as "commandant" and "chief of staff."

Romania. In Romania, the Communist Party newspaper, SCINTEIA, announced at the turn of 1959 that 35,000 youths were to be enrolled in 1,000 brigades to work on construction projects and on farms. "In all parts of our country the youth will take part in this unpaid patriotic work," SCINTEIA reported.

Yugoslavia. Among the corrective measures to combat delinquency in Yugoslavia is corrective training. One of such corrective institutions is the Vasa Stajio Institute.[36] There the gates are open for the minor and major young offenders; two thirds of them are boys and one third girls, all from 10 to 18 years of age. The staff arranges, in accordance with the local town factories,

444

to accept the inmates as apprentices under the same conditions as other youths. On Saturdays and Sundays the inmates are allowed to visit their parents, go the movies, theater, dancing, and the like. All inmates spend a month's rest at the sea every year (except for the physically weak ones who go to the mountains). The managing Board of the Institute selects its staff members from among the graduates of the Department for Delinquent Children of the Higher Pedagogic School and students of the pedagogic group at the Faculty of Philosophy. The policy is to select young rather than older teachers "who might be prejudiced against neglected and delinquent children."

For educational purposes the inmates are divided into two groups; each group (10-12 of them) has its own teacher who is also engaged in social work. The Institute also has its own psychologist who, apart from treating every indivdual inmate, also works on the determination of suitable occupations for them; he is also helped by the Consultation Center for the Selection of Professions.

The first group of about 100 inmates left the Institute about 1956. About 30 of them have become skilled workers, 24 are semi-skilled and 7 unskilled workers, while 17 are learning various trades; 3 are attending a secondary school, one is a university student; 2 are office employees; while only 7 are known to have committed new offenses. From this group of released inmates, 78 have returned to their homes, 9 are serving in the army, and 16 girls are married.

USSR. Probably the most drastic measures to handle the problem of delinquency have been taken in the USSR (where a grim political lesson had been taught to the Soviet rulers by the uprisings in Poland and Hungary led by youngsters—that their efforts of the past two decades to rear a new generation of indoctrinated communists had failed). Thus in October, 1958, a 19-year-old "stilyaga" (zoot-suiter) was re-tried and sentenced to death following public protests that the original 10 to 25-year term imposed for killing a militiaman during a robbery was too lenient.[37] And a rigid new order of discipline began to be imposed on Soviet society as it set out in pursuit of Premier

445

Khrushchev's ambitious 7-year economic goal in the fall of 1958. The leading organizations, the Communist Party, the Young Communist League and the Central Council of Trade Unions, started evolving their own strict measures in the campaign, aiming to root out drunkards and thieves, hooligans and unreliable and anti-social elements. Moves have begun to set up an armed workers' militia in all urban centers. Through the Young Communist League, work brigades are to be established in factories and on farms to compete in speed-ups of manual and clerical labor and clean-ups of attitudes and morals. In the Communist Party there is to be a new drive for vigilance against "foreign infiltration," against the leaking of State and Party secrets and against carelessness and complacency.[38]

Actually, Soviet school discipline has always been strict. If a Soviet youngster leaves a trade school against orders, he is punished by imprisonment in a labor colony. The Criminal Code of the USSR (Moscow, 1948), laid down: "Voluntary departure from the school or systematic violation of school discipline by students of trade and railroad schools and factory and plant training schools entails expulsion from school and imprisonment, prior to trial, in a labor colony for one year."

But what is to be done with the pool of juvenile unemployment in the USSR?[39] The existence of a reserve of unused labor is a serious matter for the Soviet ideological claims. On ideological grounds it cannot be allowed, since Soviet citizens are guaranteed employment—and should really work for their country. It cannot be discussed on the economic grounds, since the USSR, officially, faces an over-all labor shortage. Yet, voluntary juvenile unemployment is one of the factors behind the new educational scheme of the USSR. The reluctance of school-graduates to enter the labor market, as well as the difficulty in finding suitable jobs, have seriously troubled the Soviet authorities. To make good these defects, Khrushchev has proposed to introduce a scheme of "socially useful labor" after 7 or 8 years of school-training, for all children "without exception." (But this creates the need to grant exceptional opportunities for "socially useful" talent, although the necessity for an elite cannot be reconciled with the myth of a classless society.)

All in all, the fact remains that, in spite of the official communist propaganda to attribute juvenile delinquency to the "poisonous remnants of bourgeois morals," there are only two acceptable explanations for this problem: either the Communist educational and political system produces hooligans, or they are the result of a revolt against the system's incessant pounding.

The subject of hooliganism, at the beginning of the 1930's and the sanctions envisaged in Article 74 of the Criminal Code of the RSFSR which dealt with it, were considerably increased in recent years. On August 10, 1949, the Presidium of the Supreme Soviet of the USSR issued a decree on "Legal Responsibility for Petty Thefts and Hooliganism," under which even in extremely insignificant cases of rowdyism (those which earlier were not handled by a court, but dealt with administratively) a sentence of one year's imprisonment was imposed. In December, 1956, first the RSFSR and then the other union republics issued new decrees on petty hooliganism, reducing the sentences to 3-15 days' imprisonment. But the question was taken up again in 1958.

In line with the current stepped-up campaign against alcoholism, the new Soviet Criminal Law Code of 1958 includes a special article to the effect that intoxication shall in no wise mitigate criminal responsibility. This is especially important in view of official findings that 70% of deliberate murders were penetrated under the influence of liquor and so were 90% of all acts of hooliganism.[40]

At the end of 1959, quasi-judicial commissions with broad powers to commit young persons to reformatories and fine their parents for neglect were to be established in the USSR.[41] A draft law providing that such commissions "intensify the campaign against child neglect and juvenile delinquency" was published on October 24, 1959, and adopted the subsequent week by the Supreme Soviet.

At the same time, the Supreme Soviet enacted a law authorizing all factories, farms and organizations to establish "Comrades'

Courts." These deal with cases of misdemeanors and petty crimes by adults, violations of work rules, improper public behavior and drunkenness, refusal to work, and domestic quarrels. Both measures result from a developing theory that public organizations and neighbors should assume increasing responsibility for law enforcement. This theory is meant to prepare the population for the days of pure communism when the state will have "withered away."

Around 1958, it was proposed that petty offenders be tried at mass meetings empowered to ostracize violators from the community. Objections from legal circles against this procedure apparently led to the new forms that have now been codified.

The Commissions for the Affairs of Minors are now established in all districts and cities by local soviets. The members are deputies of the soviets, school, health and social workers, and correction officials. Their task is to care for abandoned children, try offenders, observe the conduct of minors in correctional institutions, recommend parole and supervise children after release from reformatories; they also direct reformatories, labor colonies and special medical and rehabilitation institutions in their regions.

In one way or another the commissions deal with all matters affecting minors. Factories, for instance, can now discharge persons under the age of 18 only with the consent of the local Commission for the Affairs of Minors. It has judicial authority in all cases of petty hooliganism and speculation. It tries cases of publicly dangerous acts by young persons under 14, and lesser crimes by those between the ages of 14 to 16. After proper hearings in the presence of the offenders, the commission can demand public apologies, issue reprimands or place offenders under probationary warnings for one year. It can also force youngsters over 15 to repair damage by their own labor or by payment of up to 200 rubles ($50, at the official exchange rate), if they have an income. It can place children in the charge of parents or public organizations or medical or rehabilitation institutions.

In cases of dangerous activities or malicious and systematic violations of public order by youths over the age of 11, the

448

commission can send offenders to colonies run by the Ministry of Internal Affairs (MVD) for periods up to three years. Minors placed in colonies can be released only by the commissions, after they have improved and developed work qualifications. They can be held until the age of 20.

The commission also can go before other public organizations and courts to charge adults with having created conditions leading to crimes by their children, or can fine adults up to 200 rubles in such cases. To deprive a parent of the loss of parental rights or to assess parents for damages caused by their children, the commission has to apply to regular courts.

The commission has subpoena powers and makes decisions by majority of the commissioners present; the decisions can be appealed only once to local soviets but not to courts. All materials used in the commissions must be shown to the offending minor or to his legal representative, but the draft law says nothing else about the defendant's rights.

The law for "Comrades' Courts" likewise makes no provision for legal counsel for the accused. The justification given in this case is that the courts are "friendly" tribunals and not state organs. Any group of 50 persons commonly associated in a house or work can establish a "Comrades' Court," with members drawn from their midst. At factories they are responsible to unions and elsewhere to the local soviets.

These courts try a variety of cases, including: violations of labor discipline, absenteeism and lateness at work, failure to obey safety rules and illegal use of public or state property; refusal to engage in useful labor and leading a "parasitic" existence; failure to support children or elderly parents; illegal hunting, petty speculation, plundering, and hooliganism (for the first offenders), drunkenness, swearing and illegal manufacture of liquor for home consumption; desecration of living quarters or of public property in parks and violation of order in communal apartments. The courts are also empowered to settle quarrels over such questions as the splitting of gas and electric bills in communal apartments or the division of peasant houses and resolve disputes over property up to the value of 1,000 rubles. In their

449

verdicts, the courts can demand public apologies or issue reprimands, levy fines up to 100 rubles, request the demotion of workers to lower-paying jobs for up to 3 months, and ask regular courts to evict offenders from apartments or rooms or require an offender to repair damages up to 500 rubles. The decisions cannot be appealed.

In addition to these measures, heavy penalties were to be established for drunkenness and for violation of restrictions on the sale of vodka in restaurants and stores. Regular courts are to be empowered to compel alcoholics to undergo treatment at institutions with special medical and work programs.

SELECTED BIBLIOGRAPHY *See pp. 542-545.*

NOTES

Chapter I

1. *Sovyetskoye Gosudarstvo I Pravo* (Soviet State and Law), Golyakov, No. 7, 1947, "On Strengthening the State Security," 9. Article on the State's Secret Laws, recounting the necessity for all Soviet citizens to be ever on guard against attempts of foreign intelligence services to gain information.

2. "Role of Soviet Law in Education of Communist Consciousness," *Bolshevik*, 4, 1947, 54.

3. Laquer, Walter Z. and Lichtheim, George (editors), *The Soviet Cultural Scene 1956-1957*, Praeger, New York, 1958, Chapter 22, "Conflict Between the Generations," 202-214; 23, "Uneasy Youth," 215-220; 24, "Educational Problems," 221-236.

4. Laquer, Walter Z. and Lichtheim, George, *op cit.*, 204.

5. Laquer and Lichtheim, *op. cit.*, 213.

6. Jorden, William J., "Moscow: 'Inconspicuous but a Problem,' " in The New York *Times Magazine*, February 23, 1958.

7. "Teen-Age Gangs Anger Belgrade," The New York *Times*, April 19, 1959.

8. Frankel, Max, "Russia: Unheard, Unseen Enemy," in "Global Report on Rock 'n' Roll," The New York *Times Magazine*, April 20, 1958, 24.

9. "Illicit Rock 'n' Roll in Soviet Union is Halted," The New York *Times*, CLI, 37, 244, January 13, 1960.

10. "Leipzig Presley Fans Jailed," The New York *Times*, November 3, 1959.

11. Handler, M. S., "Czechs Produce Beatnik Crop; Prague Cafes Flourish on Jazz," The New York *Times*, July 2, 1959.

12. Gruson, Sidney, "Poland: Waning, But Still Strong," *Ibid.*

13. *Ibid.*

14. "The Alcohol Problem in the Soviet Bloc," *East Europe*, VI, 12, December, 1956, 16-25.

15. *Trybuna Ludu*, April 10, 1957.

16. Lewis, Flora, "Warsaw: 'Just Having Some Fun at Last,'" in "Youth of the World: Nine Capitals Report," The New York *Times Magazine*, February 23, 1958, 16 ff.

17. Paucvo, Joseph, "Slovakia Under Communism," *Slovakia*, IX, 5, 30, June-December, 1959, 1-5.

18. "Red Satellites Admit Grave Youth Problems," New York *Herald Tribune*, June 9, 1957.

19. Although prostitution, according to the Soviet theory, is a capitalistic phenomenon, it also exists in the Soviet orbit; see, for instance: Kalb, Marvin L., "The Goings on in Gorki Park, Birds do it, Bees do it, Even Young Bolsheviki do it," *Esquire*, L, September 3, 1958, 54-56.

20. Roucek, Joseph S., "Tito's Educational Experiences and Experiments," *The Educational Forum*, XXI, January 2, 1957, 193-201; Roucek, "Reflections on My Visit to Titoland," *The Social Studies*, XLIX, December 7, 1958, 255-258.

21. Rosenthal, A. M., "Thievery Plagues Eastern Europe," The New York *Times*, February 3, 1959.

22. Reported in The New York *Times*, February 8, 1959.

23. Rosenthal, A. M., "Poland Attacks Economic Crimes," The New York *Times*, February 22, 1959.

24. *Rudé Právo*, January 11, 1959.

25. *East Europe*, VII, November 11, 1958, 45.

26. *Informativa Bucureztilor*, December 24, 1958.

27. Rosenthal, A. M., *op. cit.*

28. "Red Satellites Admit Grave Youth Problems," New York *Herald Tribune*, June 9, 1957.

29. "Crisis in the Youth Leagues," *op. cit.*, 35.

30. For the various efforts to handle the problem of juvenile delinquency in the United States, see: Roucek, Joseph S. (editor), *Juvenile Delinquency*, Philosophical Library, New York, 1958, Part III, "Evaluations of Attempted Solutions," 251-324, and the biographical references.

31. Pritt, D. N., "Juvenile Delinquency and the Makarenko Colony," *Bulgaria Today*, VI, November 22, 1957, 8-10.

32. "Bulgaria Deporting 'Hooligans' in Cities," The New York *Times*, February 9, 1958.

33. Underwood, Paul, "Czechs Resume Youth Brigades," The New York *Times*, February 13, 1959.

34. "Reds Reestablish Youth Work Units," *Christian Science Monitor*, March 19, 1959.

35. "Warsaw Worried by Young Rowdies," The New York *Times*, November 5, 1959.

36. "Institute for Young Delinquents," *Information Bulletin About Yugoslavia*, IV, 33, June, 1959, 3.

37. "Retrial Dooms Russian," The New York *Times*, October 23, 1958.

38. Frankel, Max, "Groups in Soviet Spur Discipline," The New York *Times*, November 25, 1958.

39. Maxwell, Anthony, "Juvenile Unemployment in the USSR," *Soviet Survey*, 28, October-December, 1958, 63-70; "Idle Youths Pose Moscow Problem," The New York *Times*, January 25, 1959.

40. Stevens, Edmund, "Soviet Revamp Criminal Law Code," *Christian Science Monitor*, December 30, 1958.

41. "Soviet to Set up Youth Tribunals," The New York *Times*, October 25, 1959.

Chapter II

SPECIAL CHARACTERISTICS OF SOVIET CRIMINAL LAW

In no other field of ideologies has the doctrinaire determinism of traditional Marxism been carried to such extreme defiance of reality as in the field of Soviet legal theory.

There are three great differences between Soviet law and the law of the "bourgeois" states, concerning not so much their content, as their validity. First, depending on the negation of the principle of the separation of powers, the law does not form a hierarchy in which the norms of the Constitutional law would come first, statutes second, and enactments of executive bodies third. It is true that the Constitution of the USSR (1936) made an attempt to introduce into the Soviet law the principle of hierarchy; it ordered a special procedure for constitutional amendments (Article 146), thus implicitly making the Constitution superior to other legal enactments, and declared that the legislative power of the USSR shall be exercised only by the Supreme Soviet of the Union (Article 32). But in practice these rules have not prevailed. The Constitution has been changed many times and new statutes passed in the forms departing from the Constitutional provisions with later ratification of these amendments and enactments by the Supreme Soviet.

The second difference is that, in the USSR, the law is not considered binding the officials in the same way as outside of it. In addition to the law, the officials are guided by "revolutionary expediency," which has been gradually identified with the directions of the Soviet government. The principle of revolutionary expediency was partly incorporated into the very Codes; the Civil Code, for instance, explicitly denies legal protection to the rights used against their socio-economic destination. The Criminal Code allowed the punishment of persons for offenses not foreseen by any law, but analogous to such ones. The Law on Judicial Organization declared that the courts must protect the acquisitions of the October Revolution and the interests of the State and the toilers. In consequence, the Soviet law is a system of rules applied so far as no reason arises to recur to other principles of solution, more compatible with the public interest as interpreted by the government.

Thirdly, the legal and constitutional system is not designed to protect individuals, but to advance the cause of the "workers," to serve as a weapon promoting the chimera of world communism. This is accomplished by propounding constitutional and legal fictions, and, at the same time, accomplishing these revolutionary aims by the operations of the Communist Party.

When dealing with the legality of the Soviet government and of pro-Soviet regimes behind the Iron Curtain, we must be clearly aware that we are confronted with the confusion created by semantics. A great deal of our thinking is muddled by the different varieties of "meaning of meaning" used by the pro-Soviet spokesmen and the Western observers. We especially fail in this respect to distinguish between words and the things that the words represent. We mistake abstract terms for living entities.

Differences in the ideological understanding of communist words and definitions are, furthermore, even more complicated by legal fictions. For, not only in Soviet Russia, but everywhere, legal formulas always tend to take on fictional character. Laws are a form of social rule emanating from political agencies; they are an authoritative canon of value laid down by the force of politically organized society. But the sociologist points out that it is less important to note the letter or the norms of law than to investigate what is going on behind the machinery of law-making and enforcing and to comprehend the various political interests which the law represents and seeks to serve.

Changes in the Soviet interpretations of political theory offer another dramatic illustration of the transformation in the official Soviet mentality, in inseparable association with the shifts in the reconsiderations of the ideological aspects of jurisprudence. From the original view of the proletarian state as a necessary evil destined to withering away after the revolutionary social transformation was accomplished, party doctrine has shifted to such a complete degree that it extols now the state as the highest form of social organization and a great creative force.[1] In fact, states Hook bitterly: "The development of Marxism as a movement has resulted in some peculiar paradoxes which make it difficult to retain traditional conceptual formulations. Where Marxism, as a movement, has triumphed, as in the Soviet Union, its socialist ideals have failed or have been betrayed; where it has failed, as a movement, as in the West, its ideals have made considerable headway. It seems as if history itself has been guilty of lese-Marxism."[2]

LAW ACCORDING TO MARXIAN THEORY

Law, as seen by Marx and Engels, as by the entire Marxian movement, is basically a part of the ideological superstructure rising above the material reality of the control of the means of production. Thus Engels claims: "The particular economic structure forms the real basis by which the entire superstructure of legal and political institutions and of the religious, philosophical and other production (Herstellungsweise) of every historical period must in the last analysis be explained."[3]

Hence law is not aiming to promote justice but is a means of dominance and a weapon of the exploiters using it for class interests. But both Marx and Engels did not treat legal questions in detail, possibly because they expected in the classless society of the future no need for law, and law is not even noted in the concluding statement of the *Communist Manifesto*.

According to Engels' famous formula, "the state withers away." Orthodox Marxism starts from the conception of the state as an instrument of class interest, demands the overthrow of the existing political order and expects that the dictatorship of the proletariat will follow and will make the state and its class divisions disappear. (But Stalin stepped in in the 1930's and proclaimed that the withering away of the state is prevented by a hostile capitalist world against which it must defend itself.)[4]

According to Lenin, the state is an organ for the rule of a certain class, whose interests cannot be reconciled with those of opposing classes; it is an instrument for the exploitation of oppressed classes. Bourgeois society supports its class domination by its system of criminal law, and thereby holds the exploited classes in obedience. After the revolution, the overwhelming majority of the population, consisting of the formerly oppressed classes of workers and peasants, ascends to the apex of the social pyramid, and then the law becomes an instrument for the struggle of these classes against the enemies of the working-people, the remnants of the bourgeois class and agents of the capitalist countries.

Up to about 1937, the chief legal authorities had followed Engels' general view that law was a tool in the hands of the class in control.

HISTORY OF CRIMINAL LAW IN USSR

The first principles of Soviet Criminal Code were issued on December 12, 1919, as Stuchka's Guiding Principles of Criminal Law of R.S.F.S.R.; it was a proclamation of general ideas influenced by Marxism.[5] In conformity with Lenin's doctrine of the withering away of the state and law, the first Soviet Constitution (1918) promised the abolition of state authority. This doctrine dominated Soviet jurisprudence until the '30's. The proletarian state was considered as a temporary instrument of oppression, necessary only for the period of organization of a socialist economy and the creation of a classless society. Nicholas Krylenko (1885-1938), Prosecutor and thereafter People's Commissar of Justice, denied the necessity for a Criminal Code and offered to leave a free choice of social defense measures to the OGPU.

456

Gobar, author of the Family Code, asserted that there was no need for the state to interfere in marital affairs and predicted that the family as a juridical entity would disappear. In fact, this earliest period is now called the period of legal nihilism, when Reissner, Heuchbarg and Stuchka ridiculed the law they had served in the Russia of old.

It was, however, a short-lived period. Then NEP was born and under NEP the regime again needed law. Soviet law was declared to be a combination of socialist and bourgeois law, concerned with private industry, private commerce, etc. Debates were held on such subjects as the interpretation and construction of bourgeois law in the Soviet state in such a way as would, nevertheless, serve the socialist idea. During this period Eugene Pashukanis was moving into the limelight. In line with the shift from determinism to voluntarism in the First Five Year Plan, the dynamic conception of the plan was conceived with which to contrast law. Pashukanis had to adapt to the new subjectivism in this respect and also in recognizing the increased emphasis on the role of the state in building socialism. In this respect, the Plan superseded the Law. Like Stalin, he asserted that NEP was a temporary phenomenon and that development would very quickly lead to the withering away of law (a theory which corresponded to Engels' famous words). He explained the appearance of the Civil Code in the socialist state as a temporary concession to private trade; likewise, the temporary re-establishment of the commodity of exchange and a monetary system. He predicted that the Civil Code would be replaced with regulations of a purely technical character as soon as a socialist economy would have been realized. According to this traditional Marxian theory, civil law was neglected and law schools threatened with extinction.[6] The concept of guilt and punishment was rejected as implying an un-Marxian notion of individual responsibility.

The Criminal Law of December 12, 1919, aimed to bring stability into the administration of criminal law. Most of these enactments were of a public law character, regulating relations between the state and the individual. But the whole field of legal relations between private individuals, with the sole exception of family and labor relations, remained outside the attention of the legislator. But the first Criminal Code, published in 1922, was a compromise between traditional criminological ideas and Marxian tenets. The Principles of Criminal Law of the USSR of October 31, 1924, was intended as a basis of criminal justice of the constituent Republics and forced a remaking of the Criminal Code of 1922. The basic innovations of the 1926 Criminal Code were: (1) the idea of "penalty" was replaced by that of "protective social measure;" (2) instead of "guilt" it was "social danger" which justified the application of the measures under (1); (3) "retaliation" was abolished, and "general" and "special preventions" were substituted as the aim of criminal justice with stress laid on the moral reformation of the criminal; (4) the principle that there can be no crime without a law characterizing human action as such (nullum crimen sine lege) was discarded by the admission of an analogous application of criminal repression to actions similar to those for which the application of protective social measures had been prescribed by the law; (5) if a person was socially dangerous in view of his connection with the criminal world or on account of his former activities he could be subjected to protective social measures even without having committed a crime.

Social danger thus became the leading principle of criminal justice. A socially dangerous act became "every action or omission directed against the Soviet order or violating the legal organization established by the workers' and peasants' authority for the period of transition towards the Communist order." Those committing socially dangerous acts or who were "dangerous" (under point 5) were subjected to protective social measures of a "judicially-improving" (correctional), medical or medico-pedagogical nature. (The severest measure, shooting, did not fall under these categories and was described as an exceptional measure for protecting the state of working people against the most serious kinds of crimes endangering fundamentals of the Soviet authority and of the Soviet order.)

The medical measures were compulsory medical treatment or hospital treatment connected with isolation. The medico-pedagogical measures, applied to youngsters under 18, were their handing over to the care of their parents, adopting parents, guardians, patrons or relatives, or their inclusion into special institutions for healing and education. These measures could be applied by the court at its own discretion if they considered the application of correctional measures not appropriate to the case in question or if they decided that the correctional measures should be supplemented by medical or medico-pedagogical measures.

The ordinary forms of repression were the judicially-improving measures, devised to prevent the perpetration of new crimes by the same person, or to deter other unreliable members of the community from committing crimes and to adapt those who had committed criminal actions to the "conditions of community life of the state of the working people."

In view of these aims, deprivation of liberty, imprisonment below one year, was abolished by the amendment of May 20, 1930 (in accordance with Ferri's maxim that the aim of education of the criminal to a decent life cannot be achieved by short periods of prison confinement). (The severest measure contained in the catalogue of measures for social protection—the pillorying as an enemy of the Working People with deprivation of the right of nationality and obligatory expulsion from the USSR, without any time limit, did not belong to the pattern of measure aiming to educate criminals.)

Others steps of the same kind were: deprivation of liberty in "improvement and labor camps" in far-off areas of the USSR; deprivation of liberty in general prisons; correctional working assignments without deprivation of liberty, (usually applied for minor infringements of the law, leaving the criminal at his working post but cutting down his pay). In regard to the deprivation of liberty, terms of imprisonment up to 3 years were served in prisons, longer terms in camps. The maximum term of 10 years could be extended to 25 years for espionage, wrecking and diversion (Amendment of May 20, 1938).

Other measures of social protection, in addition, were deprivation of political and certain civil rights; expulsion from the

USSR for a certain time; dismissal from employment and an order prohibiting the convicted persons from following a certain kind of employment; prohibition from occupying certain positions, from following certain professions; expression of communal contempt; confiscation of all or parts of property; monetary fine; obligation to make good the damage inflicted upon a person; warning.

Criminal acts were divided into two categories: (1) those directed against the basis of the Soviet order and considered, consequently, most dangerous; and (2) all other crimes. There was quite a differentiation between crimes against the State and State interests and those against private persons. Thus theft committed against State property by a person entrusted with it could be penalized by deprivation of liberty for up to 5 years, and there were special decrees allowing the death penalty for the thieves of socialist property (while for premeditated murder of a private person the penalty was from one to ten years deprivation of liberty). For more serious crimes against the State, the death penalty was provided for.

THE RISE OF VISHINSKY

In the early 1930's, Pashukanis was something of a god in the field of the science of law. But suddenly something unexpected happened. In the 1930's, the elite of the Soviet regime realized that the withering away of law was a theory detrimental to them, that law had then become a necessity, "although it was never officially explained why it was actually a necessity." [7] (A possible explanation is that, according to the Marxist theory, law is a function of the class society and the USSR had already seen a new social class stratification, but Pashukanis proceeded from the idea of a coming classless society in which law would wither away.)

Pashukanis did not want to vacate his position and was accused by the charges of his erstwhile assistant, Vishinsky—and suddenly disappeared.[8]

Andrei Yannuarievich Vishinsky (1883-1953), who was born of bourgeois parents in Odessa, ended his law education to enter revolutionary activities and spent years in Czarist prisons or in exile; but he was a Menshevik (not a Bolshevik) until he joined the Communist Party belatedly in 1920. He soon gained recognition as a legal orator and as Professor of Jurisprudence at Moscow University. As far as the outside world was concerned, he first gained fame in the 1930's when he was government prosecutor in the purge trials that brought death or banishment to members of the Trotsky faction. After the disappearance of Pashukanis, Vishinsky proclaimed the "new" definition of law—which consisted of a return to the theory of Ihering (a prominent German utilitarian lawyer, who dominated the minds in the 1880's and 1890's), plus a superfluous appendage from Marxist theory. According to Vishinsky (whose *Law of the Soviet State* was published in English translation in 1949) law is an aggregate of regulations protected by the state and representing the will of the ruling class. (States Timasheff: "The first part could be identified with Ihering, who had influenced Korkunov and under whom most Russian lawyers have studied. . . . The second part is an appendage. . . .")

This satisfied the rulers in the Kremlin, since they were reassured that they represented the laborers, peasants, and the working intelligentsia. The notion of the withering away of law was denounced as "wrecking" and Stalin stated, in his Report on the Draft Constitution of 1936: "We need stability of laws now more than ever," developing further his earlier pronouncement that "History demonstrates that under socialism . . . law is raised to the highest level of development." Conventional law codes and pre-revolutionary law professors were restored to their places; the concepts of "crime," "punishment," and of individual guilt were readapted.

Yet it cannot be stressed strongly enough that the new Soviet legalism has little, or nothing, to do with the protection of civil rights in the Western political sense. Soviet law left a large and elastic area where "enemies of the state" were dealt with outside the law and the courts.

During World War II, a certain lenience was shown in the sphere of law (as well as in other spheres). Publications appeared wherein the authors openly extolled Anglo-Saxon law, propounding that Soviet legal procedure is not inferior to Anglo-American; it was also maintained that the German idealistic philosophers, in particular, Hegel, exerted a progressive influence on the development of the theory of law (Hegel!—not Marx!). The contributions of that period tried to avoid philosophical discussions.

The assertion by the late Andrei Zhdanov in his famous speech, to the Writers of Leningrad in August, 1946, of the moral and cultural superiority of the people of Soviet Russia to those of the "bourgeois" world,[9] put a sudden end to all this, and a round of censoring of everything that had been previously created took place; and Vishinsky was removed from his post as editor of *The Soviet State And Law*. An utter confusion in the juristic circles followed, and in 1949 the Presidium of the Academy of Science of the USSR found the works and textbooks of such learned jurists as Lyubimov, Polyansky, Trainin, Levin, Lisovsky, Vail, and others, methodologically defective and harmful; this was explained by the fact that "the various sections of the Institute (of Law) were not assured of leaders with a command of Marxist-Leninist methodology."[10] The purge which had been carried out in the opinion of the Presidium, had been inadequate.

STALIN'S PERIOD

A sudden ray of light which might lead the Soviet jurists out of their ideological confusion was suddenly thrown on the problem by Stalin's article dealing with linguistics.[11] It would seem that linguistic problems would not concern jurists, but jurists were forced to transcribe the linguistic music into a juridical key.

Shortly, until Stalin's 1950 statement, the official line, enunciated by Academician N.Y. Marr, that language had been part of the superstructure derived from the economic basis, and subject to the same process of dialectical development. Stalin declared that, on the contrary, language was an independent phenomenon, not to be confused with the superstructure. Party spokesmen, quickly taking the cue, declared that the Russian language was the international language of the age of socialism. Today language in the USSR is not merely a philological form but is also a train of thought; in other words, thought, too, is independent of superstructure. Then it may be asserted that law plays an active role and is not unilaterally defined by the class structure of society. Moreover, Stalin casually mentioned that linguistics should develop by the comparative method, which N.Y. Marr, whom Stalin had thrown out, denied. But this meant the use of universal concepts, that there is a universal concept of bourgeois and socialist law which had been denied after Vishinsky's influence in the late 1930's.

As a result of Stalin's article, a ruthless wave of criticism and mutual recriminations appeared on the legal front; particularly sharp criticism was directed against the Editorial board of the journal *Sovetskoye Gosudarstvo I Pravo.*

On the eve of the 12th Party Congress (October, 1952), another of Stalin's works appeared: *Economic Problems Of Socialism In The USSR;* it gave a new impetus on the whole front of learning, particularly on the legal sector. From that time, the jurists were directed to appreciate Stalin's "new work of genius on economics," and to stress "the leading role of the Communist Party in the Soviet state system and in the cause of strengthening socialist legality." Roughly, this was Stalin's need to rehabilitate the law as one instrument for his policies, the strengthening of his goal for economic and administrative planning.[12]

PURGES AND BRAIN-WASHING

One of the most widely publicized efforts of Stalin's regime were his periodic purges, which in terms of judicial processes, were correct, since the regular court procedures were, for the sake of public consumption, featured. But even less doubtful, legally, were the numerous "confessions" of guilt which implicated individuals in alleged conspiracies to assassinate Stalin and otherwise overthrow Stalin's regime with foreign assistance. The method of gaining "confessions" was to use extreme and especially sustained psychological pressure and induce some form of admission of guilt from the prisoners and, in addition, to induce them to list many other persons as implicated in the alleged plots. Noteworthy was the Great Purge when the public trial of Zinoviev, Kamenev and some 14 others in August, 1936 introduced two years of terror unique in modern history.[13]

JURISPRUDENCE UNDER KHRUSHCHEV

Soon after Stalin's death, Khrushchev's spokesmen started ridiculing the very theory that had been gospel under Stalin and that had served as the theoretical justification for the increasingly repressive nature of Soviet law and of the Soviet security police.

Roughly speaking, in their efforts to establish a distinction between their own and the "bourgeois" theory of law, the Soviet jurists have been systematically denouncing traditional interpretations of the law as "unscientific." In doing so, however, they have been getting into many difficulties. The most important one comes from their vague concept of the state, or to put it more clearly, from the fact that the Soviet state is something different from what it ought to be or what it pretends to be. Some of the basic questions around the nature of the Soviet state are: Is the State an economic or a political phenomenon? Is the Union of the Soviet Socialist Republics a dictatorship of the proletariat or a People's Democracy? Is that State still a class State or a classless community? Is the Soviet state withering away according to Engels' prediction? On these questions, points out Kelsen, depends the answer concerning the nature of the Soviet law.[14] Thus, law may be an expression of property relations or of social relations in general. It may be an expression of the ideology of socialism or of an "official recognition of fact" (Marx);

it may be the emanation of the proletarian class or of the Soviet state; it may be a structural factor of socialism or belong to its superstructure.

Soviet jurists have indeed a difficult task to find correct answers to all these alternatives. Correctness here does not mean a scientific correctness. It means rather the adoption of a thesis which is identical with or very close to the opinion of the Politburo. Because everything in the USSR is ruled according to the principle of dialectics, it happens frequently that the truth of today is a lie tomorrow. Then, there is nothing else to do but purge the deviated theorist and to replace him by a new one, more flexible, more docile and understanding, and "better" the headman of the ideological machinery.

The contemporary efforts to systematize the criminal law according to the dominant ideology of Khrushchev's group received their expression in the New Criminal Code of 1958.

THE NEW CRIMINAL CODE

The long-discussed revision of the Soviet criminal law and judicial procedure was enacted into a law at the December 22-25, 1958, session of the USSR Supreme Soviet.[15]

The drafts of new All-Union codes of Criminal Law and Procedure were ready for publication by the time of the 20th Party Congress in February, 1956. But they were not published because they had been, meanwhile, overtaken by a new trend in Soviet policy—the extension of the powers of the republics. In the legal sphere this extension included the abolition of the All-Union Ministry of Justice and the transfer of its functions to the Republican ministries (May, 1956) and (February, 1957) some limitation of the powers of the All-Union Supreme Court, with consequent extension of the powers of the Republican Supreme Courts; and also an amendment of Article 14 of the Constitution in such a way as to give the Union Republics the right to promulgate their own codes of both criminal and civil law and procedure, while reserving to the Union only the right to lay down general principles for the guidance of the Republics.

In 1958, after years of drafting and months of debate, a start was finally made toward the enactment of the long-promised All-Union codes of law, aimed at the restoration of "socialist legality." A month before the 21st Congress met in 1958, the Supreme Soviet enacted a series of statutes, including Fundamentals of Criminal Law, new laws on liability for state crimes and military crimes, Fundamentals of Criminal Justice, and a new Judiciary Act.[16]

On Christmas Day 1958, eight laws were passed by the Supreme Soviet.[17] It should be noted that, apart from the Law on crimes against the state, this legislation lays down only basic principles which must be followed and implemented by the Union Republics in their own codes of criminal law and procedure. (However, some of the more important provisions of the new All-Union legislation have already been made obligatory for the Republics, even pending the completion of their new codes, by a Decree of the Presidium of the Supreme Soviet of February 14, 1959).

The changes enacted by the new laws can be divided into substantive and procedural.

The substantive changes are mainly five. (1) The minimum age of criminal responsibility has been raised from 14 to 16, except in the case of the gravest crimes, where it has been raised from 12 to 14. (2) Except where the death penalty is prescribed (hitherto for treason, terrorism, and banditry), the maximum sentence of imprisonment has been reduced from 25 to 15 years. (3) Loss of franchise and expulsion from the USSR are no longer among the penalties prescribed for certain crimes. (4) The nature of an accomplice and of an accessory before or after the fact is defined with greater precision than hitherto. (This reflects a revulsion against the abuse of the application of the conception of accessory in order to implicate as wide a range of persons as possible, practised for terrorization purposes by Vishinsky). (5) Serious political crimes, hitherto covered by the almost unlimited omnibus Article 58 of the RSFSR Criminal Code (originally drafted by Lenin) were defined with some attempt at precision.

Most important is the introduction of the term "intentionally" into the definition of treason, thus excluding from the definition the numerous cases of mere negligence or offenses without any political content which had hitherto been prosecuted under Article 58. But the new law is in other respects little less severe than the old. For instance, anti-Soviet propaganda can incur a sentence of 7 years imprisonment; refusal by a Soviet citizen to return to the USSR from abroad is now treason and carries the death penalty. On the other hand, no penalties are any longer prescribed against members of the family of a citizen who flees abroad if they were not aware of his intentions.

The procedural changes reflect, much more than the substantive changes, the objections of many lawyers against the widespread flouting of the law, and the position of privilege above the law which the party has arrogated to itself. It is true that Party policy is in theory a kind of general will, and the idea that an individual could ask protection against this will is theoretically inadmissible in the USSR. But a number of lawyers tried to propose safeguards which might handicap arbitrary action against the courts. Only a sort of compromise is found in the new laws. For instance, in regard to the extraction of confession, the new law provides that no particular form of evidence should have any greater weight than any other. In Soviet practise (as in many continental systems, and in pre-revolutionary Russia), the preliminary examination precedes the indictment and the trial and takes the place of the open presentation of the case against an accused; now defense counsel can be present at the preliminary examination of a juvenile and apparently also in the case of adults (although the law is not clear on this point) with the permission of the examining officer. Important is also the provision that the burden of proving the guilt of an accused lies upon the prosecution.

The second group of procedural enactments is a series of provisions designed to safeguard the accused during the preliminary stage of examination before the indictment is framed, or the decision taken to drop the prosecution, if the evidence should prove insufficient.[18] But none of these safeguards are new in substance.

Hence we must be especially interested in the third group of procedural provisions which are new. The much criticized principle of "analogy" has been abolished. The preliminary examinations of accused conducted by the investigators of the security organs, the KGB are now subject to the supervision of the procurators. (The KGB investigators were placed under the procurator's supervision by the terms of the statute on the procurators of May 24, 1955, but it also appears that the KGB has its own, unpublished, powers). The right of defense counsel have been extended. The courts have been given more discretionary power to be lenient; but the rules for the remission of sentences have been tightened up. A new Decree of the Council of Ministers of the USSR has also tightened up the general disciplinary administration of the penal colonies (as the former camps have now been renamed).

Liberalizing features of the Law include the dropping of the doctrine of analogy, which means that a person may now be tried for an act constituting a crime under the provisions of law in effect at the time of commission rather than, as in the past, for an act not specifically prohibited by law but analogous to one which was. The maximum term of imprisonment was lowered, but the death penalty was broadened to apply to banditry and terrorism. Terms for expunging the record of conviction were considerably liberalized. The death sentence is applied in cases of terrorist acts when the foreign or Soviet official attacked dies as a result of wounds received. (As has been the case since the early 1920's, the death penalty is not listed with the standard punishments but as an extraordinary one which will allegedly be abolished at some time in the future.)

Exile (*ssylka*), expulsion *(vvsylka)*, corrective labor without imprisonment (up to one year), the loss of some rights (the holding of certain offices and possession of honors and medals), fines, and public censure are retained as penalties. Cases in which confiscation of property may be invoked are now limited to serious mercenary crimes (large-scale theft and the like) as well as state crimes—the latter defined by All-Union law.

Being declared as "enemy of the toilers" (*trudvaschchikhsva*), coupled with loss of citizenship and exile outside the USSR, was eliminated as a punishment. (This penalty has been applied only seldom since 1930, although arbitrary use of the latter term by Stalin was denounced by Khrushchev at the 20th Party Congress in his secret speech, and although he had himself used it in his report to the Congress earlier. He also used the term in referring to Beriya in his speech at the December Central Committee plenum and Suslov used it in his November 6, 1956 speech as broadcast.)

In conformity with the contemporary campaign against drunkenness, Article 12 of the Principles of Criminal Law states that a person who executes a crime while in a state of drunkenness is not freed from criminal responsibility.

The terms for parole have been liberalized, with persons being eligible for parole after serving one-half of their sentence (instead of the former two-thirds). Those convicted of "especially serious crimes" must serve two-thirds of the penalty before being eligible for parole, and repeaters are not eligible for parole.

The minimum age for criminal responsibility has been raised from 14 to 16, except for major crimes (murder, bodily injury, rape, malicious hooliganism, etc.) where minors are responsible from age 14 (formerly 12). Persons under 18 are eligible for parole after serving only one-third of their sentence, and, in general, may receive lighter punishments.

State Crimes. Of special interest among the newly ratified laws was the one dealing with legal responsibility for state crimes (which replaced the "Decree on State Crimes," ratified in 1927). The new Code comprises of 26 articles, of which the first 10 are formed into a special section, headed "Particularly Dangerous State Crimes." These are: (1) treason; (2) espionage; (3) acts of terrorism; (4) acts of terrorism against representatives of a foreign power; (5) diversionary activity; (6) wrecking; (7) anti-Soviet propaganda and agitation; (8) war-mongering; (9) organizational activities aimed at committing particularly dangerous state crimes and participation in an anti-Soviet organization; and (10) particularly dangerous state crimes carried out against the workers of another state.

Article 1, covering treason, is extremely broad: "Treason, that is, an act deliberately committed by a citizen of the USSR to the detriment of the state independence, territorial integrity, and military power of the USSR, desertion to the enemy, espionage, the passing of state or military secrets to a foreign power, flight abroad or refusal to return to the USSR from abroad, the rendering of aid to a foreign power engaged in activities hostile to the USSR, and likewise plotting with the aim of seizing power are punishable by imprisonment for a period of 10 to 15 years with confiscation of property or by the death penalty with confiscation of property."

Thus, today, not only flight abroad and the rendering of assistance to a foreign state are classified as particularly serious crimes, but also refusal to return to the Soviet Union. The extension of the term "treason", as found in the new law, means that there is no need now for the principle of analogy. Hence, the abolition of this principle, as seen in the new Fundamentals of Criminal Legislation, has lost any meaning. The principle of analogy is thus replaced by an increase in the various types of acts qualified as treason. A liberalization step has been taken by defining treason as an intentional act; formerly the act could be either intentional or unintentional.

The pattern of stiffer penalties for more serious crimes is, however, clear in the new law. Thus, the punishment for espionage under the old law was not less than three years or death, but it is now from 7 to 15 years, with confiscation of property or death with confiscation of property. But the divulging of state secrets without evidence of treason or espionage is more lightly punished than under the 1947 law, and punishments are eased for those who inadvertently reveal or who accidentally lose such secrets; the punishment for treason is imprisonment for 10-15 years, or the death penalty, involving in both cases confiscation of property (while the earlier law provided the death penalty or 10 years imprisonment, both with confiscation of property).

The inclusion of espionage by a Soviet citizen merely legalizes a situation existing since the end of the 1930's. Espionage was regarded as an act of treason and punished in accordance with Article 1 (1-20). The main difference of Article 2 on "espionage" in the new law from Article 6 on it in the earlier laws is that the person committing an act of espionage may be only a foreigner or a stateless person. This principle is a legalization of the tendency to divide into two categories the person engaged in espionage: a Soviet citizen is brought to trial for treason, a non-Soviet citizen for espionage. The increased sentences for espionage are proof that the Soviet leaders are more worried about this problem than they were in 1927.

Certain other crimes are also more seriously regarded than previously. The maximum punishment for banditry has been increased to death. Speculators on the value of currency and valuable papers (e.g. bonds) are also subjected to stiffer penalties.

Article 8 is also very broad, and so formulated as to be capable of almost any interpretation: "War-mongering, in whatever form it is carried out, is punishable by imprisonment for a period of from three to eight years." The wording of Article 7, which covers anti-Soviet propaganda, is also very loose, including the dissemination of "slanderous fabrications derogatory to the Soviet state and social structure, and likewise the dissemination, manufacture, or storage of such literature with the same aims." "Taken together with Article 9, which covers participation in anti-Soviet organizations, a term which is particularly elastic, it shows that there certainly can be no talk of extending the presently niggardly freedoms of the average Soviet citizen." [19]

War propaganda against the USSR has, in fact, always been regarded as treason, and is dealt with by the corresponding articles of the new law, as is war propaganda against the USSR by a foreigner. The introduction of these sections into the law, the Kremlin rulers have shown their concern at the analysis of the situation within the USSR which West European radio stations transmit to the Soviet Union, the materials criticizing the system, and the very existence of anti-Soviet organizations and the need of the government to have the necessary legal means at hand should a campaign of force become inevitable to enforce its plans to embark on a new seven-year period of industrialization.

Of the 10 articles in the first section, only one—war propaganda—does not come under the jurisdiction of the Committee of State Security (KGB); in the second section of the law only the article on mass disorders fall within the purview of the KGB.

One of the most misleading sections here is the second part of the law, entitled "Other State Crimes," consisting of 16 articles, which deal with various types of crimes. Here, Article 11, on "The Violation of National and Racial Rights," deals with propaganda and agitation rousing national or racial hostility or discord, and points out that the open or indirect restrictions of such rights or the granting of privileges to any one national or racial group or individuals from such a group now constitutes a crime. Yet the historical record shows how such legislation (Article 21 (2) of the "Laws on State Crimes" of 1927 has been persistently and openly violated. The persistent outbreaks of anti-Semitism are rooted in the official appreciation of Judaism as a reactionary religious force. (Lenin, himself, described the demand for Jewish national culture as a "slogan of rabbis and bourgeois," meaning that he attached to it no predominantly religious significance). Judaism is renounced as a "counter-revolutionary force," and considerable efforts have been made to disintegrate the Jewish community life through the structural reforms of the Soviet regime, the increasing concentration of Soviet Jewry in the big cities, discrimination against Jews in Soviet life, and the announced anti-Jewish policy in 1952. Or, it is astounding how many names and histories of peoples have been erased from the record of the USSR, in spite of Article 17 of the 1936 Constitution: "The right freely to secede from the USSR is reserved to every Union Republic" and Article 18: "The territory of a Union Republic may not be altered without its consent." Yet, on June 25, 1946, the Soviet press published news in the form of a decree of the Supreme Soviet: "Liquidation of the Chechun-Ingusetian Republic and Deportation of its Population." The actual liquidation had been carried out more than two years before publication of the Supreme Soviet decree, which was thus in the full sense a post-mortem; the accusation: pro-German collaboration. In addition to the Balkarians and the

Karachayevs, two Caucasian tribes, other liquidated minorities have been the Volga Germans, Crimea Tartars, Kalmyks, plus a score of smaller groups. The "Russification" policies have also continued.[20]

Articles 12 and 13 treat "The Divulgences of State Secrets and Loss of Documents Containing State Secrets." These articles were not found in the earlier law, but for a number of years, extraordinary laws had been in force on responsibility for the divulgence of state secrets and loss of documents containing state secrets.

Article 14 on "Armed Robbery" corresponds to Article 17 of the old law, differing only in that it excludes the "stopping of trains, destruction of railroad tracks, and other means of communication." This can be explained by the fact that the term "armed robbery," as defined in the 1927 law, was taken over from earlier legislative acts issued in the first half of the 1920's, when armed bandits were still active. Article 14 on "Smuggling" is punishable by imprisonment for from 3 to 10 years, with confiscation of property. Article 16 covers "Rioting" (and corresponds to Article 16 of the former law). The death penalty has been abolished, but the maximum and minimum sentences have been increased, 15 years as opposed to 10, and from 2 years, as opposed to not more than 2 years, (the first applying to the organizers and active participants in disorders, and the latter to other participants).

Article 17 on "Refusal to be Drafted for Active Military Service" excludes in the new version refusal to enlist for religious reasons, when defining qualified refusal. Unqualified refusal has a sentence from one to three years. Article 18, "Refusal to be Drafted During Mobilization," is not found in the earlier law; the same applies to Article 20, "The Illegal Departure from and Entry into the USSR" (with the sentences from one to 3 years). Article 21 on "Infringement of International Flight Regulations" is the same as Article 17 (5) of the former law; and so is Article 26, "Failure to Report State Crimes," which had been Articles 12 and 23 of the earlier law.

The Principles of Criminal Procedure. The new Principles

473

now pay more attention to individual rights of the defendant, but the legal rights of the various organs of investigation remain. However a number of new or redefined provisions are included.

Only the courts may decide guilt or pronounce judgment in criminal cases, a provision designed to emphasize the elimination of administrative justice. Though the defendant is not presumed innocent, the prosecutor has the burden of demonstrating the guilt of the accused and not the defendant his innocence. The prisoner may be held normally only two months, but with the approval of proper authorities this may be extended up to a maximum of 9 months; formerly the legal limit was 2 months, with a month's extension permissible, but the restriction was frequently disregarded. The enactment of a longer limit is in itself recognition of frequent abuse of the law in the past. Formerly legal advice was not permitted until after the case reached the court.

Pre-trial investigation is still handled by three organs—the Militia of the Ministry of Internal Affairs (MVD), the Prosecutor's Office, and, for certain state crimes, the Committee of State Security (KGB).

The state crimes handled by the KGB are: treason, espionage, terrorism, diversion, wrecking, anti-Soviet agitation and propaganda, organizational activity aiming at the overthrow of the state and participation in an anti-Soviet organization, especially dangerous state crimes against other workers' states, and mass disorders.

There were many abuses especially in pre-trial procedure in the past and time will tell whether "socialist legality" will be enforced, particularly by the state prosecutor's office, especially since the legal rights of the various organs of investigation remain what they had been previously.

Organization of the Judiciary. The Principles of Law about the Judicial System of the USSR, Union and Autonomous Republics, represents primarily a needed consolidation of old laws and amendments. Since the abolition of various special courts, only the regular courts and the military courts remain. (Legally the military tribunals are considered a part of the regular court system of the USSR). City courts, long operative in Moscow and Leningrad, are now legally recognized. District (*uchastkovvi*) courts, already abolished in Armenia, are to be replaced by a single court in the *raion,* thus reducing the number of people's courts at the lowest level.

Evaluation. All in all, the criminal code is characterized by extreme vagueness both in its definition of offenses and in the sentences which it prescribes for them; and there is a similar failure to prescribe which levels of the system shall be competent to deal with which offenses. Even the most serious offenses by Soviet standards are all placed within the competence of the regional and equivalent courts. The procurators decide at which level it is convenient to bring any particular case (though it rests with the court to accept or refuse it). The vagueness in the other respects gives the courts wide discretion in which they are expected to be guided by analogy from similar classes of offenses in a way which cannot be found in any other judicial system, by regard for the whole motivation and record of the accused rather than the mere fact of commission, and by consideration of public educative effect in view of the administration's concern, for the time being, to suppress particular forms of conduct and inculcate particular attitudes.

While there are important changes, in substance, and more exact definitions of some legal procedures, the basic principles of criminal law and procedure and the statute on state crimes retain most of the previous provisions which could be applied to political deviation or unorthodoxy and other areas in which abuses are possible.

The educative and exemplary purpose of court proceedings—to make policies clear to the citizens—is shown in the reporting of them in the press. (Civil proceedings, having no exemplary quality, are not reported.) The great show trials of the late 1930's and, less spectacularly, since then, with their public confessions of the improbable, can only be explained by similar considerations. The prosecuting and judicial authorities are always ready to impute to an accused person theological consequences, by Marxian analysis, of his actions—even if he had himself never envisaged them. The motives which are stressed are those which induced him to the act with which he is charged. A tendency towards acts damaging to the socialist order can be revealed by acts not themselves amounting to definable offenses.

Legally, the Soviet system of justice has been liberalized. But a very great deal will depend on the spirit in which the liberalizing provisions will be carried out. The way in which even the highest-sounding provisions of the Soviet Constitution—called by the late Andrei Vishinsky "the most democratic constitution in the world"—have been trampled on by the Kremlin dictatorship is notorious. But in addition to the danger that verbal changes in Soviet law will be dead letters in practice, there are really very few apparent innovations in the new penal code.

The main difficulty is that the Soviet penal code still regards offenses against individuals by individuals as what Vishinsky (in *The Law of the Soviet State*) calls "crimes inherited from the capitalist social order," and hence of secondary importance. The Soviet statute on the judicial system, quoted by Vishinsky, says: "The task of justice in the USSR is to defend from encroachment of every character: (a) the social and state organization of the USSR . . . and the socialist system of economy and socialist property."

This means that the courts are primarily defenders of the existing order—which now means the Soviet bureaucracy and its masters of masters in the Kremlin. Moreover, whatever protection civilian courts may throw around an accused person can be wholly taken away in the military courts, which the new code characterizes as an integral part of the whole judicial system.

Under such circumstances, provisions reducing penalties, providing against "crimes by analogy"—using the law most resembling the offense charged if that offense is not statutorily criminal—and the like, appear to mean very little.

Apparently, the influence of the Soviet officials favoring summary secret procedures in the interest only of party and state still is going strong, and is shown by the fact "that even today there is no complete record of the abolition of the dreaded special conferences of the security agencies which in Stalin's day had doomed uncounted victims to deportation, prison, or summary execution." [21] A law doing away with these special conferences was enacted in the summer of 1953, it never has been abolished. (According to Wohl, "In April, 1956, a Russian-speaking French parliamentary delegation was shown the text of this law by the President of the Supreme Court of the Soviet Union, but was not given a copy.")

The basic importance of the new Code is the trend toward liberalization in its reinstatement of legality and due process, and its restoration to the courts the sole authority to interpret and apply the law, and to judge and punish offenders. While the new law does not introduce habeas corpus or exclude self-incrimination, it does provide new guarantees for the protection of the individual defendant more in line with Western legal concepts. But the rights of the accused remain limited by Western standards.

Capital punishment is retained for such crimes as high treason, espionage, sabotage, terrorist acts, banditry, and first degree murder, but no longer applies to embezzlement, corruption, and speculation. The law deals more harshly with a new group—the professional or habitual criminal, who will now draw heavier sentences than first offenders, and cannot be released on parole until he has served his full sentence.

New to some extent is the stress on persuasion as a means of preventing crimes. In practice this approach is tied to measures against juvenile delinquency which has become increasingly important in recent years; theoretically, it is presented as a preview of what the "good society" will be like, as Khrushchev now defines communism.

Just as the law of 1953, the new code makes much of the high degree of economic, social, and cultural development which has been reached and which should enable the public to prevent offenses. The philosophy of Soviet Penal Law is "more than ever the protection of the state and of society—not vengeance. Concern with reform of the individual offender, on the other hand, seems to be less in evidence than in the 1920's when the old penal code was adopted." [22]

This was clearly formulated by Premier Dmitri Polyansky of the Russian Republic, who reported to the Supreme Soviet in his capacity of Chairman of the Committee on Draft Legislation, "as opposed to the once widely accepted mistaken formula according to which we moved ahead, class struggle within the country be intensified and in this connection repression had to be strengthened and extended." This draft, he continued, "thus proceeds from the assumption that successes of socialist construction, improved material and cultural conditions of the workers, growth of their social conscience, render possible, along with the strict fight against dangerous criminals, an ever-increasing resort to measures of an educational nature." [23]

It might be interesting to remember that the main exponent of the theory which Polyansky thus discarded was a long-time chief public prosecutor Andrei Y. Vishinsky. In the introductory chapter of his *The Law of the Soviet State*, Vishinsky wrote: "The growth of the might of the Soviet will intensify the resistance of the last remnants of the dying classes . . . they will pass from one form of attack to other and fiercer forms of attack." This approach dominated the last two decades of the Stalin era.

Politically, the promulgation of the law on state crimes is the expression of the struggle for power still going on in the Kremlin. Although Khrushchev appears to be firmly in the saddle, the constant reference to the hostile acts of the Molotov-Kaganovich-Malenkov-Shepilov group, the degradation of Bulganin, and the removal of Serov from the headship of the Committee for State Security (and his replacement by A. N. Shelpin, a former first secretary of the Komsomol Central Committee and a trusted follower of Khrushchev) show that the present dictator is trying to consolidate his position. At the same time, in spite of the surface liberalizing measures, the new law grants the legal way to use the methods which might be considered necessary for the stamping out of any organized or potential opposition to the Party control.

PARTY CONTROL

All indications are that the party stresses extra-legal activities as an effective method of dealing with crime. At the 21st Party

Congress, Khrushchev was emphatic that "communal" action, both for the prevention of crime and for its punishment, must gradually take the place of the regular courts and of the police where the accused has committed an offense foreseen by the criminal law. Yet in some respects, actual Soviet practice contradicts this provision. There are innumerable provisions in Soviet law for the levying of small fines by purely administrative decision—and they remain in force.

More serious are the so-called "anti-parasite" laws.

"Parasite Laws." Among the astonishing features of the Soviet system are the so-called "parasite" laws in several republics. Every factory has its own "soviet," a self-governing body through which the workers express their desires and needs. The members are selected by their fellows; if a committee decides that a certain person within its jurisdiction is a parasite, that he is not earning his way or working as hard as he should, it can banish him to another territory within its boundaries. There is no appeal to any judicial tribunal.

Since in application the mustering of the necessary number of obedient citizens for these acts of "folk justice" can easily be ensured by the local party organs, it is evident that these laws, with their wide discretionary character (and the nature of "parasitism" is not defined), which allow the banishment for a period of 2 to 5 years, with the addition of enforced work, have in effect conferred upon the party the power of inflicting administrative exile upon anyone whom it regards as undesirable. (While drafts of the "anti-parasitic" laws have been published in all republics, they have so far been passed into law in only 8 republics—the last being Kirgizia, on January 15, 1959, after the coming into force of the new basic principles of the new criminal code.)

THE JUDICIAL SYSTEM

Since there are constitutional provisions in the USSR for at least theoretical protections for the citizens in the administration of justice, and since the government claims that it respects these provisions in non-political cases, it might be worthwhile to describe the regular process of justice.[24]

The 1936 Constitution has provisions guaranteeing the inviolability of the person, providing for arrest only upon the decision of a court or with the consent of a prosecutor, establishing public trials unless otherwise specified by law and the right to a defense counsel, and providing for people's assessors (with exceptions provided in law) and an independent judiciary subject only to the law. Each governmental level has a judicial body corresponding to that level and elected by the Soviet thereof, except for the people's courts at the lowest levels, to which both the professional judge and the two people's assessors are popularly elected. The various courts comprise a judicial hierarchy from the people's courts, at the bottom, through intermediate courts, republic supreme courts, to the Supreme Court of the USSR. The Supreme Court supervises the judicial hierarchy. Higher courts exercise an original jurisdiction depending upon the seriousness of the case and an appellate or review jurisdiction over the lower courts.

Although judicial independence is guaranteed by Article 112 of the Federal Constitution, actually the judges must serve the dictates of the Party, thanks to the manner of the judge's election and the short term of his office and the possibility of being recalled at any time during that term. (In February, 1955, for instance, 6 judges of the Federal Supreme Court were dismissed by decrees of the Supreme Soviet.) The press periodically reports on unsatisfactory verdicts, and often prints implied threats for excessive leniency by the judges in the treatment of offenders. Periodically, the Ministry of Justice instructs judges to consider press comments and recommends that they meet with press representatives to discuss complaints.[25]

Soviet court procedure has some interesting features. As in the United States, a defendant can appeal his conviction. But so can the prosecutor; if he feels that the sentence is not harsh enough, he can appeal to get it increased. He can even appeal an ordinary acquittal.

Minors and incompetents have the right to summon a lawyer

as soon as they are detained. Minors get lighter sentences than adults, although there is no formal, effective probational or psychiatric machinery for them. Some basic moral violations are not even crimes in Russia. Incest is not regarded as a crime but as a family affair, nor is prostitution a crime unless the prostitute infects her customers. (Prostitution is not officially recognized in Russia.) On the other hand, rape is severely punished. A husband can be convicted of raping his wife. So can a man who marries a woman only to gratify his desires and then divorces her. Abortion, long prohibited, has recently been legalized on the basis of mother and child welfare, though it must be performed by a doctor in a hospital. Divorce, once as simple a matter as marriage, is now difficult to obtain, for the Kremlin has finally recognized the importance of the family.

Two practices of the Soviet system of criminal law are worthy of consideration. One is the requirement that the accused must be shown all the evidence against him before the start of the trial. Another is the combining of civil and criminal trials that deal with the same incident. In Soviet procedure both cases may, at the request of the injured party, be disposed of at one time by one court.

There is no jury system at all. Instead there are two "assessors," laymen, who, however, have no legal training. They sit with the professional judge and "protect the rights of the parties." At the conclusion of the trial the three discuss the evidence and determine the guilt or innocence and the type of sentence to be imposed. These assessors serve only for 10 days every year.

As for the defense counsel, almost anyone can be one if the crime is not serious, and he gets the court's permission to do so. If the accused wants a trained lawyer, he does not necessarily get the one he wants. He must apply for him through a bar association, whose president assigns lawyers to specific cases.

Minor offenses are usually handled by reprimand. But the situation becomes severe when a form of conduct is evaluated as being dangerous to the system. In cases of misappropriation of the state, or collective property, courts have tended to deal more severely with peasants than with officials.[26]

481

THE PROCURATOR GENERAL

Formally, the judicial branch operates on the various levels, the Supreme Court being the highest court of the land. But here we meet with the power and influence of the Procurator General of the USSR, appointed for a 7-year term, and is theoretically responsible to the Supreme Soviet. His office concentrates not only the duty of state prosecutor (as in the West) but also the tasks of general supervision over the organs of preliminary investigation, an arrangement usually regarded by Soviet jurists as a vast improvement over the Western practice.[27] He appoints and directs the work of the procurators at the various lower levels of the government—the constituent republics, autonomous republics, territories, and provinces; the Procurators of the constituent republics, in turn, appoint the procurators of regions, districts, and cities and towns (but their appointments have to be confirmed by the Procurator-General). Since the procurators and their staff "perform their functions independently of any organs whatsoever, being subordinated directly to the Procurator-General," it is clear that law enforcement is, in the final analysis, focused in the office of the Procurator-General, that is, the federal government, and in the final analysis in the Politbureau.

Officially, this official acts as the protector of public property and as a most important means of checking upon corruption and sabotage within government departments and among individuals. His authority blankets the Union on all government levels. He also stands at the head of an extraordinary organization of "activist" Soviet citizens who, as an expression of civic virtue, help in ferreting out cases and situations that should be brought to the Procurator-General's attention. ". . . of all Soviet institutions the procuracy has been the most stable, the least subjected to purges, the most unanimously praised by all and every Soviet clique, and in return the procuracy has served all of them equally faithfully and efficiently."[28] And the Party understands observance of the laws to be "not a passive non-violation of the laws, but an active putting of them into practice."

SELECTED BIBLIOGRAPHY *See* pp. 542-545.

NOTES

Chapter II

1 These changes have been subject to innumerable studies, such as: Hook, Sidney, *Marx and the Marxists*, D. Van Nostrand, Princeton, N. J., 1955; Mayo, H. B., *Democracy and Marxism*, Oxford University Press, New York, 1955, and "A Guide to the Literature of Marxism," 339-353; Gurian, Waldemar, *Bolshevism: An Introduction to Soviet Communism*, University of Notre Dame Press, Notre Dame, Indiana, 1952; Committee on Un-American Activities, U.S. House of Representatives, *The Communist Conspiracy*, Government Printing Office, Washington, D. C., 1956, 5 sections, and *The Great Pretense* ("A Symposium of Anti-Stalinism and the 20th Congress of the Soviet Communist Party"), Washington, May 19, 1956, and *Soviet Total War*, Washington, September 23, 1956, 2 vols.; Mosely, P. E. (editor), "Russia Since Stalin: Old Trends and New Problems," *The Annals* of the American Academy of Political and Social Science, CCCIII, February, 1956; Wilson, Edmund, *To the Finland Station: A Study in the Writing and Acting of History*, Harcourt, Brace, New York, 1940; Borkenau, Franz, *European Communism*, Harper, New York, 1953; etc.

2. Hook, *op. cit.*, "Preface 3."

3. Quoted by Friedrich, Carl Joachim, *The Philosophy of Law in Historical Perspective*, University of Chicago Press, 1958, Chapter XVI, "Law As Class Ideology, Marx and Engels," 143-153.

4. Interestingly enough, Engels especially strengthened the philosophy of law by paying attention to the philosophical problems derived from anthropological and ethnological research. His *The Origin of the Family, of Private Property and the State*, was based on the arguments offered by the American anthropologist Lewis H. Morgan in *Ancient Society, or Researches in the Lines of Progress from Savagery Through Barbarism to Civilization*, 1877, (whose theories had been built partly on those of J. J. Bachofen, who had stressed the importance of matriarchy in *Das Mutterrecht*, 1861. Engels came to propound that at the beginning there was a kind of aboriginal communism (Urkommunismus) in which the group marriage (demanded by Plate) dominated.

5. For the Marxian approach to the concept of law, see: Friedrich, Carl Joachim, *The Philosophy of Law in Historical Perspective*, University of Chicago Press, 1958, Chapter XVI, "Law as Class Ideology, Marx and Engels," 143-153; Berman, Harold, *Justice in Russia: An Interpretation of Soviet Law*, Harvard University Press, Cambridge, 1940; Hook, Sidney, *Reason, Social Myths and Democracy*, Humanities Press, New York, 1940; Hook, *Marx and Marxites*, D. Van Nostrand, Princeton, N. J., 1955; Hook, *From Hegel to Marx*, Humanities Press, New York, 1950; Popper, Karl, *The Open Society and Its Enemies*, Princeton University Press, 1945, Vol. II.

6. Berman, Harold, *Justice in Russia*, Harvard University Press, Cambridge, Mass., 1950; Guins, George C., *Soviet Law and Soviet Society*, Mouton and Co., The Hague, 1954; Kelsen, Hans, *The Communist Theory of Law*, F. A. Praeger, New York, 1955; Sczerba, K. and von Schelting, A., "State and Law in the Soviet Union," 382-405, in *UNESCO, Contemporary Political Science*, UNESCO, Paris, No. 426, 1950.

7. Timasheff, Nicholas S., "Soviet Jurisprudence in the Service of the

Government," 93-97, in *Proceedings* of the Conference of the Institute for the Study of History and Culture of the USSR, New York, March 20-22, 1953.

8. Vishinsky's work has been translated as *The Law of the Soviet State,* Macmillan, New York, 1948. For the analyses of the changes in Soviet legal philosophy, see especially: Hazard, John N., "Soviet Law and Its Assumptions," in Northrop, F. S. C. (editor), *Ideological Differences and World Order,* Yale University Press, New Haven, Conn., 1949; Hazard (editor), *Soviet Legal Philosophy,* Harvard University Press, Cambridge, 1952; Hazard, *Law and Social Change in the USSR,* Carswell, Toronto, 1953; and, *The Soviet System of Government,* University of Chicago Press, 1957.

9. Zhdanov, Andrei, *Doklad T. Zhdanova O Zhurnalakh "Svbzda" I "Leningrad,"* Moscow, 1946, 35-36; this work is available in several English translations, for instance: *A. Zhdanov on Literature, Music and Philosophy,* Lawrence and Wishart, London, 1947.

10. Decrees of the Central Committee of the All-Union Communist Party (Bolsheviks), October 5, 1946, "The Broadening and Improvement of Legal Education in the Country," *Soviet Government and Law,* No. ·1, 1947, 73; quoted in Hryshko, Vasyl, "Academic Freedom in Soviet Jurisprudence," 46-56, in *Academic Freedom Under the Soviet Regime,* The Institute for the Study of the History and Culture of the USSR, Munich, 1954.

11. Kovaliv, Panteleimon, "Soviet Linguistic Policy," 56-64, in *Academic Freedom Under the Soviet Regime.* The reference is to Stalin's article, "On Marxism in Linguistics," *Pravda,* June 20, 1950.

12. For details, see: *Soviet Legal Philosophy,* by Lenin, V. I., Stuchka, P I., Reissner, M. A., Pashukanis, E. B., etc., introduction by John N. Hazard, Harvard University Press, Cambridge, 1951, (Hazard's introduction contains biographical data concerning the Soviet jurists whose works are included in this symposium); Kechekyan, S. F., "Social Progress and Law," 42-51, in *Transactions of the Third World Congress of Sociology,* International Sociological Association, London, 1956, VI; Levitsky, Serge L., "Soviet Law and the Press," *Journalism Quarterly,* XXXIV, 1, Winter, 1957, 51-57; Guins, George C., "Soviet Law in the Mirror of Legal Science," *The American Slavic and East European Review,* XVI, 1, February, 1957, 66-73; *Soviet Legal Philosophy,* Harvard University Press, Cambridge, 1951, published for the Association of American Law Schools; Hazard, John N., "Recent Developments in Soviet Law," 24-42, in Hoffman, George W. (editor), *Recent Soviet Trends,* College of Arts and Sciences, Austin, Texas, 1956; Kelsen, Hans, *The Communist Theory of Law,* F. A. Praeger, New York, 1955; Hazard, J. N., "Understanding Soviet Law Without the Cases," *Soviet Studies,* VII, 2, October, 1955, 121-126; Berman, Harold, *Justice in Russia,* Harvard University Press, Cambridge Mass., 1950; Gsovski, V., *Soviet Civil Law,* University of Michigan Press, Ann Arbor, Mich., 1948-1949; etc.

13. Fainsod, Merle, *How Russia Is Ruled,* Harvard University Press, Cambridge, 1953, Chapter 13, "Terror as a System of Power," 354-389; Fischer, G., *Soviet Opposition to Stalin,* Harvard University Press, 1952; Brzezinski, Z., *The Permanent Purge: Politics in Soviet Totalitarianism,* Harvard University Press, 1957; Towser, J., *Political Power in the USSR, 1917-1945,* Oxford University Press, New York, 1948; Beck, F. and Godin, W., *Russian Purge and the Extraction of Confessions,* The Viking Press, New York, 1951.

14. Kelsen, Hans, *The Communist Theory of Law,* University of California

484

Press, Berkeley, 1954. Since Kelsen has been the principal target of Soviet legal philosophers as a spokesman for "bourgeois theories," much of this valuable work is unfortunately spent on unnecessary consideration of Kelsen's own theory.

15. Bureau of Intelligence and Research, Department of State, "Supreme Soviet Approves Legal Reforms," *Intelligence Report*, no. 7946, February 6, 1959; Mironenko, Y . P., "The New Law on Criminal Responsibility for States Crimes," *Bulletin*, Institute for the Study of the USSR, VI, 6, June, 1959, 26-33.

16. Published in *Izvestia*, December 26, 1958, 2-7; and *Vedomosti*, January 1, 1959, 933, items 3-32. Among the comments and evaluations on those measures, see: Lipson, Leon, "The New Face of 'Socialist Legality,' " *Problems of Communism*, VII, 4, July-August, 1958, 22-30; Lipson, "Socialist Legality: The Mountain Has Labored," *Ibid.*, VIII, 2, March-April, 1959, 15-19; Department of State, Bureau of Intelligence and Research, *Intelligence Report*, No. 7946, "Supreme Soviet Approves Legal Reforms," February 6, 1959; Marin, Y., "Some Aspects of the New Law on State Crimes," *Bulletin*, Institute for the Study of the USSR, VI, 2, February, 1959, 17-21; Mironenko, Y. P., "The Campaign to Extend the Death Penalty," *Ibid.*, VI, 1, January, 1959, 25-30; Mironenko, "The New Fundamental Principles of Soviet Criminal Legislation," *Ibid.*, V, 5, May, 1959, 47-53; Mironenko, "The New Laws on Criminal Responsibility for State Crimes," *Ibid.*, VI, 6, June, 1959, 26-33; Lapenna, Ivo, "Socialist Legality: Soviet and Yugoslav," *Soviet Survey*, 25, July-September, 1958, 53-60; Schapiro, Leonard, "Judicial Practice and Legal Reform," *Ibid.*, 29, July-September, 1959, 54-60; Leibowitz, Judge Samuel S., "The Two Faces of Justice in Russia," *Life*, XXXXVI, 23, January 8, 1959, 147-162.

17. The text in: *Sotsialisticheskaya Zakonnost*, 1959, no. 1, 99-157; here are also reprinted the speeches in the Supreme Soviet explaining them and commenting upon them.

18. For details, see: Schapiro, Leonard, "Judicial Practice and Legal Reform," *Soviet Survey*, 29, July-September, 1959, 54-60.

19. Marin, Y., "Some Aspects of the New Law on State Crimes," *Bulletin*, Institute for the Study of the USSR, VI, 6, June, 1959, 17-21; another good analysis is: Mironenko, Y. P., "The New Law on Criminal Responsibility for State Crimes," 26-33.

20. Roucek, Joseph S., "Soviet Union's Non-Russian Nations," *The Ukrainian Quarterly*, XIV, 4, December, 1958, 327-334 and "Fictions vs. Facts of Life in the Policies Toward the Non-Russian Peoples in the USSR," *Ibid.*, XV, 2, June, 1959, 145-152. For the anti-Semitic, "Russification," and several genocide steps against various USSR minorities, see: Roucek, Joseph S., "Soviet Union's Non-Russian Nations," *The Ukrainian Quarterly*, XIV, 4, December, 1958, 327-334; and "Fictions vs. Facts of Life in the Policies Toward the Non-Russian Peoples in the USSR," *Ibid.*, XV, 2, June, 1959, 145-152.

21. Wohl, Paul, "New Soviet Law Studied," *Christian Science Monitor*, December 30, 1958.

22. Wohl, *op. cit.*

23. Quoted by Stevens, Edmund, "Soviets Revamp Criminal Law Code," *Christian Science Monitor*, December 30, 1958.

24. Fainsod, Merle, *How Russia Is Ruled*, Harvard University Press, Cambridge, 1953, 313 ff.; Gsovski, Vladimir, *Soviet Civil Law*, University of Michigan Press, Ann Arbor, 1948-49, 2 vols.; Schlesinger, Rudolph, *Soviet Legal Theory*, Kegan Paul, London, 1954; Towster, Julian, *Political Power in the USSR, 1917-1947*, Oxford University Press, New York, 1948; Vishinsky, Andrei Y., *The Law of the Soviet State*, Macmillan, New York, 1948.

25. For details, see: Gsovski, Vladimir, *Soviet Civil Law*, University of Michigan, Ann Arbor, 1948; Hazard, John N., *Law and Social Change in the USSR*, Stevens, London, 1953; Berman, H. J., *Justice in Russia*, Harvard University Press, 1950.

26. Dinerstein, H. S., *Communism and the Russian Peasant*, Free Press, Glencoe, Illnois, 1955, 121.

27. Ginsberg, George, "The Soviet Procuracy and Forty Years of Socialist Legality," *American Slavic and East European Review*, XVIII, 1, February, 1959, 34-62.

28. Ginsberg, *op. cit.*, 61.

Chapter III

CRIMINAL LAWS OF MOSCOW'S EUROPEAN SATELLITES

Although there are certain differences among the "People's Democracies" behind the Iron Curtain,[1] in their constitutional and governmental structures, in theory at least, the fact remains that all these satellite states have tried to model their institutional framework closely on that of the Soviet Union, especially in regard to criminal, police, and military institutions, the organization of propaganda and education and the economic institutions.[2]

ALBANIA

The Constitution of the People's Republic of Albania, promulgated on March 15, 1944, was almost a translation of the Yugoslav Constitution (which in turn had been based on the Stalin Constitution of 1936); the only substantial difference was that the federal structure of both models was not used.[3] Like the other constitutions in the Soviet orbit, it was based on the principle of the dictatorship of the proletariat, upheld the authority of the state, almost unrestricted in relation to its citizens, while guaranteeing, at the same time, the rights of the citizens against the state. Certain changes were made on July 4, 1950, to make the Constitution conform more closely to that of the Soviet Union; the amendments stress: the People's Republic of Albania is a state of workers and toiling peasants; all power of the Republic belongs to the town and rural workers, represented by

People's Councils; the state regulates and controls all internal trade; work is the basis of the social order of the republic; every citizen is obligated to defend and strengthen socialist property; justice is dispensed by the Supreme Court, people's courts, military tribunals, and special courts for special purposes. On June 11, 1951, the Military Supreme Tribunal was merged with the Supreme Court, and the General Military Prosecutor's Office with the General Prosecutor's Office. All in all, the Albanian Constitution "serves only as window dressing for the Communist regime." [4]

In June, 1951, a law reorganizing the judiciary was enacted and its aim has been to defend the People's Republic and its "socialist system." The law covering the organization and functions of the Office of the Prosecutor, (translated in 1946 almost verbatim from the Soviet law), was designed to "defend and strengthen revolutionary legality."

The New Albanian Penal Code of September 1, 1952, was based on the principles of "class warfare and revolutionary justice," and embodies "the basic principles of Soviet justice." [5]

BULGARIA

The Bulgarian Criminal Code was promulgated in 1951 and has been amended since then, replacing the Code enacted in 1896.[6] It reflects, in general, side by side, modern criminalistic thought, harshness and political expediency, and, above all, the influence of Soviet ideology. Following the Soviet example, the Bulgarian Criminal Code recognizes the application of the principle of analogy, and the Labor Code proclaims the principle that "acts of indictment have the force of proof until the contrary is proven"—i.e., that the individual is presumably guilty unless he proves his innocence.

CZECHOSLOVAKIA

After the Communist *coup d'état* in February, 1948, the Constitutional structure of Czechoslovakia was changed to correspond to the Soviet theory of the state, and Western democratic devices restricting the power of government (such as the separation of the legislative, executive and judicial powers, the doctrine of checks and balances, and the principle of rule by law) were rejected. A new Constitution was adopted on May 9, 1948.[7]

The Declaration to the Constitution proclaims the determination to "insure ourselves (the Czechoslovak people) of peaceful progress toward socialism." This statement is of far-reaching importance for the officials and judges, since the individual provisions of the Constitution must be interpreted "in the spirit of the whole and of the principles upon which it is based" (Section 171). The judges pledge by oath that they will render decisions pursuant to socialist legality for the benefit of the working people. In a commentary on the 1950 Criminal Code, socialist legality is defined as "the precise application and observation of such laws as are in accordance with the will of the working class and of the toilers," its aim being to "crush the people's enemies and to protect and strengthen the dictatorship of the working class in order to construct socialism and later communism . . ." [8]

The Constitution and most of the laws relating to the judiciary were amended or abolished by a series of laws in October, 1952 (Law Nos. 64-69, *Collection*) by which the courts and the administration of justice were, in effect, subordinated to the Cabinet. These laws founded two categories of courts: ordinary and special courts. The first category comprises the Supreme Court, regional courts, and People's (district) courts; the second is formed by military courts and courts of arbitration which decide on disputes between governmental agencies and those engaged in business. Theoretically, the two types of judges, professional and People's (lay) judges are elected, but actually appointed. Their task is to apply the law in the interest of "the working people," and declare on oath that they will abide not only by laws but also by orders; they are not permitted to examine either the constitutionality of laws or the legality of administrative orders.

The People's judges are appointed by the Cabinet or the

People's Committees, and only citizens "loyal" to the government and devoted to the principles of the People's Democratic Order may be appointed. As in the USSR, the Procurator General is the most effective organ of government control over the judiciary, as he supervises the application of laws and other legal provisions by ministries, governmental agencies, courts, People's committees, public institutions, public officials, and private individuals; he may protest against decisions and measures of administrative authorities and may appeal against the final decision of the courts.

Of all the satellite states, the Czechoslovak Communist regime has been most successful in warding off the fever of liberalization that began to grow in Eastern Europe in the turbulent year of 1956.[9]

Historically, the hope for liberalization, the foundation of much Western thinking, the basis of much of the hope that still remains in the area, and which is clutched like a political life-saver by those Communists who believe that their present societies can and will give their people more mental elbow room, is rooted in the "de-Stalinization" at the 20th Congress of the Soviet Communist Party and the upheavals in Poland and Hungary that followed it. The degree of economic controls, the pace of collectivization, party discipline, controls on writing and publishing and the general psychological tones, show that Czechoslovakia's communist leaders have been entirely successful in warding off liberalization. The reins of governmental power and party control are held firmly by the same man—Antonín Novotný, President of the Republic and First Secretary of the Party. On what the Communists call the "cultural front," the recent years have resulted largely in sterner rather than "softer" attitudes. The press is increasingly critical of "bourgeois tendencies" and writing that does not directly tie in to Socialist goals. Western newspapers and periodicals are not on sale on Prague's newsstands. Occasionally Western plays are produced, but they are usually about problems of life and morals in the West—such as Arthur Miller's *Death of a Salesman*.

490

HUNGARY

The Hungarian Criminal Code was promulgated in 1950 and has been amended since then, replacing that enacted in 1896.[10] Suppression of any criticism of the government is provided for by numerous measures. Article 1, Law No. 2, of the General Section of the Criminal Code, for instance, stipulates that "every act which offends or endangers the political social, or economic order of the Hungarian People's Republic or its citizens is an act hostile to society. Law No. 5 of 1950, on the Defense of Peace, makes liable to 15 years imprisonment anyone "who incites to war, or otherwise expresses or advances war propaganda." Or the new civil code, approved on July 30, 1959, stresses the obligation of Hungarian citizens regarding public property, and directors of state enterprises now bear fuller responsibility for the losses caused by "economic crimes."

In fact, Hungary has one of the most tightly-knit systems aimed to silence any opposition in the regime.[11] The series of protective laws (beginning with Act No. 7 of 1946) provides the death penalty or life imprisonment for forming, joining, or even supporting any organization that aims—even by peaceful means—to change the existing government form. Heavy sentences are applicable to those who "incite" against the state, its institutions or individuals representing it; while there is quite a category of crimes which can be committed against the people's economy.[12]

POLAND

The imposition of the pro-communist system in Poland in 1944 was not accompanied by such deep and sudden changes in the legal system as in the USSR, claims a Communist spokesman. In fact, "the new authorities did not pass any legislation invalidating in principle the whole of that previously in force." [13] On the contrary, the first Constitutional Acts clearly referred directly back to the principles of the Polish Constitution of March 17, 1921. "The Manifesto of July 22, 1944 accepted the fundamental assumptions of the earlier Constitution. The same is true of the Constitutional Act of February 19, 1947," reports Ehrlich. But Ehrlich also points out carefully that "even though whole sets of legal provisions of the inter-war period have been maintained in force (e.g. the Criminal Code, or the Code of Obligations), their social function has undergone a change. They were old rules applied to a new social behavior. Such old rules frequently had new addresses; frequently also the object of a legal relation was changed (i.e. the scope of rights and duties or the methods of carrying them out). The reading of a sentence in the lawbook remained unchanged, but the part which it started to play was new. . . ."

When reading carefully Ehrlich's article, one must be impressed with his desperate effort to promote the Marxian interpretation of Poland's law. Note, for instance, his remarks in regard to the position of the judiciary: "In the Western democracies, the principle of the independence of the judiciary, a tradition which goes right back to the theory of the division of powers, is indissolubly connected with the non-political character of the law-courts. In many cases judges are forbidden by law to take part in public life. . . . In Poland and in the other socialist countries the independence of the judiciary is conceived differently. The judges cannot be actuated by any *esprit de corps* which would make it difficult for them to understand the policy of the State, the outline of which is dictated by the leadership of the Worker's Party. The introduction of law-courts in which jurymen participate has also played its part in enabling the judges constantly to check their professional point of view against that of public opinion. Such consultation cannot but be of assistance in the interpretation of statutes and the enforcement of the law. (*Nevertheless, trial by jury has never been restored in the Polish People's Republic.* Italics ours.). Article 48 of the Constitution enjoins the law-courts to guard the political system of Poland, to protect the achievements of the Polish working people, to protect the People's rule of the law, social property and civil rights, and to punish offenders. A non-political judge, or one guided by differently conceived political aims,

492

could not fulfil such a task. This conception is universally accepted in the socialist countries, and it does not jeopardize the independence of the judiciary. . . ." [14]

The situation is viewed differently by a Western critic of the Communist regime, who stresses that the Communist regime "found it necessary to make far-reaching adaptations in the criminal law and procedure." [15]

The Decree of June 13, 1946, on Criminal Acts Particularly Dangerous During the Period of National Reconstruction (known as the "Small Criminal Code") and other statutes entrusted to the public security authorities procedure for the preparatory investigative processes in criminal acts. Since the pre-trial procedure was taken out of the court's competence, the pre-trial investigation has become more important than the trial itself. The "Small Criminal Code" supplements the Criminal Code of 1932 and embodies numerous new provisions outside the Code, and rules that the provisions of the Criminal Code are suspended insofar as they are regulated by the 1946 decree; especially Articles 55-57 provide that in matters subject to the jurisdiction of court martials, the pre-trial proceedings are conducted by the agencies of public security (the security police, which is subject only to the supervision of the public prosecutor). Arrests are permitted, without a warrant, but detention without a warrant may not be longer than 48 hours. Orders of preliminary arrest are no longer issued by the court alone, but also by the public prosecutor. Preventive arrest is limited to 3 months but may be extended up to 6 months by the public prosecutor; furthermore, the Prosecutor General may allow a further extension of arrest if, "because of the particular circumstances of the case, the investigation could not be completed within the period stated under Section 2." Officers of the security authorities are not subject to the jurisdiction of the general courts.

The Decree of December 7, 1954, on the Supreme Agencies of Government Administration in Internal Affairs and Public Security,[16] abolished the Ministry of Public Security and the ordinary police functions were taken over by a new Ministry of Interior. State security was entrusted to a special Committee for

Public Security attached to the Council of Ministers, headed by a Deputy Minister. The Ministry of Internal Affairs heads the activities of the Citizens' Militia, the Internal Security Corps, and the Military Border Guards, together with the administration of penal institutions, prison guards, civil defense, fire-prevention control, penal administrative decisions, public and civil status records, and registration and passport control, together with other matters related to public administration. Furthermore, the police and administrative functions are delegated to the People's Councils. But the matters related directly to the "protection of the system of the People's Democracy" are handled exclusively by the Committee of Public Security, a separate agency under the Council of Ministers, headed by a chairman who is at the same time a member of the Council of Ministers, appointed and recalled on the motion of the Premier, the Legislative Assembly or the Council of State.

Political expediency has replaced legal action, the belief in the omnipotency of penal sanction in regulation of social life, the need for a proper definition of legality and the principle of discretion, deficiencies in the application and interpretation of the constitution (the new Constitution was adopted in 1952), the need to curtail the powers of the Council and to promote the superior position of the *Seim,* the role of the administrative judiciary, and legal regulation of the institution of workers' councils, etc.

At any rate, a recent report from Poland stresses that "when Poles in Warsaw speak of the gains that still remain from the political revolution of 1956, the greater freedom of the law and the legal profession is almost always mentioned." Polish lawyers no longer fear to defend clients accused of activities against the state, and know that there are no more appointments of judges who never got beyond elementary school or that uneducated party hacks will turn out to be lawyers by government decree.[17] "But they know—and the defendants know, and so do the judges —that pressures and contradictions still exist. A man accused of a crime in Poland can expect the judge to protect his rights, but he also knows that the prosecutor can keep him in jail for months without ever bringing him to trial. The defendant can be sure now that it will be the judge and not the security officer who will decide the sentence. But a man accused of an 'economic crime' can read in his newspaper that the highest government body in the land is openly denouncing judges who hand down 'lenient sentences.' . . . The lawyers feel they have won important freedoms, but they are aware of a new law that gives the Minister of Justice expanded powers to suspend lawyers."

ROMANIA

Discrepancies between constitutional and legal theory and practices have been characteristic of the Romanian government since it was first established.[18] These pre-communist practices have been rejuvenated by the Constitution of 1948 and 1952 and are faithful imitations of the Soviet examples. In 1950, the Soviet system of popularly elected People's Councils was adopted, thus making the fact that the locus of power rests in Party executive committees and government leaders at higher levels. The entire government is completely subordinatd to the Romanian Workers (Communist) Party. The judiciary is entirely controlled by the Party and so are all positions of public prosecutors and most of the regular judgeships.[19]

The judicial system was built according to two special laws passed by the Grand National Assembly on June 2, 1946, and in general provisions of the Constitution. Justice must ensure the observance of the laws and "educate the citizens of the Romanian People's Republic in the spirit of devotion to the fatherland and in the spirit of the construction of socialism." Fulfillment of this task has been entrusted to the Procuratura and the regular and special courts. In addition to the defense of the fundamental principles of justice, the courts are entrusted with "hearing penal cases and application of the penalties provided by the law for the punishment of traitors to the fatherland, of spies, of those sabotaging the construction of socialism, of those

495

committing crimes against peace and humanity, of war mongers, embezzlers and those who destroy socialist property, as well as of bandits, thieves, hooligans and other offenders.[20]

The powers and functions of the Procurator General are laid down by Law No. 6 of June 2, 1952, concerning the "setting up and organization of the Procuratura of the Romanian People's Republic," a Romanian imitation of a Soviet institution. While he supervises the administration of justice, he also takes part, "with a consultative vote," in the meetings of the Presidium and of the Council of Ministers. His role as spokesman for the prosecution and the government has been changed to that of "defender of socialist legality," supervising citizens and state organs alike.

The "People's Judges" carry on a much greater function than those specified in the Constitution. The Minister of Justice may assign them from one court to another. "Thus, there are special teams of people's judges which the Ministry of Justice can use whenever the political interests of the Party demand." The courts may also hear cases outside their seats "to fulfill the educational purpose of justice." The judges of all regular courts are elected by direct popular vote (with the exception of the Supreme Court, whose justices are elected by the Grand National Assembly). But, in reality, all judges are selected by the Romanian Workers' Party and "approved" by the people and the Assembly. The Chief Public Prosecutor is theoretically responsible to the Assembly; practically, he is designated and controlled by the Party.

Among the several laws limiting the constitutional rights of freedom, of the press, of assembly, and of organization, important especially was the inclusive Law for the Defense of Peace of December 15, 1950, prohibiting "propaganda inciting to war, the spreading of any other manifestations in favor of unleashing another war, made orally, in writing, through the press, radio, cinema or by any other propaganda media. . . ." (Article 2.) Remarks against the regime, or in favor of any of its "enemies," foreign or domestic, fall within the scope of this law, and the punishment consists of "penal servitude of from

496

5 to 25 years and to total or partial confiscation of property. (Article 3.)

A new series of amendments were issued for the Criminal Code in Romania in 1957-58 which are severely out of all proportion to the transgression involved and are in clear violation of the Rule of Law. The new amendments determine as "crimes" the efforts of Romanians to regain freedom and itemized the penalties for committing them. Article 195, paragraph 5, of the Code reads: "The act of a Romanian citizen who, having a state mission or a mission of public interest abroad, refuses to return to the country, shall be regarded as treason against the fatherland, and the penalty shall be solitary confinement from 5 to 15 years, loss of civil rights from 4 to 8 years and confiscation of property. For failure to denounce acts preparatory to this offense, before the offender has crossed the frontier or has been discovered by the agencies of the state, the penalty shall be imprisonment from one to five years and loss of civil rights from one to five years."

Propaganda and agitation against the social order is punishable by 3 to 10 years imprisonment, and conspiracy against the order by 15 to 25 years imprisonment and, in exceptionally grave circumstances, by death.

Article 209 says that "undermining the people's democratic regime is a crime punishable by 5 to 25 years imprisonment, while the death penalty is provided for causing disorder or endangering the security of the state (Article 21).

The application of these harsh penalties constitutes intensified warfare against elements hostile to the Communist regime.

YUGOSLAVIA

In Yugoslavia, from World War II until the middle of 1949, the concept of legality was basically identical with that of the USSR. "Revolutionary legality" was stressed as one of the instruments of the revolution, and the "people's courts," which had sprung up into existence during the war, were almost identical with their Soviet prototypes; the public prosecutor's office cor-

497

responded to the Soviet procuracy, and the Yugoslav UDB corresponded to the Soviet Special Branch of the NKVD (afterwards MVD).[21]

The Constitution of January 31, 1946, in addition to constructing a new economic and political system, tried to destroy all vestiges of the old. It embodied three new features: (1) replacement of the old centralized state with a nominally federal structure; (2) incorporation of the judicial and administrative changes affected during the period of the National Liberation War; and (3) imitation of the Soviet Constitution.[22]

As all Communist constitutions, the document was full of anomalies and inconsistencies. In general, Article 6 asserted that "all authority is derived from the people," but the rule of the Communist Party was ensured (although, in contradiction to the Soviet document, Article 126, nothing was said on this point in the Yugoslav document).

There are also other minor differences. Individual republics and the federation are referred to as "people's" and not "socialist." Also, the Yugoslav constitution does not provide explicitly that republics may secede. Minor points of differences are also in the distribution of legislative and administrative powers. While Article 124 of the Soviet Constitution recognized freedom of religious worship and freedom of anti-religious propaganda, Article 25 of the Yugoslav Constitution, without mentioning anti-religious propaganda, guaranteed freedom of worship and only provided that "abuse of the church and religion for political purposes, and the existence of political organizations on a religious basis are forbidden." The law also provided that the state may extend financial and material assistance to religious communities, a provision not found in the Soviet constitution.

All in all, separation of powers, and judicial review does not exist in Yugoslavia, in theory or in practice. Article 115 of the Constitution provided for a unified judicial system on four levels: county courts; district courts; supreme courts of each republic and autonomous province; and the federal supreme court. The judicial system is subservient to the legislative body at the corresponding level of government. Special courts may be estab-

498

lished by law. The judiciary cannot pass on the constitutionality or validity of laws; this power is vested in the federal and republican presidia in relation to federal or republican laws. The institution of "demands for the preservation of the spirit of the law" against valid and final decisions of courts and administrative organs is provided for (Article 127). There is a detailed enumeration of basic human rights, but Article 43 provides that "the use of civil rights with the intent to bring about a forcible change in the constitutional form of government of the Federal People's Republic of Yugoslavia, or to disrupt the constitutional order for anti-democratic purposes is illegal and liable to punishment." This allows the branding of the opposition or criticism as illegal and criminal.

On January 13, 1953, the Federal People's Assembly adopted an amendment to the 1946 Constitution reorganizing the structure of the government.[23] But since these changes are not directly concerned with our topic, we shall not deal with them here. Sufficient it is to state that "the entire constitutional system rests on control imposed from the top through the League of Yugoslav Communists, who dominate the Federal Executive Council, the seat of power in the government."

The new Constitution was the result of Yugoslav criticism of the Soviet system (after the Tito-Stalin split in 1948), which forced the re-examination of the communist practices at home. Seeking "its own road to Socialism," Tito's regime also came up against the problem of legality.

Ranković's report to the Central Committee of the Party on June 3, 1958, made some revealing statements regarding the application of criminal law. The organs of the UDB (the secret police), and the public prosecutors, as well as the courts, tended to convert ordinary crimes into political offenses, and many petty offenses were treated as sabotage. Others, such as personal insults to the president of a local people's committee, were construed as counter-revolutionary offenses (as criminal offenses "against the people and the state") and punishable by several years' imprisonment. The defendant's rights were not considered, and many judgments were rendered with complete disregard for the evidence of the defense witnesses; equally frequent were cases in which too much importance was attached to the defendant's confession, irrespective of other evidence. Other cases of unlawfulness were: the meting out of punishments not specified by the law, disrespect for the provisions of criminal procedure, refusal to hear witnesses for the defense, punishments for "collaboration with the enemy" of persons who, during the occupation, were imprisoned in the invader's concentration camps, and "total confiscation," a penalty not in the law; there were frequent cases of judgments made after previous agreement with the public prosecutor, with the organs of the UDB, or party organs.

The secret police, recruited exclusively from the most faithful and disciplined members of the party, also had, according to Ranković, "great weaknesses." According to the report, in 1949 alone, 47% of the total number of arrests made by the UDB were unjustified. But even among the remaining 53%, considered legal, there was a great number of cases in which the UDB illegally exceeded its authority.

In the sphere of civil law, the violation of legality was less noticeable. The gravest errors were made in the field of matrimony, parent-children relationships, inheritance, and cases involving property, particularly when the state was involved. Abundant violations of the law occurred in the villages, especially in connection with collectivization, and the rights of urban workers were also ignored. Illegal acts involved the election and removal of judges, in the administration, in the public prosecutor's offices, in the police, and in the work of the people's committees—"in fact, throughout the entire apparatus."

Ranković attributed these unlawful procedures to the lack of legal regulations in several important spheres, the ignorance of officials, the small number of judges and their inadequate salaries, the general neglect of the courts and the undermining of their authority.

Ranković then presented several measures for "strengthening" legality (including the improvement of the quality and status of the legal profession). But, basically, Lapenna points out, "all these measures . . . were to be applied with the object of establishing, or, as the official terminology put it, 'strengthening,' not legality as such, but 'socialist' legality."

Between June, 1951 and April, 1958, greater systematization was introduced into several branches of the law and the legal system as a whole. In fact, regarding codification, Yugoslavia has surpassed the USSR. The courts and the public prosecutor's offices had been reorganized (though the fundamental principles remain the same). Two important concepts relating to the principle of legality in criminal law—the concept of analogy and that of a "socially dangerous action"—have been partially modified. According to the concept of "material crime" (on the basis of which many persons have been condemned), a crime is not only the concrete illegal deed, defined as a crime in law, but every "socially dangerous act." But since the degree of "social danger" is defined by the court, on the recommendation of the public prosecutor and party agencies, this whole area opened the door to illegality.

Although the new Yugoslav Criminal Code (Article 2) excludes this concept in regard to punishment, it appears that "the official attitude to the concept of socialist legality remained essentially unchanged," concludes Lapenna. The concept of legality, extensively dealt with and still discussed in theory, remains still linked with the "construction of Socialism" in Yugoslavia. Since 1949, the operative word "socialist" indicates in Yugoslavia that legality must serve the country's "own road to socialism"; thus legality is limited by the political ends. It is only "because the regime in Yugoslavia is less severe than before 1949, and because several important questions have now been regulated by law that the element of legality in the notion of 'socialist legality' can now take on a more significant role than formerly, and operates more effectively than in the Soviet Union at the present time." [24]

Yugoslavia's new penal law, which went into effect in January, 1960, had been under discussion for more than three years. In general, penalties for various types of crimes have been reduced. Generally speaking, maximum penalties of 20 years have been cut to 15 and those of 5 to 3, while the number of acts punishable by fines instead of prison terms has been increased.

The Yugoslav reforms follow somewhat similar lines of the Soviet changes in the criminal code, which had abandoned deprivation or limitation of civil rights as part of the court verdict against prisoners convicted of political and other anti-state offenses in the reforms of their own penal code.

The Yugoslavs explain the changes on the ground that "educational influence" during the period of sentence removes any need to limit a prisoner's rights after expiration of his prison term. Where life imprisonment had been previously a substitute for capital punishment a maximum of 20 years of "strict imprisonment" is to be imposed. Another reduction covers offenses qualifying for prison terms from 6 months to 20 years and over, which will now be met with terms of from one to 15 years.

Capital punishment is, in effect, virtually dropped altogether. In a five year period (1955-1959), only 23 such sentences had been handed down and in some cases clemency was later exercised. In the future, it is stated, they will be limited to "particularly grave crimes against the people and the state" or in cases of treason against the armed forces. Capital punishment of persons under 21 has already been discarded.

A striking liberalization of the penal provisions of the Yugoslav Criminal Code of 1959 is that it will terminate the Communist system of "loss of civil rights," which had hitherto been added to prison sentences for serious crimes, abolishes the penalty of life imprisonment and reduces other maximum sentences, and also introduces more liberal elements in the prison regime itself.

The one branch in which the new penal provisions will be more severe than hitherto is in that of so-called economic crimes; that is, cases of corruption, fraud, embezzlement in state-owned nationalized industries and enterprises. This is because crime under these headings still shows an upward tendency while most other forms of criminal activity have shown a decrease.[25]

One of the innovations of the revised Criminal Law of Yugoslavia, introduced in 1959, was the so-called "judicial warning."[26]

This measure is "corrective-educational" in character, and can be used in minor criminal offenses.

Under the earlier rules, persons serving a term of imprisonment had the right of compensation for their work, one free day a week, free medical treatment, insurance against accidents and occupational diseases, as well as the right to correspond and receive visitors and parcels. Under the new regulations, they also enjoy the right to a 14-day vacation a year, (previously prisoners used to be allowed to go on a 14-day leave and visit their relatives).

Conditions in the prison are now liberalized to the extent that prisoners will be paid for their work on the basis of an 8-hour working day, with one complete rest day a week, and 2 weeks rest from work a year in all sentences exceeding the 12-month sentence. Some relaxation of rules on letters and parcels is also included.

One of the more important new measures is the granting of leave of absence to all convicted persons after the term of 11 months. In addition, any convicted person is granted 7 days leave in the case of the death or serious illness of a close member of the family.

Other amendments allow prisoners to be released, under certain conditions, on probation or parole after serving one-third of their term. The possibilities of postponing punishments have been made more elastic, and terms of imprisonment can be interrupted in the case of difficult family circumstances. Upon completion of their prison terms, all convicts enjoy normal civil rights, with nothing to hinder their return to normal life.

Minors under 14 years of age cannot be punished. Offenders from 14 to 16 can be subjected to corrective educational measures, such as: disciplinary action, stronger supervision and confinement in corrective institutes. Persons from 16 to 18 can be punished only for serious offenses; they can be sentenced to special imprisonment which can be no shorter than one and no longer than 10 years. This punishment is served in special penal-corrective institutes where the treatment of inmates is much milder than in prisons for adults.

The new regulations also introduced some measures of protection: compulsory treatment of alcoholics and drug addicts, suspension of a driving license, prohibition to engage in a given occupation or profession, etc.

According to information given by a representative of the Federal Public Prosecutor's Offices, criminal offenses were on the decrease in Yougoslavia in 1959, particularly those committed by minor persons. In 1958, the law courts considered only 2,500 charges against young offenders. In most cases, these delinquents had come from families that had immigrated from small provincial towns and villages to cities.[27]

SELECTED BIBLIOGRAPHY *See* pp. 542-545.

NOTES

Chapter III

1. See such studies as: Taborsky, Eduard, "Government in the 'People's Democracies,' " 55-63, and Guins, George C., "Constitutions of the Soviet Satellites," 64-67, in Roucek, Joseph S. (editor), "Moscow's European Satellites," *The Annals* of the American Academy of Political and Social Science, CCLXXI, September, 1950.

2. For details, see: Szirmai, Z. (editor), *Law in Eastern Europe*, Sijthoff, Leyden, 1958, 2 vols., which includes studies of Soviet Law (Vol. I) and on Poland, Yugoslavia, and Eastern Germany (Vol. II).

3. Skendi, Stavro (editor), *Albania*, F. A. Praeger, New York, 1956, Chapter 4, "The Constitutional System," 60-72.

4. *Ibid.*, 67.

5. For more details, see: Skendi, *op cit.*, 143.

6. Sipkov, Ivan, *Legal Sources and Bibliography of Bulgaria*, F. A. Praeger, New York, 1957, 2 vols.; Dellin, L. A. D., "The Constitutional System," Chapter 4, 84-101, Padev, Michael, "National Security," Chapter 7, 147-161, in Dellin, L. A. D. (editor), *Bulgaria*, F. A. Praeger, 1957; *Das Bulgarische Strafgesetzbuch*, trans. by Thea Lyon, Walter de Gruyter and Company, Berlin, 1957; Pavlov, Stefan, *Nakazatelno Prvosudie Na Narodnata Republika Bulgariia* (Criminal Law of the People's Republic of Bulgaria), Sofia, 1951; Peselj, Branko M., "Legal Trends in the People's Democracies," *George Washington Law Review*, 513, 1954; Sharp, Samuel L., *New Constitutions in*

the Soviet Sphere, Foundation for Foreign Affairs, Washington, D. C., 1950; Union of Bulgarian Jurists, *Inquiry into the Legality of the Communist Rule in Bulgaria*, New York, 1955.

7. For details, see: Kocvara, Stephen, "The Constitutional System," 40-59, in Busek, Vratislav and Spulber, Nicolas (editors), *Czechoslovakia*, F. A. Praeger, 1957; Bohmer, Alois and others, *Legal Sources and Bibliography of Czechoslovakia, 1938-1948*, Princeton University Press, 1959.

8. *O Obecné Cást Trestniho Zákona* (On the General Provisions of the Criminal Code), Prague, 1951, 32.

9. Rosenthal, A. M., "Czech Reds Avert Liberalizing Tide," The New York *Times*, August 22, 1959.

10. Anonymous, "The Constitutional System and Government," Chapter 5, 74-103, in Helmreich, Ernst C., (editor) *Hungary*, F. A. Praeger, New York, 1957.

11. Braham, Randolph, "State Security," Chapter 7, 132-150, in Helmreich, *op. cit.*

12. Stolz, George (editor), *Forced Labor in the Soviet Orbit: A Selective Bibliography*, Mid-European Studies Center, Mimeographed Series, No. 20, New York, March 15, 1954.

13. Ehrlich, Stanislaw, "Notes on the Rule of the Law," *Polish Perspectives*, 6, October, 1958, 21-28.

14. *Ibid.*, 26.

15. Glabisz, Kazimierz, "The Armed Forces and National Security," Chapter 7, 149-177, in Halecki, Oscar (editor), *Poland*, F. A. Praeger, New York, 1957.

16. *Dziennik Ustaw*, No. 54, Item 269.

17. Rosenthal, A. M., "Court of Justice Typifies Poland," The New York *Times*, March 6, 1959.

18. Roucek, Joseph S., *Contemporary Roumania and Her Problems*, Stanford University Press, 1932.

19. For details, see: Braham, Randolph, "The Government," Chapter 5, 84-100, in Fischer-Galati, Stephen (editor), *Romania*, F. A. Praeger, New York, 1957, and Fischer-Galati, Stephen, "The Constitutional System," 101-119, and Aronovici, Serge H., "National Security," Chapter 7, 120-131, in *Ibid.*

20. *Ibid.*, 95.

21. Summarized from: Lapenna, Ivo, "Socialist Legality: Soviet and Yugoslav," *Soviet Survey*, 25, July-September, 1958, 53-60.

22. Rudzinski, Alexander, "The Constitutional System," Chapter 5, 92-111, in Byrnes, Robert F. (editor), *Yugoslavia*, F. A. Praeger, New York, 1957.

23. For details, see: Rudzinski, *op. cit.*, 103-106

24. Lapenna, *op. cit.*, 60.

25. Bourne, Eric, "Yugoslavia Moves to Ease Penal Code," *Christian Science Monitor*, June 20, 1959.

26. "Criminal Law," *Information Bulletin: About Yugoslavia*, IV, 34-35, July-August, 1959.

27. "Institute for Young Delinquents," *Information Bulletin: About Yugoslavia*, IV, 3, June, 1959, 33.

POLICE SYSTEMS IN THE SOVIET BLOC

Every totalitarian system needs an elaborate machinery of penal control and terror, which defends the "people" from its "enemies," and is glorified by the regime for its heroism and efficiency, relying on an elastic criminal code which makes the category of political crime very broad; "thus even industrial failure frequently becomes a political offense for which the guilty ones must be found." [1]

Thus many criminal cases in the USSR are settled administratively without reference to the courts. The Commission of Soviet Control and factory directors have punitive powers and can deprive workers of certain social welfare benefits; the village soviet powers and various minor departmental powers grant the right to impose small fines. Above all, the Ministry of Internal Affairs hears political cases "in private." In fact, the decree of the Central Executive Committee and the Council of People's Commissars of July 10, 1934, set up the Federal People's Commissariat for Internal Affairs and created a "special consultation" (*osoboe soveshchaine*).[2]

The most glaring deviations from the constitutional and judicial principles have been the operations carried on by the political police.

THE POLITICAL POLICE

In the tradition of the Czarist Third Department and Okhrana, the Cheka and its successors have been a thoroughly disciplined arm of the existing regime since July, 1918 when a revolt of security troops in Moscow convinced the Soviet leaders of the potentially two-edged nature of its weapon. The security have been operating as principal instruments for the enforcement of the bureaucratizing process, operating in "special sections" in factories, military units, etc., with almost unlimited jurisdiction in combating opposition to the regime.[3]

The origin and early development of the Soviet political police is credited to Lenin, although there is no good evidence for this claim. But whether or not Lenin played a direct part in forming the Cheka, he had supplied in his writings on the theory and tactics of revolution, the theoretical arguments which were used to justify its creation. He had, in particular, proclaimed that the successful consummation of a proletarian revolution depended on the effectiveness with which the resistance of counter-revolutionary classes in the period following the seizure of power was smashed under a dictatorship of the proletariat.

The Petrograd Military-Revolutionary Committee, which carried out the seizure of power, organized a security department under Dzershinsky in December, 1917. But the statutes of the Cheka were drawn up only in November, 1918, and appeared in the *Collection Of Laws (Pravda,* December 18, 1927). They declared that it was an organ of Sovnarcom, which appointed the members of its central collegium, and that it worked in close contact with the Commissariat of Justice and Internal Affairs (NKVD); they also recognized the right of Ve Cheka (the "All-Russian," central Cheka) and the local Chekas to organize armed detachments of troops.[4]

The work of the Cheka and its "glorious traditions" have become known throughout the world. According to the definition in the *Large Soviet Encylopedia,* it is the "unsheathed sword of the dictatorship of the proletariat," and according to Lenin, "it is not an institution of persuasion, but one which punishes immediately, swiftly, and mercilessly,"[5] even today the Party Central Committee holds up for present-day Chekists its cruel head Dzerzhinsky as a model (as in the greetings of the All-Union conference of leading officials of the Committee for State Security—KGB—in May, 1959):[6] "In the future too we shall constantly improve the forms and methods of Cheka work . . . , train all the members of state security organizations in the spirit of boundless devotion to the Communist Party . . . , in the spirit of the glorious tradition of the Cheka, and will introduce into all our activities the style and work methods of the remarkable Bolshevik-Leninist F. E. Dzerzhinsky."

While the Cheka (a title derived from two Russian letters for the initials of the term Extraordinary Commission) was the first Soviet security police force established after the 1917 revolution, later the same security force became successively the OGPU, the NKVD, the NKGB, the MVD, and the MGB and now is known as the KGB (initials standing for Committee on State Security) headed by Alexander N. Shelepin.

In 1959, the Soviet government tried to glorify its security police in a 500-page volume honoring the Cheka and justifying the use of terror against enemies of Bolshevism.[7] The new volume contains scores of official documents on the origins of the security police force, mass terror, labor camps, and other features of the security system of the USSR. "The whole tone of the work is glorification of the Cheka's success in assisting in the establishment of the Soviet regime." Much space is devoted to Lenin's declarations justifying terror against persons hostile to the Communist cause. Reporting on the first 15 months of activity of the Cheka, its first chief, Felix Dzerzhinsky, suggested that the labor of arrested people be put to practical use: "I propose that these concentration camps be set aside to make use of the work of those arrested, for gentlemen living without occupation, for those who cannot work without a certain amount of force being applied, or if we take Soviet institutions, such measures of punishment should be taken for careless work, sloppiness and late arrival . . ." He then asks for powers to set up regular labor camps, or what he called schools of labor. The documents picture the Cheka as ruthless in protecting the revolution but under strict orders to avoid making victims of innocents. (One such document has Lenin ordering the release of a seventeen-year-old girl arrested for tearing up his portrait.)

Issuance of the volume apparently was part of a campaign to boost the prestige of the present security police.

508

In May, 1959, an All-Union conference of leading officials of the Committee for State Security (KGB) was held in Moscow, and dealt "thoroughly with the tasks of the state security organs," as contained in Khrushchev's report at the 21st Party Congress, and "exchanged opinions on the most important problems of security work" in the period of the all-out building of Communist society.[8]

All-Union conferences of the heads of the various branches of political and economic life in the USSR usually precede either a shift in Party policy or a sharp increase in its role. There have been many conferences of the Soviet punitive organs, but nothing has ever been published about them, and the appearance of the present official report on the KGB "is an unprecedented event in the history of the Soviet state security organizations . . ."[9] An analysis of the contents of the conference greetings to the Party Central Committee contradicts Khrushchev's assertions at the 21st Party Congress that many of the functions of the state security organs are gradually being transferred to civil organizations. The message also contradicts his repeated statement to the effect that there are no political prisoners in the USSR: ". . . we Soviet Chekists . . . realize that a reduction in punitive functions within the country by no means implies that we have less to do, that the activities of our enemies have slackened."

Soviet propaganda has been trying to explain the need to step up the activities of the Soviet state security organizations by referring to the struggle against external enemies, spies and saboteurs sent into the USSR from abroad. However, the previous practice of this organ proves that its operations are still directed against internal "enemies." According to the Soviet definition, "the internal enemies of our revolution are the agents of the capitalists of all countries."[10] This definition is so broad that it can apply to any Soviet citizen. The fact that the greetings praised the "glorious traditions of the Cheka" and its "forms and methods of work," a formula dropped almost completely from Soviet propaganda in recent years, and then promise to apply and improve these methods, speaks volumes.

The conference was presumably intended to demonstrate that

the relations between the Central Committee, the government, the Army and the KGB, seriously strained since the death of Stalin and made difficult by the execution of Beria, defeat of the anti-Khrushchev group of Malenkov, Molotov, and Kaganovich, and the removal of Marshal Zhukov, have been improved.

The Abolishment of the Soviet Ministry of Internal Affairs. The Soviet Ministry of Internal Affairs (MVD) was abolished in January, 1960,[11] by the Presidium of the Supreme Soviet on recommendation of the Council of Ministers. Its responsibilities were shifted to the Ministries of Internal Affairs of the 15 Union Republics.

The Ministry once had control of all internal police units; it also had its own military forces and was in charge of all labor colonies and their criminal and political prisoners. Mr. Khrushchev had stripped the Ministry of its duties with great fanfare. He said that there are no more political prisoners. Penal colonies are now being advertised as educational institutions. Reductions of up to 40% in police forces were also reported. In effect, the police units—not to be confused with the members of the State Security Police (KGB)—were shifted to local control. The 15 Ministries of Internal Affairs of the Republics now control the uniformed civil police and internal passports, authority over prosecutors and penal colonies and the keys to important state archives.

The administrative changes do not, however, affect the status of the State Security Committee—the KGB—which remains a national organization directed by a committee responsible to the Cabinet (headed by Alexander N. Shelepin).

At various times in Soviet history the functions of the Internal Affairs Ministry and of the State Security Committee were merged or combined in different fashions. They were last combined in 1953, after Stalin's death, and headed by Lavrenti P. Beria, who was shot later that year as a traitor. The last Minister of Internal Affairs was Nikolai P. Dudorov; he is a party functionary who received the assignment in 1956. As All-Union Minister of Internal Affairs, Dudorov also fulfilled the duties of Minister of

Internal Affairs in the Russian Republic, the largest in the country (and he may retain that position).

The operation of the Ministry of International Affairs *(Ministerstov Vnutrennykh Del)* was even more strictly veiled than that of other agencies in the USSR. But it was known that at one time or another it had complete and centralized authority over all civil police forces, over the labor camps and penal institutions with their large populations of political and criminal prisoners, border guards and a special contingent of military forces. Its prisoners built many of the most famous Soviet industrial projects. The Ministry was repeatedly combined with and separated from the equivalent of the present State Security Committee, the agency in charge of the secret police.

After Stalin died and his successors had rid themselves of Beria they took measures, advertised as the assertion of strict Communist party control, over both the Ministry of Internal Affairs and the State Security Committee.

More important, many of the Ministry's functions were transferred to other agencies or decentralized so as to preclude the use of the Ministry's apparatus for forcible political action.

Khrushchev has boasted repeatedly in the last two years that there were no more political prisoners in the USSR. Others have said that the former labor colonies had been converted to educational correctional institutions.

In the Russian Republic, reductions of the civil police forces are said to have totaled 40% and the MVD military units reportedly have been transferred to the Ministry of Defense. Thus the decentralization appears to be only a confirmation of steps taken in the post-Stalin years by Premier Khrushchev. For several months at the end of 1959, the Soviet press had been conducting a campaign to proclaim the benign nature of modern Soviet justice, law enforcement and penology. With enhanced authority and prestige, the local police forces have been repeatedly represented as kindly and efficient operatives.

Furthermore, criminals, petty thieves, and even former traitors have been urged to turn themselves in for the understanding corrective action of the new police. Khrushchev himself related the case of one former thief whom he led down the path of rehabilitation.

Despite the steady whittling away of MVD authority in recent years, its initials and memory remain a symbol to the Soviet people.

THE SATELLITE POLICE SYSTEM

Most of the police forces of the satellite states are military formations, recruited, trained, and organized as ordinary armies, and include units not even known in the West.[12]

Czechoslovakia. The Czechoslovakia police force, for instance, consists of six different organizations: National Security troops, Frontier Guards, Secret Police, Prison Guards, Factory Militia, and People's Militia. The Prison Guards are subdivided into labor camp units, transport troops, (units escorting prisoners and deportees throughout the country), and ordinary prison guards. The People's Militia (in some satellite states known as "Local Militia") consists of many miscellaneous formations, including harvest militiamen, collective farm guards, and railway troops (units guarding the railway lines and stations, roads, bridges, canals, etc.).

The exact number of all these forces is a carefully guarded Communist secret, and police credits are no longer published in any of the satellite budgets.[13]

The most important of the police forces are the so-called "armed units of national security." They do not perform ordinary police duties; the People's Militia is used for that purpose. They are stationed in several strategically important districts and constitute a sort of reserve army, used in case of major disturbances. They are highly motorized; their arms and equipment are of the best quality, and they are constantly featured at military parades and party demonstrations as a reminder of the power of the Communist regimes. (They might be compared with the former Nazi SS troops.)

512

The Prison Guards, which include the labor camp troops, administer and guard the political prisons and the forced labor camps (usually called Labor Educational Camps).[14]

The People's Militia (the ordinary police) deals with the largest number of "unreliable elements": Deportees (the families ejected from their homes, expelled from their place of residence, and forcibly interned in remote country districts where they live under police supervision). Reactionaries, capitalists, and landlords form, however, only a very small proportion of the vast number of deportees, who are mostly people from all walks of life considered by the Communists as too independent in their attitudes. Then come the so-called "Kulaks" (village rich), the peasants opposing the Communist collectivization policies. (It is important to note that slave labor was introduced in the USSR on a mass scale only after the Soviet collectivization drive in the 1930's). And interestingly enough, the most recent big group of deportees have been communists and their families, expelled for anti-Soviet and anti-party activities (some half a million).

The People's Militia also keeps a careful and constant watch on every citizen. To help them, the Czechoslovak Police Ministry formed, in August, 1952, special "auxiliary guards of public safety," consisting usually of three "volunteers" working under the direct orders of a police official, even in the smallest farms or tractor stations; in some satellite states, these auxiliary police units are called "watch committees." During the summer, they form "harvest militiamen," and keep a day and night watch on all work in the countryside. A Polish decree of December, 1950 granted these auxiliary policemen special privileges protecting them from being prosecuted by their victims. In Bulgaria, children are trained to "uncover deviationists"—refugees trying to escape across the frontier.

The operations of the satellite police forces are helped by the Soviet-type laws and rules of court procedure adopted by all satellite governments. Article 1 of the Romanian penal code (April, 1949) stipulated that "actions which are considered dangerous for society can be punished even when they are not expressly punishable by law." The Czechoslovak Penal Code of

July, 1950, allows the extension of a sentence of imprisonment "if it appears from the manner in which the offense was committed that a hostile attitude towards the people's democratic regime was demonstrated or intended to be demonstrated." Furthermore, if an offender, after serving his sentence, has, "not changed his attitude" (toward the government) he can be given another two years of forced labor.[15]

There have been several administrative and, on the surface, rather functional changes in the administration of the satellite police forces.

Albania. In Albania, all police forces are commonly called "Sigurimi" but technically this applies only to the Direction of State Security (*Drejtoria e Sigurimi te Shteit*) (similar to the original Russian Cheka). In addition to the so-called General Police, the uniformed People's Police has 4 subdivisions: Police for Economic Objectives, Fire Police, Communication Police, and Detention Police (this last being the largest since it handles the many jails and the forced labor and concentration camps for political prisoners and suspects). The People's Police and the Sigurimi are administered by the Ministry of the Interior; Koci Xoxe was Minister until his purge and execution for "Titoism" in 1949. But operational and policy control is exercised by Soviet experts. Every able-bodied male is obliged to serve for a 2-month period in his own locality in the auxiliary local police (*Polici e Lokaliteit*) by a 1948 order of the Ministry of the Interior.

Bulgaria. When the Communists seized power in Bulgaria in 1944, they suppressed the Directorate of Police (in Sofia, which had been used after May, 1934 also to suppress political parties, freedom of the press, and anti-government organizations) and set up a new organization, the People's Militia, the only government department completely under the control of the Communists of the Fatherland Front regime. It did away with all prominent anti-Communists in government soon after September 9, 1949.

The Bulgarian Security Force is organized along the Soviet pattern, numbering some 200,000 men, half of whom form the Secret Police. The People's Militia is uniformed, completely

514

militarized, and all members are Party members (some 30,000) (corresponding to the Soviet uniformed militia). Corresponding to the Soviet Internal Security Army is the Motorized Militia, with armored units and artillery detachments (some 15,000), and for its loyalty to the communist regime it is often called the "front-line army of the reds." The Frontier Army (some 20,000), controlled by the Ministry of the Interior, guards the frontiers to a depth of some 10 to 20 miles; it is mainly interested in hunting down escaping refugees. This unit receives preferential treatment (in pay, privileges, rations, conditions of leave) in comparison with the other armed forces. The Transport Militia (comparable to the Soviet transport Army) guards all railroad lines, tunnels, stations, roads, bridges, and other means of communication, while the Harvest Militia watches over crops and the special Factory Guards (the Industrial Militia) operates in industrial establishments. But the most powerful is the Secret Police whose power over the life and death of each Bulgarian appears unlimited (and this includes Bulgaria's other police and military forces).[16]

The Act on the People's Militia, passed in March, 1948, divided all police forces into "general" or "special," the "special" police forces including guards for Railway, Customs, Forest and Business (Government) Enterprises, Factories and Works, and Banks and Mines, under the Ministry of the Interior, whose budgets are paid by the agencies and enterprises to which they are attached.[17] Article 52 provided for the organization by the police of the "educational camps" (forced labor camps), where the Minister of the Interior could send anyone without any form of trial, and could issue a "renewable" sentence of one year (Article 54).

In 1956, the administration of all prisons was returned to the Ministry of Justice; the administration of labor camps was assigned to a special police force (the inmates forming about 1% of the total population before Stalin's death), but this figure is not including the deportees to remote villages and small towns, and war prisoners and deportees to the USSR.

The Ukase on the People's Militia of March 29, 1955, proclaimed it an "organ of the people's democratic power in its fight for the preservation of socialist legality, socialist property, the established public order, and the freedom, security, and personal safety of the citizens" (Article 1). The police can enter any home without a warrant, issues all passports and visas for internal and international use, and "with the written consent of the Chief Prosecutor" has the power "forcibly to establish in a new place of residence for a given period of time or forever" or "to prohibit leaving the residence for 6 months" all sentenced for grave crimes, recidivists, people without fixed residence, and systematic loafers" (Article 14). Remarks Dallin: "In this respect, Bulgaria is perhaps the most sovietized captive state in East-Central Europe" (p. 158).

Hungary. The new Hungarian Police Force, remodeled in accordance with the provisions of Decree No. 274,000 of 1949 B.M., is one national state police system, without separate local or municipal police organizations. The police chief and his deputies are appointed by the Minister of the Interior. The personnel of the secret police is recruited from among the most trusted members of the Party, and Party functionaries are appointed to watch over the loyalty of the members of the force; special agents of the intelligence branch of the Hungarian Workers' (Communist) Party supplement the machinery of supervision.[18] In December, 1949, following the official establishment of the regime of People's Democracy (August, 1949), the State Security Department was separated from the Ministry of the Interior (the Cabinet Decree No. 4,353 of 1949 [268]). It amalgamated with the Frontier Guard units of the Hungarian armed forces (previously under the jurisdiction of the Ministry of Defense), and the secret police was renamed State Security Authority (AVH). Under the decree of 1949, the AVH is subordinate to the Council of Ministers which exercises its authority through one of its members.

Poland. In Poland, the decree of December 7, 1954, on the Supreme Agencies of Government Administration in Internal Affairs and Public Security (*Dziennik Ustaw*, No. 54, Item 269), the Ministry of Public Security was abolished and the ordinary police functions taken over by a new Ministry of Interior; state

516

security was entrusted to a special Committee for Public Security attached to the Council of Ministers and headed by a Deputy Premier. In particular, the Ministry of Internal Affairs heads the activities of the Citizen's Militia, the Internal Security Corps, and the Military Border Guards, the administration of penal institutions, prison guards, civil defense, fire-prevention control, registration and passport control, penal administrative decisions, public and civil status records. The decree also provided that the police and administrative functions are delegated to the People's Councils and become part of their basic tasks. On the other hand, matters directly related to the "protection of the system of the People's Democracy as established by the Constitution of the Polish People's Republic," were assigned to the Committee of Public Security, a separate agency under the Council of Ministers. In Czechoslovakia, the security forces were under the jurisdiction of the Ministry of Interior between February, 1948 and May, 1950. A new Ministry, the Ministry of National Security, was formed on May 23, 1950, and the two Ministries functioned side by side from 1950 to 1953; on September 11, 1953, after Stalin's and Gottwald's death, the Ministry of National Security was abolished and the security forces were placed under the jurisdiction of the Ministry of Interior. Secret police (STB) is responsible for ferreting out "hostile elements" and for safeguarding the regime.

Romania. In Romania, internal security is the responsibility of the Ministry of the Interior; its main branches are the Militia, the Security Troops of the Ministry, and the People's Security (secret police). The militia discharges the regular police duties necessary under any social system, plus certain duties found only in a communist state—control of movement of the entire population. The Security Troops fulfill normal army and police functions, but also totalitarian political functions (roughly corresponding to those of the former Nazi SS formations). The DGSP (secret police) is modeled after the Soviet NKVD.

Yugoslavia. In Yugoslavia, in the immediate postwar years, the first security force was the Corps of National Defense (*Korpus Narodne Obrane Jugoslavije—KNOJ*), uniformed elite troops separate from the regular army and from the secret police (UDB); they were considered as Tito's security guard, a kind of SS corps, and its task was mainly to smash any opposition to Tito. With the strengthening of Tito's regime the KNOJ lost its usefulness, and it was reduced from some 75,000 men to about 25,000 men as a special frontier force (in 1952). The People's Militia was Tito's first police force, formed from Partisan and village units in 1941; on December 12, 1946, it was proclaimed a kind of local constabulary under central government's administration (the Federal Secretariat of Home Affairs), but each of the 6 Republics had a People's Militia command within the local secretariat of home affairs. The Organization for the Protection of the People (*Organizacja za zastitu narod*—OZNA), in imitation of the Soviet NKVD, was founded on May 13, 1944. With its intelligence and counter-intelligence services, its first task was to liquidate fascist and Gestapo agents, domestic traitors and provocateurs; but one of its peculiar assignments was the combatting of national, racial, or religious intolerance, hatred, discord, and criminal offenses against humanity and international good will. Now called *Uprava Drzavne Bezbednosti* (UDB, Administration of State Security) it was transformed, in 1952, into a civil service organization. It was to the credit of the UDB that, after the Cominform split, it uncovered 1,137 Cominform agents and seized 365 armed terrorists. But it was castigated by its own chief, Ranković, in a report to the Central Committee on June 3, 1951, when, reprimanding the secret police, the judiciary, and local Party officials for neglect of duty, he accused the UDB of perverting justice and admitted that in 1949 no fewer than 47% of its arrests were unjustified.

SELECTED BIBLIOGRAPHY *See* pp. 542-545.

NOTES

Chapter IV

1. Friedrich, Carl J. & Brzenzinsky, Zbigniew K., *Totalitarian Dictatorship and Autocracy*, Harvard University Press, Cambridge, 1956, Chapter 14, "Purges, Confessions, and Camps," 150-165, 146.

2. Gsovski, Vladimir, *Soviet Civil Law*, University of Michigan Press, Ann Arbor, 1948, Vol. II, 23; Kulski, W. W., *The Soviet Regime*, Syracuse University Press, Ithaca, New York, 1954, 233-234.

3. Artemyev, V. P., *Political Controls in the Soviet Army*, Praeger, New York, 1954 Berman, H. J. and Kenner, M., *Soviet Military Law and Administration*, Harvard University Press, Cambridge, 1955 Edelman, M., G.P.U., *Justice*, Allen and Unwin, London, 1938; Glickman, J. G. (editor), *Police-State Methods in the Soviet Union*, Beacon Press, Boston, 1953; Leites, N. and Bernaut, E., *Ritual of Liquidation*, Free Press, Glencoe, Illinois, 1954; Wolin, S. and Slosser, R. M. (res.), *The Russian Secret Policy*, Praeger, New York, 1957.

4. Scott, E. J., "The Cheka," 1-23, in St. Anthony's Papers, No. 1, *Soviet Affairs*, Chatto and Windus, London, 1956.

5. Lenin, V., *Sochineniya* (Works) (4th edition), XXXXIII, 1952, 150.

6. *Pravda*, May 18, 1959.

7. "Soviet Issues Defense of Security Police Unit," *Christian Science Monitor*, April 30, 1959.

8. *Pravda*, May 18, 1959.

9. "The Conference of the State Security Organs," *Bulletin*, Institute for the Study of the USSR, VI, September, 1959, 21-23.

10. *Pravda*, May 18, 1959.

11. "Soviet Abolishes Interior Agency," The New York *Times*, January 14, 1960.

12. For the police systems in the satellite states, see: Skendi, Stavro (editor), *Albania*, F. A. Praeger, 1956, Chapter 7, "National Security," 109-124; Padev, Michael, "National Security," Chapter 7, 147-161, in Dellin, L. A. D. (editor), *Bulgaria*, F. A. Praeger, 1957; Beck, Curt, "The Government," Chapter 5, 80-100, in Busek, Vratislav & Spulber, Nicolas (editors), *Czechoslovakia*, F. A. Praeger, New York, 1957, (especially 94-97); Grothe, Peter, *To Win the Minds of Men, The Story of the Communist Propaganda War in East Germany*, Pacific Books, Palo Alto, California, 1958, Chapter III, "Propaganda by Terror," 64-71; Braham, Randolph, "State Security," Chapter 7, 132-150, in Helmreich, Ernst C. (editor), *Hungary*, F. A. Praeger, 1957; Glabisz, Kazimierz, & Gwodz, "The Armed Forces and National Security," 149-177, in Halecki, Oscar (editor), *Poland*, F A. Praeger, 1957; Barnett, Clifford R. (editor), *Poland: Its People, Its Society, Its Culture*, Grove Press, New York, 1958, Chapter 7, "Legal and Theoretical Base of Government," 114-123, & 8, "Structure of the Government," 124-140; Aronovici, Serge H., "National Security," chapter 7, 120-131, in Fischer-Galati, Stephen (editor), *Romania*, F. A. Praeger, 1957; Ziffer, Bernard, "National Security," Chapter 8, 145-165, in Byrnes, Robert F. (editor), *Yugoslavia*, F. A. Praeger, New York, 1957; Dallin, David J., *The New Soviet Empire*, Yale University Press, New Haven, 1951; Glickstein, Ygael, *Stalin's Satellites in Europe*, Beacon Press, 1952; etc.

13. M. P., "The Satellite Police System," *World Today*, VIII, 12, December 1952, 504-512.

14. For additional details, see: Beck, Curt, "The Government," Chapter 5, 80-100, in Busek, Wratislav & Spulber, Nicolas (editors), *Czechoslovakia*, F. A. Praeger, New York, 1957, (especially 94-97).

15. See: *A Red Paper on Forced Labor*, UN Information Office, 1952. Czechoslovak laws are analyzed in: The National Committee for a Free

Europe, *Population Transfers and Forced Labor in Czechoslovakia*, New York, 1951. Romanian forced labor laws are discussed in: *The Eastern Quarterly*, London, August-October, 1952.

16. Bulgaria was the first Soviet satellite to inaugurate the "legal" basis of arbitrary police repression; a decree of January 20, 1945 empowered the Minister of the Interior to organize "labor education communities" (slave labor camps) ; a special decree "for the defense of the People's government" of March, 1945, granted the police the right to impose sentences (including the death penalty) to anyone offending the regime or promoting "fascist ideology."

17. For details, see: Dallin, *op. cit.*, 157-158.

18. For frequent purges of the personnel of Secret Police, see: Braham, Randolph, "State Security," Chapter 7, 132-150, in Helmreich, Ernst C. (editor) , *Hungary*, F. A. Praeger, New York, 1957.

Chapter V

THE PENAL SYSTEM IN THE SOVIET BLOC

A. *THE FORCED LABOR CAMPS IN THE USSR*

It is difficult, from the Western standpoint, to deal with the criminal and juvenile delinquencies in the Soviet bloc, since the Soviet area includes among its definitions of crime the political aspects of deviant behavior. It is important to note that in the Soviet ideological conception of crime, there is an inter-relation between economic, political and legal matters. Hence the lack of economic or political orthodoxy, or a real or intended opposition to the current policies of the regime, becomes a crime. Thus political prisoners are joined by those who had violated economic decrees or laws; the "ordinary" criminals thus also become political prisoners, since in the Marxian theory, these were to disappear with the coming of a new society.

In this respect, the most important penal institutions in the Soviet region have been the forced labor camps.

THE MARXIAN CONCEPT OF LABOR

The forced labor system of Soviet Russia is "an *organic* element, a normal component, of the social structure." [1] It is a variety of a concentration camp, adapted to accommodate the contemporary needs and policies of the Soviet government.

Basic approach to the problem of labor in the USSR is rooted in the writings of Karl Marx, the eighth point in the Marx-

521

Engels 10 point program as stated in the *Communist Manifesto;* it calls for the "equal obligation of all to work. The establishment of industrial armies, especially for agriculture."

In the first labor code adapted by the Soviet rulers this Marxist declaration was applied at the very base of the order. The code, passed on December 19, 1918, provided for compulsory labor. Article I was entitled, "On Compulsory Labor, declaring that "All citizens in the Russian Socialist Federal Soviet Republic, with the exceptions stated in sections a and 3, shall be subject to compulsory labor." The exemptions were persons under 16 years of age, all persons over 50 years; and injured or ill persons. Those who were temporarily exempt from compulsory labor were those who were temporarily incapacitated owing to illness or injury, for "a period necessary for their recovery"; and women, "for a period of 8 weeks before and 8 weeks after confinement."

This attitude to labor as an obligation was expressed in the subsequent USSR Constitution, Article 12: "In the USSR work is a duty and a matter of honor for every able-bodied citizen, in accordance with the principle 'He who does not work, neither shall he eat.'" The principle applied was that of social socialism: "From each according to his ability, to each according to his work." (Marx, however, stated: "From each according to his ability, to each according to his needs.")

Another link in the chain of forced labor is found in the theory concerning crime. According to Marx, the nature of every society is determined by the economic relationships which exist in that society. The reason crime exists in a non-socialist, capitalistic, or feudalistic society, is that the means of production are not owned by the working classes but by the capitalistic or the feudal barons. Thus in a society with the proper economic relationships the reasons for crime and other social ills would disappear.[2]

Yet, from the very beginning of its existence, the Soviet regime had to deal with an extraordinary number of political prisoners. In theory, these prisoners had been the result of the Czarist environment, and could be corrected, re-educated, and redeemed.

Model prisons were established, but soon something went wrong. With the development of the Soviet regime, the crime rate not only did not decrease but reached unprecedented proportions. Since there were not enough prisons, by 1925-26 only 36% of all sentences imposed were actually carried out.[3] To cover up the contradictory reality, the Soviet propaganda machinery stressed this as an example of Soviet liberalism. Nothing was said, of course, about harsh treatment and brutality, summary executions and tortures— and when such stories appeared they were branded as anti-Soviet and capitalist-inspired.

THE INTRODUCTION OF FORCED LABOR

The new regime did not make the mistake of the Czarist government of sending political prisoners to Siberia where they wrote revolutionary pamphlets and books (remember: Stalin, Lenin!) and eventually became active leaders of the Revolution. Instead, the new legal codes of the Soviet Union provided for punishment for "a term of not less than three years in solitary confinement," and the idea of forced labor was introduced:

"Invention and dissemination with Counter-Revolutionary intent, of false rumors or unverified news, which could provoke a public panic, mistrust of authority or discredit the latter, is punishable by deprivation of liberty for a term not less than six months. If the actions are not proved to have been Counter-Revolutionary, the penalty may be reduced to three months of forced labor." [4]

From these modest beginnings have developed a large program of forced labor. The Czarist system of sending prisoners to Siberia has been continued by the Soviet government on an even greater scale, and, apparently, with just as much brutality.[5]

There is, however, one basic difference. Under the Czars most of those exiled were criminals in the usual sense of the concept. Under the Soviets, most of those sent to Siberia appear to be political prisoners.

The first large-scale deportation were those of the Kulaks (rich farmers), who opposed Stalin's socialization and mechanization of their farms. Many of them were assassinated, and others were packed off to Siberia. In the political purges of the mid-1930's, many of those who were not executed were bundled off to Siberia. When the Soviets occupied the Baltic States, Czechoslovakia, and Poland, many of those suspected of hostility to the Soviet regime were deported to Siberia. (It is believed that even a larger number of German prisoners of war were sent there.)

Since the Soviets have been denying such reports, there has been considerable controversy over the treatment of those sent to Siberia. Dallin, Margarete Buber and Lipper describe the Siberian conditions even worse than those under the Czars.[6]

RECENT CONDITIONS

From these "modest" beginnings the Soviet Union has developed a large program of forced labor. Though the number of inmates or prisons, camps in exile, and "model correctional centers" are not available for the early period, Herling estimates that in the 1940-1950 decade the prison camps and forced labor camps had a minimum of 8,000,000 workers, and at various times a maximum of 20,000,000.[7] Here the inmates were working in railroad construction, gold mining, the manufacturing of nursery furniture, agriculture, fishing, etc.

In 1950, the *Soviet Encyclopaedia* (vol. 57) defined Forced Labor as: "Forced Labor is one of the basic measures of punishment of Soviet socialist law. Forced labor consists in the sentenced person either being forcibly directed to work organized by corrective labor organs, or remaining at work at his normal place of work, in which case the authority sentencing that person to forced labor imposes a deduction from the wages amounting up to 25%; in the time remaining after his work the sentenced person is not subjected to any limitations."

RECENT LEGAL CHANGES

The sensitiveness of the Soviet authorities to foreign criticism induced the Soviet government to enact the Corrective Labor Codex of the RSFSSR, approved by the All-Union Central Executive Committee and the Council of People's Commissars on August 1, 1933 (Collection of Decrees No. 48, Article 208), which replaced the term "forced labor (*prinuditelnyie raboty*) by the term "corrective labor work" (*ispravitelno-trudovye raboty;*); similar changes were made in the majority of subsequent legislative acts, in particular in amendments to the Criminal Codex (Collection of Decrees 1934, No. 9, Article 51, No. 27, Article 157, No. 42, Article 259, etc.). The Code stated clearly that "Persons are directed to corrective labor who have been sentenced thereto by: (a) sentence in a court of law, (b) Decree of an administrative organ (Clause 8). Clause 129 transferred these "corrective labor institutions" from the jurisdiction of the Republican Ministries of Justice to the NKVD of the USSR. The Code provided that the forced labor can be directed toward "socially useful ends" (Clause 101) and the MVD was allowed to contract its prison labor out to various industries, cooperatives, and other enterprises and institutions.

THE TYPE OF LABOR

As a rule, forced laborers are employed in heavy work, such as mining, heavy construction work, timber work and agriculture in remote areas. In 1941, the Soviet Economic Plan disclosed that forced labor under the control of the NKVD (secret police) accounted for almost half of the total mining output of the USSR, 12% of timber procurement, and considerable quantities of gold, coal and oil. It is known that several large Soviet canals and vast stretches of railway were mainly built by forced labor during Stalin's lifetime, whilst until quite recently prisoners were employed—and possibly still are—in coal, gold, copper and nickel mining, railway maintenance, chemical factories, road building and a variety of other enterprise of economic significance to the Soviet state in camps disseminated throughout the country, including those near Inta, Pinega, Potma, Solikamsk, Chernogorsk, Stalinabad and many others.

CONTROL

Forced labor, banishment and exile in the USSR have been completely controlled by the secret police since 1934, and most camps had, until recently, MVD armed guards. Today the majority of camps and settlements are to some extent supervised by local authorities with fairly wide powers. Commissions are set up, comprising representatives of local government, and trade unions and Komsomol (youth organizations). These may engage or dismiss officials, reduce sentences, introduce punishments, organize labor schemes and seek jobs for prisoners after they are released.

TYPES OF PRISONERS

There are three distinct groups of prisoners in the labor camps: (1) professional criminals (thieves, burglars, murderers), who form a decided minority, but they are usually best treated. (2) "Bytoviks" (defined by Dallin and Nicolaevsky as "offenders against the mode of life"), mostly officials in public institutions found guilty of abuses. They are usually granted posts in the administration of the camp or in the "cultural and educational departments," and are proud of the position of preference over the "enemies of the people," or political offenders. (3) Political offenders may be classified into several categories: (a) peasants suspected of individualistic tendencies and thus evaluated as undesirable on the collective farms; (b) persons who had been abroad, or have members of their families abroad with whom they communicate (mostly Jews), and who, like the peasants, had been sentenced not by a court but simply by the secret police; (3) former inhabitants of the borderlands (mostly Russian Poles, Chinese and Koreans); (4) those condemned for their religious beliefs (mostly Catholics, Baptists, members of the Ukrainian Orthodox Church); (5) middle or high state officials sentenced for various political offenses; and (6) individuals condemned for specific Soviet wartime crimes (collaboration with the enemy, prisoners of war, nationals of countries occupied at the end of World War II).[8]

STALIN'S PERIOD

During Stalin's lifetime, the forced labor camps were largely filled, not only with political prisoners who had been guilty of actual opposition to the regime but with those who were merely suspected of being antagonistic to the Party or its policies.

POST-STALIN CHANGES

After Stalin's death, and as late as 1955 and 1956, repatriated prisoners of war who had undergone Soviet forced labor stated that the vast majority of prisoners in the places where they had been were political. In Karaganda, for instance, all 15,000 inmates had been sentenced under the article of the Criminal Code which deals with "counter-revolutionary crimes." There is no doubt that the amnesties of 1953 and 1955 set free many minor political detainees, but the statements made by Khrushchev, Suslov and others that there are no political prisoners in the Soviet Union today have been disproved by the fact that, among others, a number of Jehovah's Witnesses were imprisoned a few months ago for what were termed "crimes against the State," but which turned out to consist simply in practising their religion.

Post-Stalin changes in the Soviet system have brought also release from slave labor to a surviving few among hundreds of thousands of captives swept up especially by the MGB dragnet in the turbulent years of 1944-1947. (The deportation of the

Baltic peoples to the slave-labor camps represented the second largest group of non-Soviet peoples subjected to the slave-labor system.)

Due to persistent criticism from abroad, certain improvements in the labor camps have taken place in recent years. There are some labor "colonies" but no more labor "camps" in the USSR, reported Justice Minister Vladimir A. Boldyrev of the Russian Federated Republic in 1959.[9] (He also told a news conference that the Republic's police force had been trimmed about 40% because of a drop in the incidence of crime.) The administrative discipline in the "colonies" apparently was relaxed some time ago and then became too lax for official comfort.

According to information published in Moscow in 1957, there are now three types of regime in the corrective labor colonies. Those under the "strict" regime are possibly little better than they were in Stalin's days, but recent reports from refugees state the camps under the "normal" regime now provide adequate clothing, heating in barrack-rooms, blankets—and in at least one camp even sheets on the beds—and both reasonable medical care and payment for work. Prisoners work for about 8 or 9 hours a day, 6 and occasionally 7 days a week, and payment varies considerably. In some camps it is equivalent to that of an unskilled worker in the USSR, but in most of them about two-thirds of the prisoners' wages is deducted before payment for food, shelter, clothing, etc. In most camps, *Pravda* and *Izvestia* may now be bought and in one (Potma) prisoners occasionally see Soviet films. In some of the "mild" regime camps, prisoners can be visited by their immediate relatives, and these visitors can occasionally stay in or near the camp if they wish.

Once released, all prisoners are placed at the disposal of the authorities and these may decide to find them employment locally. In effect, this means that prisoners who have been doing unpleasant jobs in remote places can be forced to remain there, though in such cases they are invited to send for their families. However, it is probable that a good deal of the fairly extensive settlement which goes on around labor camp areas in the Soviet Union is now voluntary.

528

As a result, a number of medium-sized cities of a peculiar kind have risen in the USSR in the last few years as a consequence of the amnesties and the half-hearted liberalization, which have set free thousands upon thousands of former criminals, and among them large numbers of the worst type of bandits. Some were able to depart and submerge themselves in the vast country; others were obliged to stay in the cities near their slave labor camps and to continue work as "free citizens." Life in such places has become an eternal trial; the authorities and the local police appear to be in fear of those bandits at large, and their deeds usually go unpunished. The term "naditocracy" came into wide use.

At the same time, a substantial body of evidence has been collected by the International Commission Against Concentration Camp Practices, (with headquarters in Brussels), and the Soviet laws themselves corroborate the Commission's findings to the extent of showing that forced labor is still an integral part of the Soviet system. It is estimated that, despite substantial reductions in the past decade, there are about one million forced labor prisoners, whilst refugees state that forced labor exists in Rumania, Czechoslovakia, Albania and Bulgaria.

Whereas the 1940 edition of the large *Soviet Encyclopaedia* declared quite boldly: "Forced labor is one of the basic measures of punishment of Soviet Socialist criminal law," the 1955 edition contains no entry under this heading. Under other headings, however, reference is made to the use of "compulsion" in the USSR "towards a minority, for the purpose of safe-guarding the Socialist order." At the same time, "camps" have been renamed "colonies."

B. *THE PENAL SYSTEM IN THE EUROPEAN COMMUNIST BLOC*

Most of the provisions of the criminal laws of the satellites are carbon copies of the Soviet example, the same applies to various

529

legal and "pragmatic" steps used to handle crime and juvenile delinquency.

It is important to remember, however, that, as in the USSR, the communist states in Europe include among the definitions of crime the political aspects of deviant behavior and that there is an inter-relation between political, economic, and legal areas. Hence, the lack of political or economic orthodoxy, or real or intended opposition to the current policies of the regimes, becomes a crime. Prison camps were established for "unreliable" political groups immediately after each communist coup d'état in addition to conventional prisons.[1]

The estimates of the total number of camp prisoners in the six satellites vary between 800,000 and 1,300,000. The forced labor camps (usually called Labor Educational Camps, which guard the political prisoners) are known to number over 450. The difference in estimates is due mainly to the lack of a uniform system of "defining" and describing the different categories of camps. Some are run on the Nazi concentration camp system, and many of them (especially in Western Poland and Czechoslovakia) are housed in the old Nazi concentration camps. Originally built by the Gestapo, they form sometimes small towns of some 30,000 "inhabitants" and more. But the more recently built camps are much smaller. They are usually located near large government building projects. Still others are only barracks where the prisoners are confined only during the night; they work during the day, under escort, outside the camps. In addition, small groups of prisoners are allotted to collective farms and live in not very heavily guarded buildings, or in tents, on the farms. There are also "transport camps" which house prisoners sent from one camp to another, or deportees for whom no accommodation can be found in their enforced internment place. Special camps have been set up for women and youngsters, and camps for priests (set up usually in old monasteries). (For instance, the former Archbishop Dr. Joseph Beran of Prague was confined for some time in such a camp at the Novar Rise monastery in Southern Moravia, where there were about 300 confined priests).

There are also the ordinary prisons which, for all six satellites, are estimated to hold about 250,000 political prisoners. With the exception of those considered most "dangerous," the able-bodied prisoners are sent out during the summer months to work on government building projects while living in camps—and practically no camp prisoners are freed during the summer months.[2]

ALBANIA

Forced labor was introduced in Albania in the Labor Code, promulgated on August 25, 1947. Law no. 726 of August, 1949 widened the conscription powers of the government.[3] This method of organizing labor was integrated with the provisions of the new Albanian Penal Code of September 1, 1952, which includes among the "crimes" punishable by forced or corrective labor terms of from 6 months to 4 years: producing industrial goods of bad quality, insufficient quantity, or in violation of designated standards (Article 90); departure without permission of a worker or civil servant from a state or social enterprise or institution (Article 202); disobeying orders to work permanently or temporarily for the realization of the state's production and construction plans (Article 204).

BULGARIA

Bulgaria has extensive institutionalized Communist labor brigades, labor mobilization, compulsory labor service, "correctional labor" without confinement, and forced labor in camps or prisons.[4]

Labor brigades formed mostly of young peasants and students, provide "voluntary" labor, since service in a brigade is necessary for admission to schools or universities. The so-called compulsory labor service actually has its roots in the same institution founded in 1920-21 by the Agrarian government of Stambuliski and never abolished; it covers all men over 20 years of age and all women

531

over 16, using them in community construction projects for a period of 12 months (6 for women) and assuring them a minimum daily wage. The Communist compulsory labor service (instituted by a Decree of August 24, 1946, supplemented on May 9, 1949, and superseded by the Edict on General Rules Concerning Compulsory Labor Service on March 30, 1954) covers all young people of draft age who cannot be drafted into the armed services due to the limits imposed on Bulgaria by the Peace Treaty (1947); actually, the draftees are mostly "unreliable" elements. The service is 3 years, under the command of a special agency of the Council of Ministers (The General Administration of the Compulsory Labor Service.) The Council of Ministers direct "Labor mobilization" (Act of March 2, 1948 and subsequent legislation); its Office of Labor Mobilization can "direct individual persons or groups of citizens between the ages of 18 and 50 to perform industrial or other work" and can "mobilize specialists over the age of 50."

A vast portion of such free labor force is provided by the cadres of forced labor as a result of court sentence and administrative measures. The first group covers all convicted persons who, according to the Criminal Code, must perform "suitable work" and those sentenced to forced labor "without confinement." The second category was introduced as "forced-labor-educational work" in 1948 and included in the new Criminal Code of 1951 as "correctional labor," imposed on such offenses as "disobedience," "carelessness," "undermining labor discipline," "failure to give one's real name," or "spreading slanderous, insulting or false information likely to create distrust in the Government or social disturbances," for the term of up to one year. The sentence is served in the place of regular employment or "elsewhere," and up to 25% of the convict's pay is withheld.

The legal approval of imposing summarily the penalty of forced labor by the police was given in January, 1945 and codified in the Law of the People's Militia (Communist police) on March 25, 1948. Chapter VII of this law, "Measures Against Socially Dangerous Persons," allows the police to send to "labor-educational communities," or a "new place of residence" (deportation), all persons "with Fascist and anti-popular manifestations, those who are dangerous to public order and the security of the state, and those who spread malignant and false rumors." The places of work are defined as "projects of general utility, such as constructions of roads, railroad tracks, canals, dams, buildings, levees, river connections, forest stations, tillage of government or public farms, work in mines, quarries, factories, workshops, and the like." Thus "the frank Communist legislation gives the police unlimited freedom to arrest and confine without trial to forced labor anybody they consider politically unreliable." [5] (It is true that the Militia Law was replaced by the ukase for the People's Militia of March 29, 1955, which has no reference to "labor-educational" communities, but this does not circumvent the right of the police to arrest and deport "without trial and to unspecified destination."

According to the investigation of the UN Ad Hoc Committee on Forced Labor (1952), Bulgaria has some 50 forced labor camps with at least 100,000 Bulgarians as inmates.[6]

CZECHOSLOVAKIA

Although Section 2 of the Constitution guarantees personal freedom, which "may be restricted or withheld only on the basis of law," the Law on Forced Labor Camps of October 25, 1948, restricted personal freedom, and established regional boards of 3 members, appointed by the Ministry of the Interior, authorizing them to confine to forced labor camps "persons who are not less than 18 and not more than 60 years old, and who are physically and mentally capable of working, but who evade work or threaten the people's democratic order or economic system . . ." Such persons can be sent to such camps for a period of from 3 months to 2 years. Furthermore, the convicted person is subject to further restrictions upon the completion of his term.

The forced labor camps are now regulated by the new Criminal Code of 1950 and by the directives issued in its implementation. Before January 1, 1954, confinement in such camps could be imposed as an independent penalty by the Penal Boards of the district People's Committee; under Law no. 102 of 1953, these boards can impose a sentence of correctional labor without confinement. The Criminal Code and the Code of Criminal Procedure provides that parole boards at the Regional Courts may place a convicted person in a forced labor camp for a period of 3 months to 2 years after he had served the full term of confinement imposed by the court (Sections 36 and 279).[7]

HUNGARY

As was the case with Romania, Hungary, which had fought against the USSR until the end of World War II, was occupied by the Soviet forces. Together with the prisoners of war, about 600,000 men and women were deported to the USSR, especially to the Siberian prison camps.[8]

Law no. VII of 1946, which is concerned with the "penal defense of the democratic form of state," and military law no. II of 1939 have been used by the Communist regime of Hungary as legal justification for deporting unreliable elements to labor camps, collective cooperatives, or other areas for compulsory labor. Applied in a most arbitrary fashion, especially before harvests or at other times when serious lags, sabotages, or unfulfilled quotas are reported, these laws have been instrumental in creating one of the most oppressive features of the Communist regime in Hungary.

By a government decree of January 27, 1950, almost unlimited power over the workers was given to the Hungarian Workers (Communist) Party. This was, however, only an ex post facto step since the Communist minority government had been in control over the special police force (State Security Police—AVO) and the tribunals.

Prior to 1949, about 15,000 persons had been sentenced in Hungary for political reasons; 5,000 of them were assigned to corrective labor. When religious persecution reached its height in 1949, all Roman Catholic orders, with the exception of 4, were dissolved and their members forcibly transported to various parts of the country. Some of the 10,000 priests, monks, and nuns affected were assigned to internment and forced-labor camps. In a new mass deportation in May, 1951, about 75,000 persons were removed from Budapest and other large cities and assigned to slave labor in quarries, mines, and collective cooperatives.[9] After the Hungarian revolution of 1956, an unknown number, but reaching tens of thousands, of anti-Communist Hungarians, were placed in internment camps, imprisoned, or deported to Siberia.[10]

POLAND

The right to work has become a legal duty to work (Article 14 of the 1952 Constitution). This principle has been of far-reaching consequences since it allows the government to use coercion and compulsion when needing labor. The Decree of January 3, 1946, introduced general labor duty. With minor exceptions, every man between 18 and 55 and every woman between 18 and 45 years of age had to register with the employment office; this step was supplemented by a decree of 1947 on compulsory neighborhood help in agriculture and by two laws of 1950. These provisions have been used as an instrument of social and political persecution.[11]

A corollary law of February 25, 1948, founded a quasi-military organization, Service to Poland. Boys and girls between 16 and 21, prior to the boys' military service, and supernumeraries up to 30 years of age, are liable for service with special labor units for 6 months, where they receive preliminary labor training while working on public projects. While these provisions have social and economic aims, in practice they are often used for penal purposes. The Law of December 15, 1951, on administrative penal procedure, empowered local authorities to impose "correctional work" up to 3 months on individuals guilty of minor offenses. In the penal code draft of 1956, judges were empowered to replace improvement by correctional labor.

The most drastic form of compulsory labor was created by the

Decree of November 16, 1945, on the Creation and Scope of Activities of the Special Commission for Combating Waste and Economic Sabotage. The Commission was granted the right to impose compulsory labor in forced labor camps for a period of up to 2 years (but this term is often prolonged). While the Commission was abolished in 1955, the camps remain.

ROMANIA

The fascist regime, ruling Romania before the end of World War II, collapsed when the tide of battle in World War II had turned and Romania was occupied by Soviet troops. Some 500,000 Romanian prisoners were taken by the Red Army, and of this number only about 190,000 were repatriated. After having been held in special camps for political indoctrination and brought afterwards to Romania to provide the core of the Romanian Sovietized Army and of the Communist militia; "the remainder spent between 3 and 7 years at hard labor, in the mines and forests of Asiatic Russia."[12] In addition, beginning with January 5, 1945, a total of 36,590 men and 32,748 women, Romanian subjects of German origin, were taken from their homes by the MVD agents and deported to the USSR; the number eventually reached some 107,000. In addition, from August, 1944, until the end of January, 1948, about 20,000 Romanians from Moldavia and Northern Transylvania were deported, together with about 50,000 people from Bessarabia and Northern Bukovina, and some 70,000 from other regions, to the labor camps of Central Asia and Siberia. Around 1947, more than 100,000 Romanians, in addition, were in the forced labor camps because of their political beliefs and about 50,000 people for "economic sabotage." By September, 1950, these prisons were less crowded as they had been partially emptied by 80,000 prisoners sent to work on the Danube-Black Sea Canal.

The forced labor policies have been masked under the term "voluntary brigade," divided into four categories. The youth-brigades are divided into permanent and temporary brigades.

The permanent brigades are manned by unemployed and union-designated manual, office, or intellectual workers, who are given subsistence and nominal pay; temporary brigades are attached to the permanent brigades, and are composed of students, young magistrates, teachers, public officials, and workers drafted for the whole period of their summer vacations; they receive no pay, and only are fed. On a non-permanent basis are the other two types of brigades, employed locally for so-called "sparetime" jobs, or rural or urban areas. They are summoned, for this "free" labor, by the Communist Party or the organizations which it controls. The fourth type is composed of public officials, victims of various political purges, dismissed army officers, and anyone not gainfully employed.

Romania has laws similar to those which the USSR had enacted, and the laws defining "crimes which would endanger the security of the State and the development of the national economy" (January 13, 1949), are similar.[13] An amendment to the Criminal Code by Decree No. 187 of April 30, 1949, added to Article 1 of the Code: "The actions which are considered dangerous for society can be punished even when they are not expressly prohibited by law. In such cases the extent and limit of criminal responsibility is to be determined in accordance with the legal provisions in force for similar crimes."

The 1952 Romanian Constitution guarantees each citizen the right to work; the duty to work is seen as a corollary of this right. A worker who has left his job without authorization or has been discharged without being reassigned by the Manpower Office of the local People's Council becomes technically a vagrant.[14]

An ordinance of May 12, 1951, set up a Central Office of Labor Reserves under the Council of Ministers to provide for the training of "Labor Reserves," as well as for the distribution of "any available skilled and unskilled labor reserves . . . according to the needs of the national economy." The local People's Councils are in charge of drafting the required number of young workers for the Labor Reserves. A decree of April 18, 1953, amended certain provisions regarding Labor Reserves and established "on-the-job" training courses of from 2 to 10 months. Failure to report to a job by a government employee with "willful intent" to affect adversely the functions of a government institution is punishable with imprisonment from 1 to 3 months.

In addition to the contributions made by "voluntary brigades" (usually used for unskilled work in farming and simple construction jobs) the state's manpower is strengthened by the military labor battalions formed at the end of 1949 and placed under a Central Office of Labor Service. The government uses them to discriminate against young men of "unhealthy social origin."

Forced labor camps have existed since 1945, and "at least half have supplied manpower for various state projects." Forced labor is supplied by the Central Office of Prisons.

YUGOSLAVIA

Since Tito has been cooperating with the Western allies, to a degree, we have not heard so much about his forced labor camps as in the case of other satellites. But that they exist can be implied from several reports, and especially from Rankovic's report to the Central Committee of the Party on June 3, 1958, on the operations of the secret police, and the provisions of Yugoslavia's new penal law which went into effect in January, 1960.[15]

In October, 1959, a brief article in a small provincial newspaper reported that a Yugoslav living in a town near the Italian border had received a year's suspended sentence for "blaspheming the President of the Republic." Although this was only a minor incident, it illustrates the changing Yugoslav attitude toward political offenses. Deeds or words that in Western Europe or the United States might be frowned on but are not actionable by law are still punishable crimes in Yugoslavia. At the same time, however, the police and the courts tend to be lenient, particularly on minor offenses. This has been increasingly true since 1951, when the Tito government reorganized its legal system. At that time, the regime acknowledged that thousands of persons had been imprisoned unjustly or treated more harshly than their offenses deserved. However, "There are still some areas where the relaxation has not gone far," and "no one can work for the overthrow of the Communist system without facing harsh penalties. Equally, any attempt to stir up religious feeling or dissension among the country's various nationalities gets no sympathy from the courts."

Offenses in this latter category are taken seriously in Yugoslavia. During World War II, Serbs and Croats and Roman Catholics and Greek Orthodox people killed each other by the thousands in the name of nationalism and religion.

Although the present fashion in the Communist world is to deny the existence of political trials—offenders are generally found guilty of economic crimes—the Yugoslavs make no bones about the fact that they have political prisoners; their justification is their country's vulnerable position in the world, surrounded by hostile forces hoping for the overthrow of the Tito regime. The best known of these prisoners is Milovan Djilas, the former Number Two Man in the government, who turned against the system he helped to build. (Djilas is serving a 9-year sentence in Stremskin Mitrovica prison—about 40 miles from Belgrade). How many others there are is not a matter of public knowledge, since no separate records, the officials claim, are kept for political prisoners. But an indication of sorts can be gained from court statistics.

In 1957, for instance, 5,000 persons were sentenced to prison terms of more than 6 months. Of these, 407 were listed as political offenders. More than half of the 407 were convicted of spreading religious hatred; 70 others were charged with promoting dissension among nationalities; only about 50 were jailed for acts said to have been aimed at the regime itself. This was far fewer than in earlier years, but even so was only part of the story. There is at least one category of political prisoners that would not show in these statistics—the so-called deportees.

Under the provisions of a law first introduced in 1948, during the height of the feud between Yugoslavia and the Soviet-bloc nations, persons judged a threat to the security of the state could be "deported" for a period of up to 2 years. This action was taken

539

by police courts. The procedure is not considered a regular trial. A person deported is exiled from his regular residence and usual connections and is forced to live in a place selected by the police. This may be only a remote village or on a closely-guarded barren island in the Adriatic Sea.

Such deportations had virtually stopped by 1955, but the practice was revived in 1958, after the renewed break between Moscow and Belgrade. (A recent report—in 1959—to Parliament stated that this action was taken against 166 persons during the year that ended in June. Most of them apparently were persons suspected of pro-Soviet sympathies).

SELECTED BIBLIOGRAPHY *See* pp. 542-545.

NOTES

Chapter V—A

1. Dallin, David H. & Nicolaevsky, Boris A., *Forced Labor in Soviet Russia,* Yale University Press, New Haven, 1947, 309-320. The information on Soviet forced labor is widely scattered and usually highly colored. We might note such works as: Barhiany, Ivan, *The Hunters and the Hunted,* St. Martin's Press, New York, 1957, a novel of chivalry and valor, with unexpected themes in our grubby fiction; Krasnov, N. N., Jr., *The Hidden Russia,* Holt, New York, 1960, the 10-year Odyssey of a slave laborer in Soviet Russia that constitutes a powerful weapon in the anti-communist arsenal; Parvilahti, Unto, *Beria's Gardens: A Slave Laborer's Experiences in the Soviet Utopia,* E. P. Dutton, New York, 1960, a sound antidote to the spreading exaggerated optimism about recent developments in Soviet Russia; Nickerson, Hoffamn, *The New Slavery,* Doubleday, Garden City, 1958, based on factual solid ground; "Soviet Forced Labour Camps," NATO Letter, VIII, 3, March, 1960, 13-14; etc.
2. Dallin & Nicolaevsky, *op. cit.,* 149.
3. Herling, Albert Konrad, *The Soviet Slave Empire,* Wilfred Funk, New York, 1951, 9.
4. Herling, *op. cit.,* 11.
5. Read Dostoevsky's *House of the Dead;* Tolstoi, *Resurrection.* Details can be found in Kennan, George, *Siberia and the Exile System,* Century, New York, 2 vols., 1891.
6. Buber, Margaret, *Under Two Dictators,* Dodd, Mead, New York, 1951; Lipper, Elinor, *Eleven Years in Soviet Prison Camps,* Regnery, Chicago, 1951;

Wines, Frederick Howard, *Punishment and Reformation*, T. Y. Crowell, New York, 1919, 181-186.

7. Herling, *op. cit.*, 11.

8. Dallin & Nicolaevsky, *op. cit.*, Chapter I, "The Corrective Labor Camps," 3-19, and bibliography, 309-320.

9. "Red State's Labor 'Camp Colony,'" New York *Herald Tribune*, September 13, 1959.

Chapter V—B

1. For details, see such works: Rostow, W. W., *The Dynamics of Soviet Society*, a Mentor Book, The New American Library, New York, 1954, 212-216; and the references in the following footnotes in this article.

2. Stolza, George, comp., *Forced Labor in the Soviet Orbit: A Selective Bibliography*, Mid-European Studies Center, Mimeographed Series, No. 20, New York, March 15, 1954; Baldwin, Roger N. (Ed.), *A New Slavery—Forced Labor*, Oceana Publications, New York, 1953; Carlton, Richard K., *The Economic Role of Forced Labor in Eastern Europe*, Mid-European Studies Center, Mimeographed Series, No. 35, New York, June 28, 1954; Carlton, Richard K. & others, *Forced Labor in the "People's Democracies,"* Mid-European Studies Center, New York, 1955; Dallin, David J., *The Economics of Slave Labor*, Regnery, Chicago, 1949; Csovski, Vladimir, (Ed.), *Forced Labor and Confinement Without Trial; Study in Six Parts: Bulgaria, Czechoslovakia, Hungary, Poland, Romania, Yugoslavia;* with Supplement: *Forced Labor in the Satellite Countries as of January 7, 1955*, Mid-European Law Project, Library of Congress, Washington, 1952; Kotschnig, Walter, *Forced Labor Conditions in Communist-Dominated Countries*, Department of State Bulletin, XXIII, 510-513; Orr, Charles A., *Stalin's Slave Camps: An Indictment of Modern Slavery*, Beacon Press, Boston, 1952; United Nations, International Labour Office, *Report of the Ad Hoc Committee on Forced Labour*, E/2431, Geneva, December, 1953; Herling, Albert Konrad, *The Soviet Slave Empire*, Wilfred Funk, New York, 1951.

3. Skendi, Stavro (Ed.), *Albania*, F. A. Praeger, New York, 1956, Chapter 9, "Labor," 138-147.

4. Dellin, L. A. D., "Labor," Chapter 12, 2288-250, in Dellin, L. A. D. (Ed.), *Bulgaria*, F. A Praeger, 1957, & bibliography, 430-431; Carlton, Richard (Ed), *Forced Labor in the People's Democracies*, Mid-European Studies Center, New York, 1955; Halasz, Andrew, "Labor's Status in Iron Curtain Countries," *The Annals* of The American Academy of Political and Social Science, in Roucek, Joseph S. (Ed.), "Moscow's European Satellites," CCLXXI, September, 1950, 94-99; Mid-European Studies Center, *Presentation Made to the Ad Hoc Committee on Forced Labour*, New York & Geneva, June 18, 1952 & November 5, 1952; UN, International Labour Office, *Report of the Ad Hoc Committee on Forced Labour*, E/2431, Geneva, December, 1953; *Forced Labor and Confinement Without Trial in Bulgaria*, Mid-European Law Project, Library of Congress, Washington, 1952; Nenoff, Dragomir, *Forced Labor Camp and Prisoners in Bulgaria*, Free Europe Committee, New York, 1951; Herling, Albert Konrad, *The Soviet Slave Empire* Wilfred Funk, New York, 1951, Chapter VI, "Hungary and Bulgaria—Under the Yoke," 134-167.

5. Herling, *op. cit.*, 246.

6. The Ad Hoc Committee, *Report, United Nations Document* E/2431, June 21, 1953.

7. Kocvara, Stephen, "The Constitutional System," Chapter 3, 40-59, in Busek, Vratislav & Spulber, Nicolas (Ed.), *Czechoslovakia*, F. A. Praeger, New York, 1957; *Forced Labor and Confinement Without Trial in Czechoslovakia*, Mid-European Law Project, Library of Congress, Washington, 1951.

8. Herling, *The Soviet Slave Empire*, 134-167.

9. Legislative Reference Service, *Tensions Within the Soviet Captive Countries: Hungary*, Government Printing Office, Washington, 1954, 191.

10. *Forced Labor and Confinement Without Trial in Hungary*, Mid-European Law Project, Library of Congress, Washington, D. C., 1951; Free Europe Press, Hungarian Desk, *The Legal Aspects of Forced Labor in Hungary*, Varga, Laszlo (Ed.), Free Europe Committee, New York, 1954; Hungarian National Council, *Memorandum on Forced Labor and Forced Labor Camps in Hungary: To the Ad Hoc Committee on Forced Labor of the U.N. Social and Economic Council*, n.p., n.d.; Herling, *op. cit.*, Chapter VI, "Hungary and Bulgaria—Under the Yoke," 134-167.

11. Dolina, Joseph, "Labor," Chapter 20, 467-490, in Halecki, Oscar (Ed.), *Poland*, F. A. Praeger, New York 1957; *Forced Labor and Confinement Without Trial in Poland*, Mid-European Law Project, Library of Congress, Washington, 1951; Free Europe Committee, *Slave Labor and Slave Camps in Poland*, Free Europe Committee, New York, 1951.

12. Herling, *op. cit.*, Chapter V, "Romance in Chains," 101-133.

13. The text in Herling, *op. cit.*, 122-123.

14. Caranil, Andrew G., "Labor," Chapter 14, 248-269, in Fischer-Galati, Stephen (Ed.), *Romania*, F. A. Praeger, New York, 1957; *Forced Labor and Confinement Without Trial in Romania*, Mid-European Law Project, Library of Congress, Washington, 1951; Radescy, Nicolas, *Forced Labor in Romania, Commission on Inquiry into Forced Labor*, New York, 1949.

15. Lapenna, Ivo, "Socialist Legality: Soviet and Yugoslav," *Soviet Survey*, 25, July-September, 1958, 53-60; *Forced Labor and Confinement Without Trial in Yugoslavia*, Mid-European Law Project, Library of Congress, Washington, D. C., 1952; Gsovski, Vladimir (Ed.), *Forced Labor and Confinement Without Trial. Study in Six Parts: Bulgaria, Czechoslovakia, Hungary, Poland, Romania, Yugoslavia*, Mid-European Law Project, Library of Congress, Washington, 1952, 1955; United States, Library of Congress, Law Library, *Yugoslavia: Confinement Without Trial (Forced Labor)*, Library of Congress, Washington, D. C., 1951.

SELECTED BIBLIOGRAPHY

The USSR

Artemyev, V. P., *Political Controls in the Soviet Army*, Praeger, New York, 1954. Covers ably a neglected topic.

Berman, H. J., *Justice in Russia*, Harvard University Press, Cambridge, 1950. A systematic approach.

Callcott, M. S., *Russian Justice*, Macmillan, New York, 1935. A good introduction, but superseded by later research.

Fainsod, Merle, *How Russia Is Ruled*, Harvard University Press, Cambridge, 1953. How Stalin's genius built up the massive totalitarian apparatus. See especially Chapter 13: "Terror as a System of Power," 354-389.

Golyakov, I. T., *The Role of the Soviet Court*, Public Affairs Press, Washington, 1948. A bitter indictment.

Gsovski, V., *Soviet Civil Law*, University of Michigan Press, Ann Arbor, 1948-49, 2 vols. A good legalistic history.

Guins, G. C., *Soviet Law and Soviet Society*, Nijhoff, The Hague, 1954. An involved but a valuable survey.

Hazard, John N. (editor), *Soviet Legal Philosophy*, Harvard University Press, Cambridge, 1952; *Law and Social Change in the U.S.S.R.*, Carswell, Toronto, 1953; *The Soviet System of Government*, University of Chicago Press, 1957. By the outstanding American authority in this field.

Kelsen, Hans, *The Communist Theory of Law*, Praeger, New York, 1955. A bitter attack by an American-Austrian authority.

Konstantinovsky, B. A., *Soviet Law in Action*, Harvard University Press, Cambridge, 1953. A systematic study.

Schlesinger, Rudolph, *Soviet Legal Theory*, Oxford University Press, New York, 1945. One of the first post-war surveys.

Vyshinsky, A. Y., *The Law of the Soviet State*, Macmillan, New York, 1948. A translation of the outstanding pro-Stalinist spokesman.

The European Satellites

Adamovitch, Alexander, "Yugoslavia: Judicial Control of Administrative Acts," *Highlights of Current Legislation and Activities in Europe*, VI, 289-298.

Bain, Leslie B., *The Reluctant Satellites*, Macmillan, New York, 1960. Personal, eye-witness reports about the spirit of criticism or rebellion in Yugoslavia and Hungary; has written a report on conditions in Central Europe before and during the Hungarian revolt.

Byrnes Robert F., *Bibliography on American Publications On*

East Central Europe 1945-1957, Indiana University Publications, Bloomington, 1958(?); see especially 23-24; 67; 85; 98-99; 127-128; 153-154; 176; 187-188. Some useful, although not all, bibliographical references.

Halasz, Nicholas, *In the Shadow of Russia: Eastern Europe in the Post-War World*, Ronald Press, New York, 1959. Gives information for the understanding of the present situation in Poland, Hungary, Yugoslavia, Czechoslovakia, Romania, Bulgaria and Albania.

"The Satellites in Eastern Europe," *The Annals* of The American Academy of Political and Social Science, CCCXVII, (edited by Henry L. Roberts), May, 1958. Articles by authorities on the various aspects of the satellite world.

"Moscow's European Satellites," *Ibid.*, CCLXXI, September, 1950, (edited by Joseph S. Roucek). A similar survey which had preceded the issue edited by Roberts.

Seton-Watson, Hugh, *From Lenin to Khrushchev*, Praeger, New York, 1960. An updated edition of *From Lenin to Malenkov*.

Joseph S. Roucek, Chairman and Professor of the Departments of Sociology and Political Science, Bridgeport, (Conn.), was born in Czechoslovakia (1902–) but naturalized in the United States (1927); B.A., Occidental College (1925) and M.A. and Ph.D. degrees, New York University (1928, 1937); a member of the Editorial Boards of *Social Science, American Journal of Economics and Sociology, and Journal of Human Relations.* Is the author, editor and collaborator of more than 90 books, including such works as: *Contemporary Romania and Her Problems (1932); Politics of the Balkans (1939); Balkan Politics (1948); The Development of Educational Sociology (1956); The Slavonic Encyclopaedia (1949);·Social Control (1956); Twentieth Century Political Thought (1946); One America (1952); Contemporary Europe (1947); World Political Geography (1954); The Challenge of Science Education (1959); Automation and Society (1959); Contemporary Sociology (1958); Contemporary Political Ideologies (1960);* etc. Has published articles in the leading academic periodicals in the United States, Canada, South America, Spain, Italy, France, Czechoslovakia, Germany, Yugoslavia, Romania and elsewhere. Has taught at New York University, Pennsylvania State College (now University), Hofstra College, San Francisco State College, University of Washington College of the Pacific, New Mexico Highlands, University of Wyoming, Occidental College, University of Southern California, University of British Columbia, University of Puerto Rico, Portland State College; etc. In the spring of 1956, lectured under the auspices of the U.S. Information Service in Spain, Austria, Yugoslavia, Germany, Holland, France and also for several universities and learned bodies in these countries. The pre-communist governments of Romania and Yugoslavia awarded him the Knighthood of the Crown of Yugoslavia and of the Star of Romania.

INDEX

549